WORK, LOVE, AND LEARNING IN UTOPIA

Work, Love, and Learning in Utopia breathes new life into the age-old human preoccupation with how to create a happier society. With a fascinating mix of research from cross-cultural psychology, macro history, and evolutionary biology, the book gives new credibility to the advocacy of radical equality.

The author, a psychological anthropologist, argues that the negative emotions of sadness, anger, and fear evolved in tandem with hierarchy, while happiness evolved separately and in connection to prosociality and compassion. The book covers a wide range of human concerns, from economics and education, to media and communication, to gender and sexuality. It breaks new boundaries with its scope, arguing that equality of love is as important and possible as is economic equality. Its argument is provocative yet practical, and each chapter ends with concrete proposals that invite dialogue with any student of policy.

Written in an easily accessible style, this book will appeal to anyone who has ever puzzled over how our social world could be remade. In particular, it will be very useful to students and scholars of anthropology, sociology, and psychology.

Martin Schoenhals is an Anthropologist and Traveling Faculty for the School for International Training, USA. He has previously taught at Columbia University, Johns Hopkins University, and the University of Pennsylvania, and is the author of *The Paradox of Power* (1993) and *Intimate Exclusion* (2003).

What makes this *Work, Love, and Learning in Utopia: Equality Reimagined* such an engaging work is that it demonstrates the social nature of humanity and the importance of interdependency in realising equality in a new utopia. Using anthropological evidence, Schoenhals shows how mutual care and cooperation are what have made human life sustainable, meaningful, and purposeful for hundreds of years. By undermining hierarchy, invidious competition, and a narrow means–end logic, mutual care and love help produce the social conditions for making equality a reality in economic, social, personal, and political life. The book is not only an anthropological text however; it is also a moral one; it demonstrates how mutual care and concern for others is the 'real essence of morality'.

Professor Kathleen Lynch, University College Dublin

Utilizing his past research in China on education, class, gender, and ethnicity, as well as his broad knowledge of classic anthropology and theory, Martin Schoenhals invites us to question our present way of doing things and to consider alternative public policies, as well as social and cultural frameworks, that could lay the foundation for a happier and more just future.

Professor Ellen Oxfeld, Middlebury College

Professor Martin Schoenhals raises interesting and thought-provoking questions about the role of happiness and human interaction as important drivers of human evolution. His work connects different bodies of scholarship including anthropology, psychology, biology, and politics, into a powerful argument for thinking seriously about positive emotions, equality, and meaningful human interactions as key elements for both descriptive and prescriptive analysis of human existence.

Dr Doron Shultziner, Hadassah Academic College

Faced with insecurity and catastrophe in our neoliberal world, the best human response we can imagine seems to be resilience, the capacity to survive and recover quickly from inevitable crises and traumas. Martin Schoenhals refuses to accept this individualized answer by courageously returning to the notion of human utopia. Contrary to previous studies of utopia, however, he focuses on material as well as relational conditions for the maximization of interactive joy. He shows how human hierarchies and inequalities harm all of us, preventing people at the top and bottom from experiencing the pleasure of pleasing others, and from mutually nurturing ourselves and fellow human beings. *Work, Love, and Learning in Utopia* not only considers the evolution of hierarchies in the past and present, but also offers concrete suggestions for encouraging interactive forms of joy, happiness, and love. If you seek meaningful hope—not just coping strategies—in these dark times, this book is for you!

Professor Sean Chabot, Eastern Washington University

WORK, LOVE, AND LEARNING IN UTOPIA

Equality Reimagined

Martin Schoenhals

Routledge
Taylor & Francis Group

LONDON AND NEW YORK

First published 2019
by Routledge
2 Park Square, Milton Park, Abingdon, Oxon OX14 4RN

and by Routledge
52 Vanderbilt Avenue, New York, NY 10017

Routledge is an imprint of the Taylor & Francis Group, an informa business

British Library Cataloguing-in-Publication Data
A catalogue record for this book is available from the British Library

Library of Congress Cataloging-in-Publication Data
Names: Schoenhals, Martin, 1961– author.
Title: Work, love, and learning in utopia : equality reimagined / Martin Schoenhals.
Description: Abingdon, Oxon ; New York, NY : Routledge, 2019. |
Includes bibliographical references and index.
Identifiers: LCCN 2018041672 | ISBN 9781138549494 (hbk) |
ISBN 9781138549517 (pbk) | ISBN 9781351000314 (ebk) |
ISBN 9781351000284 (mobipocket encrypted) |
ISBN 9781351000307 (Adobe) | ISBN 9781351000291 (epub)
Subjects: LCSH: Equality. | Social change. | Ethnopsychology.
Classification: LCC HM821 .S2425 2019 | DDC 305–dc23
LC record available at https://lccn.loc.gov/2018041672

ISBN: 978–1–138–54949–4 (hbk)
ISBN: 978–1–138–54951–7 (pbk)
ISBN: 978–1–351–00031–4 (ebk)

Typeset in Bembo
by Out of House Publishing

CONTENTS

NOTE TO THE READER

Contacting me

As this book makes clear, community and interaction are central to human happiness. One motive for writing this book has been my own desire for more connection with like-minded people. Therefore, I'd love to hear from you.

Email me at mdsnewyork@gmail.com. I will try my best to reply to all messages.

About the book

This book responds to my longstanding desire to do more than report "objective" problems about society. While it is important to describe societal ills, it is, I believe, not enough to limit one's work to such descriptions. Doing so makes social scientists into voyeurs of human misery. We can, and should, do more. Imagining a better world is a key human capacity. Scholars should embrace such imaginings.

This book is my own effort to analyze social ills and suggest comprehensive solutions. It is, indeed, a proposal for a Utopia, though that word has an unfortunate negative connotation to many people. I hope this will change since the lack of a positive word with which to describe a better society reveals how infrequently thinkers attempt utopian projects—ones that are comprehensive and holistic.

The book grounds its ideas in research from anthropology (my own field), psychology, biology, and other fields in the human sciences. It is a prescriptive book, but one where prescriptions are based on scientific research.

Chapter 1 is the longest chapter, and it provides research to support the general importance of equality, another word with far less of a positive connotation than it deserves. The chapter ends with an outline of Utopia. Chapters 2 through 7 each approach a different topic. Each chapter begins with analysis of societal problems and then describes concrete solutions.

The topics covered are gender and sexuality in Chapter 2; community and invidious communities, such as the nation-state, in Chapter 3; work and Utopia's economy in Chapter 4; communication in Chapter 5; education and schools in Chapter 6; and the politics of Utopia in Chapter 7. Chapter 8 is a conclusion, addressing different human dilemmas and the ways Utopia responds to them.

I hope you enjoy reading the book as much as I have enjoyed writing it.

And, again, I do hope to hear from you.

ACKNOWLEDGMENTS

Many people spent hours discussing my ideas with me and reading various drafts of the book. For their feedback and friendship I am especially grateful to Steve Mayer, Doug Futuyma, Dyutiman Das, Eve Danziger, Nora Dudwick, and Aquil Mohammad. This book is immeasurably improved, and the writing process made so much more enjoyable, because of them.

Carlo Cafiero, Dominique van der Mensbrugghe, and Piero Conforti of the Food and Agriculture Organization, and Keith Fuglie from the United States Department of Agriculture gave critical help with my questions about food production. John Baker and Stevan Harrell read Chapter 1 thoroughly and graciously provided feedback. Doron Shultziner took time from a busy move to a new university to confirm that I correctly represented the argument put forth in Shultziner et al., an excellent article and a very important one for my own thesis about equality in Chapter 1.

Josie Dixon, Arjun Appadurai, David Borenstein, Claudia Strauss, Arlie Hochschild, Kathleen Lynch, and Suzanne Ogden contributed to the book in a variety of ways. I thank them for spending the time to give their ideas, suggestions, and general support.

Stephanie Rogers and Georgina Bishop of Routledge were extremely helpful during the acquisition and production of this book.

Two anonymous reviewers for Routledge read my work extremely carefully and provided very helpful and thoughtful suggestions. Space restrictions have precluded my responding to all of their ideas, but I hope they know how much I appreciate their help.

Above all, I want to thank my mom and dad and my sister, Julie, for discussing my ideas and reading my writings. I hope they know how invaluable their contributions have been. I am profoundly grateful to them, both for their help with the book and for their support of everything I do. This book is dedicated, with deep love, to them.

1

NEW HOPE FOR UTOPIAN EQUALITY, BASED UPON RESEARCH FROM THE SOCIAL SCIENCES AND BIOLOGY

"What, for you, would an ideal life be like?" I love asking this question and I love even more hearing the answers people give. I first raised this question among the Yi people of China, an ethnic minority living in a remote, mountainous part of the country. "Peaceful and tranquil." "Harmonious family." "A nice home and a good job." "Being liked and respected by everyone around you." Simple answers to a simple question, yet one that needs to be asked, and needs even more to be discussed in detail, and answered with specificity.

For some reason, it is not easy to do this. A few years after my research among the Yi I sat in a conference session among some very smart people who had been critiquing globalization. The session was devoted to what could replace the social, economic, and political ills we had all identified. Surprisingly, few people had solutions. Even proposals that would seem basic—an end to hunger, an end to the oppression of subordinated peoples—were not raised. Why did such smart people, dedicated activists, find it easy to criticize the world as it is, but hard to talk about the world as it should be? Perhaps it was their urbane sophistication, or even cynicism, or perhaps it was the effects of Cold War ideology that blocked these people from thinking and talking in detail about global needs. This inability to think hopefully about society must change. We ought to dare to describe what an ideal world should be like. This book is my own effort toward imagining such a world.

"An ideal world." "Happiness." What are these? Let me begin by inviting you, the reader, to think of your happiest moments and the words you'd use to describe them. I suspect your description would contain words very similar to mine: love, excitement, family and friends, play, solidarity, closeness, fun, passion, mutual care, and compassion. The only words not on my list but perhaps on yours might be peacefulness and security, words that I too would include, if I think about it. (East Asian youth whom I interviewed regularly include these words; Americans, youth in particular, are less likely to do so.) In fact the similarity of our lists might lead to a fairly banal beginning description of Utopia, but that seeming banality indicates how basic and universal are the components of human happiness: We like to be with people we esteem and love, people who also esteem and love us. We like to interact with people we love, to feel the unbridled joy we feel when we interact without constraint, without conflict, without fear of embarrassment, without the fear that we are in danger of being disrespected, dismissed, and rejected. We want to belong and to feel the multiple emotions that belonging brings: warmth, joy, fun, and a peaceful sense of being safe.

I've asked for descriptions of an ideal life from many different peoples: rural Chinese, urban Chinese, suburban Americans, and others. Their answers about an ideal life, and happiness, are very similar to my own description above. In fact the preceding paragraph's description is not only my own product, but contains many of the answers I've gotten when asking about an ideal life of people in diverse parts of the world. All answers emphasize the importance of close and good relationships with other humans, with family and friends, as key to happiness. Emphasizing the importance of our relationships to others is not surprising. We humans, like our primate cousins, are a supremely social species. We belong to an animal category known as "obligatorily gregarious" (De Waal 2005: 231). We crave intense inter-action with other humans and we feel much joy from this interaction (and often much pain too). For us and our primate relatives the quality of our relationships with others is central to our psychological and biological well-being. And so, a first approximation: Utopia maximizes affirmative relationships between people both at work and in love and friendship. I will call this the maximization of interactive joy.

So far nothing surprising here, nor controversial. But the next question is why contemporary society doesn't maximize interactive joy, given its universal appeal. What is the cause of unhappiness in our worlds today? My answer, again, is not novel, although it is controversial: Inequality is a major cause of human unhappiness.

I doubt anyone will argue against the contention that being on the losing end of society is a source of unhappiness: poor, ethnically and racially excluded, or oppressed due to one's gender or sexuality. But I will go beyond this claim and argue a more novel and less intuitive proposition. Inequality does not just injure the lowest among us. Hierarchy and inequality are fundamental sources of human unhappiness, for those on the bottom, middle, and top—for all of us. If society is to promote human happiness, a first key step is to eradicate hierarchy and inequality altogether.

Many, many others have said this before me, and many, many others have vocif-erously fought for egalitarian principles. But there are several characteristics of my argument that make it different. While progressives and leftists like me need little discussion to convince us that inequality is unfair, I decided that it is not sufficient to simply assert the virtues of equality and fairness. I want to prove that equality leads to a better society, by showing, using scientific evidence, what causes human joy, and how hierarchy quite literally impedes joy and happiness. The first half of this chapter presents the evidence. The second half describes what Utopia should generally be like. Then, in the chapters that follow, I will take on particular facets of Utopia—its gender relations and the nature of its families, how it will promote a sense of community, its economy and politics, its schools and learning institutions, and how human interaction and communication can be made more meaningful and enjoyable. And I will not just argue for basic principles, but will give proposals, as specific as I can make them, for how to change today's institutions and practices.

My thesis also differs from that of many other leftists in that I do not privilege any particular form of hierarchy as being the supreme cause of unhappiness. Hierarchy of wealth, power, gender, sexuality, ethnicity, and nation-states are all the enemies of happiness. Utopia must equalize wealth, but it also must equalize love and attention. We all deserve to love and be loved, to attract attention from those around us and to have interest in attending to them, to love and be loved for our creativity at "work" as well as for everything we do while away from work. Love/attention, home, and work should not be divided concepts.

Another difference from other progressives, not to mention conservatives, is that I make happiness and pleasure a goal, a virtue even, rather than seeing pleasure as secondary or incidental. I know some others have done this, but I also feel that happiness and pleasure are often derided by both sides of the political spectrum in countries and cultures around the world. To the conservative, pleasure connotes licentiousness and often selfishness. To the liberal, pleasure is often derided for similar reasons, or it is implicitly deemphasized in deference to seemingly more exalted virtues: Fairness, for example. More than anything else in political rhetoric, the widespread reluctance to see individual happiness—and, yes, pleasure—as a goal and a virtue puzzles me. Why should access to good schools be motivated above all by a desire to equalize individuals' opportunities in life? That's a very good goal, but why not proclaim that even more important than this goal is the establishment of schools that make learning enjoyable? After all, learning is one of the most quintessentially human activities. Why shouldn't it be fun? Why do so many people cringe at the idea that kids should enjoy school? The discourse on schooling, in fact, illustrates that there is a fundamental reluctance, perhaps at least partially a legacy of the puritans in all cultures, to recognize the importance of pleasure, including, *especially*, the pleasures of learning.

Likewise with the discourse about work. Why shouldn't the purpose of work be to please ourselves, rather than to make things, or provide services that make for a better and richer society? If we define wealth and well-being based upon happiness, then society is not rich if consumers *and* producer/workers are not happy. In our typically number-driven society today, we may decide that if consumers are really happy, but workers are somewhat unhappy, then the final result tips the scales toward a laudable result. Not so. Merely adding up individual happinesses makes a fundamental error in not recognizing that happiness comes from relationships. Thus, "work" should be no different from children at play, or artistic performance, or love. All of these succeed precisely by producing happiness and by producing it in a particular way: They give us joy from the *interaction* between individuals, not just from adding up isolated pleasures. The musicians who enjoy their playing are off to a good start, but real enjoyment comes when their enjoyment and the audience's enjoyment are mutual, and mutually reinforcing. The same with love: Love is magnified when our lover's pleasure pleases us. Thus pleasure derives precisely from an interaction between individuals, and that should include workers and consumers too, both of whom need to be simultaneously pleased. As I will argue, the human capacity for pleasure is not a selfish one at all, but is precisely the opposite. Because humans feel empathy for others, a capacity most other animals lack, our pleasure sets up a virtuous cycle in which our pleasure and the pleasure of those we please are mutually reinforcing. ("Sympathy" and "empathy" are similar but not the same in English. I prefer "empathy" because of its stronger connotations, but to me the distinctions between the two words are less significant than others might believe them to be. After all, words do not always adequately map the world at is it so they should not be given as much power as wordsmiths often like to give them.) Ultimately, if pleasure is not mutual and relational, then any pleasure we feel is only half-good, and never fulfilling. This is why hierarchy can never produce full happiness even for those at the top: It creates a vicious cycle, rather than a virtuous one, in which my win is your loss, my joy comes at your expense. And equality is necessary but not sufficient for happiness. Equality in the workplace, for example, is no good if it doesn't make as its goal the happiness and pleasure of workers and the virtuous cycle of producers and consumers in interaction, mutually pleasing each other. Work must be provided to all, not just so we can all make a living, but rather so that all people can experience the pleasure of contributing to society in a meaningful way. In addition all workers must have a receptive audience for their creations. Consumers and producers must be linked, and not just through remote monetary relationships. Instead, as with a performance, producers and consumers should be co-present, and mutual pleasuring to each other, and this is how it must be in all facets of life and society.

This is why I have called for the maximization of *interactive* joy. We know that human happiness comes from interaction with others, and so we must make Utopia's goal the maximization of pleasure, and more precisely the maximization of *interactive* pleasure, so that one person's actions can affirmatively please another, whose pleasure then further promotes the well-being of the original actor.

I am a musician, hence my fondness for performative metaphors. And I will end this section with a metaphor that I have found quite instructive. Musicians know that a performer who plays for a competition may play "well," but that ultimately the performance is often technical, cold, and lifeless. The performance may lack mistaken notes but it neither brings joy to us nor to the performer. On the one hand, it is good, in a way, but not pleasing. Really good playing, on the other hand, comes from a performer who plays for an appreciative audience. Really good performers are always aware of the audience and their moment-by-moment, barely audible, though nonetheless present, reactions. Good performers play to, and for, these reactions. It is the same with actors, who often say they want to perform before a live audience, because it makes for a truly inspired performance. In music, drama, or anything else in life, playing to earn fame and fortune corrupts the pleasuring functions of our actions. Playing to and for others, however, makes our performances, of whatever type, full of life and love.

Most of us in society today live only half-satisfying lives because we live like the competition contestant. Even if we win, our winnings are not pleasure itself, and may often impede pleasure, despite the happiness that money and fame can bring. We should live like the real musician, the real performer, instead, whose goal is to please the self by pleasing others. This is, after all, quintessentially human: Interacting and communicating, listening and talking, pleasing others and taking pleasure in another's happiness, especially happiness we have helped to bring about. This is a metaphor for Utopia, and it is what I hope to describe in the rest of this book.

The cultural and biological underpinnings of Utopia

What emotions are there?

I begin a consideration of Utopia with emotions. Beginning here seems so natural—happiness is, after all, a universal pursuit—that I first want to say a word about emotions as the basis of Utopia. Emotions seem to have evolved to make animal behavior more flexible. Humans encounter a situation and don't just respond based on "instinct," but feel, often think about what we feel, and then respond based upon what we feel. Emotions are the impetus for action (and they are implicated in much cognition too). Maximizing happiness and pleasure may seem hedonistic to some, but given the evolutionary basis for these emotions, this maximization is entirely natural. *They are there in order to be maximized.* The emphasis on pleasure might also seem too self-indulgent, and perhaps anti-communitarian, but, as I will show below, joy evolved to encourage prosocial behaviors—parenting and more general cooperation with other members of our species. Hence, maximizing individual happiness, if it is done right, leads to the general well-being of all within the community. This, then, is why we need to first understand emotions: The positive emotions are what Utopia should be all about.

What do humans feel? Do all *individuals* have the same emotions? Do all *cultures* have the same emotions? Aren't there such large cultural differences between emotions that no universal prescription for a utopian society can be made?

Let me begin with the last question, which has occupied much of my thought as an anthropological student of the emotions. Where culture enters into emotions is not so much in what people feel, but what they feel about their feelings. Anger, for example, is felt by all peoples throughout the world, but some cultures stigmatize the showing of anger greatly, while others tolerate it. Cultures also differ in what elicits certain emotions. The Yi people, a mountain-dwelling ethnic group in southwest China whom I studied, easily talked about the same emotions that I do: Happiness, sadness, fear, anger, love, etc. However, when I asked what makes the Yi most depressed, they were quite unified in answering that an inability to have children is the most unhappy situation possible, and they were quite mystified when I told them that many Americans actively choose not to have children. To the Yi, this is unthinkable.

Thus, the cultural attitude toward the various emotions differs from culture to culture, as do the elicitors of emotions, i.e., the situations viewed as leading to joy, anger, sadness, etc. However, I am nonetheless quite certain that all people in the world feel the same basic emotions, and are unified in experiencing the same emotions as negative (sadness, for example) and the same ones (joy, for example) as positive and desirable. In addition there is enough cross-cultural agreement about the emotional elicitors that it is an entirely reasonable undertaking to seek to articulate universal principles for a good, joyous society.

So, what are the universal emotions and which ones are negative and which positive (i.e., pleasurable)? Are there universal elicitors for the positive emotions? Let me begin with the most important point. Happiness, often called joy by many emotion theorists, is the main universal positive emotion, and while many different things make people happy, there is a general pattern we can discern. Consistent with our mammalian and primate heritage, interacting in a positive way (e.g., with compassion; at play) with people we mutually esteem and care for—family and friends—makes us happy. I have asked about happiness among suburban Americans, rural and urban Chinese, and rural and urban Indians. When asked to define a happy situation, the most common answer is positive interaction with friends and family and I have never encountered any informant who would view this as bad—difficult to attain, perhaps, but never bad. Of course, happiness from being with friends and family would seem obvious, and many readers might think it a waste of time to try to prove this. But aside from liking proof of the obvious (!), academics like me believe that we should take cultural differences seriously. Cultures do, in fact, differ (who counts as "family" is quite different in different cultures, for example), but on the pursuit of happiness, and the basic things that make us happy, there is basic, universal agreement.

What about other positive emotional experiences: Love, excitement, tranquility, religious ecstasy, compassion, freedom, efficacy/potency? There's no denying the importance of these feelings, but from a psychological and biological standpoint "happiness" or "joy" are terms which suffice for most theorists. Two reasons this is so: First, there are only a few discernible emotions to appear very early in infants. Michael Lewis presents a model in which infants are seen as having two original emotional states. One is "distress," marked by crying and irritability and the other is pleasure/contentment, marked by "satiation, attention and responsivity to the environment." Interest in the environment, which occurs from the very beginning of life, is placed by some analysts in the pleasure category but by others is seen to constitute a separate category. From these original two or three emotional states come the basic emotions. From pleasure/contentment comes joy, from interest comes surprise (which is not included as a basic emotion by many analysts), and from distress come the negative emotions: Sadness, anger, fear, and disgust (the latter is not included by all analysts) (Lewis 2004: 276). Thus we get the "basic" or "primary" emotions of joy, sadness, anger, and fear. Love and compassion, for example, come later in child development, as do pride, embarrassment, shame, and guilt. Many analysts see these as derivative, deriving from interplays between self-awareness, awareness of societal and group norms, and the basic emotions (Lewis 2004: 276, 278).

A second reason to use joy/happiness as a cover-all term for various positive emotions is that emotional reactions overlap biologically and psychologically in complex ways.

In general some scholars are splitters and some lumpers but it seems that most emotion theorists tend toward the latter. Most of them use joy/happiness as the largest category to which various shades of positive emotional experience can belong. For the sake of consistency with their writings, and for the sake of basic simplicity, I will follow their lead as a "lumper." I will talk, above all, about the maximization of joy/happiness and I will use that word to subsume all other positive emotional experiences, including such obvious ones as love. Excitement is one possible emotion that is distinguishable from joy since interest in novel things comes early to children and has a much more ancient evolutionary history than joy. (Attention to novel things in one's environment helps the simplest of organisms find food to eat.) But many emotion theorists have stressed the close parallels between excitement/interest and joy and so I will follow their lead in taking joy/happiness to be the main positive emotion.

As for the negative emotions, these too have been defined in a lumping way. The basic negative ones are sadness, fear, and anger. Some theorists add condescension and/or disgust, but the first three are on everyone's list, and so they will be the basic negative emotions for my list too.

The basic goal of Utopia, then, is—not surprisingly—to maximize happiness. It must do this for every individual, and it does so by providing the conditions for all people to feel interactive joy—happiness from work and love. Every individual deserves to feel pleasure from their "work" by working freely at a creative project of their own choice, a project that they feel is valuable to others, consistent with the worker's creative impulses, and capable of bringing pleasure to both others in society and the worker himself/herself. And every individual deserves to feel joy and happiness from loving others and from being loved in return, a love that is therefore mutual, interactive, and non-coerced. Any society that does not provide the conditions to each and every individual to feel interactive joy from work and love is fundamentally flawed because it is inegalitarian and hierarchical, and hierarchy, as will be seen momentarily, precludes joy, even for those provided with more money, status, or fame than others.

Regarding the negative emotions, Utopia will not eliminate them, nor should it seek to totally eliminate them. The role of negative emotions in life is a huge topic, one that might require an entire manifesto to adequately explore, but I will simply note here the following:

1. An individual's emotions can change and fluctuate without necessarily inducing depression; in fact some change is important for preventing boredom. And we all need rest, so that there will always be periods of activity followed by periods of rest. A steady-state of constant, intense joy is hard to imagine, and not really desirable.

2. Humans will experience conflict and loss since they are part of life. Communicating with others in a meaningful way about these feelings can relieve the negativity of the feelings and can become an important source of pleasure itself. As I will note later, emotional communication is a central pleasure for humans. Given this, there must continue to be nuances of feelings, and even ambiguity

and ambivalence, so that there is something meaningful to communicate with each other.

3.   And what happens to hope, that intensely positive feeling, if all is happy and joyful in the present: What, then, is there to hope for? Here we must be careful to distinguish between two kinds of situations connected to hope. The first situation is one in which present conditions are bad, and the goal of hope is to buoy oneself up with expectations that these bad conditions will eventually be overcome. The second situation is one in which the present is happy and there is also an awareness, and expectation, that the future will bring happiness equal to, or greater than, the happiness of the present. The first situation is not desirable and hope in that situation can easily turn to despair, especially if things do not improve. The second situation is the one that is desirable, and will be the situation of Utopia. If society is joy-maximizing and gives the conditions for individuals to act so as to maximize their creativity in work and love, then joy is not a momentary condition of the present, nor a far-off goal, but both a characteristic of the present and of the past and future. In work, and love, there will be present happiness, the happiness of the process, *and* there will be happiness as a result of the route traveled, what I will call for now, though with definite reluctance, the "product" or the "accomplishments."

One might still object that individuals derive their greatest happiness from emotions and conditions that are changing in a positive, hopeful direction, and from the feeling of individual efficacy derived from making good things happen for oneself. In no way does my vision of Utopia endorse static-state Nirvana, nor do I endorse societal guarantees of joy that render the individual actor passive. Instead, Utopia maximizes the conditions for individuals to act so as to experience joy. With action, i.e., life itself, conflict and problems can—even should—occur, but these can and will be surmounted because of the empowerment of all peoples and their predisposition to help those in need. If one more musical analogy can be indulged: One reason I think Beethoven's music is so moving for so many people is that while there is angst and conflict, often quite intense, there is always change and movement stirring even within the conflict-ridden musical passages, and there is an underlying sense that love, compassion, and understanding are always sufficiently present to guarantee a triumphal outcome. Utopia will be like this. Society—individuals working in concert—will provide the resources for individual joy-maximization, rather than being the obstacle to joy as society so often is today, due to the existence of hierarchy and the anxiety it generates. Angst will surely still occur, but it will be like the angst of Beethoven's music: Angst that co-occurs with faith that the resources to overcome conflict are ever-present and stronger than the conflicts that life presents.

4.   One more important point about joy in Utopia: As I write this, the word "individual" appears often and I know that some readers will see my prescription as too American in its apparent individualism. Let me remind the reader that if society becomes a resource for joy-maximization, providing the conditions for people to metaphorically perform for each other's enjoyment, then the individual versus society dichotomy breaks down, because the individual's joy, as performer, redounds

to the joy of others, the audience. Erasing hierarchy, and maximizing communication and compassion, will ensure that joy will be *both* individual and collective, as indeed it should be, given the capacity for compassion and sociality that is so characteristic of our species.

With this analysis of emotions, we can now turn to the history of the basic emotions for further substantiation of my above claims for joy and its elicitors. This evolutionary history will also allow me to consider the relationship between joy and hierarchy. How did hierarchy evolve? And is its evolutionary history indeed indicative of a fundamental conflict with joy?

The evolutionary background: Joy

Joy and happiness: When and why did they evolve? Why do we feel them? Why do we feel anything at all, in fact? These are hard questions to answer. Many biologists object to using the notion of "emotion" when describing animals other than humans because they feel it projects human qualities onto animals without evidence that animals other than human beings actually do have the capacity to feel. This attitude makes it hard to talk about the evolution of any emotions. However, other biologists point out how difficult it is to deny the existence of emotions among animals when we see our pets greet us happily and joyfully at the door when we return home. Is a jumping dog or a purring cat really not feeling anything? This seems hard to believe. So, following intuition and science as well, a number of scientists studying emotion has suggested that there are, at the very least, homologues to human emotions in non-human animals. If we observe the autonomic patterns humans display when feeling, for example, fear, we can compare these to such patterns as they are found in other animals, and note the similarities. We can also rather easily relate the human elicitors of fear—namely, things that threaten us—to analogous elicitors among animals. Thus, using autonomic data, supplemented with study of elicitors of these autonomic patterns, we can identify homologues to human emotions in other animals.

For joy our intuition provides a good start. (I firmly believe that while intuition is not scientific evidence itself, it can help us formulate hypotheses, guiding us in doing science.) Like the purring cat or jumping dog welcoming us home, animals feel happiness/joy when two conditions are met: First, the presence of other animals—same species or different ones—and second, when the other animals present are friendly, nurturing, and non-threatening to the animal's well-being. Thus there is joy in parental love, in friendship, and in the play that so often accompanies friendly, familial relationships.

With this intuition as a guide, we can hypothesize about the evolution of joy and look for evidence in support of our hypothesis. Following the work of psychologists, anthropologists, and biologists (see, e.g., Sussman and Garber 2004), and adding some of my own thoughts as well, I would argue that *joy evolved to reinforce the parental behaviors so crucial to mammalian survival.* I would add, further, that the mammalian pattern of long-term parental care of offspring facilitated another later key mammalian pattern, occurring among primates and culminating in humans: The evolution of large brains and complex behavior based upon learning. Parental care provided the possibility of long-term teaching and learning between parents and their offspring, and thus made bigger brains, and the learning they enable, a possibility.

What is the evidence for the brain size/parental care link? There is a correlation between the length of time a species is dependent on parents/caretakers and brain size. (Actually, biologists use brain/body ratio as the relevant measure, rather than absolute brain size, since larger-bodied animals have larger tissues in general, so that their large brains do not necessarily reflect greater intelligence as much as does the brain/body ratio.) Specifically, among primates, the larger the brain/body ratio, the longer the species is dependent on its parents, culminating in humans who are dependent on their parents for the greatest amount of time (Langdon 2005: 151, 275; Greenspan and Shanker 2004: 120–123) of any species. Thus, a key mammalian innovation—parenting—facilitated (and indeed was also facilitated by) a latter mammalian innovation of key importance to primates: Big brains, intelligence, and learning (Greenspan and Shanker 2004: 120–123). The correlation between these two innovations culminates in humans, who have the biggest brain/body ratio (Langdon 2005: 151) and the longest period of juvenile dependence upon their parents. Parental care is especially critical for humans because we are born with relatively undeveloped brains when compared to other primates. This is not only due to our big brain size but also to anatomical changes required for us to stand upright. Standing upright may be advantageous, but it constrains the pelvis and the birth canal, requiring humans to be born before our big brains are fully developed. As a result, we are quite helpless at birth and require a long period of parental care and teaching before we can function on our own (Greenspan and Shanker 2004: 129–130; Langdon 2005: 252–253). Parental care, crucial to all mammals, is of greater and greater importance among higher mammals and, most especially, among humans. One feature illustrating the uniqueness of human families is that we are the only species that preserves our ties with our kin even after they have moved away from us. Parent–child and other kin ties facilitate exchange networks between dispersed groups, networks that have been critical to our survival in often uncertain environments (De Waal 2009: 24).

Given how essential parental care is for human survival, it is not surprising that such care is reinforced by positive emotions—the love and compassion parents can feel for their children and the love and joy children feel being cared for by their parents. Now I can hear many readers objecting: "But not all parents are good to their kids. How do you explain that?" Some readers might add that many males don't seem to have gotten the parental bug as much as females have. My response is that there is a general trend in evolution for behavior, even behavior as crucial as parenting, to become more and more volitional, rather than automatic and "instinctive." Humans, again, are the culmination of this trend. Much of our behavioral repertoire is not programmed into our genes, but is learned culturally. And even culture does not determine our behavior; consider how many dissidents exist within any culture. We are constantly creating through our daily actions, in response to the micro and macro social situations in which we find ourselves, and in response to the thoughts and feelings induced by these situations.

Human flexibility, and our concomitant ability to learn and to create cultural norms, can no doubt be considered highly adaptive, as many, many scientists contend, even though this flexibility has some costs. But even if one is skeptical about the adaptive significance of many evolutionary changes, and/or even for those skeptical about the adaptive significance of culture, the history of emotions and their evolution is not substantially altered. I have often, myself, been skeptical about the genuine adaptive significance of culture, since many cultures today do far too many things that seem destructive to our well-being. I have also been frequently skeptical of whether evolution is, indeed, always driven by adaptation. Even so, this does not alter the fact that behavior has become more flexible, and that emotions are central to this flexibility, since we act not automatically but in reaction to what we feel about a given situation.

Thus, my basic contention is that emotions evolved to make behavior more flexible or, more exactly, emotions evolved and hence made behavior more flexible, which may or may not have had adaptive significance. Joy/happiness, those extremely positive emotions, evolved to allow parenting behaviors to be volitional yet rewarded highly with these very strong, very pleasurable emotions. I would further contend that joy and happiness also evolved in the context of, or as a reinforcement for, other extremely necessary behaviors in addition to parenting: Prosocial relationships of any kind, not just parental ones. Evidence that parental nurturing emotions widened to more general prosociality can be seen in analysis of the hormone oxytocin. Oxytocin facilitates mammalian birth, lactation, and the development of maternal bonds but is also hypothesized to underlie more general states of empathy and prosociality (see Carter, Harris, and Porges 2009: 175–176 and Sussman and Garber 2004: 180). So, being with friends and family, and engaging in a prosocial way with them and with others in our communities, became reinforced by joy. Many species cooperate with other members of the same species, including many insect species, for example. But cooperation, communality, and parental and friendly interactions are all reinforced among higher mammals, especially humans, with positive emotions of joy. This is the evolutionary history of joy: It originated in, and possibly to reinforce, prosocial interaction—interaction that is mutually beneficial and mutually pleasurable to all interactants.

Joy is distinguished evolutionarily, and in many other ways to be discussed, from other emotions. In an evolutionary sense it is distinct from other emotions in that the behaviors it is reinforcing have not only the *greatest* importance to individuals and to the group, but the *broadest* value as well. The good things we do for friends and family we usually say are done for reasons of love, not for purely instrumental reasons. The outside analyst might claim that there are broad benefits to such relationships of love but that is precisely my point: The benefits are broad, and not specified, and one of the main benefits to our interaction with friends and family is the good feelings we feel from having companionship. Companionship, and positive engagement with others, is inherently valuable. What we get and give in companionship *is* pleasure. *Pleasure and joy, thus, take on a life of their own, becoming important for their own sake.* No wonder joy is seen by a number of emotion analysts to be the same as, or very closely related to, play. Play is non-instrumental activity. It might ape adult behavior, and can often have a value in preparing us to be adults, but its real value to us, and its very *definition*, lies in its non-instrumental nature. Joy and play may have evolved to reinforce positive interaction, but they have come to be engaged in for their own sake. We seek emotional pleasure—happiness—not for some extrinsic motive but because it is intrinsically pleasurable. Pleasure is pleasurable and happiness makes us happy. This is tautological, I know, but if this is not said, many utopians will seek to define Utopia, and even happiness itself, relative to some extrinsic values, other than happiness. Our puritanical discomfort with the affirmation of pleasure, including emotional pleasure, is strong and causes us to think about happiness in a manner at odds with its true evolutionary history and true nature, namely as a positive feeling that exists broadly, for no necessary external (i.e., goal-oriented) purpose.

Now, what is the actual evidence for my hypothesis about joy: That it evolved to reinforce prosocial emotions? This is an extremely hard question to answer because of evidence problems. The events of evolution we are discussing here happened tens of millions of years ago, or more (see Bell 2001: 226), so the full history of that evolution is extremely hard to know. And since we are talking about the evolution of emotions rather than, say, the evolution of teeth, the evidence we need to reconstruct the story has not been preserved into the present.

Let me begin with the evolution of parenting among mammals and its relationship to pleasure and joy. In a fascinating article Bell (2001) discusses how parenting evolved in mammals. While there are many examples of insects, fish, and reptiles caring for young offspring, rearing of the young reaches its apex in birds and mammals (Lindsey 1994: 29). Mammals, with their unique ability to produce food in the form of milk for offspring (33), have the most complex family lives of all animals (35). How did the capacity for parental care arise? Bell turns to lizards since they are probably the most similar living animal to the mammal-like reptiles (therapsids), which evolved 240 million years ago, and from which mammals in turn evolved (Bell 2001: 218). Lizards are solitary: "[They] live alone or temporarily in male-female pairs … When food is plentiful in an area, lizards and other reptiles may live together in colonies, but their actions remain essentially solitary" (218). Reptiles such as lizards are awful parents. Only 1% of oviparous lizards give any post-egg-laying care to eggs they lay. This is consistent with the general reptile pattern where the mother lays eggs, buries them, and then goes away. Such neglect, for the offspring, is perhaps the best they could hope for since both contemporary and ancient reptiles feared strange animals and even found their own offspring to be strange. This "stranger rejection" response is based upon smell, and is processed in the emotional center of the brain, the limbic system. Smells are carried in the brain by vasotocin, which has been hypothesized to activate the fear system when predators are near and also induce competition for status. While the reptilian fear of strangers has its advantages, it is tremendously threatening to the young, since reptile parents view their own offspring as strangers and, fearful of them, *often kill them* (218–219)!

Mammals, in sharp contrast to reptiles, care for their young and, for the most part, do not kill them. (There are exceptions. Male lions will kill the cubs of a previous leader they have displaced. See Bell 2001: 219.) Bell sees the evolution of mammalian caregiving as centered in changes outside of the neocortex, since caregiving preceded most neocortex growth. He hypothesizes that reptilian vasotocin evolved into vasopressin and oxytocin, noting that the latter two peptide hormones each differ from vasotocin by a single amino acid. Oxytocin is released in female mammals when they give birth and it reduces the rejection of strangers—the response leading reptiles to ignore or attack their own offspring. Inhibiting stranger rejection was the first step toward full parental care among mammals (220–221).

The next step was the creation of a parent–child emotional bond. Oxytocin plays a key role here too. It is stimulated by an infant's sucking at the mother's nipples and, more generally, by any touch. This makes parents feel pleasure at the presence of their offspring, since the oxytocin released by sucking and touching reduces anxiety by leading to the release of opioids. Oxytocin's effect is itself supplemented by opioids, which have an important role in promoting caregiving. Bell notes that an opioid antagonist has been found to reduce the protecting of, and nurture of, infant rhesus monkeys. As the parent develops memories from interacting with its child, the positive emotions reinforcing the parent–child bond strengthen and lead to parental feelings of pleasure (220–227). The role of opioids in giving pleasure to nurturing parents is complemented in their offspring. Recent research shows mice that lack an opioid receptor do not cry when separated from their mothers, the way that mice with the receptor do. This study supports other researchers' findings that opioids help infants bond to their parents (Beckman 2004: 1888–1889).

Now the key points to note here are (1) the role of *emotions* in caregiving and (2) the *positive nature* of those emotions. First, unlike many analysts, who view mammalian caregiving as stemming from the development of the neocortex, Bell argues that research on caregiving needs to affirm the critical nature of emotions as well, especially since the evolution of caregiving came before most expansion of the neocortex (Bell 2001: 220). Second, touch and the presence of one's offspring stimulates oxytocin, in turn leading to the release of opioids. Continued parent–child interaction produces strong pleasurable memories and is further tied to opioids, for *both* parents and their offspring. Needless to say, this is where joy comes in. Opioids are the primary neuromodulators of joy/happiness/play (Panksepp 2004: 144, 149).

Thus, joy evolved concurrently with (and probably reinforced) the evolution of the parental caregiving that is so central to mammals. Our reptilian ancestors—who were solitary, fearful of strangers, and awful parents—became the mammals that we are: Animals with the strong capacity to feel joy in the presence of our families and in the presence of other conspecifics (members of the same species) more generally. This makes humans an "obligatorily gregarious" (De Waal 2005: 231) species.

Recent writing on the evolution of mammalian neural systems lends further support to Bell's description of the hormonal changes resulting in a change from fear of offspring, among our reptilian ancestors, to care for them among mammals. Newly evolved neural systems in mammals put a brake on primitive fear responses (just as do the new hormones), thus allowing mammalian conspecifics to interact with each other prosocially, rather than only seeing each other as threats. Intriguingly, the new neural systems that calm the fight/flight/freeze behaviors are also linked to the brain nuclei that regulate muscles of the face and head, those muscles used in mammalian social communication. Thus, the quick fear responses are overridden so that mammals can trust each other, cooperate with each other, and communicate with each other (Carter, Harris, and Porges 2009: See, e.g., 174).

One other study related to joy that I want to discuss is Panksepp and Burgdorf's (2003) work on laughter among rats. They have discovered play- and tickle-induced affective ultrasonic vocalization patterns in rats that they believe to be related to human laughter. They see this as a possible evolutionary precursor to the joyful laughter produced by human children when they are playing socially. Thus they tentatively suggest an evolutionary antecedent to both human laughter and human joy, especially the joy of play.

What, to me, is especially interesting about this research is that it helps demonstrate the evolution of the link between joy and parenting, on the one hand, and non-parental joyful interaction (play), on the other. Here are the two points making the link:

1. Joy is associated with parenting, as my previous discussion has demonstrated. Joy is also associated, according to Panksepp and Burgdorf's (2003) laughing rat research, with play. This doesn't prove that parental joy has evolved into broader joy deriving from any prosocial interaction, but it suggests that this might be the case. Supporting this notion is the fact that the more intelligent and social a species is, the more it plays. This pattern culminates in chimpanzees and, of course, in humans (Wilson 1980: 84–86). The centrality of play to humans, even to human adults, is consistent with a trait thought by Stephen Jay Gould to be the hallmark of human evolution: The retention of juvenile traits into adulthood (De Waal 2005: 240–241).
2. And further, Panksepp notes: "In general, the chemistries that activate separation distress tend to reduce play, while several chemistries that reduce separation distress, especially opioids, increase play" (2004: 149). Thus play, joy, and parental care are interconnected!

These two points taken together suggest what may have happened in evolution: *Joy evolved to reinforce parenting but then became more generally connected to any prosocial interaction (not just that between parent and child), especially the interaction we call "play": Prosocial, non-instrumental interaction.* This is, of course, consistent with our experience of joy: We feel it from parental nurture (giving or receiving it) and from love, companionship, and prosocial interaction of multiple kinds.

Humans are not only one example among many of the mammalian connection between nurture and joy, rather we are the *culmination* of the mammalian trend connecting joy and nurture. That connection is stronger among us than among any other primates or mammals and it is broader too, so that we derive joy from nurturing humans other than merely our own children. In support of the contention that the joy/nurture connection is strongest and broadest in humans, I will cite research on the evolution of our human pattern of parenting. Our parenting pattern distinguishes us from all other apes because of the wide range of humans who take part in caring for children. I will also describe the anatomical structures of the human brain that produce joy, and, by comparison to such structures in other primates, will show our special capacity for joy.

First, nurture: Alloparenting is the term used to describe the process of cooperative breeding. A species that alloparents is one in which offspring are nurtured and provisioned not only by their own parents, but also by other members of the community (Hrdy 2009: 30). Cooperative breeding is found in many species, including many insects, birds, and mammals, including primates. However, it is not found among any of the Great Apes—except for humans (275). Hrdy argues that our ancestors, unlike our living chimp relatives, evolved into cooperative breeders, and this paved the way for humans to have long postmenopausal lifespans, because postmenopausal women would have helped care for and provision others' children. Cooperative breeding also led to longer and longer childhood dependency and this, in turn, allowed for the evolution of the human brain, a very costly development that could only have been sustained by the kind of provisioning possible when more than one or two persons care for a child (275–280). Given the big brains of *Homo erectus*, Hrdy hypothesizes that both cooperative breeding as well as the longer childhood dependency and big brains that it facilitates were characteristic of that species, which lived 1.8 million years ago (277–278). Thus, our evolutionary ancestors took the mammalian pattern of nurture to its greatest development. The Great Apes did not alloparent and other species that do breed cooperatively have much shorter spans of childhood dependence on adults. Our ancestors survived and thrived in a very difficult early Pleistocene environment (278) by becoming the cooperative nurturers that we still are today. Cooperation, and in particular cooperation in nurture, is the distinctive hallmark of humans and our evolutionary ancestors. (See also van Schaik and Burkhart 2010 for a discussion of the connection between cooperative breeding and the evolution of prosociality among humans and ancestors in our genus, *Homo*.)

Second, joy and brain anatomy: Eccles (1989) cites data showing that the portion of the amygdala associated with positive and pleasurable emotions came to occupy a larger percentage of the total amygdala volume. This increase in the amygdala pleasure centers occurred throughout the evolution of primates, with the highest percentage of pleasurable amygdala occurring in humans (with the puzzling exception of gibbons, whose portion of the amygdala regulating pleasure slightly exceeds that portion in humans). The portion of the amygdala associated with negative emotions, however, declined throughout primate evolution, a trend again culminating in humans (102–106, 113). The sociologist Jonathan Turner (2000) reviews the data of Eccles and others and offers an evolutionary scenario to explain all of this. He speculates that the pleasure centers of the brain grew early in hominid evolution, before the expansion of the neocortex. He further connects the evolution of our capacity for joy to the importance of our social bonds. He explains that negative sanctions relying on anger and fear are disruptive to social harmony, whereas positive sanctions are not nearly as disruptive. Because of our ancestors' cooperative nature, they evolved a greater capacity for pleasure in order to pave the way for positive sanctions, which in turn allowed them to maintain social harmony (Turner 2000: 48–49, 54, 91–95).

As I have explained previously, the evolution of emotions is extremely difficult to describe with certainty, so the evidence presented here could never be taken as definitive proof. Such proof is simply impossible to find. But the evidence, taken as a whole, suggests a consistent pattern. Our ancestors developed a tremendously advantageous ability to cooperate with each other, especially the critical capacity to cooperate in the raising of children. Cooperative breeding, in turn, facilitated the evolution of our big brains. And our ancestors also evolved an enhanced capacity for joy.

It is our special capacity to nurture broadly, and our enhanced capacity to feel joy, that suggests to me that humans are the culmination of the mammalian joy/nurture complex. We nurture most broadly and our greater capacity for joy reinforces our nurturant tendencies.

Human happiness derives from, and even is tantamount to, mutual nurture. And from a biological and evolutionary perspective, the emotion of happiness is not derived from, nor related to, the domination of others in hierarchies, despite the feeling of satisfaction—an illusory satisfaction, I will argue below—that many humans seem to experience when dominating others.

More evolution: The history of hierarchy

With this history of the evolution of joy, we can now look to hierarchy, and its antagonism toward joy. I begin with a synchronic observation: When a challenge to the established dominance hierarchy rears its head among chimpanzees, the first casualty is play (De Waal 2005: 63). This is consistent with our own intuition, I think: *Threatening interaction, such as dominance and hierarchy, preempts play and joy.* I do need to confess here, however, that some analysts have pointed out a relationship between play and dominance; Panksepp even says "social dominance is also learned through the dictates of play systems" (2004: 149). This point could be a serious challenge to my assertion of an antagonism between play/joy and hierarchy but in fact I do not believe the challenge is real. This is because I part company with Panksepp in the definition and characterization of play. I follow many scholars, and probably the reader's intuitions as well, in defining play as non-instrumental and inherently non-serious. Therefore, interaction truly functioning as a means to the end of establishing dominance cannot be seen as play. It is true, of course, that much play apes adults and adult interactions, but children dressing or acting as adults is funny to adults precisely because they are not adults, and their behavior makes light of and even mocks behavior that we adults take so seriously. And children's own laughter at their mockery shows that they recognize what they are doing. Much play functions this way: It mocks and subverts threats and fear, as when we playfully fight or tease each other, knowing all the while that the conflict is not real. Even my own cat easily knew that my play-fighting with her was play and not serious. Thus, play is subversive of conflict and dominance, not supportive of it. That is, after all, what makes it "play."

Let me now turn to the evolution of hierarchy. When and why did hierarchy evolve? The evolutionary origins of hierarchy have not been extensively investigated by evolutionary biologists (Douglas Futuyma, personal communication), but one thing is fairly clear: Hierarchy, or what biologists call "dominance" and "dominance hierarchies," *evolved much earlier than, hence separate from,* mammals and their practice of giving long-term parental care to their offspring.

Dominance hierarchies were first observed in the 1920s among domestic hens, where highly linear hierarchies are established based on pecking, hence the commonly known term for the phenomenon among hens, "pecking order." Dominance hierarchies are present in most social vertebrates and also among invertebrates such as crickets, ants, wasps, and shrimp (Hall 1994: 98). Hierarchy evolved among group animals as a substitute for fighting. Fighting over food and/or sexual mates can result in injury or death. An alternative is for two animals (within the same species) to develop a relationship in which one defers to the other, letting the other have primary access to food and/or sexual partners. The animal that routinely defers is the subordinate one, while the one who gets preference is "dominant." The dominant–subordinate relationship exists between pairs of animals but out of these pairs a larger ranking arises, albeit not always in a clear, linear fashion (97–98, 100–102).

Many factors can lead one individual to dominate another individual. These include size (bigger individuals dominate smaller ones), age (usually older dominate younger), inherited status (among baboons and macaque monkeys a female has the rank of her mother, "inheriting" status from her mother), and alliances (99). A common primate pattern is for two or more subordinate animals to band together to overthrow a dominant individual (99).

Now what is most relevant for the purposes of my argument is the concomitants of hierarchy. We could imagine a passionless hierarchy in which, say, the smaller animals always deferred, without hesitation, to the larger ones. But in reality, because food and sex, fundamentals of survival, are at stake (101–102), dominance hierarchies reduce conflict but never eliminate it, nor do they eliminate the threat of conflict. (The persistence of conflict also stems from an apparent paradox of hierarchy: If it is not periodically performed in some way, it will eventually cease to exist. So, at a certain level, conflict, plus dominance and submission displays, must be endemic to hierarchy. This is true for human hierarchy as well. Human hierarchy requires some periodic performances of status differences, in order to be perpetuated.) Therefore, subordinate/dominant interactions (and even fighting) can, and sometimes do, happen. While it is difficult to read the emotions involved, the fight/flight modality of interaction suggests a mapping onto anger and fear, with the frequent displays of subordination and submission hinting at something like sadness or depression. In chimps the fear grin of the subordinate chimp or the presentation of the rump by subordinates in many species of monkey (98) further suggests the states of mind of subordinate and dominant individuals.

While some scholars object to using emotion words for animals, more are willing to do so than in the past, and I think it is appropriate to identify the submission as homologous to fear, or self-deprecation (which in humans becomes depression). And so here is the key point: *Hierarchy as it has evolved is infused with the emotions of aggression/anger, fear, and sadness/depression. It is not connected to such positive emotions as joy.* Animals *do* feel joy/happiness but these positive and pleasurable emotions are connected to interactions devoid of conflict and self-interest. It is interactions of positive sociality—play among age-mates or parent–child nurturance—that lead to good feelings. In sum, hierarchy is based on a more primitive drive for individual survival, and is tied to the fight/flight modality of anger and fear. Joy, as described previously, is connected to prosociality.

Hierarchy among humans: An antagonist to joy

Now what does this mean for hierarchy and emotions among humans? What I aim to show is that hierarchy in humans incites negative emotions in all of us, just as is the case with animals. Whether we are on top, in the middle, or on the bottom of any hierarchy—of class, race, gender, sexual orientation, ability, looks, etc.—we will feel negative emotions such as fear, anger, disgust, and condescension. Further, we will not feel the positive pleasurable emotion of joy/happiness. I will also show, most importantly, that not only is hierarchy *not* a source of pleasure and joy, but that its existence actively interferes with the joy that might be felt from other sources: Hierarchy crowds out happiness and joy, even among those of high status— sometimes *especially* among those of high status. Hierarchy precludes happiness. Thus, its elimination is a necessary (though not sufficient) condition of Utopia.

The claims made in the preceding paragraph will be divided into three separate contentions:

1. The evolutionary connection of hierarchy to negative emotions continues among humans. Fear and anger and additional negative emotions of depression, contempt, and disgust are fundamental aspects of human hierarchy.
2. The positive pleasurable human emotions of joy/happiness and interest/ excitement are not aroused by hierarchy.
3. Most importantly, hierarchy diminishes the feelings of joy, play, and excitement that humans might otherwise feel in the absence of hierarchy.

With this background to human emotions we can proceed to the evidence for the three contentions.

Contention 1: Human hierarchy, like animal hierarchy, is based on negative emotions

Obviously, human hierarchy is extraordinarily complex and I could devote this entire book to elucidating this complexity. But one critical characteristic that human hierarchy shares with non-human hierarchy is the emotions that infuse both. Human and non-human hierarchies alike are infused with negative emotions. For animals it is fear and anger/aggression. Humans add condescension (seen by many emotion scholars as a basic emotion), such as the condescension of class systems. We also add disgust, a prime constituent of race and caste systems, where uppers feel they will be contaminated by intimate contact, eating together, or living together with lowers. Finally, animal submission is perhaps closely related to human low self-esteem and depression. These, then, are the emotions of human hierarchy—all negative ones.

Now what is especially interesting about human hierarchy, and a difference between such hierarchy and animal dominance hierarchies, is that in many forms of human hierarchy it is quite explicitly the higher-status individuals whose positions are characterized by negative emotions. One can see this among non-humans too. I will give evidence in the next section to show that negative emotions are experienced by dominant rats. But with human hierarchies the very nature of the hierarchical system itself is often premised on the greater dangers experienced by high-status individuals and groups, dangers coming from lower-status individuals and groups. The reason that this is important is that it supports my contention here (contention 1) by illustrating that among humans, in many cases, it is *the entire hierarchical system that is infused with negativity*. Negativity is not just relegated to the lower status.

A classic example is race and caste systems. Such hierarchical systems as American race or caste in India seek to prevent contact between uppers and lowers and it is *uppers* who suffer most from cross-status contact, being polluted by contact with lowers (as when Indian "Untouchables" encounter high-caste Indians). As a result, the system is built out of the anxiety of the uppers, anxiety about what will happen if they encounter those of lower status (and the anticipation of disgust should an encounter occur). I might add here, too, that there is another difference between human caste and animal dominance hierarchies. While animal uppers usually gain from their superior status because it gives them greater access to food and sex, in human dominance the situation is often more complex. Many caste systems actually restrict the sexual privileges of high-caste members in comparison to low-caste members. While this restriction is most commonly placed on high-caste females, there are caste systems, such as that of the Yi, an indigenous group I studied in China (Schoenhals 2003), in which both female and male uppers are more restricted than their female and male lower-status counterparts in terms of sexual license. Hence, here too everyone who is part of the culture faces anxiety (in this case anxiety pertaining to sexual violations), not just those of lower status.

What about anxiety and social class systems? I don't think I will have to convince the reader that being poor is a source of anxiety, since the poor in many countries often face the prospect of not having enough to eat. But the wealthy, and other elites, are not relieved of anxiety. In fact, as in caste systems, many class systems place their upper-status individuals and groups under the greatest explicit anxiety-producing pressures. I have written of this pattern in meritocratic China, where status is conferred upon those who are meritorious (at least in theory) but where such merit is constantly being tested. As a result of the performative nature of Chinese status, those with the greatest status usually live with the greatest fear that in a wide variety of contexts they may perform badly, and hence lose their status and reputations, what the Chinese refer to as "losing face" (Schoenhals 1993). Also, in contrast to the animal pattern whereby an angry and threatening superordinate confronts the fearful and submissive subordinate—a confrontation that serves to remind subordinate animals of their proper place—in Chinese culture there is cultural permission and even encouragement given for anger displays among *subordinates* while a *non*-angry and often benevolent posture is required of superiors (Schoenhals 1993).

One of the reasons human hierarchy is so thoroughly infused with negative emotions is because we humans have culture. Human hierarchy is not just played out between individuals seeking food or sex, it is often taught and talked about endlessly by the socializing institutions of society. In schools, workplaces, religious institutions, and in the home and in the media, hierarchy is constantly being portrayed and propagated, and sometimes contested. Hierarchy and its negative emotions may characterize non-human dominance, but hierarchy and negative emotions are even more significantly spread throughout any human society due to culture. And two more human features that lead to the spread of negativity: Human hierarchy adds group over group dominance to the individual over individual dominance of animals; and, of course, our dominance systems span not just generations but centuries.

One final characteristic of human hierarchy showing that it is at least as infused with negativity as is the case with animal hierarchy: Humans have added to fear and anger several powerful emotions to reinforce hierarchy. As mentioned above, we add condescension and disgust. Perhaps most quintessentially human of all, humans add shame to the arsenal with which hierarchies are enforced. While not all shame comes from being in a hierarchy, both the lower status and the upper status confront shame in hierarchy: The lowers for what they are, the uppers for what they fear they could become, if they lose their status. And since we can think about the future, humans add worry and anxiety about our future social status to the long list of negative emotions that are endured by all animals living in hierarchical systems.

Contention 2: Hierarchy among humans does not produce happiness

This contention is the hardest to argue. After all, if hierarchy is not pleasurable, why do we manufacture hierarchies so readily and why do we pursue places at the hierarchical peak with such obsession? First, an answer that appeals to the reader's intuition. We all know people who persist in doing things they don't really enjoy—drinking too much, gambling excessively, working too much, or pursuing money and material goods too fervently. Some of these pursuits—of money, hard work—are often connected to our survival. And thus, as with animal hierarchy, human desire to obtain a top spot stems from an understandable fear and anxiety: The anxiety that if we are not on the top, our survival will be endangered. But readers will also know, all too well, how easily any fear, especially existential ones, can run amok, leading to obsessive-compulsive behavior. Even if we're on top, we don't feel happiness but continuing fear, fear that we must keep working or we'll lose the top spot, or fear that we're really not top enough—even guilt that we're on top at someone else's expense. In fact the higher we are, the *more* vulnerable we often are, a phenomenon I described in my work on China as the "paradox of power" (Schoenhals 1993). Among caste systems it is uppers who fear being polluted by lowers, a reflection that, in a sense, the uppers are still vulnerable, and still anxious, perhaps even more anxious than lowers. I do not want to minimize the pain that lowers genuinely feel, but it is important to point out that earning the top spot is not the key to happiness, because it often does not end the craving and anxiety. In fact I have often thought that the relentless seeking of fame and fortune is an addiction just as much as any addiction to drugs or alcohol. Money-obsession, like substance abuse, is driven by anxiety and compulsion. Money, like drugs, doesn't give us real happiness but only temporarily calms us, and gives us the illusion of contentment. We may even know the truth of our dissatisfaction and unhappiness, but we continue the addiction nonetheless, even at the expense of our real well-being. It is important to add here that the folk view of addictions—that people engage in addictive behaviors such as drug taking because they give pleasure—is wrong. Recent research indicates that there are two separate brain reward systems in mammals. Nesse and Berridge (1997) call these systems "liking" and "wanting." "Liking" occurs upon receiving the reward, whereas "wanting" anticipates the reward and motivates instrumental behavior. Liking brings pleasure, but wanting motivates a quest for something, whether or not that something brings pleasure. These two reward systems are neurologically separate as well as functionally distinct. The authors explain that pleasure is "mediated by certain opioid forebrain systems and by brain-stem systems" while wanting is "mediated by ascending mesolimbic dopamine neurons." "Liking" and "wanting" are needed for a full reward and normally co-occur. But this is not always the case. What happens in addiction is that the wanting system is activated in the absence of the pleasure motivation, so that behaviors are pursued relentlessly, addictively, even though they do not actually produce pleasure (Nesse and Berridge 1997: 64; Berridge 2004: 194–196). My point in citing this research is to give further validation for my contention that the pursuit of hierarchy is not proof, by any means, that it brings us pleasure. The obsessive pursuit of hierarchy, like the obsessive taking of a drug, is a non-pleasurable addiction, destructive to ourselves and to those around us.

My feelings about money being an obsession are by no means original, of course. The majority of world religions recognizes these obsessions as a primary cause of human individual and collective unhappiness, and hurtfulness to others. Although there is much about religion that is damaging, the insight about the addictive destructiveness of the pursuit of fame and fortune is one of religion's genuine contributions to human well-being.

Hierarchy also induces low self-esteem and depression. We know this is true for those who are low on the status ladder, but it is true for uppers too, and for the society as a whole. Why? One of my Yi student-informants explained this to me brilliantly, when arguing the negative consequences of Han Chinese feelings of superiority. (He believes the Han look down on others more than do the Yi, despite the existence of castes among the Yi.) His argument is: If your society doesn't condone looking down on others, there will be much less of a likelihood that individuals will look down on themselves. Only with the presence of feelings of superiority and inferiority in a society can there be such a thing as a feeling of self-inferiority and low self-esteem; basically, when an individual becomes accustomed to looking down, that looking down can be turned inward, toward oneself. If there are no such feelings of condescension in a society, then low self-esteem and its accompanying depression are much less likely to occur.

All of the previous discussion strongly suggests that hierarchy does not produce happiness and joy, and augments anxiety and depression, but is there any scientific evidence that this is so? First, I would remind the reader of the evidence presented on the evolution of joy and of hierarchy. These evolutionary stories are completely separate, strong evidence to support the disconnect between hierarchy and pleasure. Second, fascinating research on rodents has been done recently in order to model causes and consequences of anxiety and depression among humans. Not surprisingly, rats who are subordinate in a dominance hierarchy feel anxiety and depression. (It should be noted that the authors explain that human anxiety and depression are interconnected—Arregi et al. 2006: 398.) Arregi et al. (397) write:

> In specific terms, it has been found that repeated experiences of social defeat or subordination is a psychological factor that provokes behavioral and physiological alterations in rodents that are related to neuroendocrine changes coupled to a negative emotional state typical of anxious/depressive symptoms in humans … and are sensitive to antidepressant treatments.

The subordinate rodents' depression decreases their social interaction with other rodents and decreases their sensitivity to rewards, such as sucrose (398). All of this should sound familiar to humans who, when depressed, find less joy in normal activities, such as contact with friends and family, and who frequently withdraw from such normally pleasurable interaction.

But there is more to the rodent research that is not necessarily intuitive. The authors review research showing that it is not only subordinate rodents whose emotions are negatively affected by dominance hierarchy. Dominant rodents—those on the top of the hierarchy—can display significant stress from maintaining their dominant position (401–402). Even more interesting is that dominant individuals in a wide variety of species, all cooperative breeders, show *greater* stress than subordinates (Creel 2001). Ferrari et al. (1998) have found higher anxiety among socially dominant Swiss male mice than among social subordinates. Sapolsky (2005) reviews the stress literature and the complex factors at work in stress, concluding that sometimes dominants are the most stressed while at other times it is subordinates who are most stressed. Wittig et al. (2015) find that dominant chimpanzees have higher urinary glucocorticoid levels following aggressive interactions than do subordinate individuals and they argue that this is due in large part to psychological reasons rather than due to the need for energy for aggressive encounters (the conventional explanation). In addition there is also research showing that dominant rats experience what the researchers say is a model of a (human) manic state, and researchers find that treating rats with an anti-manic human medication suppresses dominance behavior (Malatynska and Knapp 2005).

All of the above evidence is consistent, of course, with my argument that hierarchy is related to anxiety (and also, in this case, to the agitation of mania), but not to genuine pleasure and joy; the finding of anxiety in dominants shows that hierarchy is anxiety-inducing for them as well. Mania, it should be noted, is an elevated mood that is different from happiness in that humans who are manic remain in an elevated mood regardless of whether there are good or bad stimuli to which they are exposed—that is, it is a mood indifferent to external pleasure or displeasure. Mania is also characterized by recklessness and sexual disinhibition. And, of course, it cycles into the depressive episodes characteristic of bipolar disorder. Some people think that mania and depression are not just related in bipolar disorder, but are actually similar emotions, both responding to loss or fear of loss, but with depression being a fearful withdrawal from the loss or impeding loss, but mania being an aggressive (the fight rather than flight modality), confrontational approach response to loss or impending loss. (My characterization here draws not only from the psychological literature but also from web blogs. See, for example, the fascinating discussion on the mania–depression relationship, posted by Sandy Gautam at http://the-mouse-trap.com/2010/03/19/am-manic-will-focus-am-sad-will-drift/. Accessed on January 30, 2011.)

Contention 3: Hierarchy interferes with joy; it "crowds out" joy

As above, I begin with an intuitive appeal: The reader knows how anxiety produced by zero-sum competition (where if X wins, no one else wins) can make us tense up, diminishing the joy, pleasure, and excitement we would otherwise feel. This is a common experience of performers, such as those speaking, acting, or performing musically in public. Performance anxiety is also a common experience in sex. When men, for example, feel the pressure of sexual performance and anticipate sexual failure, they end up not able to function sexually and not able to fully experience sexual gratification. I think it is especially revealing that the Internet is filled with men advising other men that the way to overcome such performance anxiety is to refocus their attitudes on the pleasures of sex, rather than seeing sex as a proving ground for one's superior masculinity, or rather than seeing sex as an obligation or a job, as one male clinical psychologist described it on his web site (www. stanleyducharme.com/resources/anxiety.htm. Accessed on April 18, 2011). Here we have the clear antithesis between pleasure and hierarchy. Hierarchy and a desire for dominance leads to anxiety and hence crowds out pleasure, in this case sexual pleasure. And a refocus on pleasure is the common treatment for performance anxiety, since this focus works, in turn, to crowd out anxiety. One musician writing to other musicians experiencing performance anxiety makes the focus on pleasure and joy one of his "six golden rules" for overcoming their anxiety. He counsels that "your performance ... [should be] a time of joy and not a time for correcting errors or other faults" (http://davidleisner.com/six-golden-rules-for-conquering-performance-anxiety/. Accessed on April 18, 2011).

Another intuitive appeal regarding our attitudes toward "work": I often ask my students what they do on weekends. I then ask them if they would enjoy these activities as much if I made them part of their homework assignment. The reader can guess the answer: "No way." One of my students, getting the point, said that a genre of fiction she formerly loved to read became a chore when one of her professors assigned it to her one day. The point here is clear: A pleasant and joyful activity, no matter what its inherent content, can be made unfun if it is turned into "work," into an obligation. And the basis for the obligation is hierarchy. Students know if they do not do their "work," they will fall down the hierarchical ladder (by getting a bad grade), which in turn can push them down the career ladder into a lower-status job. The anxiety and fear that pervade threats to one's status all come into play once an action, however pleasant, becomes wedded to hierarchy. Thus, hierarchy crowds out joy.

Scientists confirm our intuitive feelings. Among primates De Waal has found that play stops when there is a challenge to the established dominance hierarchy among chimps (2005: 63). Panksepp summarizes research on joy and play among mammals by saying that "*any agent that promotes negative emotions reduces play*" (2004: 144; emphasis added).

Anthropologist Victor Turner describes two opposing types of human interaction, structure—equivalent to hierarchy—and what he calls "*communitas*"—a sense of community derived from an egalitarian lack of hierarchy and the presence of generalized selflessness (1977: Chapter 3, see, e.g., 106, 126–127). Turner identifies structure with mundane emotions and *communitas* with joyful, ecstatic and often religious experiences. He describes how egalitarian community leads to transcendent positive emotions. When structure and hierarchy displace *communitas*, the special joy of *communitas* ceases (128, 138–139, Chapters 3 and 4).

Research on the human brain supports the antagonistic relationship between anxiety and other negative emotions, on the one hand, and pleasure, on the other. This research supports contention 3 because of the association I've already described between anxiety (and other negative emotions) and hierarchy. That is, hierarchy produces anxiety and other negative emotions, and these decrease human pleasures and happiness. In a recent definitive work on pleasure in the brain, the various authors discuss whether pleasure and pain are on opposite ends of a continuum or whether they are different kinds of brain response. While there is uncertainty about the answer to this issue, they all agree that pain and pleasure are clear antagonists. Petrovic describes two examples of the antagonism. He says that sadness suppresses the opioid system, a system that gives pleasure. He also notes that the CCK (chole-cystokinin) system, which induces anxiety, is antagonistic to the opioid system. If the CCK system is active, the opioid system is inhibited and vice versa. That is, the production of anxiety by one system reduces the feelings of pleasure and well-being in another brain system, the opioid system (Petrovic quoted in Kringelbach and Berridge 2010: 12–13). I know that some readers may hasten to argue here with the idea of pain and pleasure as opposed by citing the fact that pain can produce pleasure, for some people, in sex. The same can be said about dominating others sexually, or being dominated. However, just as playful hierarchy among children is not the same as real hierarchy, pain and domination in sex are not the same as actual pain and domination, and this observation is one that I have heard SM (sadomaso-chism) enthusiasts assert frequently in defense of SM—often claiming SM to be subversion of pain and domination, or a parody of them. Sometimes their assertions seem suspiciously defensive, to me, and I wonder if a more nuanced explanation might be this: We all have endured pain, humiliation, and domination and have experienced the hurt these engender. Some people try to heal this hurt by taking control of it, and by reenacting the hurtful episodes in quasi-playful form during sex. This is an understandable response to hurt, but it does not prove that hurt/pain and pleasure are the same thing. In fact it really shows what the researchers cited above are saying: That they are distinct. After all, if pain and pleasure were interchangeable, then there would be no such thing as SM to begin with since the whole dynamic of SM depends on taking something that is painful and transforming it into something pleasurable. I know SM enthusiasts may disagree with me here, but I think that an ideal world, ultimately, should try to minimize pain and domination altogether, so that the cathartic pursuit of pain and domination would no longer be necessary, and so that pleasure can be pursued for the sake of pleasure, and pain avoided. If we lived in an egalitarian world, then the humiliations we all endure would diminish, and there would be less craving for healing through reenacting and recreating pain and domination in SM sex, and pleasure could be returned to its purest (hence most pleasurable), pain-free form.

For me, the strongest evidence for the tendency of hierarchy to crowd out joy can be seen in the observation so often made that exuberant joy is much more often displayed among some oppressed peoples than among their oppressors. My good friend and colleague, Kant Nimbark, frequently remarked to me that he felt upper-caste Indians were more emotionally constricted and challenged than were members of many of the lower castes, such as Kant's own lower-ranked caste. (I would add, with fondest memories, that anyone who knew Kant before he died knew how real were his capacities for joy.) I have heard black Americans say the same thing about white Americans, gay men say the same thing about straight men, and have read that upper-class Brazilians believe that the one thing they can learn from Afro-Brazilians is how to enjoy life and be happy. I would add that I was impressed by the joyfulness of Dalit (Untouchable) Indians whom I met in 2006 during research among them.

Why is there such joy among the oppressed? Clearly, I do not believe the oppressed are joyful because they are oppressed. Rather, the reason that disenfranchised peoples often more easily display joy than do their overlords is because they have learned to seek emotional satisfaction from sources other than social status, and from relationships that have less to do with status—from a playful sense of community, for example. Upper-status people, who are much more invested in maintaining status, spend more time thinking about their high status, honoring it, and trying, in vain, to derive joy from it. They lack the resources to make their own critique of hierarchy, to realize—as many disenfranchised people do—that true pleasure and joy in life come from avoiding status issues altogether.

Final thoughts

I want to finish this discussion by analyzing how hierarchy not only crowds out joy, but also interferes with the potentialities of joy to solve a longstanding evolutionary dilemma, the dilemma of altruism.

To most of us, altruism has a good ring to it. The idea of people helping others at their own expense is appealing, especially to all of us accustomed to self-interested social behavior. But altruism is hard to explain with evolutionary theory, since benefiting another at one's own expense does not seem biologically sustainable.

Joy changes the altruistic calculus. Like altruism, it reinforces benevolence, but it does so in an evolutionarily innovative way. With altruism, X benefits Y at X's own expense. But joy sets up a new dynamic in which there is a feedback of positive benefits going in *both directions, so that the benefits from the giver benefit both the giver and the receiver.* The reason this feedback occurs is due to another, related, evolutionary innovation: Compassion. Because of compassion—which only humans and apes, and perhaps also dolphins and elephants, possess (De Waal 2005: 194–195)—humans and our evolutionary ancestors know what others feel, and our feelings are reinforced by theirs. Thus, if we give another conspecific pleasure, we *know* that they feel pleasure, and we feel pleasure from their pleasure, they from our enhanced pleasure, etc. This is the essence of joy: It generates positive feelings that spread in a positive *virtuous cycle* to others. Benefit is no longer a zero-sum game. Beneficial actions no longer have to cost anyone anything. This should sound familiar to the reader. It is, indeed, the dynamics of ideal love (pleasing the other pleases the self), and it is also the dynamics of aesthetic pleasuring, where the artist pleases the audience, and their pleasure increases the performer's pleasure, ad infinitum. (I'll leave it to the evolutionarily inclined reader to speculate on the quite obvious advantages of a system in which benefit is mutually reinforced in a virtuous cycle.)

Now here is where hierarchy so clearly impedes joy. *Hierarchy, by its very nature, impedes joy's feedback dynamics.* That is, in a hierarchical situation, X can give money or praise to Y, but *the giving is limited.* If X overdoes it, then the hierarchy is destroyed, because X gives away all his money, or praises so much that Y rises beyond X in status. Hierarchy is about self-interest and perhaps altruism too (on the part of subordinates), but not unbridled joy, with its virtuous cycle of well-being, that is, well-being for all. Ultimately, in hierarchical systems one person's happiness is often another person's loss, which is why hierarchies so commonly engender feelings of what the Germans call *Schadenfreude*, or what the Chinese refer to as *xing zai le huo*: I feel good precisely by knowing that you feel worse. This is a powerful emotion, to be sure, but it is not one that can be described as joy. Only with the elimination of hierarchy can joy truly flourish. Only then can we all benefit from each other's prosociality.

On hierarchy and human nature

Perhaps the strongest objection to my proposed good society is that hierarchy, even if based on objectionable emotions, is nonetheless ubiquitous. Can any society possibly get rid of hierarchy, since it seems to be inevitable? And can compassion for others really predominate over the self-interest that is at the core of hierarchy? Given the horrific extent of war and genocide during the 20th century, the bloodiest century in history, it would seem that the prospects for compassion and egalitarian community are slim.

First, an intuitive appeal: Though our 20th-century history makes us feel that humans are warlike, violent, and greedy all the time, this is not true. We sometimes act with great compassion, even in the face of trying circumstances. Two examples familiar to me: After 9/11 people came from all over America to New York City volunteering their efforts to help with disaster recovery at the 9/11 site. They did this out of sheer kindness, not because anyone paid them. Many did this at great risk to their own health and well-being, on behalf of victims and victims' families whom they had never met. Another example: As I was beginning to write this chapter, I was in India studying *Velugu*, a program for extremely poor, rural women in southern India. *Velugu* women come together in groups to help each other. It amazed me to see the kindness these women offered to each other but even more astounding was their kindness to strangers. Though many struggled just to have enough money to buy the basics of life, like food and shelter, they took up a collection for the victims of the tsunami that had hit South and Southeast Asia in 2004. These women were nowhere near the site of the tsunami victims but were inland, in a semiarid region often plagued with water shortages. Nonetheless, their compassion for other humans, strangers to them, led to their heartwarming generosity.

Yes we can: Humans can cooperate, share, and live peacefully

Can humans share? Can we live cooperatively, without hierarchy? I always begin the discussion of these questions by asking my students if humans have always lived as we do today—selfishly, greedily, with hierarchy and oppression as central characteristics of our society. My students quickly respond that society has always been as it is today. "Greed is a central part of human nature," they say. "Cave men" were just as selfish as we are today. After all, we all know that cave men walked around beating each other up with clubs to get what they wanted. The very image of the "cave man," in commercials and in such cartoons as *The Flintstones* (my own childhood reference point!), contributes to stereotypes of ancestral humans as being brutal and hardly different from contemporary humans.

My students' beliefs—and those of many readers I'd guess—are dead wrong. Humans actually lived a sharing, cooperative, and egalitarian life for most of the time we've been on earth. This is worth repeating: Hierarchy is the anomaly. We've only become hierarchical *very* late in our history on earth—only in the last 5% of our time in existence. For 95% of our earthly presence, humans lived cooperative and egalitarian lives. To the extent that there is such a thing as human "nature," we would have to characterize it based on our biological evolution, and based on our history, as caring and compassionate. To me, the realization that humans have almost always lived cooperatively and without oppression is an enormously hopeful finding, hopeful because it suggests that we can once again live this way.

Cooperative hunter-gatherers/foragers

What is the evidence to support these claims about how humans lived in the past? First, two concepts and three dates. All animals need to eat, and the way they procure food can strongly influence how they relate to each other. This is especially true of humans. One food-gathering method is called "hunting and gathering" or "foraging." (I'll use the latter term from now on.) In this method, humans do not alter the environment to produce food—no planting crops or raising animals. They simply walk from place to place picking the nuts, fruit, and other vegetable foods that are there, supplemented by the hunting of animals in the wild. The other food-gathering method is different in that humans do alter the environment. This is called "agriculture." Agriculturalists grow food and raise animals. Today all of us get food that has been grown or raised, except in rare circumstances, so our mode of living today is a farming one, not one of foraging.

And here are the dates: Humans first appeared on earth approximately 200,000 years ago, in Africa. From that time until the "invention" of agriculture 12,000 years ago, all humans worldwide lived exclusively as foragers. "The history of modern hunters and gatherers is as long as the history of any human group or way of life. [It is] a legacy common to all of humanity" (Smith 2004: 384, 389).

At approximately 12,000 years ago agriculture began for the first time. The very earliest evidence of agriculture comes from the Eastern Mediterranean, and includes present-day Syria, Lebanon, Israel, Palestine, and Jordan, with the very earliest cultivation dating to 13,000 years ago. While this is the very earliest evidence, agriculture originated independently at about the same time in several parts of the world, including the Eastern Mediterranean, southern China, Ethiopia, New Guinea, and several parts of the New World. While the dates of agriculture are agreed upon, the reasons for its occurrence are in dispute. Many researchers point to climate changes. Others have argued that increasing population caused a shift to agriculture, although there is no consensus on population pressure as a causal factor (Stock and Pinhasi 2011: 2–3).

Only a short time after the advent of agriculture, hierarchical societies arose in human history for the very first time. Hierarchies were formed in several different parts of the globe when previously independent agricultural villages were subjugated, probably forcibly, by one ruling group—which Carneiro (1970) hypothesizes was the community victorious in battles with neighboring communities. The subjugated peoples were forced to pay tax or tribute, or to work as slave laborers for the rulers. This process of the unification of multiple villages and peoples under the control of a single ruler or ruling people is most commonly referred to as the origins of the "state" (Carneiro 1970).

The first state in human history appeared around 6000 BP (BP stands for "before present" where the present is 1950) in Mesopotamia. (I am following Carneiro's dates here. Other scholars put the origins of the first state at 5500 BP or later.) Other states in the ancient world, each with origins independent of the others, soon followed Mesopotamia, most notably those states located in what today are the nations of China, India, Egypt, and Mexico. (The classical civilizations of ancient Greece and Rome developed a little while later than these first early states.) Thus:

200,000 BP to 12,000 BP: All humans lived as foragers.

12,000 BP: Agriculture begins for the first time in several parts of the globe.

6000 BP: The state, with its characteristic hierarchy, arises for the first time, in Mesopotamia.

Millennia following 6000 BP: More states arise, and more and more foraging societies diminish as they are displaced by agricultural societies, or as they convert to agriculture.

Today: Virtually all societies live by agriculture and none by foraging.

Noticing that hierarchy arose almost simultaneously with agriculture, the reader would be right to surmise that there is something about farming, as innocuous as it seems, that promotes hierarchy and, conversely, that nomadic foraging must somehow promote cooperation. More about this momentarily but the reader will probably guess that the settled life of farming might lead to notions of ownership of the land one lives on, the land one grows crops on, and ownership of the animals one raises. And one might also guess that such ownership leads to inequality and war in some fashion. Both guesses are correct (Stock and Pinhasi 2011: 1; Carneiro 1970).

And so one would also guess that a nomadic life might somehow be inconsistent with ownership and inequality. This is true: Foragers, the mode of living followed by all humans worldwide for approximately 95% of human existence (200,000 to 12,000 BP), lived cooperatively and without hierarchy.

How do we know all of this? How do we know that ancestral humans lived by foraging, and, most importantly, how do we know that foragers are egalitarian, both today and in the remote past? Evidence of how foragers lived comes from two basic sources. First, there is archeological evidence of how prehistoric foragers lived. Second, there are studies of peoples living in the 20th century as foragers. The latter evidence has the advantage that virtually all aspects of society can be observed directly, whereas studies of prehistoric societies must rely on many inferences about the nature of their social interaction. But because by the 20th century very few pristine foraging societies remained (some scholars would say none of the foraging societies studied by anthropologists in the 20th century was pristine—free from contact and influence from agricultural societies), there are few studies of such societies. The Kung people, who lived as foragers in southern Africa well past the middle of the 20th century, are one group that has been studied especially well by a number of excellent anthropologists and other social scientists.

Let me begin with a review of the archeological evidence, followed by a discussion of ethnographic studies of contemporary foragers. My aim is to demonstrate that foragers lived an egalitarian life, thus showing that such a life is not just a figment of the imaginations of utopian thinkers.

Shultziner et al. (2010) give a masterful synthesis of the evidence for egalitarianism during the Last Glacial, 74,000 years ago to 11,500 years ago (the latter date being the time agriculture originated). They begin with a review of data on the global climate and conclude that the climate during the Last Glacial was "highly unstable over even decadal time scales" and was also more arid and colder than during the Holocene. The instability of the climate and its arid nature would have led to scarcer and "more unpredictable" rainfall and thus required animals to migrate frequently to find food and water. Humans too would have had to migrate—in search of water, animals, and edible vegetation. The unpredictability of food and water for humans, and their relative short supply due to the arid weather, would have limited group sizes of humans and compelled a nomadic life (321–325, 336).

Smallness of group size and nomadism are significant because they suggest a lack of significant political stratification. As Shultziner et al. point out, sedentism is usually seen as a "precondition of hierarchization" (335). Thus, demonstrating that ancestral peoples were nomadic is tantamount to showing that they were non-hierarchical.

Shultziner et al. (320) provide additional evidence, direct evidence, for ancestral egalitarianism. They define political egalitarianism as

> a social organization in which decisions are reached through deliberation and consensus; individuals do not command authority over, or coerce, other group members; social status, honor, and positions (if and when they exist) are voluntarily granted or withdrawn, and not inherited; and individuals can freely leave their group peers or residence.

Anthropologists typically demonstrate egalitarianism by showing an absence of evidence of political hierarchy. The signs of political hierarchy and social stratification in the general archeological record are: (1) differences in how people are buried (with people of high status given elaborate burial conditions, while low-status people are given simple burials); (2) differences in size or elaborateness of houses; (3) presence of prestige goods; (4) evidence of conspicuous consumption of resources; and (5) monumental architecture. But such evidence of hierarchy is lacking in the ancestral record. There is no monumental architecture at all found before the onset of the Holocene (at about 12,000 years ago) and very little evidence of types 1–4 during the Last Glacial so that "the indications for political hierarchy during the Last Glacial are too few and inconclusive to lend support to a common presence of this type of social organization" (333, 332–336). Archeology supports the view that ancestral foragers were egalitarian.

Consistent with this archeological evidence are the findings from physical anthropology. First, some background: In primate species where males mate with more than one female, males fight over sexual access to females. This leads to the establishment of male-dominance hierarchies. It also means that those males who are bigger and have longer canines are more likely to win in sexual contests, so that "polygamous" hierarchical primate species, on the one hand, have males who differ significantly from females in canine size and body size: The species is "sexually dimorphic." Baboons are a typical example of this pattern. On the other hand, "monogamous" primates (where one male mates with only one female) have few conflicts, are much more egalitarian, and have much less dimorphism. Thus, looking at canine and body size dimorphism, or its absence, can tell us whether an ancestral species was hierarchical or egalitarian.

The trend in hominin evolution has been for a reduction both in body-size dimorphism and in canine-teeth dimorphism. This trend strongly suggests that our ancestors were egalitarian rather than hierarchical. In fact the virtual lack of sexual dimorphism among *Homo erectus* supports the interpretation that our hominin ancestors were egalitarian at least as long ago as the origins of *Homo erectus*, dated at about 1.9 million years ago (Shultziner et al. 2010: 330–331). Further, Darwin's explanation that canines reduced in human ancestors because of the invention of tools does not hold up for a number of reasons, perhaps the most compelling of which is that tool use began after canine reduction (Plavcan and van Schaik 1997: 346, 370). The climate data, and evidence from archeology and physical anthropology, all point to the egalitarianism not only of humans but also of our hominin ancestors.

Contemporary forager societies

Studies of contemporary foragers further demonstrate forager egalitarianism. Studies show them to be profoundly egalitarian. There are a very few contemporary exceptions, such as Northwest Coast American Indians, who are sedentary, larger in population, and inegalitarian. While a minority of anthropologists have wondered if ancestral foragers could have been like Northwest Coast foragers, the climate data from the Last Glacial show this to be virtually impossible because the climate was too harsh for sedentary or even semi-sedentary life. Therefore small nomadic present-day foragers can be used as a good model for what ancestral human social organization was like (Shultziner et al. 2010: 325–326).

To understand more about ancestral humans, let's turn now to what studies of contemporary foragers have shown. (Shultziner et al. 2010 also has a nice summary of contemporary forager life. See 325–327.) In the *Cambridge Encyclopedia of Hunters and Gatherers* (Lee and Daly 2004), the editors summarize the primary characteristics of contemporary foragers as follows:

1. They are politically egalitarian. Leaders are constrained by popular opinion and, quite importantly I think, cannot command their followers. They can only try to persuade them (Lee and Daly 2004: 4; see also Ingold 2004: 407 on leaders being prohibited from dominating "followers" in forager societies, and the requirement that good hunters never make their superiority obvious. See also Boehm 2012: 84–85 on group killing of deviant individuals in forager societies, what he calls "capital punishment." He finds in a calculation of cases of capital punishment among 50 forager societies that the most commonly punished individuals are those who attempt to intimidate the group. Foragers do not tolerate "tyrants" and sometimes inflict the death penalty upon them. Also see Boehm 2001: Chapter 4, for a good summary of the literature on forager egalitarianism).

2. They are mobile. People move their settlements several times a year, and they will move away from unpopular leaders rather than submit to their will. Conflicts are often resolved the same way. People simply move away to avoid continuing conflicts with someone in their community (Lee and Daly 2004: 4).

3. Groups concentrate and disperse throughout the year, rather than living in groups of stable size and composition. The concentration/dispersion pattern occurs for both social reasons and for ecological ones (Lee and Daly 2004: 4).

4. Land is held collectively by a kinship-based collective. While individuals may possess personal moveable property, they do not own land privately and individually. In addition, rules of reciprocity allow an individual to have access to several other groups' land (Lee and Daly 2004: 4).

5. Sharing is a universal and central rule among foragers and "there are strong injunctions on the importance of reciprocity" (Lee and Daly 2004: 4).

Another list, a similar one (Leacock and Lee 1982: 8–9):

1. "Collective ownership of the means of production—the land and its resources—by a band. ..."

2. "The right of reciprocal access to resources of others through marriage ties, visiting, and co-production. The necessity of obtaining formal 'permission' to use the land of others in a crisis situation does not imply 'ownership' in the sense of being able to withhold access; granting permission often takes the form of hosts telling guests to help themselves. ..."

3. "Little emphasis on accumulation. The land is the larder and the emphasis is on mobility and adaptability to the land rather than on accumulation. ..."

4.   "'Total sharing' or 'generalized reciprocity' within the camp as well as with others who come to visit or to seek help if food shortages exist in their terrain. This does not mean that each item of food is divided, or that all eat together out of a common pot. Indeed, eating may be quite individualized much of the time. However, it does mean that no one goes hungry if there is food in camp."
5.   "Access of all to the 'forces of production'. Virtually everyone possesses the skills for making essential tools. ...."
6.   "Individual 'ownership' of tools. However, tools are easily lent and borrowed, and the fact that people generally possess the resources and skills necessary for replacing them means that such ownership does not divide haves from have-nots as it does in class societies."

Although this list of forager characteristics may seem hard for the average reader to imagine, given the absence of sharing in our own societies, there are a couple of corners of our own societies that can help us to think about forager societies. Our relations with our families differ significantly from our relations with non-family members. One of the key differences is that sharing of property, and mutual care for each other, is the basic norm in families. This is perhaps a defining feature of the family and a reason "family" is so often invoked positively by politicians and others (e.g., the nation-state as "family"). A classic analysis of forager societies, that of Elman Service, describes family and society as coterminous in forager societies, in contrast to our own societies, in which families are separate from the rest of social intercourse (see Ingold 2004: 400). Ingold (401), summarizing Service, writes:

> [F]or Service the essence of the hunter-gatherer band lies in the extension of familial relations which, in other societies, are internal to the household, across the entire community. Such a society is not internally differentiated by boundaries of segmentary exclusion into relatively close and relatively distant sectors, nor is access to the resource base divided between its constituent units. The [forager] band is conceived as one big household, whose members enjoy unrestricted use of the resources of its country and who labor in common to draw a subsistence from them.

Another model helpful for understanding forager societies is, I believe, friendship in our own societies. When we are among a group of friends, one person may become an informal leader, but they are not formally given such a position, by a process or voting or any other overt social process. In addition, if the leader decides we should go to see movie X, s/he would be loath to command us to see the movie, knowing that were s/he to do so, we would view the command as unfriendly. Most likely, a person trying to force us to abide by her/his wish would not remain a leader very long. Moreover, someone having the gall to try to require us to heed his/her wishes would probably no longer even be included in that circle of friends in the future. In fact I can think of many persuasive people in friendship circles in the societies with which I am most familiar—the US, China, and India—but I can't ever recall anyone even daring to try to lead by commanding others. This is precisely true of forager leaders too. They lead by persuasion, and never by command.

Humans and hierarchy

There is no disputing that humans became hierarchical with the origins of the state approximately 6000 years ago. With the origins of the state, humans showed our dark side. Slavery, war, sexual inequality, political and economic hierarchy, and a refusal to share even when we encounter starving conspecifics—these are all the legacy of the state, or "civilization."

But the lateness of the origins of the state is instructive and optimistic in its implications. That it took so long for humans to arrive at the conditions to produce hierarchy suggests something fundamental about our capacities and, indeed, perhaps something about which way these capacities lean. That is, the extremely late origins of hierarchy strongly suggest (although not with absolute certainty) that something monumental must occur to make humans show our darker side. If our dark side had occurred earlier and frequently in our 200,000 year history, we could conclude, conversely, that we are easily incited to hierarchy and selfishness.

But just what is it that led to hierarchy? If we can know this, we might know how to end it. The answer, unfortunately, is in dispute, although there are many fascinating hypotheses. Carneiro (1970) gives a classic, widely cited explanation, and one that I find convincing. He explains that in the first few millennia following the origins of agriculture, humans lived in independent villages, until roughly 7000 years ago, when the first aggregations of villages into "larger political units" occurred. By 6000 years ago the aggregation process had accelerated to such an extent that the state arose for the first time in history. The state is a "centralized government with the power to collect taxes, draft men for work or war, and decree and enforce laws" and one of its primary characteristics is a division of labor—with not all people working as farmers any longer—and differential political and economic power, such as slaves and masters. Thus we have the existence of social classes, i.e., hierarchy, for the first time in human history (733, 736).

The fact that states and hierarchy developed, and that this was its first occurrence, is not in question, but we do not know for certain the cause or causes of this process. To address the question of causes, Carneiro suggests that we examine the areas in which states first arose, to see what distinguishes these areas from places where states did not arise. He notes that states developed in agricultural areas where geographical features such as mountains, oceans, or deserts prevented people from fleeing to nearby unoccupied areas if they lost a battle with neighboring communities. He notes that humans do not readily and voluntarily submit to rule by others (734), so that where there is no geographical "circumscription" (or what he terms "social circumscription," a situation in which the layout of communities prevents those communities surrounded by others from escaping), peoples who lost a battle would simply flee to unoccupied land.

Thus circumscription, plus rising population pressure on the land, led to wars over land. The impossibility of escape in circumscribed areas meant that the victors could subjugate the losers, with the victors in war becoming the upper class, and the vanquished peoples being either enslaved or compelled to pay tribute to the victors, their new overlords. The role of war in the formation of the first states is supported by the fact that historical or archeological findings from many early states show evidence of warfare during the early stages of state formation (Carneiro 1970; see 734 on warfare's presence during early state formation).

One of the aspects of Carneiro's hypothesis that is so appealing is that it explains why states arose in certain places but not others. His hypothesis is also consistent with the widespread reluctance of humans in small-scale agricultural societies to willingly submit to other humans. And it gives an explanation of the origins of hierarchy, an explanation often lacking, or deemphasized, in other hypotheses about the origin of complex social formations. The reliance on war to explain hierarchy is appealing, too, because it is consistent with what we know from historical times, when warriors were rewarded with land for their victories, with vanquished peoples enslaved. Carneiro also nicely refutes other theories, such as the idea that agricultural surpluses led to a division of labor and of power. The problem with this theory is that farmers did not usually produce surpluses in early agricultural societies (734), until capitalism impelled them to do so.

Egalitarianism among contemporary non-state societies

It is important to say that although state societies led to hierarchies, small-scale non-state communities, even today, retain an egalitarian ethos. There are still many parts of the world where people live primarily by subsistence agriculture, and among such peoples it is common to find much less hierarchy than exists among states. One even finds some egalitarian characteristics reminiscent of foraging societies. Among the Yi people I studied, an ethnic minority in the high mountains of southern Sichuan Province in China, there is a recent history of household slaves (ending in the late 1950s) but among non-slave peoples there were no formal leaders—no one who could compel anyone to follow their orders. Leadership was, and still is, informal; sometimes a consensus will develop among people that someone should be listened to as an informal leader and these people are designated as *ssa hxuo*. *Ssa hxuo* are respected for their beneficence and one of their main responsibilities is to help settle disputes. What is interesting about *ssa hxuo* is that the two most important characteristics required for earning this informal designation are modesty and generosity. Also, *ssa hxuo* have no formal right to compel others to follow their wishes. They can persuade but not command and they do not receive compensation or special privileges for the roles they play (Schoenhals 2003: 43). The Yi pattern is strikingly similar to that found among forager leaders, such as Kung leaders, who must be humble, and who can only suggest what should be done, rather than commanding that it be done (Lee 1993: 95).

The egalitarian nature of Yi leadership is similar to leadership in countless small-scale agricultural societies described in the anthropological literature. A common characteristic is that leaders have the ability to persuade but not to compel others. Among the Warm Springs Indians studied by Philips (1985: 389), for example, the author writes:

> [A] person is not a leader by virtue of holding a particular position, even in the case of members of the tribal council and administration. Rather, he is a leader because he has demonstrated ability in some sphere and activity, and many individuals choose to follow his suggestions because they have independently each decided they are good ones. If, for example, an individual plans and announces an activity, but few people offer to help him carry it out or attend it, then that is an indication that the organizer is not a respected leader in the community at the present time. And the likelihood that he will repeat his efforts in the near future is reduced considerably.

Interestingly, Philips finds consequences for the non-coercive nature of Indian leadership in children's play. She says that Indian children are reluctant to play games in which they must tell others what do to, games such as Simon Says, or Green Light Red Light. Indian children are especially reluctant to take up the leadership position in such games, while non-Indian children eagerly vie for the role of the commandeering leader (379).

Other evidence of the human propensity to cooperate

Research on children complements the above anthropological research. Michael Tomasello (2009) has devised a number of ingenious experiments to show that children willingly help others from a very early age, at around 12–18 months old, and this leads him to conclude that children have a "*natural* inclination to sympathize with others in strife" (13; emphasis added). Cooperation is a capacity and tendency that children have naturally, not something that they must be taught by parents or by their cultures (13).

In one experiment, infants of 14–18 months old see an unrelated adult encountering a difficulty, such as trying to open a cabinet door when the adult's hands are full. Of 24 18-month-olds studied, 22 helped "at least once, and they did so basically immediately" (6). Tomasello then tried giving rewards to children, a small toy, to see how rewards would affect children's motivation to help. It turns out, remarkably, that the children who received rewards were *less* likely to help in subsequent trials than those not given a reward, thus showing that intrinsically satisfying behavior is actually subverted by extrinsic motivations such as the rewards (9–10). The author cites work by Warneken and other researchers with 14–24-month-old children, who were engaged in an instrumental task with a reward at the end. Children sometimes turned the instrumental task into a cooperative game for its own sake by putting the reward back into the apparatus so that the task could start all over again, showing, according to Tomasello, that "the collaborative activity itself was more rewarding than the instrumental goal" (63–64). That is, the children were willing to forsake the reward so that they could continue the cooperative experience, strongly suggesting that cooperation is a greater reward for these young children, due to the pleasure it brings them, than the external reward the researchers offered. This shows, as I will be arguing throughout this chapter and in subsequent chapters, that the joy of cooperation is innate among humans. It is only as we grow up in societies where external rewards are given greater emphasis than intrinsic rewards that we come to forsake cooperation in our pursuit of such externals as fame and fortune.

Perhaps one of the nicest illustrations of the persistence of our capacity for egalitarianism comes from answers to my questions about the ideal life. I've asked this question of people of various statuses and varying cultures: Han Chinese, minority Yi in China, American students, etc. Despite the heavy presence of hierarchy among the Yi, the Chinese, and the Americans, no respondent, out of scores and scores of respondents, has ever said that his/her ideal life was to attain a status above others. Many informants cited material comfort as a component of a good life, but their answers were never phrased in a hierarchical way. That is, no one ever said, "My ideal life would be to have more money than (or 'more possessions than') others around me." The desire to have more than others is a very real desire and I know all three cultures well enough to know that many people would like to be better off than others. In fact the Chinese have a saying that translates roughly that "people take pleasure in others' sorrows." *Schadenfreude*, the German version of this concept, is indeed not just a Western phenomenon. Yet what my respondents' answers show gives me hope. The Yi, with their open and unabashed system of inherited caste status, along with extremely capitalist and class-conscious post-Mao Chinese, and equally status-conscious urban Americans, all refuse to openly admit any *Schadenfreude* feelings or ideals. This illustrates that even the most hierarchical of societies contain a strong egalitarian element—an intuitive sense among people that somehow it is wrong to admit wanting to be better than others or have more than them and that having good morals means you should not seek superiority over others, at least not openly.

The primate evidence

But even if humans lived for most of our existence as egalitarian hunter/gatherers, isn't the real heritage of humans clear in how our primate relatives live today, and isn't that a hierarchical and often violent way of life? Chimpanzees are indeed hierarchical and they can be stunningly violent, but this is only part of the story. World-renowned primatologist Frans De Waal has conducted brilliant research that completes the story. He begins by noting that the animal capacity for empathy has been largely, and wrongly, overlooked because of both popular and scientific tendencies to portray humans and our animal relatives as selfish and ferocious (De Waal 2005: 1–3). De Waal begins a recent book with the following touching story:

Truly remarkable is the bonobo, a little-known ape that is as close to us genetically as the chimpanzee. When a bonobo named Kuni saw a starling hit
the glass of her enclosure at the Twycross Zoo in Great Britain, she went to
comfort it. Picking up the stunned bird, Kuni gently set it on its feet. When it
failed to move, she threw it a little, but the bird just fluttered. With the starling
in hand, Kuni then climbed to the top of the tallest tree, wrapping her legs
around the trunk so that she had both hands free to hold the bird. She carefully unfolded its wings and spread them wide, holding one wing between
the fingers of each hand, before sending the bird like a little toy airplane out
toward the barrier of her enclosure. But the bird fell short of freedom and
landed on the bank of the moat. Kuni climbed down and stood watch over
the starling for a long time, protecting it against a curious juvenile. By the end
of the day, the recovered bird had flown off safely.

De Waal 2005: 2

De Waal also recounts the story of a gorilla in a Chicago zoo who rescued a three-
year-old boy who had fallen into the primate exhibit. After carrying the boy to
safety the gorilla took him in her lap and gently and reassuringly patted his back
before returning him to zoo staff (3). Primate behavior such as this shows a capacity for compassion. This is a capacity that only appears in higher primates and in
humans.

In addition to recognizing the compassionate capacities of our primate relatives,
a few other similarities should be noted:

1. Like humans, chimps also do share food with each other (De Waal 2005: 205–
   208) and stinginess is remembered. Others share less willingly with a stingy
   individual than with a generous one.
2. Also, like humans, a common dynamic is for chimps to fight against superiors.
   While monkeys tend to support dominant individuals, chimps often "rally for
   the underdog" in fights, creating an inherent instability in chimp hierarchies
   (79). Male bully chimps are often punished severely, including the severe punishment of ostracism (80).
3. Alpha status among chimps is never absolute. De Waal reports Jane Goodall's
   surprise that her alpha male had to beg others for his food; he could not automatically commandeer their food (207).
4. Chimp conflict prevention also reinforces a certain chimp egalitarianism.
   Dominant chimps break up fights by supporting the weak against the strong or
   by intervening impartially (81). The most respect and love goes to those chimp
   males who support the weak and the oppressed (87).
5. In fact in the chimp colony De Waal studied, the "second-in-command" played
   the role of arbiter of disputes and he was the one getting the most pantgrunts
   (given toward those of high status) rather than the alpha male. But the arbiter
   gains respect and community support only if the arbitrations are fair and in
   support of "the weak against the strong" (82, 85).

While biologists might see hierarchy everywhere, it is important to note that the egalitarianism seen among human foragers was already developing among higher primates: "What we see in the chimp, then, is a halfway station between the rigid hierarchies of monkey on the one hand, and the human tendency toward equality on the other" (83).

In fact research among primates shows that conflict among all primates has been exaggerated. Sussman and Garber (2004) review information from 78 studies of primates, "much, but certainly not all, of the literature" (168), to determine how much cooperation versus conflict exists among the diversity of primates. They find that rates of agonism among apes are "extremely low" at .09 events per hour (174, 175). They conclude for primates as a whole (including apes) that "affiliative interactions represent the overwhelming majority of primate social interactions and form the basis of individual social bonds" (176). With this data in mind, plus the finding from MRI brain scans showing that mutual cooperation activates brain areas connected to pleasure (179–180), the authors assert the primacy of cooperation, rather than conflict, in primate behavior (180–181) and they suggest that the pleasures of cooperation have made it a "reward in its own right" (180).

Much recent debate about chimpanzees has focused on whether they engage in "coalitionary killing" of conspecifics, an action seen as analogous to human warfare. Power (1991), in a carefully researched and remarkable book that has not received the attention it deserves, reexamines Jane Goodall's evidence from the Gombe National Park, Tanzania, as well as work by other chimp experts such as Toshisada Nishida's research in the Mahale Mountains, Tanzania. Power questions Goodall's startling findings of war among chimps, and the implicit characterization of them as warlike and violent, by noting that the violent chimp actions she and other researchers described occurred only *after* wild chimps were provisioned with bananas by their human observers.

Goodall's early observations were of chimps in the wild. The wild chimps, able to join and leave groups at will, avoided conflict and lived peacefully. However, the difficulty of getting close to chimps in the wild led Goodall in 1965 to begin "provisioning," to provide bananas to the chimps, in order to attract them to a location where she could observe them. (See Power 1991: Part 1 for a description of the naturalistic versus provisioned methods of observing chimps.) Power analyzes Goodall's writings and finds that there are profound differences between the wild chimps and the post-1965 "provisioned" ones. She attributes the transformation in chimp behavior to the frustration the chimps felt when they were forced to compete for a limited supply of food in a concentrated area, frustration only exacerbated by the fact that Goodall's assistants placed the bananas in concrete boxes with steel lids, which were open and shut by the human observers so as to control chimp feeding on the bananas, due to the limited supply of bananas that could be procured by Goodall (28). Goodall herself noted that the new feeding system led to "a great deal more fighting than ever before" and the system caused what Goodall called "chaos" and "bedlam" (Goodall quoted in Power 1991: 29–30). Thus, notes Power, all post-1965

Goodall research is based on an artificial situation (29), a situation that brought about a radical transformation from peaceful coexistence to conflict and violence (241):

> The (simulated) prolonged food crisis brought about by the methods in which the bait foods were supplied at Gombe instigated a change to a set of negative behaviors, which led to a cultural crisis. When the chimpanzees began competing directly and aggressively for resources, the old open, cooperative, nonacquisitive system no longer operated ….The observers took control of access to a desired and scarce food and, through the frustrating and (to the apes) incomprehensible method of distribution, added the tension of anxiety over food to the artificial feeding situation. Unintentionally, the Gombe and Mahale apes were pushed into competing directly and aggressively against conspecifics for the bait foods.

Power theorizes that when the chimps were forced to compete directly over provisioned food, this led to anxiety, tension, and, especially, extreme frustration. Drawing on psychological theories of frustration, she asserts that frustration in turn engendered aggression (136–150). It also may have led to a kind of obsessive (my word; she uses the word, "fixated") behavior pattern among chimps that was clearly *maladaptive*, in which they waited for provisioned food for hours when the surrounding forests were full of edible food (141–142).

The pre-provisioned chimps in their natural environment could not have been more different from the provisioned chimps, forced to compete over bananas and frustrated and incited to aggression by this situation:

1. *From no dominance hierarchy to despotism*: No observations of pre-provisioned natural chimps contain evidence of a dominance hierarchy or a closed group, or an alpha restricting sexual access to receptive females. Chimp groups in their natural context are flexible and "ever-fissioning and fusing." Only Nishida senses in his early observations some vague signs of dominance (cited in Power 1991: 23, 66). Likewise, natural chimp groups had their own ranges, but they did not defend these ranges as their own territories, especially since there was such flux in group size and composition (60–67, 70). Power notes that in no naturalistic (nonprovisioned) accounts of chimps is there any case of chimps attacking or chasing chimps who are strangers (146) and there was a pattern of easy visiting between chimp groups and migration from one group to another (62–67, 114–117), a "pattern of youthful chimpanzees of both sexes migrating to other groups" that "both results from, and facilitates, friendly intragroup relations" (116).

After provisioning was instituted, a new pattern of migration arose, one in which males remained with their natal groups for life, and it was only young females who migrated (105, 116) (I cannot resist noting the resemblance to patrilocality among humans. While foraging people of both sexes move freely between groups, among agricultural societies a preference for only female out-migration develops, in which women move from their natal homes at marriage to live with their husbands. Anthropologists see in the shift to patrilocality a fundamental source of the debasement of the status of women, since men live for life among family and acquaintances, whereas adult women are outsiders, and outsiders among strangers, in their husbands' world.) The chimps in Gombe split into distinct separate communities and chimps started to patrol the borders of their new territories (70–71). Chimps who had previously been companions started attacking each other with an intent to kill their new competitors. Whereas group encounters pre-provisioning had resembled human "carnivals," the new encounters were entirely different: They resembled war (64, 72–73). Power hypothesizes, intriguingly, that the excitement of "battle" has replaced the pre-provisioned encounters with new chimps that led to the excitement of "carnival" (147). The provisioned Gombe and Mahale chimps, as is now well-known, engaged in group killing, with the Mahale groups killing all males in a neighboring group and the Gombe chimps killing all members of a neighboring group (145).

Since territoriality and dominance hierarchy are two signs of the same coin, it is not surprising that provisioned chimps developed hierarchy, which had been absent among the nonprovisioned chimps. Goodall's earlier observation about the chimps was that dominance was not a useful concept, because any mature chimp, in Goodall's own words, "may from time to time be the highest-ranking individuals of a temporary association" (Goodall quoted in Power 1991: 74). But Goodall later abandoned this position, influenced by what she saw happening among the provisioned chimps. In her later writings Goodall talks about discerning the rise of a dominant, alpha male. Interestingly, two of the earliest despots were nervous, aggressive animals who had been shunned by others pre-provisioning (75), a finding consistent with the fear/aggression that I have described as central to hierarchy. Both of these new despots not only acted aggressively toward adult males but they also began to attack juveniles, a sign Power characterizes as the dysfunctional nature of the new hierarchy (76). Power notes that "Goodall does not report either of these dominant males taking on a society-maintaining, protective role" and she suggests that "it seems possible that their aggressive behavior toward the vulnerable females and young was frustration-inducted scapegoating, and that these domineering males were simply aggressive, *uncontrolled* despots" (77; emphasis in original).

2. *Changes in chimp sexual behavior*: Sex among wild chimps is unanimously described as "relaxed, non-competitive and amiable" and there is no competition for access to estrous females or any attempt to monopolize them (77). Copulation pre-provisioning was solicited by either sex. This all changed after 1965, with males at Gombe taking the initiative 83% of the time (78). In addition males post-1965 threatened females with attack if they did not agree to copulate (79, 81) and despotic males began to attempt to monopolize access to females, although they were not often successful in these attempts (82). In addition "abductive" consortship was observed between 1966 and 1969 at Gombe, a situation in which males displayed and attacked females who hesitated to follow them (83). Summarizing, Power writes that "the once autonomous female chimpanzee has lost *her* sexual rights, which

are the freedom of choice to accept or reject sexual solicitation" (83; emphasis in original).

3. *Reactions to the young*: In contrast to the easygoing and caring nature with which natural chimp juveniles are treated by all adults, the reaction to the young by provisioned chimps ranged from "affectionate acceptance to … murderous attack" (88–89, 84–95). Power describes the multitude of killings of infants and eating of them by adult chimps. All of these cases occurred after provisioning (95–103). (All of the killers were males except for one female Gombe chimp, who killed and ate four infants—96.) Although negative evidence is never completely conclusive, Power notes that there is only one case of cannibalism among wild, nonprovisioned chimps (96–98).

One reason Power fascinates me is because her description of the origins of hierarchy and war among chimps is amazingly similar (though not the same) to the process anthropologists have described for the origins of human hierarchy. The reader should note the many similarities between Carneiro's (1970) theory of the origins of hierarchy among humans and Power's description of, indeed documentation of, this process among living chimps. *In both chimps and humans, when conspecifics are brought into direct, rather than indirect, competition over food, the result is a major transformation in the nature of society.* Direct competition becomes especially potent when barriers prevent some conflicting group members from moving away from the site of conflict. Among humans, environmental and social circumscription prevents such movement, according to Carneiro. Among chimps, Power cites human encroachment on areas to which chimps might retreat as a factor exacerbating the crisis brought on by direct competition (244, 248). *Direct competition and some form of circumscription have the same result in both species: Peaceful coexistence is replaced by war, increased territoriality and aversion to strangers, patrilocality, male dominance over females, and despotic hierarchy.*

The significance of the chimp evidence

There has been a great deal of writing on what the behavior of chimpanzees means for our understanding of human behavior. One recent summary of both sides of the evidence is presented in Sussman, Marshack, and Wrangham (2010). Their debate centers on the significance of coalitionary killing among chimps for understanding of humans and war, with Sussman and Marshack arguing that coalitionary killing is so infrequent as to be insignificant, and Wrangham arguing that its existence among chimps is, in fact, relevant for understanding the occurrence of war among humans.

What *both* sides are at great pains to say, however, is that the chimp evidence of coalitionary killing does not in any way suggest that chimps and humans are both destined to be warlike. In fact Wrangham is the author of a book written with Dale Peterson, *Demonic Males: Apes and the Origins of Human Violence* (Wrangham and Peterson 1996), that has staked out the chimp/human violence connection most clearly (and controversially), and yet Wrangham clearly sees his own work as supporting the possibilities for human peaceful coexistence (Sussman, Marshack, and Wrangham: 2010).

And this is what I am saying as well. Chimps and humans are capable of being warlike, but both species are capable of living peacefully as well. The reason that I have focused so much attention on Power's book is that her careful analysis not only shows *both* sides of chimps, but she also suggests a possibility for *why* chimps might have gone from being peaceful to warlike, open to strangers to hostile to them, a loose group to one tightly bound around a core of males living together for life, and from little hierarchy to despotism. She sees provisioning as having led to direct competition where none existed before, and having created an intensely frustrating situation that led to a major transformation of the Gombe chimps.

In the wake of Power's work, some primatologists have looked for evidence of chimp killing among natural, nonprovisioned chimps. One publication that documents a case of chimps killing one member of another group among wild, *nonprovisioned* chimps is Boesch et al. (2007). However, this case does not contradict Power's general important findings that some form of food frustration can cause chimps to change from peaceful and conflict-averse animals to aggressive and often despotic ones. Clearly, provisioning in Gombe and Mahale made a significant difference in the behavior of the chimps and one or more cases of killings among nonprovisioned chimps does not contradict this finding. And, it should be noted, Power ends her book by hypothesizing that any severe food crisis—not just provisioning per se—can lead to the changes she describes. This is especially true if the food crisis exists alongside conditions preventing some chimps from breaking away from the group in search of less conflict, conditions such as human encroachment on chimp areas (Power 1991: Part 7). So it is not enough for Power's critics, such as Boesch et al., to describe killing among nonprovisioned chimps as evidence that Power is wrong.

In any case the central point made by Power is that environmental conditions—provisioning in the Gombe and Mahale cases—are sufficient to turn the same group of peaceful chimps into aggressive killers. The environment matters and can make the difference in the kind of society that chimps have. That this is true of our closest living ancestors, whose social lives are less flexible than that of humans, is strong proof that humans, too, are not by nature warlike, or peaceful, egalitarian, or hierarchical. We are, like chimps, capable of diverse social lives and how we act depends on the kinds of social conditions we create for all of us. (Other esteemed analysts have made a similar point. Christopher Boehm, in his work on the evolution of morality and altruism among humans, shows how humans have evolved a mix of egotistical and altruistic propensities that coexist, with environmental conditions helping to explain shifts in the balance between these propensities. See Boehm 2012: Chapter 10, 310.)

My proposal

Primate compassion, forager egalitarianism—these give strong evidence that an egalitarian and sharing society is humanly possible. It is true that humans can be horrific toward each other but, as De Waal notes, the cruel aspects of our nature have often been emphasized by scholars at the expense of our caring abilities. He writes:

> With both cruel and compassionate sides, we stand in the world like a Janus head, our two faces looking in opposite directions. This can confuse us to the point that we sometimes oversimplify who we are. We either claim to be the "crown of creation" or depict ourselves as the only true villains. Why not accept that we are both?
>
> *De Waal 2005: 5–6*

And given that our altruistic sides can come into play under the right conditions, it becomes incumbent on us to try to maximize those conditions.

So what, more specifically, are those conditions? And what is the nature of Utopia? Let me summarize my proposal in point form. This will also help introduce some of the ideas that are to come in subsequent chapters.

Utopia should:

1. Minimize hierarchy. This is because hierarchy, though masquerading as a form of pleasure for superiors, is actually evolutionarily based on anger and fear, emotions that it regularly produces along with anxiety. These negative emotions crowd out joy. To feel full joy, we must arrest the joy-interfering dynamics of hierarchy, and that requires us to minimize it in all its forms.

    Ending hierarchy will end zero-sum dynamics among humans. Because we have the unique capacity to empathize with others, we can please them and ourselves at the same time—the essence of love. A more egalitarian world encourages the virtuous cycle of making ourselves and others happy simultaneously.

2. Begin the elimination of hierarchy with a basic guarantee to every human of decent food, housing, health care, and clothing. Fear of not earning enough to guarantee one's survival, and the survival of one's loved ones, is a timeless fear. This fear must be eliminated to reduce joy-precluding anxiety, and to give individuals the freedom to work for pleasure and by their own volition, rather than out of obligation, or due to coercion by richer individuals or by family members. Freedom and joy can only occur in an environment where all humans are free from want.

    My idea that economic deprivation constrains our freedom is consistent with Nobel Prize-winner Amartya Sen's analysis of the aims of development. Sen argues that individuals are not free unless they have the capacity and conditions to live the lives that they seek (Sen 1999).

3. Change the nature of work. With the basic guarantee, work is no longer done for subsistence and status, and no longer obligatory. We are free to work, to create and interact, to please ourselves and others. The nature of the "economy" also changes since its new goal will be to provision all of us for creative work, and organize the audiences we want and need to appreciate our creations.

4. Change the nature of school. Like work, learning need no longer be diminished by being a means to an end. We will work and learn, all throughout our lives, for the fulfillment this brings. As such, work, play, and learning are intentionally confounded, and lifelong learning likewise blurs many (but not all) distinctions between childhood and adulthood—those artificially created by the current means–end nature of schooling.

5. Eliminate other invidious hierarchies besides those based on money. Hierarchies of men over women, one race over another, one sexual orientation over another, one religion or ethnicity over another, and so on cannot be tolerated. Gender distinctions must be minimized, if not eliminated. So too with distinctions between nations and nationality. Subsequent chapters will, like this one, explain the principles behind current hierarchies in order to formulate specific suggestions for how each of them can be challenged.

6. Challenge inequalities of love as well as of wealth. We all deserve to be loved and society can help to make this happen. Equality of love can be, and should be, every bit as much of an agenda item for the utopian as is equality of wealth.

7. Minimize shame in favor of compassion so that the divided self that shame produces—along with insincerity and inauthenticity—can be overcome. Communication is central in Utopia and good communication requires that shame, so often an adjunct to hierarchy, be diminished.

This is a lot to do! But doing it all in a comprehensive manner—by challenging all forms of inequality—is not only desirable but perhaps also more feasible than non-comprehensive change. Above I have discussed Carneiro's theory connecting warfare to hierarchy. Other anthropologists note the connection of war-induced hierarchy to the beginnings of serious gender inequality. And gender inequality connects to the oppression of LGBT peoples. And so on. Therefore, all hierarchies must be challenged, because they are so intertwined. It is a lot to do, but we have an egalitarian legacy to encourage us.

The challenges to hierarchy will be detailed in subsequent chapters and specific proposals will be described. For the remainder of this chapter, let's focus on the more general principle of interactive joy—what it is, how ending hierarchy facilitates more genuine interaction, and what kinds of general social changes can promote interactive joy.

What is interactive joy?

What, exactly, is interactive joy? First, a clarification: Interactive joy does not only occur in musical or other performative contexts; I invoke the performance metaphor because it is useful and instructive. But interactive joy can derive from any kind of interaction between humans in any context—the kind of dense interaction that all humans enjoy—as long as it is not based on hierarchy and fear/anger but on joy and pleasure. Scientists, for example, will find interactive joy by eschewing hierarchical esteem and by pursuing the truth about the world for the pleasure it brings to find out this truth. Scientists will also want to share this pleasurable knowledge—and will be encouraged to do so. I firmly believe in the importance of communicating one's ideas to a receptive but not facile audience—an audience that challenges not to reduce the status of the idea-generator but for the pleasure involved in playing with the ideas themselves, by debating their pros and cons. This kind of intellectual play is key because it is a good way to test ideas, refine them, and improve them. The same is true of any field. Policymakers and politicians, for example, will hold public discussions and debates so that all people can debate public policy—the equivalent of the pianist and her/his proactively engaged audience. The point here is that many of the professions of current society will remain but they will operate in a fundamentally different way—maximizing the *interaction* between the worker/performer and a metaphoric audience and basing this interaction on the enjoyment wrought by back-and-forth communication between performer and audience.

How Utopia fosters interactive joy by its challenge to hierarchy

If interactive joy is the key, how should society be reorganized to foster it? Ending hierarchy and hierarchic esteem is a huge start, and should not be underestimated. Even those motivated by non-hierarchic motives find these motives crowded out as long as hierarchy exists. That is, those who create for self and others' pleasure but who earn no money or formal professional recognition for their creations have a hard time feeling pleasure and esteem when all the societal signals tell them they have failed since they are only unpaid "amateurs." And as long as there is hierarchy and a concomitant cult of celebrity, audiences will be unlikely to attend performances by "amateurs" or non-celebrities, even though these performances may actually be superior to those of the celebrity. (As I write this, I've been listening to one such performance, by an unpaid pianist whose performance outdoes recordings by "professionals." It is so sad that the audience for his extraordinary performances is exceedingly limited because he is not a well-known celebrity.)

Eliminating hierarchy is also key to the fostering of interactive joy because its elimination will allow for the kind of meaningful exchange of ideas at the core of interactive joy. How so? Let me explain by describing how currently existing hierarchy precludes meaningful discussion in one sector of society where the reader might expect such discussions to be most robust: The academy. Not all scholars in all disciplines will agree with the following characterization of the academy but I know that quite a few will admit that it rings true.

Hierarchy in the academy precludes meaningful discussion both between those of different status—between students and professors—and between those of the same status. First, different status and communication, based upon a personal example: In 1989, while I was conducting dissertation fieldwork in China, the student democracy movement occurred. It was a fascinating time to be in China. I was living on an active university campus in a large city, and was friends with several of that city's student movement leaders. I returned to America after the movement's tragic demise, when the Chinese army killed more than 1000 civilian protesters in Beijing. It was with both exhilaration and sadness that I recounted what I had seen and heard in China to my American friends and neighbors, who plied me with questions, eager to hear China news from someone who had been there.

I expected even more eager curiosity from my professors in graduate school. After all, their job was to learn about societies and cultures abroad, so of course they would be more curious than anyone else. But I was wrong. They did not ask me about my observations during the 1989 student movement, or its aftermath, despite the fact that the movement had been the front-page story every day that spring and the subject of endless discussions by the international media. (Apologies to those professors of mine who were not around that summer and toward whom this critique does not apply.)

In trying to understand their disinterest, and the analogous disinterest of those same teachers toward one of my classmates who had observed a fascinating protest movement in the Soviet Union, I came to the conclusion that the hierarchy of the student–teacher relationship was at fault. Normally, professors are the ones with the fascinating stories to tell, and students are the listeners. In fact the basis of professors' prestige, and the ostensible reason we get paid, is because we are the ones with fascinating knowledge and understanding. My classmate and I had turned the tables, inverting the normal relationship that gave our professors their status and income. We did this because *we* were the ones with something interesting to say. Because this inversion challenged the normal status hierarchy, our professors could not acknowledge their interest in what we had to say. I suspect, and hope, that they *were* curious, but hierarchy precluded them from showing it.

Because of the importance of eliminating hierarchy in order to foster interactive joy, I hope the reader will indulge one more analysis about the negative effects of hierarchy in the academy. (I know that hierarchy has similar effects in other sectors of society but I use the example of academia because, of course, it is what I know best.) This one is the effect of hierarchy on communication between status peers. My friends who are not academics always say they envy those of us who are professors, because they imagine us spending hours each day in stimulating discussions and debates. It should be this way of course, but it rarely is so. I have taught at elite and non-elite institutions and at both types of places there is little intellectual dialogue among professors, at least in the social sciences, an irony given what we study. When analyzing the reasons for this, it is helpful to analyze the ways intellectual exchange is avoided. One way is through over-specialization. I have often heard colleagues (again, this does not apply to several close friends, who know that I am not talking about them) say something like the following: "You are an expert on X. I know *absolutely nothing* about X." Does the person ignorant of X then seek to learn more about it? Almost never: That would be too threatening, not only for the scholar ignorant about topic X but even more so for the one who is the expert. What happens then is that no one talks about their expertise much with non-expert colleagues, so that everyone can maintain a belief in each other's expertise based on hearsay, what we've heard about our colleagues' reputations, rather than by our own considered judgment of them. This is the use of mystification to maintain prestige. We maintain our high place in the hierarchy by cloaking ourselves in mystery and this mystery tends to enhance rather than diminish prestige. Non-communication maintains the whole system of status.

We do talk issues with some people, of course, but we limit these discussions to a smaller and smaller circle of people in our ever-narrowing subfields. And when we do talk to people in our own narrow fields, our discourse becomes more like that of gang members or fraternity brothers, who exchange handshakes and other signs to signal allegiance to each other. The professoriate version is to use jargon, and repeat disciplinary and subdisciplinary clichés that are true but trivial. We might say: "My theory is that culture makes us who we are as humans," which is certainly true but not controvertible and therefore formally insignificant. The point here is that the need to preserve our reputation and place in the hierarchy makes us communicate with very few people. Moreover, it makes what we do say become like the words of the politician—pretty words (e.g., "I'm in favor of improving education"—well, who isn't?) that are, at base, devoid of any genuine meaning or specificity. Our discourse is intentionally calculated so that no one can possibly disagree with us in any substantial way—since such disagreement might threaten our status. The casualty of such a situation is real communication, communication that means something because it is detailed, controvertible, and based on logical analysis and facts.

How Utopia fosters interactive joy proactively

Ending hierarchy, then, goes a long way toward promoting the kind of interaction that I've found sadly lacking in the academy and which, I'm sure, is lacking in many other creative workplaces today outside the academy. All people deserve interactive joy; apathy and inattention are nothing but signs of perverse and perverted sociality.

Steps that might be taken to proactively foster interactive joy:

1. Democratize access to jobs and end the cult of celebrity: Anyone wanting to perform as a pianist for others should get access to an auditorium and audience, perhaps in part through a lottery if necessary. Anyone wanting to do scientific research should be allowed to do so, and allowed access to facilities to enable it. Many readers will fairly object that such facilities are limited, so how can just anyone be allowed access? My response is that the goal of society should be to accommodate people's creative desires, and this might mean building more facilities, more auditoria, etc. So be it. Also, many of the facilities that currently exist could, no doubt, accommodate more people, people who could work as assistants to scientists at scientific laboratories, for example. I know, as an anthropologist, that if I lived in a different world, I could easily take many interested people along with me to the field as assistants and I would love

doing that. Unfortunately, in the world the way it is currently structured, most "amateur" anthropologists can't afford the time away from their "real" jobs to do fieldwork, and I don't have money readily available to pay them. But with money not an issue and more time available, these people would be able to come to work with me and I would welcome them.

2. Maximize audiences and audience attention to all: Society should encourage people to attend to others' creations. Multiple physical and cyberspace perform-ance venues could be established—with the important stipulation, as always, that "performance" is used broadly. (Therefore, one kind of "performance" venue would be a place for scientists to discuss their current theories with lay audiences. Another such venue would be a place for policymakers to routinely engage citizens in debates about public policy.) Volunteers could be recruited to attend performances, or hear lectures—even by non-famous people and even in fields that are not their (audience members') main interest. If someone gets too much attention, attention could be "redistributed" through barter and reciprocity. An organization might say: "If you volunteer to be an audience for an under-recognized person, you will be guaranteed an audience of such people to reciprocate by attending your creations/performances." Perhaps the more hours you spend as an audience member, the more hours you might be guaranteed to have as your own audience when you are the performer. I'm sure astute readers will think of others ways to solve the problem of how to equalize attention given to all. I invite readers to do so!

3. Link "performers" with each other: Encourage collaborative research, for example, or collective discussions of societal policy. Break down barriers between audience and performer. In schools the teacher should not just be a lecturer/performer but a senior co-collaborator in research with students. (More on this in Chapter 6.) Thus teacher and student become performers and an audience for each other—again democratizing roles and eliminating hierarchy. The goal here is to foster community through communal creations. Community cre-ativity will not replace individual creativity, but will nicely supplement it.

4. Further enhance community ties by making the audience–performer relation-ship a personal one, and a source of ongoing relationships: An important point to make here is that the giving and receiving of interactive joy can become a new basis for significant communal feeling, replacing many of the detrimental ties of race, caste, class, etc. Rather than performances being anonymous and fleeting contacts between people as they usually are today, performers and audiences will come to perform regularly for each other, thus getting to know each other personally and professionally, as creators and as individuals.

5. Create audiences where none exist: Citizens should routinely hear politicians' plans and be both audience and "performer" in the planning process. Debate and disagreement should be institutionalized in all domains—politics, educa-tion, science—so that theories or policies are never accepted based upon power but upon fact, argument and logic. In fact debate should be an ultimate form of play. If no disagreement exists, individuals should be recruited (voluntarily)

to play devil's advocate. If a scientist comes up with a new theory, an audience of other scientists or even amateur-scientists (well, there will really be no distinction between them) should be routinely formed to test the theory through debate.

6. Break down the artificial boundaries between work and play: Activity versus rest is a dichotomy that I think can remain and could replace the play versus work dichotomy. Break down the boundary between love versus work. Erasing play versus work might seem intuitive, given my general proposal, but love versus work's erasure is more problematic. However, note that if hierarchies of physical beauty are challenged (more on this in Chapter 2), then the mutual attentions between two people based on their appreciation for each other's compassionate and creative communication becomes the basis of real love. Such mutual creative communication is also "work," and hence work and love can be merged. And this is a worthy goal because the compartmentalization of work and love, and of the productive sphere versus the domestic sphere, is a prime basis upon which current hierarchies—men versus women (the former who "work" and the latter who are often home "not working,") for example, or good, prosocial activity ("work" and "industry") versus indulgent activity (love and sex)—are based. Ending the false dichotomy of work and love will lead to much more holism in society and in individuals' lives as well.

7. Make space to listen to everyone's life story: Not everyone is creatively productive, which raises the question of what to do about someone who might not have anything to perform, or someone too shy for the limelight. As an anthropologist, whose job is to listen to people tell their life stories, I'm obviously fascinated by autobiographies and biographical storytelling. I would propose that telling life stories of oneself is a very special activity that deserves an important place in my proposal. Individuals could tell their stories; groups could too. People could learn to interview others they don't know—even others from backgrounds quite different from their own—and tell their stories. Biographical narration would then be a prime way for people to communicate with each other and, I might add, a great way to foster the mutual empathy that all too often lies dormant in human nature.

Interactive joy is a human specialty. We like attention, we crave it, and we want the esteem of others, and their meaningful affirmative interaction with us. This can all be done. Some of my ideas may seem far-fetched but it is important to think creatively, without unnecessary constraint. The next chapter begins this process by looking at gender and love and ways to dramatically reconfigure them in Utopia.

Bibliography

Arregi, A., A. Azpiroz, E. Fano, and L. Garmendia 2006. Aggressive behavior: Implications of dominance and subordination for the study of mental disorders. *Aggression and Violent Behavior*, 11: 394–413.

Beckman, Mary 2004. The mice that don't miss Mom: Love and the [mu]-opioid receptor. *Science*, 304: 1888–1889.

Bell, David C. 2001. Evolution of parental caregiving. *Personality and Social Psychology Review*, 5: 216–229.

Berridge, Kent C. 2004. Motivation concepts in behavioral neuroscience. *Physiology & Behavior*, 81: 179–209.

Boehm, Christopher 2001. *Hierarchy in the Forest: The Evolution of Egalitarian Behavior.* Paperback edition. Cambridge, MA: Harvard University Press.

—— 2012. *Moral Origins: The Evolution of Virtue, Altruism, and Shame.* New York: Basic Books.

Boesch, Christophe, Josephine Head, Nikki Tagg, Mimi Arandjelovic, Linda Vigilant, and Martha M. Robbins 2007. Fatal chimpanzee attack in Loango National Park, Gabon. *International Journal of Primatology*, 28: 1025–1034.

Carneiro, Robert L. 1970. A theory of the origin of the state. *Science*, 169: 733–738.

Carter, C. Sue, James Harris and Stephen W. Porges 2009. Neural and evolutionary perspectives on empathy. Pp. 169–182 in *The Social Neuroscience of Empathy.* Jean Decety and William Ickes, eds. Cambridge, MA: MIT Press.

Creel, Scott 2001. Social dominance and stress hormones. *Trends in Ecology and Evolution*, 16: 491–497.

De Waal, Frans 2005. *Our Inner Ape.* New York: Riverhead Books.

—— 2009. *The Age of Empathy: Nature's Lessons for a Kinder Society.* New York: Harmony Books.

Eccles, John C. 1989. *Evolution of the Brain: Creation of the Self.* New York: Routledge.

Ferrari, P.F., P. Palanza, S. Parmigiani, and R.J. Rodgers 1998. Interindividual variability in Swiss male mice: Relationship between social factors, aggression, and anxiety. *Physiology & Behavior*, 63: 821–827.

Greenspan, Stanley I. and Stuart G. Shanker 2004. *The First Idea: How Symbols, Language, and Intelligence Evolved from our Primate Ancestors to Modern Humans.* Cambridge, MA: Da Capo Press.

Hall, Marion J. 1994. Hierarchy. Pp. 97–103 in *Animal Behavior.* Tim Halliday, ed. Norman: University of Oklahoma Press.

Hrdy, Sarah Blaffer 2009. *Mothers and Others: The Evolutionary Origins of Mutual Understanding.* Cambridge, MA: Belknap Press of Harvard University Press.

Ingold, Tim 2004. On the social relations of the hunter-gatherer band. Pp. 399–410 in *The Cambridge Encyclopedia of Hunters and Gatherers.* Paperback edition. Richard B. Lee and Richard Daly, eds. Cambridge: Cambridge University Press.

Kringelbach, Morten L. and Kent C. Berridge, eds. 2010. *Pleasures of the Brain.* New York: Oxford University Press.

Langdon, John H. 2005. *The Human Strategy: An Evolutionary Perspective on Human Anatomy.* Oxford: Oxford University Press.

Leacock, Eleanor and Richard Lee 1982. Introduction. Pp. 1–20 in *Politics and History in Band Societies.* Eleanor Leacock and Richard Lee, eds. New York: Cambridge University Press.

Lee, Richard B. 1993. *The Dobe Ju/'hoansi.* 2nd ed. Fort Worth, TX: Harcourt Brace College Publishers.

Lee, Richard B. and Richard Daly 2004. Introduction: Foragers and others. Pp. 1–19 in *The Cambridge Encyclopedia of Hunters and Gatherers.* Paperback edition. Richard B. Lee and Richard Daly, eds. Cambridge: Cambridge University Press.

Lewis, Michael 2004. The emergence of human emotions. Pp. 265–280 in *Handbook of Emotions*, 2nd ed. Paperback edition. Michael Lewis and Jeannette M. Haviland-Jones, eds. New York: The Guilford Press.

Lindsey, Terence 1994. Rearing the young. Pp. 29–39 in *Animal Behavior*. Tim Halliday, ed. Norman: University of Oklahoma Press.

Malatynska, Ewa and Richard J. Knapp 2005. Dominant-submissive behavior as models of mania and depression. *Neuroscience and Biobehavioral Reviews*, 29: 715–737.

Nesse, Randolph M. and Kent C. Berridge 1997. Psychoactive drug use in evolutionary perspective. *Science*, 278: 63–66.

Panksepp, Jaak 2004. Emotions as natural kinds within the mammalian brain. Pp. 137–156 in *Handbook of Emotions*, 2nd ed. Paperback edition. Michael Lewis and Jeannette M. Haviland-Jones, eds. New York: The Guilford Press.

Panksepp, Jaak and Jeff Burgdorf 2003. "Laughing" rats and the evolutionary antecedents of human joy? *Physiology & Behavior*, 79: 533–547.

Philips, Susan U. 1985. Participant structures and communicative competence: Warm Springs children in community and classroom. Pp. 370–394 in *Functions of Language in the Classroom*. Courtney B. Cazden, Vera P. John, and Dell Hymes, eds. Prospect Heights, IL: Waveland Press.

Plavcan, J. Michael and Carel P. van Schaik 1997. Interpreting hominid behavior on the basis of sexual dimorphism. *Journal of Human Evolution*, 32: 345–374.

Power, Margaret 1991. *The Egalitarians—Human and Chimpanzee: An Anthropological View of Social Organization*. Cambridge: Cambridge University Press.

Sapolsky, Robert M. 2005. The influence of social hierarchy on primate health. *Science*, 308: 648–652.

Schoenhals, Martin 1993. *The Paradox of Power in a People's Republic of China Middle School*. Armonk, NY: M.E. Sharpe.

—— 2003. *Intimate Exclusion: Race and Caste Turned Inside Out*. Lanham, MD: University Press of America.

Sen, Amartya 1999. *Development as Freedom*. New York: Knopf.

Shultziner, Doron, Thomas Stevens, Martin Stevens, Brian A. Stewart, Rebecca J. Hannagan, and Giulia Saltini-Semerari 2010. The causes and scope of political egalitarianism during the Last Glacial: A multi-disciplinary perspective. *Biology and Philosophy*, 25: 319–346.

Smith, Andrew B. 2004. Archaeology and evolution of hunters and gatherers. Pp. 384–390 in *The Cambridge Encyclopedia of Hunters and Gatherers*. Paperback edition. Richard B. Lee and Richard Daly, eds. Cambridge: Cambridge University Press.

Stock, Jay T. and Ron Pinhasi 2011. Changing paradigms in our understanding of the transition to agriculture: Human bioarchaeology, behaviour and adaptation. Pp. 1–13 in *Human Bioarchaeology of the Transition to Agriculture*. Ron Pinhasi and Jay T. Stock, eds. Hoboken, NJ: John Wiley and Sons.

Sussman, Robert W. and Paul A. Garber 2004. Rethinking sociality: Cooperation and aggression among primates. Pp. 161–190 in *The Origins and Nature of Sociality*. Robert W. Sussman and Audrey R. Chapman, eds. New York: Aldine de Gruyter.

Sussman, Robert, Joshua Marshack, and Richard Wrangham 2010. Are humans inherently killers? A critique by Robert Sussman and Joshua Marshack followed by a response by Richard Wrangham. *Global Non-Killing Working Papers*, 1: 7–47.

Tomasello, Michael 2009. *Why We Cooperate*. Cambridge, MA: MIT Press.

Turner, Jonathan H. 2000. *On the Origins of Human Emotions: A Sociological Inquiry into the Evolution of Human Affect*. Stanford, CA: Stanford University Press.

Turner, Victor 1977. *The Ritual Process: Structure and Anti-Structure*. Ithaca, NY: Cornell Paperbacks.

Van Schaik, Carel P. and Judith M. Burkhart 2010. Mind the gap: Cooperative breeding and the evolution of our unique features. Pp. 477–496 in *Mind the Gap: Tracing the*

Origins of Human Universals. Peter M. Kappeler and Joan B. Silk, eds. New York: Springer.

Wilson, Edward O. 1980. *Sociobiology: The Abridged Edition.* Cambridge, MA: Belknap Press of Harvard University Press.

Wittig, R.M., C. Crockford, A. Weltring, T. Deschner, and K. Zuberbühler 2015. Single aggressive interactions increase urinary glucocorticoid levels in wild male chimpanzees. PLoS ONE, 10(2): e0118695.

Wrangham, Richard and Dale Peterson 1996. *Demonic Males: Apes and the Origins of Human Violence.* New York: Houghton Mifflin.

2

EQUALITY OF GENDER, SEXUALITY, AND LOVE

All hierarchies must be challenged. Some inequalities, such as differences in wealth, are overt; it is, therefore, fairly easy to think about how to challenge them. But other hierarchies are less overt, even hidden. This is true, for example, with the stigma associated with LGBT people. This stigma leads to an erasure, through silence and censorship, of positive media and public discourse about LGBT people. With little discourse about gay issues, the inequality affecting LGBT people is often hidden. Those of us who are LGBT must affirm our identity publicly in order to begin to challenge the inequalities that affect us.

So, in a process analogous to the coming out of gay people, hierarchy must be outed and unmasked. How do we do this? I know many scholars will look for me to start with a definition of hierarchy. How can we understand it without knowing, in a sentence or two, what it is? I will resist this temptation. Just as "art" is something that can't be defined in words, due to the inherent limitation of verbal language (a limitation needing much more space than I have here to explain adequately), so too with hierarchy. Instead of defining it, I want to give examples of hierarchy that the reader might not have thought of, or might have thought of but not realized were that destructive. I do this in order to model how hierarchy can be unmasked. In reality, this process of its unmasking must be an ongoing process. It is not something that can be accomplished with a simple equation. In fact in Chapter 6 I will describe the role I believe education can play, and should play, in enhancing our understanding of the various forms of hierarchy in our midst.

Gender hierarchy

Let me start with a familiar topic: Gender. Discrimination in the workplace needs to be challenged in order to strive toward gender equality. But consider, as well, the following examples of gender discrimination. They will be recognizable to many readers, but might have been overlooked by other readers, because of their subtle and somewhat hidden nature. Despite their less overt nature, they are toxic if left unchallenged:

1. Boys get teased by peers and often family members too if they cry, or act in other ways too much "like a girl." This phenomenon varies culturally but is nonetheless pervasive. (An example of a partial exception: One male Chinese informant told me that in China many of the positive traits of "civilized" people are also those most commonly associated with women, so that a boy who is quiet, gentle, and studious—traits often associated with women—is not likely to be teased for his feminine traits because his character is seen as more generally laudable due to his civility.)

2. Women's sexual freedom is more limited than sexuality among men (with the notable exception of same-sex relationships). On the one hand, women are defamed as "sluts" if they have multiple sexual partners while men are called "studs," a positive word in many circles. On the other hand, women are lauded for showing sexual "self-control," while men who are too controlled are reviled as sexually troubled, not "real" men.

3. Men, in general, take less of an active role than women in childrearing and in anything associated with children or the home. This manifests itself in strange ways. Men often don't cook, but when it comes to starting up the family barbeque in suburban America, the man is king, and his wife is often not party to the outdoor cooking. It is interesting that cooking inside is womanly, associated with the home and the indoors, while cooking outside is masculine, associated with outside, the street, and the public domain so often controlled by men. The association of women and femininity with the home and the private domain, and men with the public and the outside, is a major form of gender inequality.

I could go on and on with similar examples, of course. What the above examples all share, however, is that they are forms of hierarchy not just of men over women, but of *maleness over femaleness*, as well as discrimination based on the notion that a masculine female is somehow unnatural, as is a feminine male. Clearly, then, while ending discrimination against women in work and politics is an absolutely necessary step toward ending gender hierarchy, it does not go far enough.

Gender, indeed, is like a caste system and the separations of caste must be eradicated in order to achieve full equality. Let me explain with reference to caste in India. In a caste system, such as India's, groups of people, castes, are both separated and ranked. The separation does not just occur in the workplace, with workplace discrimination, but also in the intimate sphere of home and family. Upper-caste Indians do not (usually—there are exceptions) marry the lower castes, nor do they interact in any intimate context with them where they could be seen to be equals. (This is changing, of course, but the changes are slow in coming.) The upper castes, especially in the countryside, won't live with lower castes, and the quintessential manifestation of caste ranking is often said to be who will take a glass of water from whom. If A will not accept water from B, but B will take it from A, then A is higher than B. This is part of a larger system of belief that holds upper castes to be purer, and close to the sacred—the highest Indian caste, Brahmins, are the ancestral priestly caste—while the lower castes are seen as profane. The lowest people in caste rankings are the Dalits (Untouchables), whose ancestral and often contemporary jobs are seen to pollute them through contact with the profane: Sex, bodies, and mortality. Dalits do such jobs as working with leather, which is polluting because it requires contact with the skin of dead animals, and other reviled jobs such as garbage collecting and toilet cleaning. Dalits in rural India live separately from non-Dalits and a visit by a Dalit to the village well, located in the non-Dalit sector, can incite non-Dalits to injure, and even kill, the well-going Dalit.

I raise the caste analogy for my analysis of gender in order to illuminate a key characteristic of both of these hierarchical systems. Caste is based upon both separation as well as hierarchy. There has been a great deal of debate in the literature on India about whether separation or ranking is primary. I think this sets up a false division between the two. In point of fact, caste hierarchy is manufactured through separation. The whole rationale for upper-caste dominance rests on notions of pollution, a separation metaphor as well as a dominance metaphor. The pollution ideology requires the separation of uppers and lowers, so as to keep the uppers clean, and it legitimizes upper dominance because they are seen as purer, and holy (see Schoenhals 2003).

Gender hierarchy is like caste hierarchy in that it too requires separation and segregation of the sexes. In many societies women are seen as polluted, and they therefore threaten the purity of men. Many societies ban women from the male sphere and from religious institutions because of their ostensible impurity, often seen as a result of menstruation.

For anthropologists, one of the best-known examples of gender-pollution beliefs comes from New Guinea. In the classic case of the Sambia, only one of the many groups in New Guinea with such beliefs, women are viewed as inferior to men in large part because they are polluted. While young boys are raised almost exclusively by women, they are also viewed as contaminated by women, even their own mothers. (Girls, however, grow up "naturally," without any risk of pollution from either their mothers or other adult women.) The pollution of boys begins in the womb, a result of contact between the male fetus and his mother's blood. As babies, boys are believed to take in additional female contaminants through their noses. These pollutions are considered so severe that all Sambia boys are taken away from their mothers at 7–10 years old by adult men, who bring the boy-initiates into the male clubhouse to begin a series of rituals seen as critical to making them grow into men. From this point on the boys live with other men in the clubhouse and they cannot have any contact with women (they cannot even look at them), including their own mothers. This taboo lasts for more than 10 years (Herdt 1982).

The rituals are serious business. Older men take the initiates away from their mothers and other women. They go out into the forest, where men nosebleed the boys, putting sharp cane grass up their noses so that they bleed out feminine contamination, which is thought to reside in the nose. This is seen as purging them of feminine pollutants. In addition to this pollution purging, the Sambia believe all boys need male essence, which they acquire during their initiation by ingesting semen (performing oral sex on older male youths, which Herdt describes in much greater depth in his other publications) (Herdt 1982).

The New Guinea nosebleeding practices and the underlying belief system in feminine pollution sustaining them might seem extreme, but they are by no means unique. My students respond to the New Guinea beliefs and practices by saying they are strange and exotic, but I remind them that American schoolchildren hold similar beliefs, as seen in what they (or we, for all of us who are American) call "cooties." This belief seems to hold throughout America based on my informal survey of the subject, and the essentials of it are roughly the same in different regions. Girls fear cooties from being touched by a boy and boys fear it from being touched by a girl. If you are touched by a person of the opposite sex, you are polluted with cooties. There is an escape from the pollution, however. You can get rid of cooties by touching a person who is the same sex as you, thereby transferring the pollution to that person. (And in New York, students believed that there is a "cooties shot" that you can give yourself, as a protection from cooties. In suburban Detroit, where I grew up, we did not have such protective devices!) Often, there is also a belief that any undesirable classmate can give cooties to everyone else.

The point of the above discussion is to note that gender, like caste, is about both separation as well as hierarchy; separation and the pollution rationale for it create a higher caste of males and a lower caste of Untouchables, females. The separation of gender caste takes myriad forms. It is a separation of men from women, based on the heterosexist assumption that they are two categories properly relating to each other as sexual attractors. Men and women avoid touch as pre-adolescents and avoid easy interaction as adults out of anxiety about the power of the potential attraction between them. But the separation is not just one of men and women but of the masculine and the feminine, and the consignment of each to its proper place. Just as a Dalit going to a regular village well for water is often courting death, a feminine male or masculine female is likewise subject to being attacked violently for confounding societal divisions. And to my mind, the very fact that the challenge is so threatening is an indication of how necessary is its eradication. Gender hierarchy cannot really be fully overcome as long as males and females are separated and as long as separate categories of masculinity and femininity, the symbolic and potent extensions of the male/female divide, continue to persist.

My conclusion is one that some readers may see as radical: *True gender equality requires the abolition of the categories of men and women*. Also required is the abolition of "masculinity" and "femininity." No personality trait, ability, or job should be seen as "naturally" female or naturally male.

I know that many readers will object that my prescriptions here are unreasonable, and impossible to carry out: "Women and men are different. That is simply a fact of nature. Ignoring this fact is imposing ideology onto reality." But think of some other distinctions: Black versus white, for example. A century ago, this distinction was seen as real and natural, and was the basis for an odious hierarchy of racism. Scientific thinking since that time has challenged the very distinctions upon which racism has been built. While no scholars would deny the existence of differences in skin color among peoples, we also point out that these differences do not conform to ideology: There are not "black" peoples and "white" peoples but people with varying degrees of pigment in their skin. These differences occur between populations (the word now replacing "race"), but also within populations. In any family, one sibling might have darker skin and one lighter skin. We point out how ideology distorts biological reality. In the American ideology of race, my sister and I, born of the same "white" parents, are members of the same race, "white," even though she and I have somewhat different skin tones. That reality is ideologically denied. The same is true among American blacks, whose own skin tones vary but who are all defined as "black." And those who have one "black" parent and one "white" parent are assigned to one or the other category (usually to "black"), due to the American belief that says one is "black" if any part of that person's ancestry is "black." That this is an arbitrary classification is further reinforced by the cross-cultural study of race. In Brazil, mixed-race peoples are culturally acknowledged, in contrast to the US situation, and skin color is only one component used in defining a person's race. In addition, in the Brazilian ideology money can change one's racial classification, reflected in the Brazilian saying, "money whitens" (Pitt-Rivers 1971). In the caste-like US belief system no amount of money can change someone's racial classification.

So, yes, there are physical differences based upon skin, but US racial ideology distorts these differences, and minimizes other physical differences that it might have focused upon (why is there no "race" of tall people and "race" of short people?). The ideological distortions are arbitrary with respect to biology and reality, and they are promulgated in order to contrive a separation between two groups. This separation between blacks and whites was integral to, and remains integral to, the hierarchy of white over black. If we are to attack racial hierarchy, we must eradicate any odious cultural significances attached to the difference between blackness and whiteness, and we must challenge the arbitrary divisions that culture makes between black and white.

The same is true of gender. Yes, there are males and females. But as the intelligent reader will know, biology itself is not so simple. There are countless examples from biology of animals that fall in-between the female/male dichotomy, or change from one gender to another. Roughgarden cites many examples in her book of the complexities of gender, complexities that run counter to our received belief in two clear-cut opposing genders of male and female. She says that in fact there are three or more genders in many species "with individuals of each sex occurring in two or more forms." She also notes that in half of the animal kingdom the common pattern is for an individual to be both male and female at the same time or to change between genders at different times during its life (Roughgarden 2004: 27–28).

Among humans, several things about gender are noteworthy:

1. Biologically, not all humans clearly fall into the category of either male or female. Roughgarden reviews the diversity of human genetics (such as XXY or XYY) and conditions such as genital ambiguities. While doctors often deem such individuals, commonly referred to as intersexed, to be abnormal and in need of treatment, Roughgarden argues persuasively that this is not the case. Humans who do not clearly fall into "male" or "female" categories exist throughout the world (Roughgarden 2004: 288–305).

2. The biological trend in the evolution of humans from our ancestor hominins, a trend occurring over millions of years, has been one in which the physical differences between males and females have *diminished*. This is true of body size and of canine-teeth size (Shultziner et al. 2010: 330–331), two especially significant traits. While the casual observer may focus on the physical differences between human males and females, the reality, from the perspective of evolution and comparative primate anatomy, is that human males and females exhibit greatly diminished sexual dimorphism compared to other primates. (See Chapter 1 for a discussion of the relationship between our evolutionary ancestors' reduced sexual dimorphism and their egalitarianism.)

3. Culture, ideology, and human intelligence introduce a significant element of flexibility into the way humans define the gender to which they belong. On one end of the continuum, culture can play an extraordinarily gender-dichotomizing function. It is rather amazing to me that many Indo-European languages assign genders to things that aren't even alive, so that evening (*le soir*) is masculine in French, while night (*la nuit*) is feminine. Similar gendered divisions, though not present in language, are made by the yin yang system of thought of ancient China, where the moon is considered feminine and the sun is masculine (although yin yang recognizes that the two forces are complementary and that there is a bit of yin in yang and a bit of yang in yin). An American example of gender-dichotomizing that I love to cite to my students, mentioned earlier, is the kitchen stove versus the outside barbeque grill. While the former is traditionally the sole province of women, the latter is the sole province of men. Why is cooking inside a female activity while cooking outside is a male activity? Clearly, there is no necessary reason for this division. It is an arbitrary artifact of culture's gender-dichotomizing tendencies.

4. But just as culture can divide gender into two categories, it can also do the opposite. Many cultures recognize more than two genders. There are many such cases (see Herdt 1996). One example often cited by anthropologists is the berdache, or two-spirit person, found among 150 North American indigenous societies (Roscoe 1996: 330). The two-spirit person is a culturally recognized practice in which individuals of one sex take on the activities and dress of the other sex. However, Roscoe demonstrates that the two-spirit is best seen as a separate gender, because in some cases they dressed differently from both men and women (335, 339). The existence of native terminology for the two-spirit

supports the view that they are both culturally recognized and that they constitute a third gender or a third and fourth gender. Some languages, such as the Shoshoni term "man-woman" (*tanowaip*), reference gender while still giving the two-spirit their own label. Other languages have words for the two-spirit that have no etymological relationship to "men" or "women" at all (338–339). In some cases two-spirit persons lived together with each other in groups (347) and in many cases they engaged in activities not pursued by any non-two-spirit persons (338) and they were honored for surpassing others in their occupational and religious capacities (335).

5.   Individuals, regardless of the culture to which they belong, can identify with a gender different from the one to which they are biologically and/or culturally assigned. The capacity to do so should not be dismissed lightly, since it is part of the hallmark of humanness: The ability to have a sense of self, and a sense of identity that may, or may not, conform to how we are seen biologically or culturally by other individuals around us. (Many scholars lacking in anthropological awareness believe that only Westerners from industrialized "modern" societies think about their identities robustly. This is incorrect.)

What all of this tells us is that human gender is intrinsically flexible, just like so much else that is human. We can assign gendered traits to people and even to things, in ways more dichotomized than any non-human animal could ever do. But we can also transcend dichotomized gender more than any such non-human could ever do. The dichotomization of people into two genders based on two anatomies is neither natural nor inevitable. This dichotomization, the foundation for a caste-like gender hierarchy that privileges men over women and maleness over femaleness, can be transcended with the same human capacity that enables their rigidification in the first place: The capacity of humans, through human flexibility, to transcend a two-gender system.

Before discussing the details of how we might transcend gender, let me ask the reader to reflect on how much of a liberation it would be for so many people if being "masculine" or "feminine" were no longer a supreme measure of one's success or failure as a human, as a man or woman. I don't think I have to tell the reader how much angst and energy is expended, and tragically wasted in my opinion, by people worrying about their masculinity and femininity (a worry, incidentally, which gives the lie to the assertions of natural gender divisions: If gender were so natural, men would automatically be "masculine" and women would automatically be "feminine"). Males in cultures throughout the world suffer the incredible burden of having to prove their maleness, feeling that they are losers if they are not high on the masculine, or macho, status ladder. Pollack has written eloquently about the American boys he has encountered and the price they pay emotionally for having to maintain a pretense of masculine invulnerability—a pretense that one is not vulnerable to "fear, uncertainty, feelings of loneliness and need" (Pollack 1998: 5). Some of my students, especially female students, have talked about how liberated they have felt in mixing up gender attributes in their own identities, daring to like sports while also liking clothes, for example.

I know there are more dramatic examples I might cite of how we might be liberated from gender—especially examples from highly gender-segregated and patriarchal cultures. The reader will know, from many media and academic accounts, of the desperate situation of women in many such cultures, where those who deviate from normative sexuality face ostracism and even death for their deviations. The same is true for LGBT people. But my point in citing less obvious examples of the possibility of gender liberation is to illustrate that the damage wrought by gender and gender segregation is not always conspicuous, but is nonetheless extremely painful—and sometimes painful precisely because the hurts are hidden from us and viewed as products of individual failure.

Given how much importance cultures, families, and individuals invest in gender, and sexuality, gender/sexuality changes offer as much potential for increased happiness and genuine liberation as changes in any other sphere of hierarchy. This is why I started the first post-introductory chapter of this book with challenges to gender and sexuality, rather than with changes in power or wealth. Hierarchy of the latter is definitely hurtful, but these hurts are more often clear. I do not mean to diminish any hierarchical hurts because they are more dramatic or more obvious, but instead wish to call attention to all hierarchies, even those less obvious. And gender, and the damage of gender segregation and hierarchy, is a quintessential example of the obscuring of hierarchy and its damages. This is because societies promulgate norms of proper femininity and masculinity and most members of society come to accept the view that failure to conform to proper gender norms is, indeed, a failure of the individual, rather than seeing it for what it really is: A failure of the society that created the constraining norms in the first place.

Ending gender

If culture can rigidify the two-gender system, then culture, and the human imagination, can end it as well. How can this happen? I advocate that Utopia should:

1. *Promote a new kind of sexuality, one not based on gender distinctions*: I will have more to say about this below, but I wanted to put it as number 1 because sexuality reifies the very gender distinctions that Utopia should seek to eliminate.

2. *End all segregation of men and women*: Just as culture can segregate or integrate "blacks" and "whites," so it has the capacity to segregate or integrate males and females. The association of the public space—the street and the plaza, for example—as male, and the domestic sphere as female, must end, especially since it is a cornerstone of so much gender oppression (see Rosaldo 1974). And, yes, even bathrooms and locker rooms should be integrated. The assumption that sexual attraction exists between only men and women—the basis for this segregation—is, of course, an assumption that erases the existence of LGBT people. (In fact homophobia is the handmaiden of sexism and sexual segregation.) All people should be considered to be humans first, rather than first as men and women. (When a baby is born, we

should ask if it is healthy, rather than showing our gender obsessions by asking the parents if they have had a boy or girl.) In that case all people could share a locker room or a bathroom with other humans.

3. *Use radical enforcement to prevent "work" discrimination*: Even though work will no longer exist as it does today, productive activity will continue. There can be no discrimination in who gets to engage in such activity.

Laws against discrimination mean nothing unless they are enforced with great strictness, which is not currently the case in many countries. In the US a lawyer fighting a slip and fall accident can earn far more money than one fighting gender discrimination. This must change. In Chapter 7 I will discuss how the principles of Utopia will be enforced, but for now it must be said that the strictest enforcement will apply to violation of any egalitarian principles, including those applying to gender.

4. *Teach equitable gender roles*: Games and clothes will become unisex. Television will produce shows celebrating parents who display exemplary methods of socializing children for gender egalitarianism. Web sites will do likewise. Companies that produce toys, games, and movies showing kids in non-stereotypical roles will be given favorable air time and shelf space.

5. *Strongly enforce laws against rape*: Women are not only subjugated in the economic and political spheres, but in the sexual sphere as well. Therefore, laws punishing rape and domestic violence (including violence and rape directed at men) will be promulgated and enforced globally. While Utopia will aim to end war (Chapter 7), should rape occur during conflict, as it does today during war, the perpetrators will be punished strictly. The toleration of rape during war, and its use as a means to punish an opponent or enemy people, must end.

6. *Promote new views about LGBT peoples*: It is often said that homophobia helps teach sexism. One only has to look at a world map of countries with discriminatory laws and policies toward LGBT people and overlay it with a map of countries mistreating women: There is a clear correspondence.

This is not surprising. Heterosexuality reinforces gender distinctions and gives them the greatest emotional charge possible—that of love and sex. Homosexuality, bisexuality, androgyny, and transgendered peoples threaten the distinctions made between men and women, and the wall heterosexuality so often erects between maleness and femaleness.

Thus, anti-gay teasing/bullying must be ended not only because it is a form of anti-gay prejudice, but also because it is a means to sustain gender prejudice. In many societies boys first learn to enforce gendered segregation through the act of teasing each other for being girlish, or gayish. Such teasing socializes them to refrain from interaction with girls and encourages the stigmatizing in boys of anything feminine. Through anti-gay teasing boys learn to promote gender segregation and hierarchy.

I must note here that there are many, many more things to be said about ending gender discrimination. The reason I do not give more of these issues here is because others have done such a good job discussing the issue. In addition my goal is not just the promotion of equity between men and women. Rather, I want to eradicate gender altogether. And to do this requires instituting not only rules for equality between men and women, but also a new kind of sexuality that deemphasizes attraction based on gender—whether to persons of the opposite or same gender.

A new kind of sexuality

Heterosexuality promotes and sustains gendered distinctions. Men try to be masculine to appeal to women, and women try to be feminine to appeal to men. Homosexuality presents a clear challenge to this dynamic, but it is not free of complicity in reifying gendered norms. Although I would like to advocate, as a gay man, that Utopia should simply "tolerate" homosexuality as well as heterosexuality, I must admit, if I am honest, that both heterosexuality *and* homosexuality can reify gendered dichotomies. When a gay man says, "I am attracted only to men, and to the masculinity of men," the fact that it is a man making this statement does challenge traditional sex and gender notions, but the man's attraction itself, nonetheless, is based upon gender and gendered dichotomies. I suppose something like bisexuality might take the place of other sexualities, although calling it bisexuality still emphasizes the division of people by gender.

Let me, instead, coin a new term for a new sexuality, one that will erase gender and the hierarchy based upon gender. This is a sexuality that will also promote a more general end to the hierarchies often sustained through sex. I will call the new sexuality "egalitarian sexuality."

I will outline the general principles of egalitarian sexuality here and, in the next section, I will describe my ideas for how Utopia can promote this new kind of sexuality.

Four features of egalitarian sexuality are described here:

1. Gender will be equalized by erasing the division between men and women, and the concomitant sexualities that go with this division. That is, to be specific, Utopia will encourage people to be attracted to other people without regard to their gender. All humans will be encouraged to feel attraction to any other human, whether that human is male or female.

I have to admit here that I don't know if a genderless sexuality is truly feasible. Those who still base their sexuality upon gender—being either straight, gay, bisexual, or transgendered—will in no way be compelled to relinquish their sexual attractions, although all people will be encouraged to rethink their attractions, as discussed below. I do suspect, given the wide variation in sexuality so typical of the animal kingdom (Roughgarden 2004), that humans are probably more capable of genderless sexuality than we would like to believe. Our cousin bonobos are famous for using sex with both same- and opposite-sex partners; sex is used to reduce tensions and promote reconciliation when there is conflict (De Waal and Lanting 1997: Chapter 4). This suggests that humans, too, may have a strong capacity for sex without regard to gender. In fact I believe that it is only the cultural elaboration of gender dichotomies that creates and reinforces a distinction and hierarchy between sex-with-opposite-sex versus sex-with-same-sex partners.

The one notable exception to a lack of classes of people to whom one can be attracted is children. Their age precludes them from being consenting sexual partners and therefore renders them a category separate from all adults and off-limits to sex with adults.

2. Egalitarian sexuality not only ends the male–female distinction by challenging sexual attraction based on gender but also, even more importantly, it helps eliminate within-gender hierarchies based on sex. The notion that specific sexual characteristics and actions make one more of a real man, or more of a real woman, is one of the most odious and angst-producing dynamics that exists. Among males, for example, there is often the tendency to prove one's masculinity, and move up the ladder of masculine success, by having multiple sexual partners. Sex is sought not for enjoyment but for the sake of conquest, to "score," in a process that degrades both the women (or men) who are the man's sexual partners, as well as the men with whom he competes to show off his superiority. The idea of a "score" illustrates the hierarchy at work, a hierarchy as odious as any other hierarchy. This is a hierarchy too that, like all hierarchies, crowds out genuine pleasure, because sex to score means it is pursued to achieve status rather than for enjoyment. (And to the reader who thinks male scoring behavior is an intrinsic, adaptive biological trait and, therefore, one not open to change, I would suggest taking a look at Roughgarden 2009, especially 194–195, 241, and 245. She argues that "promiscuity" is not "an inherent male characteristic" of male mammals and that among males promiscuity is only a "strategy of last resort that occurs when males are excluded from control of offspring rearing." And among humans women are not acting out an evolutionarily adaptive script either, when being attracted to the promiscuous male. Their truer advantage comes in choosing a male partner based upon "effectiveness at raising offspring.")

In Utopia both men and women will be encouraged to have sex not to prove something to themselves or others, but instead to please their partners and themselves. As with other forms of interaction, sex will be seen as a form of compassion. Individuals who do not desire to engage in sex will be free to abstain, without being acclaimed (the "pure" woman; the saintly monk or nun) or vilified (the sexless man) for their abstinence. The only real constraint is that anyone trying to put themselves above others will be pressured to give up the pretense.

Think how much freer we will all feel, indeed how much of a liberation it would be, to live without the pressure to be something, or do something, in sex and love that is at odds with our real selves and our real desires, and perhaps at odds with our real sexual and romantic capacities. To me, this kind of honesty and authenticity is the real meaning of "coming out of the closet." The closet metaphor might be most appropriate for LGBT people, but closets can constrain all people, gay and straight. The real constraint of the "closet" is that it forces us to have sex we don't desire (with the undesired gender, in the case of gay people, or with more partners than are really desired, in the case of men trying to prove themselves). Sex serves the sole purpose of demonstrating our ostensible self-worth to ourselves and others, and our superiority over other ostensibly sexually flawed peoples. This is undesired sex, coerced on us by societal or peer dictates, or even something which we force upon ourselves, in our quest for superiority. And if rape and child abuse are centrally evil because they coerce sex, then the closet, in its widest definition, must be seen as evil and immoral too by the same logic.

Coming out (of the closet) will free us to live authentically, in accord with our genuine sexual and romantic desires, with no outside societal or peer pressure forcing us to attempt to attain some hierarchical perch through our sexual actions. That kind of coming out is, indeed, a true liberation.

3. There will be no socially created, nor socially condoned, hierarchy of physical attractiveness in egalitarian sexuality. (More about how to bring this situation about, in the next section.) Just as all humans deserve to live free of hunger and deserve to work freely and have their work valued by others, so all humans deserve to love and be loved in return. And just as no one should be allowed a monopoly on money or power at others' expense, so no one should be allowed to monopolize a claim on attractiveness, leaving others with diminished access to romantic love and the affirmation that goes with it. (I owe these insights to my good friend, Kant Nimbark.)

I know many readers will respond: "But some people are attractive and some are not. How can I be forced to think of unattractive people as attractive? I'm just attracted to certain people and that's the way it is." The belief that our desires come only from inside our individual, idiosyncratic selves is a seductive belief, but it is a naive one, because it individualizes attraction and overlooks the role of culture and society in defining what is attractive. And that role is substantial. Many readers will know that chunkiness was considered attractive at certain times and places because it was emblematic of wealth. Thin people were seen as malnourished and thinness was a sign of poverty, an undesirable and unattractive trait. (Now that nutrition is significantly better in much of the world, thinness, rather than chunkiness, is in vogue.) Many readers will know, too, that in the Europe and America of the past fair skin was considered more beautiful than tanned skin, because the latter signified one who was obligated to labor outdoors. Today, these notions have changed, as tanned skin has come to symbolize the possession of enough wealth to travel to tropical tourist locales.

The role of society in creating attraction continues unabated in our own time. Moreover, as in the past, notions of attractiveness reflect and reinforce hierarchy. Those on top status-wise are often also the ones considered to be most attractive. This is obvious, of course, with regard to skin color. People of color get marginalized in movies and news and are too infrequently portrayed as beautiful. Those who do make the cut are often lighter-skinned African-Americans. This is true on American television and even in children's cartoons. The enormously popular Disney movie,

The Lion King, is amazingly insensitive to this issue, portraying villains such as Uncle Scar as darker-skinned while the heroes of the story, Mufasa and his son, Simba, are lighter-skinned. The skin color difference is reinforced by making the villainous Scar have dark hair, compared to the lighter brown hair of the heroic Mufasa.

I like the above examples because they show the complex way in which social conditions shape sexual desire; even more importantly these examples demonstrate the *central place of hierarchy in this shaping*. The connection between sexual attractions and the nature of society apart from sex is a connection all too often overlooked. I have often heard many gay men, for example, dismiss their attraction to neo-militaristic or even neo-fascist clothing and shoes, or their predilection for "master-slave" roles, as just "play." I am not convinced. The eroticizing of hierarchy both reflects and reinforces very real hierarchy in society. A truly egalitarian society should encourage all people to see equality and compassion, not hierarchy or attributes of wealth and status, as the most sexually attractive of all traits.

4.   Finally, egalitarian sexuality will replace what I will call "compensatory love" with reciprocal love. Sex and love will be equal, reciprocal, and not a compensation for low self-esteem—low self-esteem so often caused by the casualties inflicted upon us by living in a fundamentally inegalitarian society. The goal of sex and love will not be to gain a sense of self-esteem by finding a perfect, godlike sex or love object for one's possession. Such love and sex, which I call "compensatory" because it is compensating for past hurts, is so common today only because of the fundamental unequal societies in which we live. It seeks to compensate for past hurts by replicating, in often highly destructive ways, the very hierarchies that should be undone. Perhaps the paradigmatic example is the battered spouse, who keeps returning to the very person who emotionally and physically degrades her, or him. What makes this paradigmatic is that the relationship, and even possible attraction, is based upon hurt and fear rather than love.

As a way to describe a different approach, egalitarian sex and love, let me discuss in more detail the causes and many manifestations of its opposite—compensatory love and sex. One such manifestation is the attraction to the "bad" boy or "bad" girl as sex partner. Why does this occur? Previously, some sociobiologists posited that the "bad" boy is a better potential protector to the woman, but I hope the reader sees the lack of common sense in this view. What bad boy really is a good love object for oneself, or for one's potential progeny?

Based on the new evolutionary thinking, I would posit that feelings of sexual attraction can arise from love, following the mammalian propensity for bonding. But this love and sex dynamic coexists with evolutionarily prior dynamics. Many species have sex and then die soon after. Pacific salmon, for example, swim upstream for hundreds of miles, lay eggs, and then die. Death follows the first mating of several marsupial mice species. And, when mating, the female praying mantis bites off her partner's head. Evolution does not have any incentive to preserve those who have already reproduced, hence there is a strong temporal and functional link between sex and death (Kearl n.d.). In humans this dynamic is partially overridden since post-reproductive humans play such an important role in raising the young, and in tending to the community more generally. We therefore live long after sexual maturity and reproduction, fulfilling roles as nurturers of our own or others' off-spring, and in old age we are taken care of by those our generation has previously raised. Sex can lead to the new lives that represent new opportunities to nurture and be nurtured and this accounts, in part I believe, for the loving and life-affirming feelings that people often feel due to love and sex.

But the sex–death connection remains underneath. Many readers will know this is a widespread theme throughout Western literature (Dollimore 1998). Psychologists have also noted the strength of this connection. Although I disagree with some of their studies' terminology (anthropologists are uncomfortable with stigmatizing labels, such as "neurotic"), Goldenberg et al. (1999) report several studies showing that many of us associate sex and death, primarily, the authors surmise, because the corporality of sex reminds us of our own more general corporality (which the authors see as linked to our view of ourselves as animals) and hence mortality. (This hypothesis is, perhaps, not as far-fetched as it might seem since a common belief in major religions—I'm thinking in particular of Hinduism, but the Christian connection is no less strong—is that sex, death, and the body are opposed to the spirit, the sacredness of asceticism and/or virginity, and the immortality of heaven or reincarnation.) The terror of death thus infuses sex with anxiety. But the authors argue that collective cultural beliefs, such as a belief associating sex with love, can override the anxiety of sex and its connection to death, and can give sex a positive meaning.

Thus, to summarize my argument: There are two types of sex and love, one that is life-affirming and connected with nurture and love, and one that is driven by anxiety and fear, and their concomitants—obsession and compulsion. It is fascinating to note the existence of such dynamics among our chimp cousins. As Power notes, when new hierarchies arise among chimps, sexuality changes. Males begin to force females to have sex, and the newly elevated despotic males monopolize females in a manner fundamentally at odds with the easy-going non-competitive sexuality that existed prior to the advent of more general hierarchy (Power 1991: 77–83).

For humans, sex driven by anxiety, including (or especially) the anxiety induced by hierarchy, leads not to pleasure but to agitation and stimulation and cycles of fear and (hoped for) release from fear. The pursuit of this type of sex and love can be triggered not only by our own actual death anxieties, but also by any substantial existential threats. Thus, if we are ostracized or ashamed—facing the prospect of social death—this can lead one to act out sexually in search of sex and love. The quest here is not for the real desire and happiness that sex and love brings, but rather is an attempt to diminish the social threats we face. But, like the battered wife returning to her abusive partner, the dynamic is not a healthy one, nor one that is pleasurable, to say the least. Like the trauma victim who so often yearns to go back to the site of trauma or compulsively seeks to recreate the trauma itself ("trauma reenactment syndrome"), the person hurt by society puts himself/herself back into fear-producing situations, through sex and love, as a way to try, however vainly, to overcome past traumas.

I have seen this pattern often among my gay friends. So many LGBT people face the threat, or reality, of being rejected by family members due to our sexuality. And we have all had to confront the low self-esteem caused by the societal and religious stigmas attached to being gay. I know many gay men who seek redress for their negative experiences through the pursuit of compensatory sex and love. Their pursuit is agitated and driven by an unhappy obsessive cycle, the familiar cycle of the trauma victim, who is driven back into fearful and unhappy situations, ironically, in an attempt to find relief from fear and unhappiness. It is a pursuit driven too by a desire to find self-esteem in another domain, when one has lost it, or been denied it, by natal family or by society at large. Unfortunately, the hurts of being at the bottom of society's hierarchy are also sometimes compensated for by creating our own hierarchies. A familiar pattern is the re-creation, among our own gay circles, of the very exclusive and exclusionary types of hierarchy that we have all endured in wider society. Many gay men (I know this is not limited to gay men, but I use them/us as an example, since this is what I know best) try to attain a perch on the "A-list" of the gay community and, in true caste-like fashion, those with "A-list" pretensions refuse to interact with anyone but other "A-listers." We recreate the very sense of exclusions and exclusiveness that have hurt us, by seeking the uber-sex object, and by excluding all others, just as we have been excluded from love and touching by our heterosexual male peers.

I can categorically say that none of the men I've known engaging in these compensatory patterns has ever been made truly happy by them. They may have a feeling of temporary elation, but the elation dies down, and the drug needs to be taken again. The result is not pleasure but obsession and further pain, sometimes leading to a spiral of depression and lack of satisfaction. This is, indeed, a worldwide pattern, and it is not one limited to gay people.

Another related compensatory love pattern, all too familiar, is falling in love with someone who is unavailable. I know there might be many reasonable psychological explanations for this, but I cannot resist the obvious cultural, or sociological, explanation. Any kind of social rejection or outcasting is so hurtful that for many it becomes traumatic. And one response to trauma is to try to regain control of the explosive traumatic feelings by re-entering the traumatic situation. Hierarchical society is composed of traumatic exclusions, and the more we experience these, the more we may try to gain control over past traumas by reenacting them. The familiar response is to pursue in love and sex the person who is unattainable, the person too "good' for us, the person likely to reject us. By doing so we try to reclaim the dignity we have lost in past hierarchicized rejections and outcastings. But the attempt is ultimately in vain. The person too good for us often shames us, and humiliates us by rejecting our affections. That is why women who are especially beautiful are referred to by the term "femme fatale." Their beauty is toxic, even deadly, to self-esteem and well-being.

Without strong distinctions between men and women, a new egalitarian sexuality becomes possible. It is a sexuality that eschews all forms of hierarchy and segregation, especially sex based on the hierarchy and segregation of men and women. It challenges hierarchies of maleness and femaleness based on sex. It encourages more egalitarian notions of beauty and attractiveness, so that all humans have the chance to experience love and sex, and so that no one group of people can monopolize the right to be loved. It is a humane view of sex, encouraging people to be themselves, liberated from the terror and humiliation so often driving them to prove themselves as a man or woman. It is a sexuality that seeks to diminish compensatory sexuality, the seeking of sex in a frenzied state of trauma, as a balm to heal the hurts of inequality. It is a sexuality that seeks to replace such sex with sex and love based on true reciprocity, equality, and compassion for others.

How to implement egalitarian sexuality

A key theme of Chapter 1, and of this chapter, is that all forms of hierarchy must be eradicated. Eradicating wealth and power inequalities is necessary, but it is not enough. All people should get the attention and love that they need, and attention and love need to be redistributed if necessary. Equality of love is every bit as important as equality of money.

But how can people be loved equally? Should those who get too much attention surrender that attention by force, so that others can have their share? Should those who cannot find a romantic partner be given one? Isn't that prostitution of love? Isn't it a coercion of sorts?

These are, indeed, vexing questions. Let me start by saying that no one should be forced to love anyone else, nor forced to have sex with anyone else. However, Utopia will aim to establish love equality, and the simultaneous eradication of gender distinctions, by socializing new values for whom one loves. In particular Utopia will encourage everyone to feel romantic love and attraction not based on gender, nor based on other criteria connected to overt hierarchy. Beauty may be in the eye of the beholder, but notions of who is sexually attractive get constructed too often in a way that privileges a few people, at the expense of everyone else.

Instead, two principles will prevail, in the socialization of attraction:

1. attraction to those who are compassionate; and
2. attraction to those who are undervalued.

By encouraging attraction based on these two values Utopia will seek to equalize love, and encourage compassion. It will also seek to eradicate gender as the means by which individuals feel attraction. I know many of my readers and friends will call my proposals here hopelessly naive, working against human nature. But as I've already argued, attraction is much more socially malleable than any of us want to admit. We should be free to love whom we want, but we should also be receptive to learning new ways to love, especially ways consistent with equality and compassion. In any case the reader should recall the earlier analysis of how hierarchy leads to compensatory hierarchical sex today. With the end of all societal hierarchies, we will have no need to crave entry into the society of A-list sex and love objects, and reject and spurn those we deem as unworthy non-A-listers. We will follow our desires, buoyed by a newfound tendency to seek those who are compassionate—those who can truly love us and whom we can love back. This description of Utopia's love seems so simple and intuitive that I find it hard to believe it cannot be realized and I find it even harder to believe that any thinking person would not see it as a goal toward which a humane society should strive.

To encourage egalitarian sex and love, I make the following points:

1. Promote attraction to those who are compassionate and those who are undervalued.

a. *Increased attention to the compassionate*: Utopia will establish a television channel, Internet web site, and other media portals for the celebration of compassionate individuals. In order to ensure that this channel does not get commandeered by a new elite, the channel will be open to all people to tell stories of anyone they know whom they deem truly compassionate. The goal will be to make the nice person, the compassionate person, of any gender, seem truly appealing—making compassion literally sexy.

Inevitably, there will be more stories told than any viewer could ever read about on the web or watch on television. Stories will make it to the top of what might be a huge stockpile based on the following formula. Luck will play 50% of the role in determining what stories make it to the head of the newscast, or the top of the web site. This way, anyone's story has a chance of being heard. The other 50% determination of who gets headlined is based on viewer ratings. Viewers will not be allowed to rate stories about themselves or friends or family, but they will rate stories about those they don't know, based on how compassionate they find the story and the individual described in the story. This way the most compassionate stories, and the most compassionate individuals, will rise to the top, based upon democratic rankings by the viewing audience.

But how can facile rankings of compassion be thwarted? Will the young guy helping the older woman across the street get all the attention on these programs, at the expense of less obvious, but equally valid, forms of compassion? To counter facile and conventional definitions of compassion I propose that a computer program will search for reviewers who are counter-conventional in how they rate others. For example, ordinary acts of compassion, such as the compassion expected of parents, especially of mothers, is often overlooked. Thus, if persons X, Y, Z rank stories of compassionate parenting highly, and indicate their counter-conventional reason for doing so—because of the overlooking of parenting as compassionate— these rankings, and the stories of those so ranked, will be weighted, thus moving those stories up toward the top. This way minority rankings, and unconventional views of compassion, can coexist along with majoritarian views.

And both majoritarian and unconventional rankers will be able to comment on each other's reasons for ranking someone highly, so that a robust discourse and debate about what compassion is will develop. The whole goal of the new compassionate media is to give attention to compassionate individuals and, yes, even more attention to them than to lesser compassionate individuals. (This is one type of "hierarchy" that would be permitted.) This way, compassion itself will come to be valued as attractive, and new values for sexual and romantic attraction based on compassion will replace attraction based upon gender or based upon inherently hierarchical characteristics such as looks, money, race, nice clothing, etc. The result will not be perfect but by encouraging robust dialogue about what compassion is, and using luck and counter-conventional weightings, the average person's seemingly ordinary compassion has a chance to be recognized, thus socializing in us that most desirable of ideas—that ordinary kindness, and the nice man or woman, is not a fool but the real hero whom we should both admire, and love.

b. *Media portals for the unloved*: In addition to a channel portraying ordinary acts of kindness, will be a channel, and web site, with stories about anyone experiencing a deficit of love and attention. The goal will be to equalize love and attention to all humans, regardless of their looks, their wealth, their fame or fortune.

The goal will be not only to bring love to the unloved but also a related goal will be to change the way that all of us think about love and attraction. Today we all act out our attractions in pure hierarchical fashion. Despite the possible beauty in the unattractive (and for readers doubtful of such beauty, recall how many poets have found beauty in things and people normally deemed to be ugly), we think of those at the bottom the way former generations of Westerners thought of bad people and the devil—as pure incarnations of badness, clearly *dichotomized* from the good. We denounce the ugly devil with certitude, a certitude born of our belief that our own convictions are shared widely among all our peers. In fact we know that consorting with the devil is not only bad for the harm the devil brings upon us, but also bad because of what it will make our peers think of us. Thus our denunciations of the looks-devil are not private; in fact we make those denunciations quite publicly, so that our friends know *we know* what is truly bad. (At least I know this dynamic happens among men, who must make a very public display of their revulsion at seeing an ugly woman.)

And we know, concomitantly, how many hierarchical points we can score by striving for the attention of the beauty gods. Having such a god on one's arm, or even winning a look from a god, transfers their godliness to us. The look and touch of the upper caste, the beautiful, blesses us in our friends' eyes, while contact with the ugly pollutes us, so we avoid their looks, and avoid looking at them, at all costs. We say that our feelings are only coming from inside us, but this is no more true about beauty than it is about fundamentalist religious beliefs. We pretend that our desires are innocent, when in fact our rejection of the "ugly," our scapegoating of them, is what gives us increased status. In fact I'm absolutely certain that there is a potent politics of attention at work in the New York streets and subways (one at work in most major cities, too, I'm sure). By almost ritualistically disattending to the "ugly," we are trying to raise our own status through that familiar but odious social dynamic: Scapegoating others we define as unworthy.

I make my metaphors here quite consciously. We all know that scapegoating is odious, and is a fomented hatred of one group designed to elevate another group. This is no less true of the beauty caste system.

My other metaphor, the implication I've put forth above that beauty is a kind of secular religion, has more reality to it than the reader might imagine. Anthropologists studying urbanization have noted a shift from a search for marital partners in rural areas based upon their dutifulness (in southern Spain, the woman's sexual purity; in China the man's filiality—both notions bound up with morals and religion) to the quest among the urban (and those who feel they are urbane) for physical beauty (Collier 1986; 1997). If one needs further evidence for the religious metaphor, look on the Internet and note how often "god" is the word used to describe the beautiful and the sexy.

My ultimate goal in using these metaphors is to underscore that what we esteem as great and wonderful is a creation of society and a product of the dynamics of hierarchy, and this is no less true for what we deem to be attractive, despite our strong desire to naturalize our notions of attraction. And the point of saying this is to pave the way for my proposal immediately below, to show that, in fact, hierarchies of attractiveness can be undone. Here are the details of that proposal:

First we need to decide how to determine who counts as the unloved person, or the person deprived of needed attention because of the hierarchies of attractiveness we all help to create. The definition of the needy person must be multipronged, as with the definition of compassion. I would suggest that as a first step in this definition of the needy that individuals can nominate themselves if they are single, widowed, orphaned, or friendless. Story producers will then focus on telling their stories—not just their stories of loneliness, although that will be part of the telling—but their life history, biographies, desires, hopes, and daily life, both sad and happy.

A second way to find the needy is to have a computer program that will monitor all media. Anyone who has not appeared in media stories will be targeted to have programs made about them. This will promote a cult of the anti-celebrity or the uncelebrity, a desire to hear about the neglected person, the ordinary person. I must say that this is not as far-fetched an idea as it might seem. The whole spirit of my own discipline, anthropology, is to tell the stories of marginalized peoples. The periodic waves of popular fascination with anthropology give me hope that the average viewer does, indeed, find compelling the recounting of the lives of those typically neglected by the media.

Those who lack compassion will, of course, be neglected by media portals devoted to compassionate people. Should they and their stories be portrayed, as examples of people overlooked? It is tempting to say no, but I would make no exception to the rule that anyone overlooked should have their stories told, even if they are deemed uncompassionate. This will be a further check on the development of facile and conventional definitions of compassion. Maybe on the overlooked channel people will find compassionate individuals whom the compassion channel neglected!

c.   *Media portals for the macabre and the satirical*: Human fascination with the anti-compassionate—with tales of mass murderers, for example—seems widespread worldwide. It is tempting to say that there should be a prohibition of, or strong discouragement of, media portrayals of those who are uncompassionate, cruel, and/ or violent, but Utopia should avoid the temptation to censor out the darker side of human action. In fact I think that stories about the macabre might actually help to reinforce values for compassion. How so? By portraying extraordinarily unkind individuals as well as extraordinarily kind ones (albeit those who are ordinary in other respects), the media could establish compassion as the dimension of significance for judging people. On television now conventional good looks is one of the main ways by which people attract positive attention, and evil characters or the unloved are often portrayed as having particularly bad looks. The new media should make compassion or anti-compassion the relevant dimension to which viewers attend, and looks or bad looks will become merely incidental, and orthogonal to goodness or badness.

The new media can also seek to parody the compassion channel. Allowing such parody might, again, seem risky to many readers, a forum for undercutting the very emphasis on compassion which Utopia seeks. But I believe that true compassion, as opposed to facile or fake compassion, cannot be easily satirized. Thus, satire will be a healthy means by which the dialogue about compassion can be further opened up. What is most important is to have that dialogue in the first place, so that compassion becomes the object of societal attention and attraction, replacing attraction to characteristics such as clothing or "beauty," which often have nothing to do with compassion, and which often derive from their connection to hierarchy.

Although organized religion has often become a force for hierarchy, the emphasis on the overlooked and on compassion is central to the world's main religions. I think there is, indeed, a desire for people to attend to compassion and equality, and even to humility. This desire has become side-tracked as hierarchical values have continually reasserted themselves after the establishment of the world's major religions—ironically often using the those very religions to perpetuate, rather than counter, hierarchies of wealth and power.

One other currently existing tendency that gives hope that the ideas I espouse will succeed is meritocracy. In wealth terms, the notion that your status at birth is fixed has been replaced by a belief that it is fairer, and better, for society to give everyone an "equal" chance. Of course, there is a long discussion one could have on whether equality of "chances" is sufficient, but that is not my reason for bringing up meritocracy here. Instead, I want to point out that the notion that everyone should have an equal chance at wealth appeals cross-culturally and it has gained widespread currency even in places, such as caste India or feudal Europe, where it wasn't previously the norm.

So, too, then should there be increased popularity and receptivity for the idea that everyone should have an equal chance at love. And what better way to make these chances equal than by basing sexual attraction on a quality that all individuals can, as humans, achieve—the ability to love others? This is, indeed, a simple proposition: We should be attracted to, and love, those who are compassionate, since those with compassion are most likely to sincerely love us back. Love of the compassionate, thus establishes real, reciprocated love, and replaces the dynamic of attraction to the "bad" boy or "bad" girl who seems so sexually attractive to so many now precisely because they stimulate fear in us, the very real fear that they might not love us, and might instead do us harm.

2.   Reduce the attraction of the uncompassionate "bad boy" or "bad girl."

By establishing equity and explicitly valuing equality and compassion, Utopia will go a long way toward reducing the attractiveness of the "bad boy" or the "tough guy" who is violent and domineering. I owe to several of my students, nice guys all, the observation that the attraction of some women to the feigned tough masculine pose is responsible for its continuation. After watching the brilliant video *Tough Guise* (Katz and Earp 1999), which analyzes the masculine pose men adopt and its extremely negative consequences, one male student turned to a group of female students with a rebuke. He told them that if women would no longer fall for the "bad boy" and would go for the nice, compassionate man instead, then there would be less incentive for men to try to act tough, violent, and bad. His point was a simple one, yet profound. Nice guys shouldn't finish last. In fact in Utopia they will finish first.

What about the female equivalent to the bad boy, the "bad girl" to whom many heterosexual men are attracted: Will this attraction diminish with the change of values in Utopia? The bad girl is one who, like the bad boy, flouts overt societal values requiring her to be good. She might be sexually "loose" and uninhibited, an ultimate antithesis to the suffering virgin or the all-compassionate and sexually controlled (if not virginal) mother celebrated in popular and religious thought—the virgin versus the prostitute. Now while I want Utopia to encourage compassion, women should not have to give up their sexual passion in order to become compassionate. In fact I owe it to another of my students for identifying the extreme conflict women feel to be both sexually attractive and yet also mother-like. For this student the conflict between these two identities made her feel extreme angst.

It need not be this way. Many of the problems for women, as for men, will be solved by erasing the straightjackets of gender, in this case allowing someone like my student to feel no necessary contradiction between being sexy and being compassionate and mothering. Also, as the sexual inequalities that exist today between males and females diminish, in particular the double standard making a sexually loose woman an outlaw to conventional values, there will be no dichotomy remaining between sexual passion and compassion, since a good woman can be both. Compassion should become seen as sexually attractive for all people. And the person valuing displays of their superiority, or valuing any form of hierarchy, should become viewed as ugly and vile, rather than alluring. Snubbing others should be one of the most condemned of behaviors, because it lies at the core of the attempt to elevate oneself above others.

In fact sexuality based upon compassion should allow for a new honesty in sex, and a balance between martyrdom and narcissism. If compassion is the core of sexual ethics, and compassion is a positive value in Utopia, then sexual passion and desire need not be considered shameful, or selfish. There need be no duality between the "good" self that one presents to the world versus the "bad" and hidden self that motivates sexuality; sexual desire will not be aroused by being "bad," by the breaking of publicly acknowledged virtues during the secretive sex act.

Notice the pattern today, in contrast: In a hierarchical world where compassion is not valued, hierarchy, selfishness, and toughness are the prominent values, and this has been the case since the origin of the first hierarchical societies 6000 years ago. While early religions celebrated sexuality and fecundity, the major religions, at least in their original incarnations, arose in many ways as an antidote to selfish and hierarchical post-6000 BP values. They trained their ethics on both the hierarchies of power and on the concomitant selfish narcissism of the resulting sexualities.

However, as the major religions gained power, they dropped the challenge to societal hierarchy (this is certainly true of Christianity, for example in its American fundamentalist incarnation) and in fact used their critique of sexuality more rigidly, as a way to assert the power of the priest, whose role became one of sexual judge. Being "bad," being selfish, being a sexual rebel—these all became arousing, as is still the case today, especially in those societies that enforce sexual mores most intensely. The problem is that this rebellion, like so many rebellions throughout history, did not genuinely and holistically challenge the mores of every sector of society, a challenge that might have resulted (I'd like to believe) in a world more like the one I'm describing in this book. Instead, the rebellion *confirmed the very significance of the values it pretended to challenge, by simply violating whatever those values were, rather than creating new ones.* If religion advocated sex for reproduction, "bad" men and "bad" women set out to have sex for pleasure, reveling in their secretive violations and feeling an imagined, albeit fake, intimacy in doing something with each other that no one else would know about, or could know about, because of its "badness." But this kind of intimacy is founded on the very notion that there is something shameful about sexual pleasure in the first place, and hence its intimacy confirms, rather than challenges, the anti-pleasure manifestos of religion.

And when "badness" means men treating women like sexual objects (or gay men treating each other this way), this is hardly a true rebellion, since such behavior—being a "bad boy" through "scoring," as the American idiom describes it—is entirely *consistent* with the gender hierarchies of patriarchy. This is true even for gay men who, if they are trying to find multiple sexual partners in order to prove their masculinity (as is so often the case), are simply aping a very conventional patriarchal image of masculinity. Treating others without compassion is not a rebellion, nor a "badness" at all. It is, in fact, entirely consistent with the selfishness and anti-compassion of hierarchy (and, I would add, consistent as well with the objectifying and anti-humanist stance of modern consumerist capitalism, a point so very nicely described in Schur 1988).

I feel a need to say all this because I know that the word "compassion" today has, for many readers, a slightly insipid sound, and might seem to mean I am advocating muzak intimacy. But if one realizes that compassion is the *real* challenge to contemporary society, then there is nothing insipid or trivial about compassion in sex at all. Compassion is a challenge to hierarchy in economic and political power and a challenge to patriarchy and sexism. It is a challenge to the notion that we can only be aroused through secretive and shameful sex, and to the dishonesty and insincerity that results from such sex. And it is a challenge to the notion that there are only two opposed poles in sexuality: Selfish indulgence (usually gendered male) versus martyred abstinence (usually gendered female). Since compassion, unlike selfishness or shame/martyrdom, should include care of the other and of the self, compassionate sex introduces a balance into sexuality, and ends the false dichotomy of self/selfish versus other/self-denial. We care for ourselves by caring for all people—both ourselves and others in balance, and this care permeates both our economic and creative lives as well as our intimate life.

3.   Does egalitarian sex necessitate an end to monogamy?

This is, indeed, a difficult question. Many leftists have noted the connections between the jealousy and possessiveness of sex and sexual partners, and the existence of property and the hierarchies it creates. Engels (2010 [1884]) is the canonical reference for connecting property and monogamy. He argues that property plus patriarchy yields monogamy—specifically of women but not men—since men and the society they increasingly dominate require their wives to be monogamous in order to guarantee that property can be passed on to children whom a man knows to be his own. (Engels differs, however, from many contemporary writers, in that he sees socialist communal property as leading to egalitarian marriage and monogamy of both men and women, rather than polygamy for both.) But does all this spell a society of free love, love for everyone and love for all? First, let me say that the anarchy of such a situation is frightening and upsetting to so many of us partly because it is parallel to the free-for-all nature of obsessive, compensatory sex. I'm going to remain agnostic on the pansexual issue because I do feel what is, admittedly, an American middle-class bias but one I feel strongly nonetheless, namely that love can be shared, but that there's a limit—in time, in energy, etc.—to how much romantic love and sexualized love one can feel for multitudes of other humans. Perhaps some readers will weigh in on the issue on one side or the other—arguing that true egalitarianism necessitates pansexuality and a foregoing of any and all sexual possessiveness, or arguing that pansexuality creates such conditions of anonymity among people that the attraction and love cannot be anything other than compensatory—trying to "accumulate" as many lovers as possible. After all, if you really know nothing of your sexual partner, then how are they not then less human and more like a possession or a piece of property, than if you know them, and care for them over the longer term? These are questions I'll leave open.

4.   Provide judicial enforcement to promote fair treatment.

Finally, any individuals who believe that they are being treated unfairly in love and sex can take the matter to court. Courts will adjudicate such cases, and will be the final means to guarantee that all humans have the love they need. The nature and functioning of these courts will be described in further detail in Chapter 7.

The next chapter expands on the themes of this chapter by examining how reconfiguring love and sex, and marriage, can make the romantic and sexual dyad compatible with, rather than a challenge to, the community and its solidarity.

Bibliography

Collier, Jane Fishburne 1986. From Mary to modern woman: The material basis of Marianismo and its transformation in a Spanish village. *American Ethnologist*, 13: 100–107.
—— 1997. *From Duty to Desire: Remaking Families in a Spanish Village*. Princeton, NJ: Princeton University Press.

De Waal, Frans and Frans Lanting 1997. *Bonobo: The Forgotten Ape*. Berkeley: University of California Press.

Dollimore, Jonathan 1998. *Death, Desire and Loss in Western Culture*. New York: Routledge.

Engels, Friedrich 2010 [1884]. *The Origin of the Family, Private Property and the State*. London: Penguin Classics.

Goldenberg, Jamie L., Tom Pyszczynski, Shannon K. McCoy, Jeff Greenberg, and Sheldon Solomon 1999. Death, sex, love and neuroticism: Why is sex such a problem? *Journal of Personality and Social Psychology*, 77: 1173–1187.

Herdt, Gilbert 1982. Sambia nosebleeding rites and male proximity to women. *Ethos*, 10: 189–231.

Herdt, Gilbert, ed. 1996. *Third Sex, Third Gender: Beyond Sexual Dimorphism in Culture and History*. New York: Zone Books.

Katz, Jackson and Jeremy Earp (writers) 1999. *Tough Guise: Violence, Media & the Crisis in Masculinity*. [Documentary film.] Northampton, MA: Media Education Foundation.

Kearl, Michael C. n.d. Sex and death, connection of. In *Encyclopedia of Death and Dying*. Accessed December 29, 2012 at www.deathreference.com/Py-Se/Sex-and-Death-Connection- of.html.

Pitt-Rivers, Julian 1971. The color of race. Pp. 171–184 in *Conformity and Conflict: Readings in Cultural Anthropology*. James P. Spradley and David W. McCurdy, eds. Boston: Little, Brown and Company.

Pollack, William 1998. *Real Boys: Rescuing Our Sons from the Myths of Boyhood*. New York: Henry Holt and Company.

Power, Margaret 1991. *The Egalitarians—Human and Chimpanzee: An Anthropological View of Social Organization*. Cambridge: Cambridge University Press.

Rosaldo, Michelle Zimbalist 1974. Woman, culture, and society: A theoretical overview. Pp. 17–42 in *Woman, Culture, and Society*. Michelle Zimbalist Rosaldo and Louise Lamphere, eds. Stanford, CA: Stanford University Press.

Roscoe, Will 1996. How to become a berdache: Toward a unified analysis of gender diversity. Pp. 329–372 in *Third Sex, Third Gender: Beyond Sexual Dimorphism in Culture and History*. Gilbert Herdt, ed. New York: Zone Books.

Roughgarden, Joan 2004. *Evolution's Rainbow: Diversity, Gender, and Sexuality in Nature and People*. Berkeley: University of California Press.

—— 2009. *The Genial Gene: Deconstructing Darwinian Selfishness*. Berkeley: University of California Press.

Schoenhals, Martin 2003. *Intimate Exclusion: Race and Caste Turned Inside Out*. Lanham, MD: University Press of America.

Schur, Edwin M. 1988. *The Americanization of Sex*. Philadelphia: Temple University Press.

Shultziner, Doron, Thomas Stevens, Martin Stevens, Brian A. Stewart, Rebecca J. Hannagan, and Giulia Saltini-Semerari 2010. The causes and scope of political egalitarianism during the Last Glacial: A multi-disciplinary perspective. *Biology and Philosophy*, 25: 319–346.

3

INCLUSIVE COMMUNITIES AND NEW SOLIDARITIES

Not all animals live in groups. Many carnivores, such as the leopard, exist in the wild as isolated individuals (Estes 1991: 272–273). But humans and our primate relatives live in groups and we crave social interaction. Humans belong to a category of animals who are "obligatorily gregarious" (De Waal 2005: 231). In the apt words of primatologist De Waal, we are

> intensely social creatures who rely on one another and actually need inter-action with other people to lead sane and happy lives. Next to death, solitary confinement is our most extreme punishment. Our bodies and minds are not designed for lonely lives. We become hopelessly depressed in the absence of human company.
>
> *De Waal 2005: 6*

A sense of belongingness is among the most intensely positive emotional experiences for most humans. This is true in every culture I know of. In fact the emotion of belongingness is so intense that a common way to punish people in many cultures in different parts of the world is ostracism—expelling an individual, temporarily or permanently, from the family and even community to which s/he belongs. If a society is to be good, it must promote the formation of groups and the intense sense of belongingness so central to human satisfaction and happiness. This should be easy to do. After all, if we crave sociality, we ought to know how to find it. And yet, the feeling of not belonging is as intense worldwide, in both large-scale societies and small ones, as is the desire to belong. Belonging, though so desirable, turns out to be extremely hard to achieve.

If we are to increase belongingness, we must first analyze what interferes with it in contemporary societies. This will help us to answer this chapter's central question: How can interactive joy, or what others might call "solidarity," "community," or a sense of "family," be promoted? The first part addresses the tensions and conflicts that love, sex, and marriage create within and between groups and discusses how Utopia can overcome these tensions so that group feelings can be full and robust. The second part is on a topic familiar to most readers: In-group and out-group dynamics and their toxic effects, which are especially pronounced in the modern era. I show how hierarchies within and between groups lead to racism, ethnic prejudice, and the invidious and sometimes genocidal nation-state. I then give solutions to these toxicities. The third part focuses on the subjective feeling of belongingness. I ask what happens if feelings of belongingness are absent even in otherwise objectively inclusive groups. How can we really be made, by utopian social forms, to feel we belong, and to feel the joy of such belonging?

Social dynamics that preclude greater group unity: How romantic and affinal tensions challenge the solidarity of groups

Why do we so often feel we do not belong? Why are groups to which we belong seemingly weak in their operation, and in the feelings of solidarity for which we yearn? Let me be anthropological and begin with the diagnosis given by average peoples in diverse parts of the world, especially worlds distant from Western academics.

The unity of the group is of great concern in China, so it is interesting to hear the Chinese analysis. The Chinese regularly say that group unity suffers when the individual's interests are too prominent: Selfishness and individualism are seen as the bane of the group. Those who do not adequately sacrifice for the group are deemed "selfish," which is a much, much stronger criticism than the word used in English by Anglo-Americans. Although there is a barely covert admiration among many Chinese, especially educated youth and their teachers, for Western individualism, the Chinese regularly castigate the West, and America in particular, for a failure to adequately cater to the group and for rampant attention to individual needs, at the expense of group needs. (I must add here that there is a very strong group versus individual tension in China itself, one outsiders such as me can see clearly but which is not normally acknowledged by the Chinese themselves.)

But this is not the end of the story. If one presses the Chinese about what *really* causes conflict between the individual and the group, the nearly ubiquitous response is the tension between one's obligations to parents (aka the group) versus one's indulgence in the pleasures of love and sex (aka the individual—that is, the individual's pleasures) and allegiance to affines, i.e., one's spouse and in-laws and, among the young, potential love interests. This is an observation virtually absent from Western scholarly analysis of why East Asia values groups and what is really at the heart of group solidarity and its antagonists.

The Chinese are onto something key: The real threat to group solidarity is not the individual alone but rather conflicting forces of kinship—forces of love for children and parents versus forces of love for romantic partners. Anthropologists refer to these respective forces as those of loyalty to the "natal family" (family of birth, parents etc.) versus the loyalty to one's "affines" and "affinal family" (family formed through marriage). This is a tension found throughout the world and hence is second nature to anthropologists but it is no doubt less known to other readers, so let me expound on the issue by describing traditional China as an example, an especially clear example, of how groups, in this case family groups, were affected by marriage, love and sex. I will be describing the Chinese family group known as the "lineage." Lineages—especially their patrilineal variant—have been an extremely common family form throughout the world, and they continue to exist in many parts of the world today. Therefore, it is worth describing in detail the Chinese case to illustrate lineage dynamics and the tensions they produce. But even where lineages do not occur, natal/affinal tensions are nonetheless intense, even if less conspicuous. Therefore, the reader should keep in mind that the Chinese lineage example is meant to illustrate a *universal* human pattern: The tension between natal and affinal family and its implications for groups (family groups above all but also non-kin groups since groups of friends, or groups of students, for example, are challenged by the forces of love between any two individuals within these groups).

Traditionally, for many Chinese, "family" meant the lineage—or more precisely the patrilineage. When people say that the Chinese are family-oriented they are often referring to the patrilineage, a huge extended family group, sometimes numbering thousands of people, who all considered each other as family. Lineage members, being family, undertook familial functions, many of which will be familiar to Westerners but some of which are not. The lineage took care of its members who were poor, orphaned, and widowed. The lineage was responsible for the education of its member youth, and schools were often established for lineage male (but not female) youth. Lineages, such as the patrilineal Yi lineage, regulated who lineage youth could marry, just as parents today often intervene, albeit less obviously, in the romances of their children. Lineages also protected their members, and among large lineages in southeastern China violent inter-lineage feuds were common. Lineages also established temples to celebrate the ancestors of the lineage.

Given the central place of the lineage in carrying out so many important societal functions, from education to welfare to protection, it is not surprising how carefully the lineage protected its prerogatives. Given the central place of sons to parents, a direct outgrowth of the lineage principle emphasizing descent through males, it is also not surprising how carefully parents protected their prerogatives. In fact parental prerogative was backed up by the lineage. A son who failed to care for his parents in their old age, one of the most immoral failings of any man in China, was punished by the lineage, often at the lineage temple (Liu 1959: 55).

The primary way for the lineage, and parents, to protect their prerogatives was through the control of marriage. This is because love and sex by a young man for a woman was seen as threatening the man's loyalty to his lineage and his parents. Marriage, and a man's spouse, took a clear back seat to filial obligations. In fact the purpose of marriage was not to satisfy a man's needs, nor his wife's, but rather to give the family sons. Marriage legitimized any sons born of the union, giving the lineage a claim on them. This claim was crucial because male offspring were the ones who would continue the family line into the next generation. The bearing of sons was also critical because it was sons who were, traditionally, charged with the duty to care for ailing parents and worship them upon their death, along with more remote ancestors such as grandparents and great-grandparents, at ancestral temples. Filial obligations—obligations to parents and to one's natal family, to the *group*—were thus linked to that most basic of human desires: The desire for some kind of immortality, in this case the immortality of being remembered by, indeed worshipped by, one's descendants, after one's death.

Marriages were arranged by the parents of a young man and woman and "love marriages," marriage based on a young man and young woman's love for each other, were forbidden. This helped guarantee that parental prerogatives trumped individual desire, that is, the romantic and sexual desires of the young married couple.

The wife, an outsider from another family and often another village, was distrusted by the patrilineage, despite having been picked by a man's parents as a suitable spouse for him. There was often the fear that she might win her husband's heart and take him away from his own parents, emotionally or even physically (by moving him away from his family). A reflection of this fear is the social opprobrium directed at public spousal affection. It was forbidden and was considered to be almost immoral. The wife was also reviled due to her status as an outsider to the lineage. (She must be an outsider; if a man married a lineage female, this would be incestuous since all lineage members are considered family.) The abuse of young women by their mothers-in-law and by their husbands and husbands' lineage-mates served to unite the lineage group through scapegoating of the young woman/outsider. (Mothers-in-law were also outsiders but once they bore sons, they had a stake, albeit a stake never formalized, in their sons'/husbands' lineage.) Such abuse of daughters-in-law was legendary in China and in other patrilineal societies.

Anyone who has studied anthropology will recognize arranged marriage, as well as the prerogatives of the lineage, since both are so common in much of the premodern world. But the reason it is worth studying the natal/affinal conflicts of lineage societies is because they are an excellent representation of a nearly universal conflict that continues to this day even where lineages are absent. In China, for example, the Communist Revolution challenged traditional family forms, banning arranged marriage and breaking up lineages throughout the country. These were among the first actions taken by the new government after its ascension to power in 1949. Yet in the China I encountered in the 1980s, the group/individual tensions were still clearly present, often expressed as a tension between one's obligations to study versus the pull of romantic love and sex. Schools are a prime site for such tensions, since one studies to achieve status in order to bring respect, "face," to one's parents and family. Romantic feelings are believed to conflict with the concentration needed for studying (or I should say "known" to conflict, not just "believed," since I clearly see in my own American students the way that thoughts of love and sex, and relationships, dramatically affect academic performance). While Americans usually tolerate the study/dating conflict, the Chinese in the 1980s forbade dating in high school and often college as well.

The school and studying represented the natal family/parents—the group—and its prerogatives. Dating represented unseemly individual desire, desire at odds with the group. And consistent with traditional China's valuation of group over individual, the school actively interfered in students' potential romances to assert group rights over individual ones.

Specifically, students knew that they could be expelled from school, a huge embarrassment, if caught dating. One of my friends in China, dating a recent high-school graduate, was confronted by a senior administrator of the college he was attending. He was told that dating his girlfriend was ruining the harmony of her relationship with her parents. He was to end the relationship or be expelled. Needless to say, he did as he was told. Another student, at the same college, was caught by his dormmates having sex with his college girlfriend. The dormmates turned the couple in to the school by notifying administrators of their affair. Both students were expelled. I was told that the young woman returned to her village in disgrace, and she, her mother and father all committed suicide. What is revealing about this story is the intensity of the social obligation to one's parents and, even more tellingly, the willingness of anyone not party to the romantic dyad to constitute a group to challenge the romance seen as antithetical to the group. In this case it was the young man's dormmates who turned him in. I have seen this dynamic repeatedly: Groups of age-mates bonding with each other non-sexually, and viewing any sexual or romantic feelings among their members as antithetical to the solidarity of the group.

To return to the central question: What makes it so hard for humans to maintain unified groups, and a sense of belongingness? One reason, one of the main reasons, is that there is a conflict, probably primal and universal, between allegiance to one's family of birth versus the strong feelings of sex and love that one feels for those who are not members of one's family of birth. And families and society prevent one form of potential reconciliation of this conflict, an incest reconciliation, by thwarting the young child's desire to establish affinal/sexual feelings with natal family.

Psychology discusses the individual manifestations of the incest avoidance. Anthropology gives the evidence for its cross-cultural nature, by showing its existence, and the existence of the correlative natal/affinal conflict, that is present in diverse cultures. Despite the extreme difference between forager societies and those that formed in agricultural times, with their property and hierarchy, forager peoples do seem to experience some version of natal/affinal conflicts. Among the Kung foragers discussed in Chapter 1, there is a great deal of freedom of youth, who cannot be told to work or do anything else by their parents. However, when it comes to the love and sex realm, possessiveness takes over: Parents arrange all first marriages for their children (Lee 1993: 79–87).

Natal/affinal tensions in modern urbanized society are not as conspicuous as in lineage societies, but they exist nonetheless, and with perhaps even greater potency. As my good friend, Kant Nimbark, pointed out when one of his daughters left for college, in India—Kant's homeland—a child leaving for college causes less sadness because "family" is extended, so no child ever fully leaves the nest. But in America the child leaving is growing up, and moving on, which Kant knew to be the cause of his own very strong sadness at seeing his American daughters moving off to college. Such sentiments are expressed poignantly by many writers. Here is just a small sample I found easily and quickly in searching the Internet. Journalist Michael Gerson writes in his article "Saying goodbye to my child, the youngster" that "I was cautioned by a high-powered Washington foreign policy expert that he had been emotionally debilitated for weeks after dropping off his daughter at college for the first time." He says that dropping his eldest son off at college "is the worst thing that time has done to me so far … The adjustment is traumatic" (Gerson 2013). Editor Shelley Emling laments that "nothing prepared me for the moment on the morning of Thursday, August 29, when I had to give that final goodbye hug to my son in the driveway, already dreading the walks by a now quiet but not-quite empty bedroom." She comments that "I always knew this phase would be hard. But I guess I never knew it would be *this* hard. A few weeks ago, I was melancholy down to my bones" (Emling 2013).

Although marriage is not arranged in most modern societies, with South Asia and parts of the Middle East the most notable exceptions, parents and their children often clash over the children's choice of dates, with both sides feeling much angst at this quintessential manifestation of natal/affinal tensions. I know this from my own students' accounts, with many white students being told implicitly or explicitly not to date African-Americans. I know it all too well from gay friends from around the world, for whom the pull toward a member of the same gender causes great consternation for virtually all parents if and when they find out they have a gay child. Although many reasons might be given for parental objections, there is no doubt in my mind that a major part of the objections stems from the realization among parents that feelings of love and sex pull their children away from natal allegiances; perhaps this parental fear is just more pronounced in the case of the maturation of their gay children.

For many individuals, the transformation into adulthood is empowering but for others, parents and children, it is one causing sadness and loss. Such feelings, as well as post-marriage in-law conflicts, may have primal roots, but society has the capacity to overcome many of these tensions, the topic of the next section.

Overcoming natal/affinal tensions

Based on the above discussion it is clear that the natal/affinal tensions that exist in most societies must somehow be overcome, or at least mitigated, in order to foster a greater sense of belonging among all humans. With these tensions present, the group always feels vulnerable to the pull of the romantic outsider on members of the group, and the group always comes to sense that it can never satisfy the full range of positive human emotions, since it lacks the ability to make us feel romantic love. At the extreme, members of the group experience jealousy and concomitant fears of abandonment—fear that other group members will, one after another, desert the group for love.

The romantic dyad suffers too from group/love tensions, since it doesn't have the warm and fuzzy feelings of the group and group belongingness, nor does it have the sustainability and permanence of natal families, which, by definition, are with us from birth. In the extreme, the romantic dyad finds itself in great conflict with natal family members, setting up that vexing in-law tension that is the cause of so much unhappiness and a frequent cause of the dissolution and divorce of married couples.

Is there any hope of overcoming these tensions? It is interesting that one way many groups, especially groups of youth, have tried to bridge the group/individual gap is by involving the peer group in sex and romance. Peer pressure is exerted by one's age-mates to be sexually active, and groups seek to experience that activity vicariously as audiences for tales of peer sexual exploits. This is a familiar way in which friends and age-mates try to reconcile the group/individual gap opened up by sex and love. This is, however, only a partial solution at best, since it widens the divide between parents and their children and is the cause of a generation gap, something again not limited to the West. (Some young Chinese believe their conflicts with parents exceed the conflicts of American youth; I cannot judge whether that is true, but I know the Chinese generation gap can be an intense one.) Moreover, peer pressure establishes hierarchical and gendered sexual norms, as described in Chapter 2, and these norms are totally antithetical to Utopia. I will consider below, however, ways that the group might be involved in promoting individual group members' love and sex, in such a way that the group/romantic dyad tensions are lessened, and so that the sexualized hierarchies that peer groups promulgate—teen boys who compete for status among each other by trying to "score" more than each other, for example—do not occur.

There is perhaps greater hope for the possibility of overcoming the natal/affinal conflict, however, if we think of the tremendous happiness that the entire group, or groups, experience during a wedding, a happiness expressed in some cultures by days of celebration. Despite the tensions marriage introduces into societies, it also brings two strangers together, making them kin, and in addition brings two *groups* of people who are non-kin—bride's and groom's respective families—into kin relationships. The natal/affinal tension may be primal, but so is the idea of turning strangers, individuals and groups of individuals, into family. This, too, is no doubt a primal reaction. Recall that the ultimate mammalian triumph over that of our own reptilian ancestors is that, unlike the latter, we do not view our own offspring with fear and seek to kill them. Instead, the stranger introduced into the world by birth is nurtured by family and others, and birth itself, the introduction of a stranger, is a cause for great happiness and celebration. Marriage is yet another form that brings a stranger into our midst, and turns them into family.

I would ask the reader to reflect on the whole panoply of ways in which societies valorize the stranger and, especially, the introduction of the stranger into our own group, and our own family. Not only is there marriage, but most societies have formal and informal ways to make strangers into kin. In many cultures good friends become kin. They may also become metaphoric parents, such as godparents. Religions often celebrate the universal brotherhood and sisterhood of mankind, and the transcendent emotions of these feelings, feelings so eminently expressed in Beethoven's Ninth Symphony, are an eloquent testimony to the power of the quest to make strangers into family.

To further this process, I think it is critical to challenge, as much as possible, the distinctions we make between strangers and family. I begin with several suggestions for explicitly addressing the natal/affinal conflicts, first by recreating arranged marriage in a non-coercive manner, so that friends and family can help each other find ideal romantic partners. I also redefine the nature of marriage. By taking the sexual component out of marriage—or at least sex as the defining feature—I aim to overcome the primal tensions caused by the way sex and love pull us away from natal family. Marriage can thus become the ultimate instrument for bringing strangers into our families, for building upon family and groups, rather than pitting groups and lovers, or the group and the individual, against each other. Here are my suggestions:

1. *The group as assistant in love and marriage*: Arranged marriage is, as noted above, an attempt to reconcile the natal/affinal conflict where the parents of a young person pick a spouse for them. A major rationale for parents exercising this function is to guarantee that the spouse will be suitable to the parents.

The problem with arranged marriage, however, is that parental prerogatives trump the young person's prerogatives, rather than harmonizing with them. No wonder, then, that arranged marriage was one of the first targets of the Chinese communist revolutionaries. The idea of denying one's own romantic and sexual needs in deference to parents had built up a stock of resentment and unhappiness among a whole generation of revolutionaries.

Underpinning arranged marriage is a desire for families to secure a spouse and in-laws who are equal or superior to one's own family in status. Thus, if hierarchy is abolished, one of the main motivators of parental self-interest will dissipate. This should help parents be arrangers in a manner that is helpful to their children, a manner that addresses the latter's needs and desires.

What I imagine is that there will be a marriage-helper group for any young person so desiring the help. This group will be composed of one's parents, friends, other family, and anyone else with a strong interest in assisting the young person to find a suitable mate. The group will use its knowledge of the person to find potential mates. It will use its large size, and its networks, to find a larger number of such potential mates than any individual could find on his/her own. The group will function in a helpful, non-binding manner. Should it ever violate this require-ment that it be non-coercive, any person with knowledge of the violation, whether a group member, the young person being matched, or someone else, may refer the matter to courts for adjudication. Further, should it ever make mate choices based upon ethnicity, race, gender, or other invidious and divisive features of personhood, the matter may also be referred to the courts. (See Chapter 7 for a description of Utopia's judicial system.)

The group could also have an ongoing function as marriage counselor. You and your new soulmate can continue to belong to the marriage-helper group. If you and your soulmate experience problems, the group, who know you well, can intervene to repair conflicts and prevent a divorce, or help you find a more suitable soulmate if that seems necessary. In cases of unrequited love, seemingly so common worldwide, the group could operate non-coercively to get to know the unrequiting partner. If they feel the reasons for unrequiting are not rational, as is so often the case, then they can gently intervene to bring the couple closer together. It is, after all, a universal human tendency to feign disinterest precisely when we feel most potentially interested in someone, and the presence of outsiders to this dynamic can help ameliorate it. (This very human tendency is, no doubt, a non-human one too. At least I know that cats, like humans, love to play hard-to-get. They won't jump on your lap as long as you are coaxing them. It is only when you feign disinterest yourself that they quietly, in that funny cat-like way, make themselves available to you, and to your lap!)

I have left unsaid whether the group will help other group members besides you, or be devoted solely to you. I can't decide which approach is better, and I can see merits in both approaches. So I will encourage both types of groups to form—those that function as matchmakers for all group members in turn, and those that are devoted just to matchmaking for one member. Different individuals may find they prefer different approaches. Being the sole center of group attention may be too much for some people, and they may want to be part of a group that matches all group members. Others may find appealing the purity of a group that works just for them, and their interests, without any other conflicting obligations.

2. *New forms of marriage*: Marriage must not only be open to all people, including members of the LGBT community, but also it should be reduced to its real essence: *A bonding mechanism for making non-kin into kin.* As such, marriage should not be preserved for those with whom one wants to have sex. Sex and marriage will become orthogonal: You can have sex with a marriage partner, or your marriage partner might be someone with whom you choose not to have sex. This does not mean that individuals cannot chose to maintain monogamous sexual relationships. It simply means that marriage will no longer be the vehicle through which this will happen.

Instead, the *incorporative essence* of marriage will come to the fore, so that one can marry anyone and everyone with whom a *mutual* (i.e., mutually consenting) kin relationship is desired. If you have the time and energy to take care of someone, and if you have the desire to do so, and if the other person reciprocates those feelings, then you can and should marry them. This means that you can marry more than one person but that you can also marry no one. One thing you cannot do is marry children, since they cannot give full consent. Likewise, you cannot marry people who are already your own family members, since the whole point of marriage is to formalize and institutionalize caring connections with those *outside* your own family. In fact the reason I have made marriage the key to institutionalizing relationships with non-kin, rather than something like blood brotherhood or other fictive kin arrangements, is because marriage as it exists today has the reaching out to non-kin, and the building of egalitarian and affirming alliances with those outside your own circle—whatever that circle is—as a core feature. (Of course, marriage today is egalitarian within a hierarchical system. That is, person A may marry status-equal B but A and B may refuse to marry status inferior C. This refusal makes non-Utopian marriage into an odious mechanism that concretizes today's social hierarchies. By ending hierarchy in wealth and power, the role of marriage in reifying status differences will be eliminated and its incorporative and egalitarian-affirmative potentiality can come to the fore.) Other fictive kin relationships don't have this incorporative project as their essence.

One other virtue of my proposal: By taking sex out of the definition of marriage, and making marriage and sex orthogonal to each other, there will no longer be a fundamental distinction between spouse(s) and one's natal family, such as one's parents. In all societies today one's family has to be seen as implicitly inadequate, because one takes another, new family, through marriage, in order to satisfy sexual desires, desires that cannot be satisfied at home with natal family members. For some people, this is felt to be a normal process, but for many others, both adult children and parents, the break that sexualized marriage brings is wrenching. I have seen this clearly in America, where parents know that as their children leave home for college, they are also cutting their natal ties. I've seen this same wrenching trauma in many other parts of the world. Why not, then, mitigate the break by saying that one marries people to add on to family, not because one's family can't provide something essential (sex) that one desires? By desexualizing marriage, much of the tension between sexualized affines and non-sexual natal family will be reduced, and much of the trauma from creating this distinction will, likewise, be diminished. Marriage can then be about joining two individuals and their families (and respective friends), without the inherent individual and group trauma and conflict present in today's non-Utopian marriage.

I want to stress that this is not an anti-sex manifesto. People can still have sex and they might very well have sex, perhaps exclusively, with their spouse. The key is that the idea of marriage as an institution to add family will not be bound up with the notion of sex and sexual exclusivity.

3. *Blurring of the family/non-family line through care for non-kin*: When thinking further about what really makes for powerful groups and group experiences, I have begun to realize that it is not only family groups that do so, but even more so groups that mix family and non/family in powerful ways. As noted above, the real power of marriage is that it is the taking of a non-family member who is turned into family. Birth, likewise, expands the family. Notions of universal brotherhood and sisterhood—the universality of humankind—enchant us because these feelings extend a sense of family over the widest circle of humans possible.

Less exalted, perhaps, but no less powerful, is the common occurrence of cross-cousin marriage in many small-scale societies. In the West, we define all cousins equally as being kin, but in many small-scale societies the father's sisters' children or mother's brothers' children are non-kin enough that one can marry them, but informally kin enough that they are attractive mates in societies where the strengthening of kinship ties through marriage matters. The widespread nature of such marriage, "cross-cousin" marriage, is to me a clue that it is not only sociologically attractive, but also psychologically appealing. This appeal extends to others who are kin/non-kin. While many cultures require stiff and formal relationships with one's parents and other kin—relatives on one's father's side in the case of patrilineal societies—there is a joyful and playful relationship (actually called a "joking relationship" by anthropologists) with such kin/non-kin as your mother's brother. Something about those who are formally non-kin, yet informally kin, elicits a great deal of joy.

In fact when thinking of the bases for group joy, I kept returning in my own mind to one of the most joyful experiences of my childhood—playing with my cousins. While I also had great fun playing with some neighborhood kids, cousins have an added intimacy built into their nature. They are peers, friends, playmates, *and* family intimates.

Where I'm going with this is simple: There is great joy in building relationships that somehow transcend, bridge, or blur the family/non-family line. We must think through the source of this joy, and then use this knowledge in Utopia to foster more such groups.

It seems to me that there are at least two key reasons kin/non-kin groups are joyful. First, they take the power of kin, and add the power of openness—opening out the intimate feelings we have for close kin to those further afield. The joy, thus, is the joy not just of belonging to a meaningful group, but of belongingness that is dynamic, alive, and *growing*. To the security of family is added the excitement and novelty of having new family—the basis for the power of romantic love.

Second, kin/non-kin relationships combine volitionality and obligation in powerful ways. Family ties can obligate, and obligation can be a potential—though not inevitable—source of resentment, of unfreedom. But by adding the non-kin element, we add a touch of volitionality that lightens the sense of obligation. Cousins, fictive kin, friends whom we consider family, surrogate family—these all combine obligation and volitionality. There is the obligation that we like about family—that the relationship is one of "blood" and therefore is dependable. But there is volitionality in that we have *chosen* to activate family ties, or to create them, with *these* individuals in particular, individuals who are distant kin or those, like friends, who are not even actual kin.

So how can we combine kin and non-kin in a *joyful and non-exclusionary way*? There are several ways to do this:

a. First, my proposal above to widen marriage is key. By widening marriage as described, Utopia can realize the full incorporative potential of marriage, doing so by breaking down the customary divisiveness that marriage conventionally stirs up: In-law tensions, for example, and the conflict between natal and affinal allegiances.

Utopia's incorporative marriage—the ability to marry friends and others—will be a key means to form healthy, nondivisive, and joyful kin/non-kin groups.

b.   But I want to add a new proposal here. In Utopia, just as there is a small minimal work requirement for all people (see Chapter 4 for more on this), there will also be a small, minimal "family" requirement, which must be carried out toward *non-kin*. All able-bodied members of Utopia will be required to give minimal family service. This will consist of either caring for a sick person and/or giving companionship to someone who is lonely. Of course, this proposal will be especially helpful in addressing the needs of the growing population of elderly, but it will not be limited to care for the elderly.

The recipient of your family service will not be someone you choose. Instead, community organizers will identify those in need of care due to incapacities such as illness. They will also identify those in greatest need of companionship. Individuals will be allowed, *and encouraged*, to self-nominate themselves as needy: "I am lonely and want some company."

Caregivers will then give their care to several needy individuals, chosen based upon need and not based upon a kin relationship with the caregiver (thus expanding kin actions onto non-kin). If a caregiver develops a friendship with someone, they can continue the care and companionship for more time than is required of them (this is the volitional element), but those who receive care but develop no friendships with caregivers will not be shortchanged their basic care. In fact it is precisely those needy individuals receiving the least volitional extra care who will move to the head of the line for receiving care in the next round of caregiving.

The idea behind this is simple yet critical: Just as there must be general equality of wealth, so that all people have their basic human food and housing needs met, so *all* humans must have their basic needs for attention, affirmation, and care met. And, in meeting those needs, equalizing processes must be at work just as forcefully as with the distribution of food and housing. No one should go hungry—either physically or emotionally.

c.   Surrogate families: Any time I have heard members of 12-step groups talk about what the groups do for them, I've been sincerely impressed by how much genuine mutual concern exists in these groups of people who were once strangers to each other. A student 12-stepper told me the solidarity is so appealing that there are non-alcoholic people who have joined her group, pretending to be there for drinking problems.

I propose bringing together groups of people who agree to care for each other as family. Like family, the members of the group would care for any of its members who are sick, or unhappy. And like family, the group would have a sense of shared fate, so that if someone in the group has a particularly good thing happen, the whole group will celebrate this happiness.

For those of us who are Americans, especially males, the idea of mutual care among strangers, or even among friends, feels awkward. But friendship in many other parts of the world has mutual concern, even love, as a central feature. Among Chinese friends, especially males, there should be willingness to help each other in any way, even to the extent that friends should, at least ideally, be willing to die for each other. This is the traditional value about friendship in China, and I heard my friends articulate it (even though I never saw friends dying for each other).

Of course, the astute reader will note that loving and concerned friendship is most common in gender-segregated societies. Lindholm describes friendship among the Pukhtun of northern Pakistan and cites a poet who writes: "Separation from the friend for one moment is like Judgment Day. Should their love take them to Hell, for the friends Hell is paradise" (Lindholm 1982: 240). Smith-Rosenberg describes 19th-century female friendships in America. She takes as a case study two such "not atypical" friendships that were "intense, loving, and openly avowed." She continues:

> For nearly half a century these women played a central emotional role in each other's lives, writing time and again of their love and of the pain of separation. Paradoxically to twentieth-century minds, their love appears to have been both sensual and platonic.
>
> *Smith-Rosenberg 1975: 3–4*

So, can such loving friendship occur in less segregated contexts? I believe the answer is yes. Clearly, humans are capable of love and concern that transcends traditional boundaries of love (by "traditional" I refer to what American middle-class readings think of as the typical loci for love: Love for partners, children, parents, siblings). Where the nuclear family has supplanted family groupings emphasizing the primacy of same-sex bonds—bonds such as those found in patrilineal China or Afghanistan—same-sex friendship has lost its emotionality. And, quite ironically, as overt sexual attraction between same-sex individuals has gained some acceptance— as in the US or Europe—fear of being labeled gay has terrorized many heterosexual males, making them afraid to show too much care and concern for same-sex friends. This is why Utopia's attack on homophobia and its ultimate challenge to gender itself seems to me to be critical: Without gender, people can treat each other as humans caring for other humans, regardless of the other's anatomy.

4. *Parenting*: One of the central ways humans cooperate in many societies is for adults to help each other with child-rearing responsibilities. Hrdy points out that human cooperative parenting is one characteristic, and a key one, setting us apart from all of the other apes (and she argues that it is the precondition for the development of our big brains and our prosociality) (Hrdy 2009: See especially 275–286). Thus humans are biologically primed to share the joy and burdens of parenting. I, therefore, suggest the following:

a. Utopia should organize volunteers to help care for the children of others. The volunteers would be trained by more experienced parental caretakers and would be those who find genuine joy in caring for children.

I know that sharing of caretaking responsibilities happens within families or among neighbors but I want mutual childcare to be a responsibility of the entire community, and one shared equally by males and females. I also want groups based on potentially invidious categories, such as proximity (neighbors) or close kinship relationships, to be *overridden*, with caretaking a responsibility of non-kin and non-neighbors as well as kin and neighbors. Since humans are genetically related to one another, we are in fact all family to each other, and we should thus act with responsibility to any and all children. While the extended family and the inclusion of grandparents as parental caretakers is a nice notion, an even nicer one is the entire community, kin and non-kin, as parentally involved.

I know my suggestions here strike at primal issues, and will make many people feel uncomfortable. I should say that I am not advocating communal childcare. But childcare must be a responsibility of as large a group as possible, and it must be one not seen as limited to those who are kin, or those who are paid (or, often, underpaid). This leads me to my next suggestion:

b. Utopia should make parenting fun. I am not a parent, so I cannot know its full frustrations, but I can say I am shocked, based upon my observations of American parents in public settings, at how joyless many parents seem in interacting with their young children.

This can't be good for anyone. It should come as no surprise, then, that I believe access to birth control and abortion should be widespread and free for all, so that parents bear children because they genuinely want them, not as a covert punishment for having sex.

And one more suggestion: I want to consider the possibility that parents who feel overly stressed by their children can temporarily give them to others to take care of. Parents should be able to take a parenting break without enduring a huge societal stigma. These breaks should be mutually agreed upon between a child's parents and the children involved.

The temporary caretakers could be people who want the temporary responsibility of caretaking, without its permanence. Thus, they need not be experienced parents but could be a childless individual or even a group of individuals. I would also like to see teachers take on the role of temporary parents to any of their students, if they so desire this role. Parenting is a teaching role, and so having teachers take on this role (as they often do in China) helps bring the parenting and teaching functions more closely into alignment.

What if the child wants to stay longer with the temporary parent? While I would not allow a permanent transfer of parenting, I do believe that children should have a greater say in who parents them, and I would allow them strong input into deciding when to end a temporary parenting arrangement.

c. Utopia should teach parenting, teach compassion: I hope that parenting, like anything else in life, will be something people will be curious to learn about, and curious to discuss with others. Utopia will convene parenting discussion groups, for parents to discuss their approaches with each other. Parenting classes, with older and experienced parents as teachers, should also be established.

One key question, of course, is how to teach compassion, both compassionate parents and compassionate parenting. It might seem a dodge on my part by some readers, but I do not have elaborate plans for how to do this. Since humans have the capacity to be compassionate if their surroundings are so, compassion in all spheres of life should lead to more compassionate parenting. I also believe that relieving parents of the worry and stress of having to provide financially for their children will allow them the real opportunity to enjoy parenting.

One method, though, might be the compassion-highlighting media, as described in Chapter 2. Just as there will be media portals to portray compassionate individuals, there will be special media portals to portray especially compassionate parenting, and more generally, compassionate caretaking of any kind.

Social dynamics precluding greater group unity: How hierarchy within and between groups creates the toxic effects of racism, genocide, and nationalism

Groups and hierarchy: How are they related? Does eliminating hierarchy foster community, or does it hinder it? The reader can guess my response: Hierarchy has a pernicious effect on community. Eliminating hierarchy and fostering genuine community and belongingness go hand in hand.

In considering this dynamic further, it is useful to divide the analysis between within-group hierarchy and between-group hierarchy.

Within-group hierarchy: This is the easiest relationship to describe. Many hierarchies such as caste and race are structured *precisely* by forbidding closeness and community between those of different statuses (Schoenhals 2003). The Jim Crow laws in the US forbade any mixing of blacks and whites, especially in intimate contexts—bathrooms, drinking fountains, schools, marriage. (Bathrooms and drinking fountains may not seem to belong with schools and marriage but caste and race systems use everyday intimacies as well as less mundane ones to foment separation.) Similar intimate separations are true of caste in India, and were true of apartheid in South Africa.

Even in hierarchies based on money and power—rather than on pollution and taboo—poor and rich, the downtrodden and the powerful, may interact, but infrequently with any sense of intimacy and belongingness (with, perhaps, the exception of patron–client relationships, where the patron and client model their interaction, metaphorically, on that of father and child). Latin Americans, for example, have told me of how rigid class differences in their cultures prohibit a coming together of people, except in contexts where everyone is of the same basic status. Anthropologists have written frequently of the opposition of hierarchy and community. Victor Turner wrote an entire fascinating book that catalogued the huge variety of contexts in which hierarchy and community, or what he called structure and *communitas*, exist as two poles of human interaction (Turner 1977). These contexts include rituals, religion, politics, and much more.

Between-group hierarchy: Although the distinction between within-group and between-group is by no means always clear-cut, I do want to separate out for special consideration cases in which one group bonds *precisely* by putting down, by denigrating, a group it considers *external* to it, and inferior. This process is all too familiar. In fact the 20th century probably saw the climax of such dynamics. The nation-state is one of the prime examples of this phenomenon (Schoenhals 2003), since it seeks to exclude from its borders those whom it deems outsiders, those who are different culturally, racially, and/or ethnically. Outsiders are not seen with neutrality but rather are viewed in the same way upper castes view Untouchables: Outsiders are beneath those who belong in the nation. If they were to enter the nation, their presence, like that of Untouchables, would pollute the nation's purity. The nation bounds a community more clearly than the frequently porous empire did and it thus creates the us–versus–them dynamics that give us racial/ethnic hatreds (see Schoenhals 2003 for my analysis of racial prejudice as an extreme, caste-like form of prejudice partly induced by nationalism) and, in the extreme, the horrors of genocide.

The nation, in dividing people so clearly, also creates extremes of love and hate, loyalty and hatred. Members of the national community are expected to sacrifice everything for the nation only, including (especially) their very own lives in that ultimate national sacrifice known as war. Many social scientists, me included, see the 20th-century devastation of warfare, which exceeded in death and destruction everything in previous centuries, as a direct result of the rise of nationalism (e.g., in Germany) in the decades leading up to the two world wars.

So where does this leave my thesis on community? It would seem that between-group hierarchy hinders belongingness between nations but fosters it within a given nation. Doesn't this, then, implicate community as something to be abhorred, since it was the cause of so much misery in the last century? Can humans ever really bond without a scapegoat or enemy? Can we be as united in peace as we are in war?

These are vexing questions and they troubled me for a long time as I thought about community. But then I thought deeper about the causes of genocide and nationalist war, forms of community that I will call anxious community or, better, terrorized community. As Mann so clearly points out, and as a cursory review of history confirms, terrorized community (my phrase) is a new phenomenon, a product of modernity. Mann implicates that otherwise sanctified concept of democracy. The darker side of democracy—especially failed democracy—is the 20th-century horrors of mass genocide (Mann 2005: See especially Chapter 1). I concur with Mann. As the multi-ethnic colonial empires ended, replaced by the notion of rule by ethnic insiders who are in the majority, majoritarian triumphalism arose, culminating in ethnic genocides in the many new nations and malignant nationalisms of the post-imperial 20th-century era.

Let me be clear: Democracy and the end of colonialism are good things, but they have a very dark side. The question is why? And what does this do to our hopes for benign community? For me, one key is to note that ethnic killing often (although not always) occurs in seemingly cosmopolitan settings. In India, for example, 96% of the ethnic violence outside of Kashmir occurs in urban areas, even though two-thirds of Indians live in the countryside (Mann 2005: 475). The anomie and other challenges of urban life are, indeed, anxiety-producing and they impel people to form malignant communities, based on newly aroused notions of ethnic difference.

Where I'm going with this is actually straightforward: The breakdown of community in the modern world leads to a frenzied, anxiety-driven quest to create new community. But just as anxiety-fueled hierarchy does not lead to a feeling of peace and security but rather to ever more desperate and obsessive assertions of hierarchical privilege, so too for community. Anxious community, terrorized community, is anxiety-driven, even infused with the trauma of a loss of genuine belongingness. It leads to the obsessive response to anxiety that is manifested as racism, ethnic hatred, nationalistic warfare, and, in the extreme, ethnic genocide.

This leads me to one of my overriding prescriptions for fostering community: If we are to end racism, if we are to end genocide, if we are end the dark side of nationalism, *the nation-state must be abolished*. It must be abolished because it is both cause and consequence of anxious community. As a substitute for joyful community, it impedes and precludes such real community. The nation-state teaches us to exclude others from the group, fostering what I will call invidious groupism. The nation-state system makes a rhetorical pretense of the equality of nations, but in fact national borders and national armies protect privilege—the privilege of wealthy nations and the privileges of the elites within each nation. Nations, and the concept of settling disputes between them based on which nation has the greatest power to carry out violence (war), must be replaced by a nation-less world, a world where disputes are settled as they are (at least in principle) within nations—based on notions of fairness and justice. Warfare led to the first hierarchy 6000 years ago, so it is fitting that Utopia should end war, and the exclusionist system of group privilege that is the nation-state.

Is the end of the nation-state and of war feasible? I will have more to say about this in Chapter 7, but the answer is a clear affirmative, especially with the end of property and hierarchy. To see why this is so, let me begin by asking the reader to indulge in a thought experiment: Imagine that there was no more ownership of land and no more property. Imagine again that you were protected not by your nation but by a council of nations, like the United Nations. Imagine that your food, housing, clothing, medical care, entertainment, and everything else was provided for you, so that there was no one, nor any group, nor any nation, which might have more than you and your group/nation.

Now try to imagine war occurring. It's hard to imagine: What would be the warring group, after all, if there were no nations defined as in competition with each other? What would be the purpose, if all of your needs were guaranteed? Without nations that own land, and erect boundaries, it's even hard to imagine anyone feeling the kind of intense nationalism that exists today.

Likewise, try to imagine whether invidious groups of any kind—nation-state, race, ethnic group—would persist. After all, so often people foment ethnic hatred over things like employment. "Those immigrants from outside are taking my job." "People from that group don't deserve jobs as much as people from my group. We're hard-working and intelligent. *They* are not." Can you, without the existence of a jobs motive, continue to imagine ethnic prejudice? Perhaps so. You might see it based, as it often is, not just on zero-sum conflicts over employment, but also over issues of sex and love: "I am not attracted to those people." Or: "I don't want those people marrying my daughter: I don't want *them* to become my family." (See Schoenhals 2003 on race and caste as forms of exclusion operating as much, or more, in the sphere of marriage, family, and intimacy than in the public economic and political sphere.)

Now imagine that sex and love was democratized in the ways that I've described in the previous chapter. Recall that compassion will be the new basis of attraction rather than "looks," which is more odious than it seems since attention to "looks" in a multi-ethnic society serves to reify racial difference through sexual attraction. Thus, with new bases for love and sex, and without land and jobs as a motive for creating prejudice, can you still imagine prejudicial feelings? It's hard to imagine this, isn't it?

Animals bond with each other over shared territory, and they fight over food and sex. When these are issues for humans too, we do the same, to a much more hor-rific degree. We will try to eliminate the other in ethnic cleansing, wage warfare—obsessively to kill off all of our enemies, and spend much of our cognitive capacity trying to rationalize hatred of ethnicities and races different from us.

But there's a *big* if/when here: When zero-sum sex and subsistence are issues for humans, we develop invidious groups. But if there is no property, if every-thing of value is shared, and our subsistence and sex needs are taken care of in an equitable way, then it's a different story. Under those conditions we will come together to engage in our supreme human capacity, our signature virtue as humans: Cooperation and solidarity.

Invidious groupism

Not only must the nation-state be abolished, more generally, too, groupism based on the denigration of other individuals and groups—what I will call invidious groupism—must be challenged. In the language of social science, feelings of group solidarity should not be based on a distinction between "in-group" and "out-group."

When I described my plans for a society that would bring people together in solidarity and community, a good friend challenged me. This is my own rendering of my friend's very thoughtful challenge to me:

> People only unite in opposition to an out-group. It is the out-group, deemed an enemy or an inferior caste, that unifies people in the in-group. Without it, people never will come together. So you'll never have the kind of joyful

groups and solidarity you want—unless, of course, you promote inter-group conflict and hatred.

My friend's challenge to me is a good one, unfortunately. I've so often told my students to be wary of politicians who raise the alarm about an enemy, and the need to wage war against enemy peoples. Politicians unify their own nations, and shift dissent away from themselves, by inventing or exaggerating external threats, or internally hidden ones. Thus, I tell my students, be skeptical of fear-mongering politicians, who are trying to create fake solidarity by fomenting inter-group dissensus.

I continue to warn them about fear-mongering to this day, since the in-group/out-group dynamic, first described by Sumner (1906: 12–15), is a potent one and seemingly omnipresent. So I must ask: Is the out-group, and hatred or fear of them, the only way groups can be unified? If so, is there any real hope to achieve my ideals for solidarity in the utopian society?

I thought about this question for many weeks. Finally, one night I asked myself a question I will ask you, the reader: When have you felt most joyfully connected to other humans, aside from dyadic connections with parents, children, or romantic partners? When have you felt the joy of being in a group, sustained by it, and affirmed by it? Think about these occasions and answer the following key question: *Did your feelings of solidarity depend upon the presence of a hated and/or feared or despised out-group?*

My answer to my own question pleasantly surprised me. In all but one case my best group experiences have *not* depended on the existence of an out-group.

Examples of inclusive groups

Now let's look at some examples from social science research of real group solidarity achieved without out-groups, examples that I will call inclusive groups:

- Festival time: Festivals in many societies are times of great solidarity and it is a solidarity that is not necessarily exclusionary. I'm thinking here of such inclusive rites as harvest festivals or festivals to celebrate the new year.
- Shared parenting: The sharing of parenting responsibilities, not only among kin, but among neighbors and, in some cases, all adults in the community is another example of group cooperation and apparent group solidarity that happens without the existence of an out-group. Among forager Kung, for example, children usually do not accompany their mothers or fathers on gathering expeditions. The mothers will go off to forage without their children in tow, secure in the knowledge that Kung adults who stay back in the camp with the children will take responsibility to watch over any children in the community, not just their own children (Draper 1976). In other African societies, nonforager ones, communal care of children is also common, as illustrated by the well-known African saying, "It takes a village to raise a child."

- Age-based groupings: Age-based groups are often not based on explicit exclusion since in age-grade societies everyone passes from one age-grade to the next; if you live long enough, you will be a member of all age-grades in the society. (This is in contrast to, say, racial or ethnic groups, which are defined based upon birth and descent, so that one cannot easily transition, or often never transition, from one group to the other—hence making ethnic and racial groups exemplars of exclusion).

  An example of non-exclusionary age-based solidarity is Chinese student groups. In China students are divided into classes of about 50–75 students, or more, called *ban*. *Ban* stay together for all classes they take at school. *Ban* students are not only together for all classes in one semester, but also all classes over the three years of junior high school (roughly ages 12–15). In senior high school new *ban* are formed, which stay together again for all classes, for all three years of school, until graduation, at age 17–18.

  Having conducted two years of research in Chinese schools, I can attest to the genuine solidarity of these groups. Decades after graduation Chinese will often turn to high-school classmates, i.e., *ban*-mates, when they need help. There are implicit yet powerful expectations of permanent reciprocity between any *ban*-mates, such that X will ask for a favor from Y and Y will later ask for a favor from X, or from Z, another *ban*-mate. Students were not wrong when they excitedly and breathlessly told me, "All of us in our *ban* will help each other."

- Hunter-gatherer groups: Hunter-gatherers move from group to group, sometimes due to conflicts within their own group and sometimes just for a sense of variety. A single person will have relatives in a variety of neighboring groups. As a result of such networks, and the movement of individuals between groups, group boundaries are not fixed. I find this to be really important, since it is the fixity of group boundaries that lays the foundation for in-group/out-group dynamics. The fact that humans evolved biologically living in porous non-invidious groups (see Ingold 2004: 403) suggests our potential to refashion these dynamics in the modern world.

- There are many more examples I could list here. One that deserves mentioning is 12-step groups, those groups that meet to support members in their journey to end an addiction to alcohol, drugs, or to addictive behavior of other kinds. I know there is great solidarity in these groups, and great helpfulness among group members, since I've heard this described by students and acquaintances in 12-step programs. Several times I've come upon such groups in meeting places where I was going for other meetings, and I admit to being slightly envious of the tremendous warmth and solidarity I saw among the 12-step members. Clearly, these are great examples of humans' capacity to come together in groups for mutual helpfulness and mutual support not driven by a need to denigrate outsiders.

- I want to add, too, that in-group/out-group dynamics need not always be toxic, i.e., with an in-group maintaining cohesion by disparaging the out-group. Sometimes the feelings toward the out-group can be neutral. Allport, in his well-known classic investigation of prejudice (Allport 1979), says that groups need other groups to define their own group boundaries, but the attitude toward other groups need not be one of disparagement (Allport 1979: 41–42).

Admiration of other groups: LeVine and Campbell, in their classic study of ethnocentrism, rightly point out in their chapter critiquing Sumner's theory (LeVine and Campbell 1972: 60–71; also 56–57 on different dynamics of in-group-out-groupism in stateless societies) that sometimes groups look up to other groups, in comparison with themselves, rather than always looking down on them (LeVine and Campbell 1972: 63–71). This is, of course, the case with many minority groups, who feel self-hate and a desire to become part of the majority. I do not, of course, hold up this phenomenon as an important model, but it does illustrate the capacity to admire, rather than denigrate, the other.

A complementary phenomenon, and an interesting one, is *majoritarian* admiration of, and even emulation of, *minority* groups. In the US, for example, American readers will know of the longstanding pattern of some white youth unconsciously and/or consciously emulating blacks, especially lower-class urban blacks. The baggy jeans, the hand gestures, the warm greetings, and the music of many of my suburban white students are directly appropriated from elements of black culture. Whites trying to act black are called, by my students, "wiggers." Students of sociolinguistics will also recognize the issues I'm describing here, since they are common in language.

Recommendations for ending invidious groupism

If groups today need not lead to invidiousness, then it gives us optimism for even further limiting invidious groupism in Utopia. Here are some suggestions for how to do it and how Utopia can promote inclusive groups:

1. *Formalize exchange of members between groups*: There is a universal human urge to travel the world, to learn about other peoples. We see this urge today in the huge numbers of people traveling globally as tourists. We see this urge too in the popularity of college study abroad programs. Those of us who are professors see it in the yearning of so many students to come to America, in order to experience a culture and society different from their own. And my own field, anthropology, is based on the belief that there is something inherently interesting, pleasurable, and humanizing about knowing how other groups live.

In Utopia people will be organized into groups who study together, work together (Chapter 4 will describe work groups in much more detail; Chapter 6 will describe learning groups), and live together, with some groups encompassing all these functions. But a prime additional function of groups will be to travel together. A person, or several persons, who belong to any group in one place will travel to other places, near and far, to visit other groups. They will join those groups temporarily, to understand life among them. Members from the group visited will travel too, either to groups in the place where the guests are from, or to the actual group that sent the guests.

This way groups can learn about each other's experiences. This will lead to inter-group compassion. Groups may also help each other by, for example, working on a common project. Mutual group help, greater compassion, and group travel will break down any us–them dynamics between groups. By implementing group visits and exchanges, Utopia will be utilizing a basic sociological principle to break down invidiousness. When people visit different groups, and belong to more than one group, they develop multiple group loyalties. Such multiplicity of loyalty is a paramount way to temper in-groupism (LeVine and Campbell 1972: 47–50; see also Tajfel 1982: 29–30 on criss-crossing group membership and its role in reducing group competition).

2. *Family care*: Because in-groups bond through metaphors of "family," if any in-group/out-group dynamics remain, there will be temporary exchanges of children between in-group families with out-group families—voluntary exchanges, of course. That is, if an in-group child and his or her parents agree, that child would go to stay, temporarily, with an out-group family. That family would send one of its children, if willing, to stay with the in-group family. Even in the absence of in/out-group distinctions, I think children staying with other families—aside from families of their friends—can be salutary for all concerned, since it will help bind all people, across different groups, into real family. My ideas here may seem outlandish to American middle-class readers but fictive kinship and "fictive" parenting—godparents, apprentice/master relationships, mentoring by teachers or other adults who take over many or most of the functions of parenting from a child's caretaker/parents—are all common in many parts of the world, even today.

3. *World festivals*: People derive great joy from festivals. But festivals, while not depending on in-group/out-group distinctions, are often limited to members of one community or one religion.

So, why not have world festivals? How about a worldwide festival day, or two or three, to celebrate world unity and happiness? This would be a time for people to let down their normal guard, break any barriers that do still exist in Utopia (hopefully few, but inevitably some, may remain), meet new people, interact in new and unbounded ways, and, above all, revel in play and joy. Although festivals are temporary and sometimes have been indicted by anthropologists as reinforcing conventional social boundaries precisely by making temporary playful mockery of them, this need not be the case in a society dedicated to the thoroughgoing and day-to-day repudiation of boundaries and hierarchies. The festival time would be a time to officially celebrate this process.

4. *Group pilgrimages*: The reader by now may have noticed that I like taking conventional cultural forms, such as marriage, the arranging of marriage, etc. and transforming them to fit egalitarian and inclusive principles. Pilgrimages are

important group-bonding experiences, but they limit themselves to those following one religion. To have non-divisive pilgrimages, I'd suggest that groups of people could be organized to make a visit to a place not seen as holy by a group or religion, but by an ordinary person. For example, let's say that you have a special place you've visited during your childhood. A group of people might then make a pilgrimage to this place, and the group could be as wide and exclusive as possible, limited only by the time and willingness of people to join the group. This is just one example of how to take an invidious practice and make it inclusive.

Social dynamics precluding greater group unity: What makes us feel we really belong?

Even as I've thought through the causes of a lack of belongingness, and ways to address this lack in Utopia, I've continued to worry that my proposals would not suffice. Won't we still feel alone, even among all these good groups? What if we are with others with whom we feel we have nothing in common, with whom we can't identify? We all know that there is nothing worse than being in a group in which we feel excluded, either because the group pushes us out or because we don't feel we have anything in common with other group members. What then?

I must confess that I don't feel I've entirely solved this most universal of dilemmas, the existential feeling that, after all is said and done, we really are still alone. I do believe that groups made innocent of affinal tensions can be a source of joy. I do believe that eradicating group hierarchies can produce profound feelings. And yet will these changes induce belongingness intense enough to satisfy all of our belonging needs? Or is it simply the case that the human need to be part of a group exceeds the capacity of all of us, collectively, to satisfy each other's needs?

Here are ideas to make the inclusive groups that exist not just objectively and formally inclusive but functionally and subjectively so:

1. *End group-shaming and outcasting*: The power of groups is so strong that they also have a potent negative force. They can scapegoat or outcaste, or simply shame, any of their members. If Utopia is to have groups that actually fulfill positive needs for group belongingness, then the anxiety, indeed terror, of being abandoned or scapegoated by the group must be thwarted; this is essential to produce a genuine sense of belongingness, rather than a superficial sense undercut by the terror that comes with the possibility of being scapegoated or outcaste by one's own group.

How can this be accomplished?

a. First, anyone who studies caste knows the intimate connection between outcasting and hierarchy. Outcastes are the downtrodden, and the downtrodden can become further outcaste. Were hierarchy to be challenged in every domain, so that all humans were secure that their basic physical and social needs could be met, this would be a great help in ending scapegoating and outcasting. After all, if there really is no hierarchy, then the downgrade in status that is outcasting could not happen.

Further, without the indignities that we all suffer due to hierarchy, the cycle of hierarchical abuse would be ended, and replaced by new inclusionist values.

b. But more is necessary to prevent groups from outcasting and scapegoating. I propose that voluntary group monitors, chosen for their generosity of spirit and impartiality, will be appointed to make sure that groups do not outcaste. If outcasting occurs, the monitors will bring the outcastes back into the outcasting group, or into some other more suitable group. Outcastes will receive the most attention from group monitors so that there is always a thwarting of this invidious and inegalitarian dynamic.

Since newcomers into groups are often ones most likely to be a source around which the group forms exclusionary feelings, the voluntary group monitors will also make sure that any visitors to the group, whether temporary or longer-term, will be welcomed into the group. The monitor will introduce the newcomer to some of the group members with whom the newcomer might share common interests or temperament.

I hope this process can address what is one of the most common yet insidiously painful experiences of contemporary life, especially as lived in large societies. We attend an event without knowing anyone, feel too shy or awkward to talk to those in the group—or they are too cliquish to talk to us—and we go home having been in a group but never part of it, because we did not have meaningful interaction with anyone in the group. This common occurrence must end. Groups should welcome newcomers, and not bond by excluding them.

c. Just as the media will be used, as described in the previous chapter, to celebrate those who are compassionate, so the media will be used to celebrate anyone who is isolated from membership in voluntary groups, and/or anyone scapegoated by groups. Lest the reader think this is a novel and strange idea, I would remind readers that attention to the outcaste is at the core of the Christian story. The story's widespread appeal demonstrates a human joy that derives from witnessing, or experiencing, processes that make the low into the high, and the outcaste into the person of central attention.

Of course, my idea here is not simply to retell ancient stories of outcastes, but to celebrate all contemporary non-conformists and isolates (with their consent, of course). One might object that isolates and shut-ins will never want attention, but I doubt this is the case. Every isolated individual I know, without exception, is not isolated by genuine choice, but because they are genuinely social and sensitive individuals, who have isolated themselves because they have not received the attention and affirmation given to more inauthentic personalities. A media channel that helps to champion such individuals need not be patronizing, but can showcase the very genuine warmth, compassion, and even sociability of some of the most isolated individuals around us today. In addition to leveling the attentional playing field, so that all humans receive attention and affirmation, a media channel devoted to the nonconformist will help to establish new values, in which nonconformity and individualism are given real value, rather than the lip service so common when people today claim to value "Western" individualism and autonomy.

d. Groups must also be formed explicitly based upon difference, divergence, and dissensus. One way to do this is for educational institutions to teach the scholastic value of nonconforming thought (as is sometimes done today, in discussions of Beethoven or Galileo). Schools should foster much more debate, so that any consensus that exists is forged because it fits the facts, rather than because facts are made to fit group consensus.

The analogues to nonconforming thought—nonconforming personalities and nonconforming actions—must likewise be fostered. One way to do this would be for group monitors to routinely bring in nonconformists who might challenge group conformity. For example, those holding differing views, those different from the usual group members, etc. can prevent groups, whether they be work groups or "hobby" groups (actually, there will be no difference between these), from hewing to conventional beliefs and conventional personalities. It might even be helpful, as an experiment, for monitors to form groups that are explicitly made up of people who are as divergent from each other as possible. I'm envisioning a music interest group made up of an opera singer, a young rapper, a hard rocker, a jazz player, and someone with little knowledge of music at all. I'm also envisioning a group made up of people with different personalities: Quiet people, loud people, funny people, serious people. The goal here is to socialize all of us to get along with people who might be different from the norm, and different from us. Although we all crave people like us, we should not let anyone in Utopia reject, stigmatize, or shame anyone who is different.

2. *Group mediation*: Conflict between two or more people is both a human universal and a universal source of angst, since it undermines the love and belongingness we crave. Chapter 7 describes in detail courts that will address imbalances in love among people, but this process should be regularized at the micro level as well. That is, all groups, at all times, and all couples (friends or lovers) should be afforded access to conflict mediators. There is nothing new to this notion, of course, since conflict mediation exists today. But today mediators are often paid and they are not seen as essential as food.

Utopia will change this. In fact it might be the case that part of the basic guarantee to all people will be a guarantee of access to a conflict mediator. Working as a mediator might have to be considered, along with the requirement to work at growing food (see the next chapter) and the caregiving requirement (this chapter), to be part of the obligation of all members of Utopia. Not everyone will do all this work but all people will have to spend a small number of hours weekly tending to one of these obligations.

3. *Group sharing*: Belonging to a group that is objectively Utopian may not guarantee individual group members a sense of belongingness. There are a variety of reasons for why this is so, but one that might especially need to be addressed

is intra-group emotional inequality. While no differences in wealth will exist in Utopia, members of a given group may experience different levels of emotional well-being. While some of these differences and inequities cannot be ameliorated, some can be leveled through non-zero-sum redistribution.

Let's say in a given group person X has many friends while another group member, Y, does not. Utopia could encourage a non-coercive practice whereby the two individuals trade places, so that the friendless one, Y, can experience social interactions with the many friends of X. And X will temporarily relinquish his/her claims on the time and energy of her/his friends. At the end of the set time period the friend-loan ends (although, of course, Y may gain new friends through the interaction).

This proposal is by no means a perfect solution to guarantee that everyone in a group, or in Utopia itself, will be equally happy, of course, since something like happiness cannot easily be shared fully. But the principle is an important one. Anything making one person happy should be shared with others if possible. The sharing should be permanent as long as no loss accrues to X in trying to compensate for Y's unhappiness. And if permanence is not possible, at least Y can stand in X's shoes temporarily—to experience X's friendships, loves, creative conditions etc., even if this experience requires some simulation. After all, actors simulate the conditions and emotions of those very different from themselves. The proposal here simply encourages all of us to be actors. By doing so we can experience happiness by acquiring someone else's happy conditions. And those who are emotionally content can stand in others' less happy shoes, thereby increasing empathy for them.

Above all, the group can take on a function of genuine mutual help. That is, members will help each other feel as happy as possible, by "loaning" each other the circumstances contributing to individual happinesses. This will further strengthen group solidarity by making group members mutually helpful to each other in the absence of money and power, two social elements that in today's world are at the center of mutual help. Sympathies within the group will be strengthened and emotional inequalities within the group—a threat to group cohesion—will be reduced, a reduction that will occur through art—in this case the capacity of humans to simulate each other's circumstances, stories, and emotions.

4. *Work and groups*: Today many of us spend most of our hours in groups at our workplace. In Chapter 4 I discuss how work groups will form. But here I want to advocate an important principle. Work, play, and family must not be separate societal spheres. This separation, largely a product of industrialization's separation of the home from the workplace (think, by contrast, of the preindustrial small-scale craftsman—the shoemaker or the farmer who lives and works at home), reinforces the valorization of unfun coerced activity (work) over freely engaged in fun activity (play). Likewise, the emptying of larger social functions from the family, such as families' contributions to the wider economy, isolates families and deprives them of a feeling of having functional societal significance. Thus, Utopia must encourage family, work, and "play" (although the work/play distinction will no longer hold in Utopia) groups to overlap and cross-cut, thus giving greater meaning to all Utopian groups.

To do this a voluntary rotating position of local group advisor might be created. The advisor could make nonbonding recommendations for altering groups and group membership to make sure that creative groups and kin groups are merged. Utopia may foster other interventions and experiments, such as having a group of people living together engage in collective creative projects. Thus, creating and family life would overlap, which is the goal.

5. *Group performance binds groups*: Groups will also pledge to become audiences for the performances of other groups, especially other groups as different as possible in interest, culture, geography, age, etc. from themselves. For example, an interest group in rock music and an interest group in opera might give presentations, or demonstrations, to each other. People will be encouraged to be interested in new things, even if only temporarily.

Because of the centrality in Utopia of *interaction* and the pursuit of *interactive* joy, all groups will interact with others outside their own groups and will be "performative." I use performative not in the literal sense, but in the metaphoric sense: All groups will strive to learn new things, and create new things, and then they will interact with those outside the group to present what they have learned, to teach what they have learned, to others, to an "audience." This performative dimension is extremely important in order that the group acquires a sense of significance and purpose. Performance will bind groups together with that sense of purpose and it will enhance the pleasure in their own work, because they will interact not only with each other but also with the widest groups of others possible.

Bibliography

Allport, Gordon W. 1979. *The Nature of Prejudice*. Unabridged, 25th anniversary edition. Reading, MA: Addison-Wesley.

De Waal, Frans 2005. *Our Inner Ape*. New York: Riverhead Books.

Draper, Patricia 1976. Social and economic constraints on child life among the !Kung. Pp. 199–217 in *Kalahari Hunter-Gatherers: Studies of the !Kung San and Their Neighbors*. Richard B. Lee and Irven DeVore, eds. Cambridge, MA: Harvard University Press.

Emling, Shelley 2013. 4 things they never tell you about Empty Nest Syndrome. *Huffington Post*, October 8, 2013. Accessed June 9, 2014 at www.huffingtonpost.com/shelley-emling/empty-nest- syndrome_b_3956231.html.

Estes, Richard Despard 1991. *The Behavior Guide to African Mammals, Including Hoofed Mammals, Carnivores, Primates*. Berkeley: The University of California Press.

Gerson, Michael 2013. Saying goodbye to my child, the youngster. *The Washington Post*, August 19, 2013. Accessed June 9, 2014 at www.washingtonpost.com/opinions/michael-gerson-saying-goodbye-to-my-child-the-youngster/2013/08/19/6337802e-08dd-11e3-8974-f97ab3b3c677_story.html?utm_term=.376d9c931bdc.

Hrdy, Sarah Blaffer 2009. *Mothers and Others: The Evolutionary Origins of Mutual Understanding*. Cambridge, MA: Belknap Press of Harvard University Press.

Ingold, Tim 2004. On the social relations of the hunter-gatherer band. Pp. 399–410 in *The Cambridge Encyclopedia of Hunters and Gatherers*. Paperback edition. Richard B. Lee and Richard Daly, eds. Cambridge: Cambridge University Press.

Lee, Richard B. 1993. *The Dobe Ju/'hoansi*, 2nd ed. Fort Worth, TX: Harcourt Brace College Publishers.

LeVine, Robert A. and Donald T. Campbell 1972. *Ethnocentrism: Theories of Conflict, Ethnic Attitudes and Group Behavior*. New York: John Wiley and Sons.

Lindholm, Charles 1982. *Generosity and Jealousy: The Swat Pukhtun of Northern Pakistan*. New York: Columbia University Press.

Liu, Hui-chen Wang 1959. *The Traditional Chinese Clan Rules*. Locust Valley, NY: J.J. Augustin.

Mann, Michael 2005. *The Dark Side of Democracy: Explaining Ethnic Cleansing*. New York: Cambridge University Press.

Schoenhals, Martin 2003. *Intimate Exclusion: Race and Caste Turned Inside Out*. Lanham, MD: University Press of America.

Smith-Rosenberg, Carroll 1975. The female world of love and ritual: Relations between women in nineteenth-century America. *Signs*, 1: 1–29.

Sumner, William Graham 1906. *Folkways: A Study of the Sociological Importance of Usages, Manners, Customs, Mores, and Morals*. Boston: The Atheneum Press.

Tajfel, Henri 1982. Social psychology of intergroup relations. *Annual Review of Psychology*, 33: 1–39.

Turner, Victor 1977. *The Ritual Process: Structure and Anti-Structure*. Ithaca, NY: Cornell Paperbacks.

4

WORK IN UTOPIA

What is a good life? The conventional answer is an economic one, and more specifically a consumerist economic one. If lots of things are produced for consumers, then consumers are happy. And if consumers are happy, then the economy is a good one, as is the society that produced it. In this view of the good life, material production for consumers is the goal, and work is the means to achieve that goal. Even some progressive thinkers are, unwittingly I think, influenced by the consumerist position, since their prescriptions for economic reform focus on getting more goods and services to those who now lack them. Again, work is a means, but not an end in itself.

Given that more and more of us work longer and longer hours, spending much of our lives at work, the above equation has always puzzled me. If work is what most of us spend so much of our time doing, then shouldn't the goal of a good economy be happiness at work, with the satisfaction of the consumer a less important measure? It might be heretical to say it, but isn't an economy of happy but less-efficient workers better than a highly productive economy of unhappy workers? After all, who says that consumers and consuming should take precedence over workers and work?

I do not, in any way, overlook the need to satisfy people's basic needs, of course, but to me, work is one of those needs, and a paramount need at that. In this chapter I argue that the truly utopian society is one that provides the conditions so that all people can work, and so that all people can work at activities they choose and they enjoy. The provision of enjoyable work for all is the prime goal of the good economy and production of consumer goods takes a back seat to the goal of making work enjoyable.

How can work be made enjoyable? To start with, I will argue that what makes work "work" in the first place is that it is not freely chosen. It is something we must do to make a living. Almost any task can be turned into work if it is made obligatory. I often ask my students what would happen if I gave them the following homework assignment over the weekend: "You must go to the beach" or "You must go see a movie." They get the point. When I require it, things they do for fun turn into work. No activity is inherently odious; it only becomes so when coerced. Whether an activity is coerced or freely engaged in makes a difference—something we recognize about sex but fail to recognize when it comes to work.

To make work enjoyable then, it must be turned into something that is not obligatory. Currently, most of us work so we can earn a living, and we join institutions—our workplaces—in which people with more power than us become the ones to tell us what to do, with the power to deny our access to subsistence needs if we do not follow their bidding.

This can change. We can, and should, be given the basic means of subsistence. All people throughout the world should be guaranteed food, shelter, clothing, health care, and other basic means to live, whether they "work" or not. This "basic guarantee" to all will then free us to engage in productive activities not because we have to do so, but because we want to do so. Productive activity, freely chosen, will no longer be "work."

I know my ideas about work and the economy will have automatic appeal to many, but to even those to whom they might appeal, overwhelming objections will be raised. Therefore, before giving the details of my plan, let me first deal with these objections.

A response to objections

Objection 1: The welfare objection

This objection goes as follows: People only work because they have to work, in order to make a living. If everyone's livelihood is guaranteed, it will be like welfare for all. No one will have any reason to work, and with everyone lounging around all day, we will all starve (or at the very least suffer declining standards of living).

This is a serious objection, of course. It is not only familiar to Americans, like me, who have grown up during the heyday of neoliberal economics; it is also something I heard repeatedly from the Chinese in the late 1980s. My "socialist" Chinese friends were eager to school someone like me, a denizen of a capitalist country, about the dangers of socialism. Little did they know the irony: Though from a capitalist country, I am far more of a socialist, in its pure form, than most of my Chinese friends! Each side wanted to convince the other of the dangers of their own system.

My Chinese friends told me about the "iron rice bowl"—the guarantee (no longer in existence today) by the government of a lifelong job to hundreds of millions of urban workers, a guarantee that meant that none of them had to worry about the basic necessities of life. My friends disliked the iron rice bowl because they said it allowed people to lounge around in the workplace without fear of getting fired, and without fear of ever losing the basic subsistence that came with the guarantee of lifelong work.

Here is my response to my Chinese friends, and to American friends too. I would first ask this question: "Do humans only work when forced, whether it be the force of a person, an institution, or the force that is the specter of starvation?" The answer is no. In Chapter 1 I cited the example of people coming to New York from all over the US to volunteer their help with the tragedy of 9/11. People will, in fact, put out great effort, will "work," in response to *non-coerced, non-survival motives*. Parents know this best. Parents don't need pay or the threat of being fired to make them do one of the most arduous tasks in the world. Parental care for children is surely the most profound example of labor there is and it is labor done totally (except for paid childcare) without coercion or survival motives (that is, the parents' immediate survival does not depend on doing work, even though when children are infants their survival does depend on someone else's work).

People will work, and they will do it for a variety of reasons: Some to earn a living, others to help friends, others to care for family. None of this is surprising, in fact, given that one of the great mammalian innovations was parental caretaking. And since parental care for children became extended, as I argued in Chapter 1, to a more general propensity to care for other humans besides our children, it is clear where our species' real potential lies: We can and do work best for the genuine benefit of others. We will work if coerced, but not very well. I think most of us know this instinctively, how we resist coerced work, disliking it, sometimes finding ways to cut corners, etc. We all also know that if we love what we are doing, we don't call it work, but rather "play" or a "hobby." In fact if we could recognize pleasurable creation for the work that it is, and not cast aspersions on it because it is non-coerced and enjoyable, then we could see far more clearly how much labor gets done voluntarily. Think how much "work" actually is done that is never called work, such as all of the hobbies people engage in. I'm in a good amateur choir in New York and we work very, very hard at our rehearsals, but we do so out of love for the music, not because we must earn a living. For me, doing it for love of the music frees me up a great deal, and allows me to enjoy what I am doing in a way that I wouldn't if it were my job. I know most readers will easily understand what I am saying.

Where I'm going with all of this is to not only establish that we will work for reasons other than pay, but that we will often work better and with greater enjoyment: Parents do so, amateur enthusiasts do so too. Thus, I am going to make a strong claim here. Not only *can* work for survival be replaced by work for joy, but it *should* be replaced, because the latter work is done better (as well as being enjoyed by the worker). The basic guarantee I propose, in freeing people from the specter of starvation, will not lead to inactive and lazy people, and incompetent and unmotivated workers. I know very few people who really want to sit at home doing nothing—maybe for a while, but not for a lifetime. So the basic guarantee will encourage us to work at that which we enjoy, making us better workers in the process. After all, who would you rather have growing your food, or teaching your children: A farmer or teacher for whom farming or teaching is a passion and joy, or farmers and teachers bitter about their work, because it is something they are compelled to do? I know who I'd pick in a heartbeat.

This is how I usually end my arguments with the Chinese. I point out to them that work, in Utopia, is nothing like the kind of work they lived with. Contrary to American stereotypes about "communist" China, workers in China were never freed to do what they wanted. For starters, no one was given a basic guarantee or an iron rice bowl so they could follow their own passions. The Chinese, culturally, would have had a hard time allowing this because they would have seen it (wrongly, as I argue) as "selfish" and "bourgeois." Ironically, both capitalists and communists cast aspersions on workers who work freely and without obligation, even more ironic given that "freedom" and "worker empowerment" are their respective favorite slogans. The Chinese iron rice bowl, the lifelong job, did free many people from basic want (although I'm sure its real motive was to convince early skeptics, among whom urbanites and urban workers were the most threatening to the government, that they would be taken care of much better by the new communist government, than by the former one, the Nationalists). But it didn't give them the freedom to do whatever work they wanted. They were obligated to be at the factory, or make a pretense of that, and there were ways to reward or punish those conforming or not conforming to work demands. Workers might not have been subject to losing their jobs, but they could, for example, be denied good housing if they didn't work hard. If they did work hard, there were all kinds of non-monetary honors too that they could earn.

So if someone says that my plan is "communism" and that communism didn't succeed, my response is that I don't know what to call my plan, but I do know that it's never been tried, least of all by those communists most respected for their innovative approaches to communism, the Maoist Chinese.

And if someone calls my plan a welfare scheme I would say that most people want to work, if given the opportunity. If I am wrong, and many people take their basic guarantee and sit around, feeling content, then that is their choice. I do not believe in capital punishment for laziness, which is what the neoliberal view amounts to: "If they don't work, let them starve." After all, many people can't work—people incapacitated in various ways, for example—yet we never let them starve. Children can work, but we don't require them to work, nor do we even want them do so, since the world has come to a shared consensus about the evils of child labor. If we can tolerate the relatively new, 20th-century conception that the best childhood is one devoted to "play" and learning, rather than obligatory labor, why not accept a new 21st-century notion that the best life for all, children *and* adults, is one where play and learning take precedence, and replace compulsory activity of any kind?

Objection 2: The scarcity objection

Central to Utopia is the basic subsistence guarantee. Food, housing, and other basic necessities will be given to every human in the world. Skeptics might raise the following two issues:

1. Food scarcity: Is there really enough food and housing for everyone in the world? And will there be enough in the future?
2. Too much work to do: And can the world feed itself, and provide the other necessities of life, without requiring everyone to work long hours? If not, Utopia's goal to make work optional and non-coerced would fail.

While this book focuses on the human sociological and psychological possibilities and constraints to Utopia, here I will discuss technological potentials and constraints, since they are so central to two fundamental Utopia characteristics, the provision of food to everyone and the reduction or elimination of obligatory work. (I know true skeptics will wonder whether any Utopia is possible with declining energy sources or climate change. Good questions, but I cannot address every possible issue, although I will look at food and climate change.) I also feel it is important to discuss these issues because the scarcity refrain, "There's not enough to go around," is often used to justify poverty and compel workers to work longer hours. In reality, there is enough food to end hunger, and food to feed the world can be produced with so little labor that most of us can be freed to work voluntarily, without obligation.

To challenge the above objections—food scarcity, and too much work to do—I will begin with a worst-case scenario for each one, and then work up to more rosy scenarios. Readers who have less interest in the technical details discussed here may wish to skip to Objection 3.

Worst-case scenario for 1 (food scarcity): Some people say food, in particular, will not be produced in sufficient quantities for the world's population of the future, either because that population will grow too fast, outstripping food supply, or because global climate change will adversely affect food production.

My response: Utopia's basic guarantee is essential. If there is not enough food for everyone, then the world's population must be controlled. Many people might feel that it is their right to have as many children as they want, but I am arguing that there is an even more basic right, the right of every child and adult to be able to eat enough to be free from the threat of hunger. Therefore, in the case of decreasing or insufficient global food supply, Utopia will institute mandatory population controls, to reduce the population to match the carrying capacity of Earth.

A rosier scenario: There are many doomsday predictions about the availability of food in the future, some plausible, but most research indicates that even with the increase in world population from over 7.5 billion today to 9.7 billion in 2050 (DESA 2017: 1), the world will produce enough food to feed all people. In particular a detailed report by the United Nations organization responsible for research on food, the Food and Agriculture Organization (FAO), summarizes work by a group of food experts who concluded that there will be sufficient food for a world population of more than 9 billion in 2050 (FAO 2009: 4). This report considers many different factors affecting food availability, including climate change.

The above report does *not* consider another factor, the huge amount of food that could be saved by reducing waste. Recent research by the FAO estimates that each year *one-third* of food produced globally for human consumption is lost or wasted due to being thrown away by food sellers and consumers, and by inadequate harvesting, storage, and cooling (FAO 2011: v, 11–12). Food that is produced but not eaten has a huge carbon footprint, ranking third behind the carbon footprints of the US and China (FAO 2013: 6).

Also not considered by the FAO food predictions for the future are new technologies that could increase production. Although these ideas are speculative at this point, they have the potential to increase food production significantly. Among such ideas are desert agriculture using low-energy conversion of sea water for irrigation and newly engineered rice that increases yields by 50% (Rosner 2009).

Worst-case scenario for 2 (too much work to do): Most readers probably are not farmers, while many of our recent ancestors lived as farmers. Our intuition that agriculture has become so efficient in the past decades that most of us don't need to farm is correct.

But let's return to gloomy skepticism: What if the mechanization of farming occurring in developed nations in the 20th century did little to reduce the numbers of people farming? Or what if that technology can never be used in developing countries, even if they are provided with it for free?

My response: Let's assume the above doomsday issue is true, and that farming simply requires too many workers, even if fully mechanized. If that were true, we could never free ourselves from the burden of "work" because humans would have to spend a significant amount of time farming.

If this were the case (it isn't, but let's assume the worst), one option would be to *maintain* the basic guarantee, but require everyone to farm and build houses for a significant part of their waking hours—reluctantly giving up the idea that work can be freely chosen and optional. But while work may be required, it need not be configured in a manner that maintains today's hierarchies. In particular, Utopia can arrange farm work so that no one has the power to compel others to work, or the power to supervise them. To do otherwise would be to bring about hierarchy, and the elimination of hierarchy is the central goal of Utopia.

To prevent hierarchy, Utopia, in the unlikely case of farming requiring too much work, could give a plot of farm land, and materials to build a house, to all people (with the handicapped, elderly, and children assisted by the more able-bodied). The global population will be controlled, or reduced if necessary, so that there is enough land per capita and enough housing materials for all people. Thus, we will all independently grow our own food and build our own houses, on land we are allotted, and with materials distributed to us. In cases where environmental catastrophes strike one area, Utopia will redistribute surplus food from areas where food is plentiful to those areas with too little.

I might add that this idea, giving land to every person, or to vast majorities of people in a nation, is not just an imaginary one. Many countries have carried out such policies under the banner of "land reform." China did it in 1950, undid it in the later 1950s, and then reinstituted the allocation of plots of land to all rural families in the early 1980s so that there was general equality of landholding among all Chinese peasant families. (Unfortunately, tragically I feel, very recent real-estate land grabs are, once again, undoing the Chinese policy of land to all rural residents, thus re-creating a landless peasantry in many areas.) Most analysts of China's growth in the past several decades see the early 1980s distribution of equal plots of land to all as being a major factor leading to vastly improved agricultural outputs.

The fact that land could be given to all Chinese peasant families, who at the time of the distribution represented about 80% of a population of one billion people or more, suggests that Utopia, with far fewer people per acre than in China, could do likewise and thrive—even more than the multitudes of Chinese peasants who thrived in the 1980s following land reform.

A rosier scenario: Lee writes about foragers that "it is becoming clear that, with a few conspicuous exceptions, the hunter-gatherer subsistence base is at least routine and reliable and at best surprisingly abundant" (Lee 1968: 30). Even though the Kung of southern Africa, whom Lee studied ethnographically, live(d) in a harsh environment (30, 43), they met their food needs by working *only 12–19 hours per week* to obtain food! Even the very hardest-working individual worked only 32 hours per week seeking food (37). Lee found that the Kung averaged a per person share of nine ounces of meat per day, plus a large variety of vegetables and nuts. Most importantly, he calculated that the Kung were able to *exceed* the US recommended daily allowance for both calories and protein (39). And this all occurred in a harsh environment and, moreover, during one of the most severe droughts in South Africa's history (39). As Lee notes: "One can postulate that their subsistence base would be even more substantial during years of higher rainfall" (40). In summary, the Kung foragers ate very well, probably better than many of us in industrial societies, and with little time devoted to food procurement.

I am *not* advocating that we return to being foragers but I cite this to show that foragers and their plentiful leisure demonstrate that even in harsh environments, and even with pre-agricultural food production methods, it is possible to live more leisurely than the vast majority of us, since in industrial society we work more than 40 hours a week to obtain our daily necessities (for those of us in New York even 40 hours might not be enough for our necessities, given the extremely high price of housing). If they can do it, we can at the very least use some mix of foraging and agriculture, and whatever sustainable agriculture technologies exist, to do even better—probably far better than their requisite working week of less than 20 hours.

As I have already pointed out, the fact that most readers are probably not involved in food production suggests quite strongly what has happened in so many nations: Food production *has* become far more efficient, so that fewer and fewer of us are needed to produce food, that most basic subsistence item. (I will focus on food here, rather than housing construction, since there is so much information available on increases in food production. Further, food is the most basic biological requirement we face.)

What data support this claim? I will start with more intuitive data, from the movement of people to cities, and then give the precise data on declining percentages of the population working in agriculture. In the US in 1900 nearly half of all American workers were farmers. By 2000 only 1.9% of American workers were farmers (USDA 2005: 2). I know many readers may share a story similar to mine. My paternal grandparents both grew up on farms in northern Michigan. They became teachers and all of their descendants have lived as non-farmers, in suburbs or cities. This pattern is one being replayed the world over. Over 50% of humans live in cities and this is estimated to grow to nearly 70% by 2050 (DESA 2012: 1–2).

These data are indirect of course since the movement of people from farms to cities does not prove a decrease in hours worked at agriculture. Some people living on farms do not actually work on them (often because their labor is not needed there; these people are often the ones who migrate to cities), and some urban dwellers grow some food.

So, more direct statistics: Let me begin with the past, worldwide, to show a widespread pattern of declining percentages of people working as farmers. In 1950 the percentage of the economically active population working in agriculture for developed countries was 35.7%. In 2000 it had decreased to 7.3%. For developing countries the figures were 81.8% in 1950 and 55.4% in 2000. For the world as a whole the figures were 67.1% in 1950 and 44.8% in 2000 (FAO 2000: 13). A different report by FAO gives even more impressive declines for 2010 (FAO 2000 had only estimated 2010 whereas FAO 2012 gives actual figures. Note, however, that FAO 2000 and FAO 2012 may differ somewhat in the way "developed" versus "high income countries" were defined. FAO 2000 does not specify which countries count as "developed," so comparison between the reports must be made with some caution.) By 2010 only 3% of the economically active population worked in agriculture in high-income countries, while for the world as a whole 40% worked in agriculture in 2010 and 47% for low- and middle-income countries (FAO 2012: 114, 118). The reader should note that "economically active" in agriculture also includes those who are producing food only for their own family consumption (FAO 2012: 15). (Readers may wonder, as I did, if the work in high-income countries was merely shifted to foreign migrant workers. Taking the US as an example, hired farm workers make up less than 1% of the US workforce and over half of these are US citizens. See USDA 2016. Therefore, foreign migrant workers represent, at most, less than .5% of the US workforce. Clearly, few people in the US, citizens or foreign migrant workers, are involved in growing all of the nation's food.)

But is food still being produced? Did the farm population reduction hurt production? In fact, not only did production not decrease but it increased, concurrent with the movement of people out of farming. Between 1950 and 1973 the world grain harvest doubled!

Brown notes that the "expansion during these 23 years equaled the growth in output from the beginning of agriculture until 1950." The vast majority of this remarkable growth occurred due to increased yields, and not due to increasing the land under cultivation (Brown 2012: 72). The adoption of new plant breeds, called the Green Revolution, along with increased fertilizer use, and increased irrigation, are the major changes leading to the huge growth in the grain harvest. The development of dwarf wheat, which devotes a greater part of the plant to the edible part, led to huge increases in wheat production. In Mexico, for example, there was a fourfold increase in the wheat yields between 1950 and 2011 (75). Dwarf rice led to similar massive increases, doubling yields in many nations (75–76). New corn was bred to grow under conditions of greater crowding, so that more corn could be grown per acre. In the US new corn breeds enabled a quintupling of corn yields from 1940 to 2010 (76). In addition to new breeds, the world area under irrigation tripled since 1950, further raising grain yields (76). Fertilizer use grew from 14 million tons in 1950 to 177 million tons in 2010, also leading to the massive increase in grain yields (77).

But is there still more room for growth? Can the less developed nations reduce their agriculturally active populations to percentages closer to 3%, as developed nations have done? (Note here that I am asking a different question from Brown 2012, who is mostly raising the alarm about a plateauing of yields in developed countries, an alarm he raises in order to spur needed change in agricultural practices. My question is whether agricultural labor required in developing countries could be reduced with mechanization, so that fewer people need to work on farms than at present, following the situation in developed countries over the past half century or so.) If so, this would mean that the whole world could produce our needed food with most of us not working in agriculture. If we could spread out the work to all of us, each of us would only need to spend, say (these figures are just for the sake of argument), three days out of 100 farming or roughly one day in every 33 farming. That would leave 32 days free, minus whatever time it takes to build our housing and provide other basic needs. Thus it would be possible for most of us to not work at all, or the hours we would be required to work for our basic subsistence would be very few. Based on a 40-hour work week we would spend only a little over one hour per week farming!

If Utopia prioritizes labor-saving efficiency as it will do (see Chapter 7), then there is no reason that developing countries' non-mechanized farmers cannot be freed from most of their required farm work. That is, the world can produce food with only a small percentage of humans working in agriculture, as indeed has already happened in the developed world. The reason developing countries have not yet significantly reduced their agricultural workforce has to do with politics and economics, not with the constraints of science and technology, according to the top agricultural experts I contacted (personal communications from Carlo Cafiero and Dominique van der Mensbrugghe of the FAO and Keith Fuglie from the United States Department of Agriculture).

I wish there were a study that quantified the percentage by which developing countries could reduce their agricultural labor force due to mechanization (e.g., greater use of tractors), but there is none. I know this because I looked long and hard for such a study and also because the expert I consulted on this issue said that the FAO (the definitive source for such studies) has not conducted one (personal communication from Piero Conforti of the FAO). As Clarke and Bishop note, it is too complex to calculate all of the labor that can be saved in developing countries throughout the farming process. They concentrate on calculating potentials for mechanizing the preparation of the fields for planting, which they describe as being "the most arduous" activity in "manually based systems" (Clarke and Bishop 2002: 1). I might note that, among other difficulties, data on hours worked in non-mechanized agriculture are extremely hard to estimate because to do so would require researchers to intensively study the farm practice and hours worked of smallholder farmers throughout the developing world, and there are too many of them and too many variables to make sampling easy.

Nonetheless, using available data I have arrived at a non-definitive yet, I hope, convincing argument for the possibility of reducing agricultural work worldwide to a single-digit percentage of all working people (and, recall, this is percentages of people who are economically active, not the entire world population). First, I will give a summary of the argument, which will be followed later by the details:

1. Many people in developing countries do the most time-consuming work by hand, or by animals, even today. (I see this all the time on farms in China, despite China's reputation for modernity.) Mechanize these processes, as has already happened in the developed world and as is already happening in some, perhaps many, developing countries, and we're almost there.

2. Farmers, whether manual or mechanized, often do not need to spend 40 hours per week year-round working on their farms. Estimate how much time they really spend and then recalculate the work figures.

3. Many who appear in national farm censuses as farm workers are really not laboring on farms. In densely populated nations such as China, for example, there are hundreds of millions of people living on farms, counted as farmers, but who really are a surplus population of non-workers. Estimate the "surplus population" in agriculture.

4. Finally, additional labor reductions are also possible due to new discoveries, or by use of recently developed technology that has yet to be deployed even in high-income countries.

I know there are those who abhor many of the efficiencies existing in agriculture today. Some of these bother me too, and I hope Utopia can find ways to more humanely raise animals, for example. However, following the logic of this book, it is most important to reduce obligatory labor, principally farm labor and other work pertaining to the basic guarantee, to a minimum, so that the means–end nature of work is eliminated, replaced with action for pleasure. I know there are those who prefer hand labor in agriculture and they would be free in Utopia to engage in this as a pleasure, if they so choose, but they may not "choose" for other humans to do so. For those for whom a return to a technology-less world is a virtue in itself, Utopia will necessarily disappoint, although I hope that the end of hierarchy, the end of compulsory work, and the return to social action engaged in freely and for its own sake, will more than offer sufficient consolation.

Now for the details:

1. In a very detailed case study on Africa, farmers themselves ranked the most time-consuming farming activities. Often on top as most time-consuming was digging i.e., preparing the soil for planting, followed by weeding (IFAD and FAO 2003: 9). Both of these activities can be quite significantly transformed so that they require very little time. Take digging. Soil preparation by hand (done with a hoe) takes 100 times longer than when done by a tractor, and six times longer than when done by animals (IFAD and FAO 2003: 16). Other estimates show even more labor saved through use of animals or tractors for plowing. At a site in Nebraska in 2006 a team of four horses was timed and compared with plowing done with a modern tractor. The horses took 55 hours to plow a 40-acre field at the rate they were plowing, while the tractor worked at a rate of a little over an hour to plow the same field (Ganzel 2006). The FAO's labor-saving technologies and practices data indicate that plowing by human labor power alone takes 10 to 20 times as long as when done with a pair of oxen (FAO 2007).

In the developing world my calculations based on Clarke and Bishop's data show that 39% of all land in all developing countries is cultivated by hand, 30% with animal labor power, and 31% using tractors. (See Figure 2, Clarke and Bishop 2002: 4. The percentages I cite here are my own calculations based on the data from Clarke and Bishop 2002. I have used 1998 World Bank figures for arable land in each region in the developing world—since 1998 is the year of Clarke and Bishop's data—and Clarke and Bishop's Figure 2 to calculate an overall percentage of land-cultivation methods for the whole developing world. For World Bank figures see World Bank n.d. The year of Clarke and Bishop's data, 1998, is a bit old, but it is the only data I have found giving percentages of land cultivation by hand, animal, and machine worldwide. Figure 1 in Foster and Rosenzweig 2010: 32 gives more recent data for India only, for tractors, plows, and threshers. It shows a situation in 2007–2008 for India that is even worse than Clarke and Bishop's 1998 data for South Asia, despite India's role as a leading producer of farm machinery.)

Now according to the more conservative estimate cited above, hand preparation takes 100 times longer than tractor preparation and six times longer than animal preparation, and land preparation is perhaps the most time-consuming activity in farming, so *for the sake of argument*, let's assume there are three equally sized plots of land (this approximates the developing world situation I've cited, where over a third of land is cultivated by hand) and preparing the land is all that needs to be done (not the case, but remember this is for the sake of argument, to make calculations simpler). Plot A, done by hand, will take one person 100 days to prepare. Plot B, by tractor, will take 1 day to prepare. And plot C, by animal, will take about 17 days. (The 100 days by hand divided by six.) This is 118 person-days of labor. If we have tractors used on all three plots, only 3 person-days of labor will be required. That means the work would be reduced by mechanization to 2.5% of the current work done using a mix of methods!

If all economically active people worked in agriculture in developing countries, under this hypothetical scenario, we could reduce that 100% number to 2.5%. Given that in actuality 47%, not 100%, work in agriculture, *with tractors, we would now have 1.2% of the economically active population working in agriculture in the developing countries! This is even better than we could have hoped for and is even better than the current situation in developed countries.*

Of course, I have assumed land preparation is the only time-consuming procedure. But farmer respondents also mentioned weeding as significantly time-consuming (IFAD and FAO 2003: 9), which can also be made less labor-intensive with mechanization, or with fairly simple processes such as mulching or covering the soil with clear or black plastic (Mechanical weed control n.d.).

2. I could stop here, but it is also the case that the one tractor-operator/harvester-operator is not spending 40 hours per week, year-round, on farming. Even without tractors this is true, especially in colder climates, where farmers might plant only one crop per year. When no crops are planted, farm workers have free time, and when crops are growing, little needs to be done until harvest time.

So how much time is available to our now mechanized farmer? This is very hard to estimate but a proxy can be had by looking at American farmers. Of 2.2 million principal farm operators in the US, 900,000 report working off the farm more than 200 days a year (USDA 2007: 3) (and 1.2 million list something other than farming as their principal occupation, a figure I will not use due to its ambiguity). For the sake of being conservative in my estimates, let's say the 1.3 million not working off-farm 200 days a year are working every day on the farm. Let's say their work week is 40 hours a week, year-round (unlikely, but this is for the sake of conservative estimation). Then let's calculate, again conservatively, the 900,000 as working 165 divided by 365, or 45%, we'll say 50%, of their time farming. This means that farmers average 80% of the work week at farming (at the very most—far less in reality). This further reduces the amount of person-hours worked at farming.

3. Surplus labor: I have heard time and time again from Chinese farmers that there are too many of them on the land. For example, one family told me that one or two people are more than enough to farm the small plot of land they have (all families are allocated similar-sized plots), even though there may be four people (two children is now quite common in the countryside) available to farm the land. This is the case in many densely populated areas of China and it is the reason some 200 million peasants have been able to move to cities as factory workers and construction workers. The existence of surplus labor in densely populated developing countries such as China and India further reduces the number of developing-country farmers needed for agriculture, without doing anything other than admitting contemporary reality. There are too many people living on farms. There is not enough work, even if done manually, for them to do. They should not count as farmers, since they are idle.

4. Many new technologies exist, or are being developed, that can significantly reduce the need for human labor further. Often discussed in the popular press is the use of robots to weed fields, prune vines, monitor moisture and soil over vast areas, harvest fruit, herd livestock, and milk dairy cows (see Rosner 2009; Harvey 2014). Tractors that can drive themselves already exist and are in use (Dobbs 2013).

The final upshot: There is enough food for all of us, and it can be produced with so little labor that all of us can have the majority of our hours free to work creatively at non-subsistence pursuits.

Objection 3: The no one wants to farm objection

This objection goes as follows: Schoenhals makes a good case for speculating that people will work even in the absence of coercion. But what if he's wrong? What if we institute a basic guarantee and absolutely *no one* chooses to farm, or to build houses? Where will the food and housing, guaranteed to all, come from if there's no one working to produce them?

Okay, in this case I'll be slightly un-utopian. Work that needs to be done, like growing food, building homes, etc., can be assigned to those who are able to work. I might have a system whereby minimal work requirements, say five hours of work per week, are assigned to all those capable of working. See the last section of this chapter, 'My plan: The details', points 2 and 8. Number 8 addresses what happens if some people refuse to work, a situation I believe will be uncommon and which, therefore, does not concern me, but one which, I know, will concern many readers.

Objection 4: The fairness objection

The fairness objection runs along the following lines: Redistribution schemes are profoundly unfair. They take money from morally virtuous, hard-working people like me, and give it to the undeserving, lazy poor. If Utopia guarantees the same basic guarantee for all, this is unfair to those of us who work harder and produce more: If we work more, we should earn more, and not have anything taken from us to support non-workers.

My response to this objection is to make an end-run around the whole question of the fairness of how money is allocated. Rather than debating who should get what, and whether inequality is fair or not, my overriding strategy is to reframe the issue altogether by saying we *should* gain recognition for our creative efforts *but* money is a terrible form of such recognition. Utopia must give birth to a new currency: The pleasure we feel in pleasing others, others who are in our presence as audiences to our creative work.

I know all too well the responses: "What kind of pay is that?" "You can't eat pleasure." The very fact that people belittle the value of getting pleasure from pleasing others is a sad commentary on how far money has displaced pleasure as a legitimate motivation for human productivity. When we recognize that we should really live for interactive joy, the whole issue of who gets paid what loses its centrality. The distribution of money and status is important—it must be equal (or rather minimized or zeroed out, as I am proposing) lest hierarchy result—but this issue is not the central issue that should concern anyone in reforming the economy, even those of us on the left. A truly good economy is one that provides creators plenty of opportunities to create and have their creations attended to by audiences, so that both creators and those for whom they create can be interactively pleased.

I know my answer here will not assuage the deep-seated resentment among so many people who will feel that they might work hard in Utopia while others loaf. My final response is to say two things: First, the very fact that this resentment exists indicates to me that there is profound unhappiness underneath high-earning people and dissatisfaction with their work, even if they say otherwise. For *if your work were indeed pleasurable*, why wouldn't you pity non-workers, rather than being angry at them? Why wouldn't you recognize that they lack something fun that you have—an enjoyable job, making feelings of pity the obvious response to the non-worker? And why wouldn't you then be indifferent to any money taken from you, rather than feeling it somehow debases your very existence? The very fact of your focus on money, and your anger at others, to me is proof that money has trumped your ability to enjoy your job, and proof, further, of how vital is the need to eliminate money, status, and any extrinsic values as the rewards for work, because they clearly have crowded out your ability to feel unbridled pleasure from your employment. Only changing the meaning of work can rescue you from this overt, or perhaps covert, fundamental dissatisfaction.

And, second, a challenge (to the holdouts): If you truly think my plan is unfair, then perhaps you believe "fairness," rather than "happiness," is the ultimate criterion for Utopia. Good enough. But in that case I urge you not to critique the "unfairness" of my proposal, but to offer your own fairer one, and to further make the case for why your type of fairness trumps happiness as a measure of Utopia. I know you will get into the weeds on fairness over happiness and even more so trying to justify why one person should really get more money than others. Why should a hedge-fund manager be paid more than a teacher, for example? You might argue the case, but you can never fully win such an argument. Philosophy, and math, will bring you back to the only *unassailable* way to distribute society's resources: *They should go to each of us in equal measure.* And that brings you back to my Utopia where equality is a necessary, albeit non-sufficient, criterion for what a good economy should look like.

Objection 5: The technology objection

This objection states that without paid labor, and without the incentives of a market economy, Utopia will not be capable of building the technologies that people today so desire.

I will say, first, that happiness derived from being a creator will trump the current desire to consume. However, I know many people for whom the idea of living in a world that has no iPhone, and no Internet, is unthinkable. The invention of ever-new products is something that truly pleases most of them, and many of my own progressive friends too. So I want to take seriously the issue of how this can continue to occur in Utopia.

Let me begin with a concessionary amendment to my basic proposal. While Utopia must clearly eliminate paid work that could lead to status differences, those who want iPhones or other such products could volunteer their labor time to do whatever jobs might need to be done, and are done today, to support those technological industries. So let's take Apple as an example. Its labor force will likely *grow* in the future, rather than shrink. This is because all the people who want to work for them today, but can't do so, will be able to do so in Utopia because money to hire workers will no longer be a limitation. Anyone willing to work for Apple will be able to do so, unlike today.

What about the people in lower-level assembly jobs—who will do those jobs? This is not a problem unique to Utopia. Workers at Apple's China contractors have quit in past years because they are so unhappy (and suicides at the factories have been a serious problem). Now imagine if there were no market pressures on Apple to please its shareholders by using cheap and desperate workers. Instead, those individuals who enjoy its products could volunteer their time to work in the factories (after they have fulfilled their obligations to Utopia for working to grow food or build housing; the basic subsistence work requirement is obligatory and comes first). They would be working as volunteers, so they could and would leave if conditions were intolerable. Therefore, it's unlikely conditions would remain intolerable. A large part of the creation of intolerable conditions in any factory in the first place is because workers are not there entirely voluntarily. A huge supervisory apparatus is instituted to discipline and punish workers. But this would not be necessary with the Apple enthusiasts working at the company.

Objection 6: The ownership objection

This objection asks: What if there's a new medical treatment? Who gets it? What if there's a great painting produced—who gets to have it?

The elimination of hierarchy is so essential that if there are, in fact, goods or services deemed by everyone to be especially valuable—a new medical procedure to be tried out or a great painting to be hung on one's wall—then they either must be shared publicly if possible (e.g., the painting could be put in a museum or public place) or they must be given to people based upon luck. In the case of a new medical procedure that everyone wants, the only fair solution is to have a lottery to choose who can go first. Some readers might believe that the most moral or meritorious individuals should have first crack at the medical procedure in order to reward them for their morals and good work, but such rewards are exactly the kind of phenomenon Utopia must avoid. Valuing people's creative productions, and total human worth, differentially is anathema to Utopia. If someone's work is better, it *can* receive more attention, and it may please the audience more than someone else's work, but the creator of the good work cannot be rewarded in any other way, since that promotes exogenous motives for creation and work.

As the reader must know by now, equality in the basic guarantee cannot be overridden either. Everyone will get the same amount of food, housing, etc. Does this mean everyone's house will be exactly like everyone else's, or the meals eaten will be the same? No, variety can exist, as long as equality isn't violated. For example,

I might be guaranteed a house requiring X number of hours of labor and Y value of materials, but I could play with the actual house design, as well as adding my own labor to the project. Meals will guarantee basic nutrition, but the foods eaten can vary from person to person, and place to place.

Natural resources, of course, will be collectively owned and collectively available. Natural resources include land and water, as well as anything else central to the production of the basic guarantee. First priority will always go to the production of the basic guarantee. But once those needs have been met, other creators needing access to natural resources for their creations (e.g., if one person wants to build an architectural monument, or if another wants to open a restaurant) will have access to them, using a lottery to preserve equality in this access.

What about other kinds of things: Can you own anything besides a house, and what happens if someone tries to commandeer too many material things—too many clothes, too many shoes, etc., or too many services—excessive numbers of plane flights, etc.? The answer is that there can be some ownership of personal items, although goods deemed desirable will be kept publicly available whenever possible. Also, schools will socialize new values discouraging anyone from accumulating more personal items than they can actually use. Since status will no longer be a central motivation of human desire, I would hypothesize that most cases of excessive accumulation of personal property will end, and the same should be true of excessive use of services. If, however, there is someone who still violates these principles, that person will be persuaded by conflict-resolvers to forego their excessive consumption. If necessary, conflict-resolvers will develop guidelines to limit how many personal items one person may accumulate, so that no one is able to use an accumulated surplus to promote renewed status distinctions, or to use their accumulated surplus as a form of wealth at the expense of others.

Rethinking work

One of the greatest enemies of utopian and progressive thought is the belief that the only state of affairs possible is the present one. "There is no alternative" destroys the possibility of thinking imaginatively.

In the previous sections I have refuted various challenges to the idea that work can be different. This has laid the foundation to describe my proposals about transforming work. But an even more pernicious challenge to my proposal has yet to be confronted and that is to refute the idea that the present nature of work—obligatory and therefore a burden to endured, and only rarely enjoyed—is natural and inevitable.

Nothing could be further from the truth. Therefore, in the following section I will show that work is already tending toward the transformation I propose here. The present state of affairs is not "natural" because, in fact, it is already in the process of changing. While my approach in this book has been to prescribe changes based on what is known about humans and our needs, an added rationale for the proposals in this chapter is that they are already coming about.

After this journey into the future, I will turn to the past and describe something many readers may already know: Our puritanical views of work and our opposition to redistribution are products of history, just as is hierarchy itself. (In fact hierarchy and our views of work are related, not surprisingly.) Because the past was different, the present need not exist in perpetuity, and the difference of the past suggests the possibility for a different future conception of work.

Let's start with the present state of affairs and how it is already beginning a massive, and desirable, transformation.

"We must work to make a living": This present truth will inevitably change

Today most readers share with me the recognition that if we want to survive, we must work. This is literally true for many people, and we believe it must always have been thus. After all, animals need to work to feed themselves. So must we. Work is as natural and inevitable as nature itself.

Or is it? Most of us visit museums and marvel at the arts of the ancients. Many of us read their philosophical tracts, their literature and plays, and more. So we also know that at least some people in ancient times were freed from the burdens of full-time farming. Agriculture, we suspect, provided enough food to feed not only the farmers, but philosophers, rulers, warriors, priests, artisans, and more. When we see the Parthenon or the Coliseum, we know that there must have been enough food to feed those designing and building these monuments. Civilization could not have existed if we were all burdened with the requirements of food procurement.

Our consideration of the ancients should make us realize the beginnings of a truth about work: Not all humans have had to engage in subsistence farming to survive. Even in the past, there have been many times when food surpluses allowed for engagement in other activities, a full-time engagement for many people. And the 20th century, we also know, has seen the greatest worldwide transformation in agriculture yet, allowing in a few decades a majority of people to move off farms into cities and into non-farming occupations, a topic discussed in detail near the start of this chapter.

Those of us growing up in industrial centers, such as my hometown of Detroit, will know too that agriculture is not the only sector producing more with fewer and fewer human labor inputs. The increased mechanization of the auto industry led to dramatic declines in the number employed by that industry, a trend still continuing in industries and services worldwide. As I write this I am looking out at New York's harbor, where ships previously steamed up to Manhattan, so that a multitude of dockworkers could unload them. Today containerized shipping has moved the docks to New Jersey and the vast majority of the dockworkers into unemployment or other jobs. My most vivid impressions of the changes happening in employment came when I graduated from college in the early 1980s. Unable to easily find a job despite a great education from a great university, I ended up becoming, ironically, a "job developer." My task was to find jobs for unemployed youth on the West Side of Chicago, one of the city's poorest areas with an adult unemployment rate in many neighborhoods above 50%. I soon learned that the jobs were gone, many to East Asia of course, but also gone forever due to mechanization. Nothing hammered home this truth to me more vividly than the day a local factory owner told me he'd had 200 full-time adults working in his shampoo factory the previous year, but had let them go because that year a new computerized machine rendered all of them obsolete.

If this trend toward reduced human work inputs continues, might we reach the point where unemployment soars to permanent double-digit levels? Might we even reach a further point, as has already happened in agriculture, where we can produce what we need with only 2–3% of the population working? If it happened on farms, why not in factories, and offices? Work could very well end for most of us. (For a convincing discussion of the possibility of the end of work, see Rifkin 1995).

Some readers will characterize these predictions as doomsday sensationalism on my part. "Don't worry, there will always be enough jobs for most of us." This attempt at reassurance has puzzled me ever since, as a child, I heard liberal politicians suggesting we should create work so that all Americans could work. Why, I wondered then and now, is it bad that most work is done by machines? Why fabricate work for humans? Why not view this condition more correctly as the liberation that it can and should be? After all, wasn't the whole point of industrial capitalism to use machines to produce more goods with less labor than in the past? And doesn't capitalism aim at ever-increasing efficiency (even if it doesn't always achieve it, something I know every time my computer crashes)? After all, if the Chicago shampoo factory owner I met in the 1980s had replaced 200 workers with 200 technicians to run the new machines, he wouldn't have lasted long in business. We shouldn't be surprised that the Industrial Revolution set us off on a path toward producing more and more with less and less human input. That's the goal of capitalism—increased profits through, in large part, greater efficiency. (Saying this in no way denies the immiseration caused by capitalism.)

My point here is simple: Our economy *should* produce more and more unemployment, as machines and other efficiencies reduce human work to a minimum. And, even more, we should not panic at that situation but should celebrate it. If all our needs in the future are met by machines and robots, then doesn't that free humans to pursue philosophy and poetry again, like the ancients who were freed from subsistence farming burdens? If work ends, then we have been massively liberated from a huge obligation and we have been freed from the threat that we must work or die. To me, that is one of the greatest liberations I can imagine because it gives us our lives back so that we can create not because we must do so to avoid perishing from starvation, but because we find joy in creation, and in creating to please other humans.

Let me underscore an obvious point here: The new economy not only should but *will* (fact, not just wish), if it is working properly, end, or at least radically diminish, menial and tedious work. *The people who are living in a fantasy world are those who refuse to accept this obvious and inevitable coming reality, not those of us who see the need to refashion society to accommodate this reality.*

Why is this inevitability not perceived more often, and why, even more import-antly, is its liberatory potential so often overlooked by those on both the left and the right? I don't know the answer for sure but I think so many of us who are scholars, writers, or policymakers take pride in our work, and also accept the notion that not "working" is morally debasing. As a result we have been blinded to the possibility, to the desirability, of a world without work as we know it.

And to the freedom-lover on the right: I've never quite understood why right-wing economists, with a professed reverence for freedom, see freedom as only existing in market capitalism, while viewing any kind of distribution as "unfree" socialism. If I am freed from the obligation to work for others, isn't that a funda-mental freedom? If I am freed from the burdens of making a living, and allowed instead to engage in activities of my own choosing, isn't that a fundamental freedom?

Of course, right-wing thinkers deemphasize the importance of worker freedoms, and put all their eggs in the basket of the freedoms of property. Freedom comes to mean the right to keep as much money as you make, even if others are starving. Not only is this patently unethical, but it is rather ironic. The right-winger can only see capitalism as equivalent to freedom by diminishing the importance of work while exaggerating the importance of income and the consumption that income facilitates. But in industrial capitalism, there is no production of consump-tion items without work. So there is no justification for ignoring freedom at work, while extolling its existence in consumption and earnings. In fact extolling the freedom of income but ignoring the freedom of the process by which one earns it, work, revivifies pre-capitalist aristocratic notions, notions that valorize wealth made without work—inherited wealth, for example—rather than wealth made through work.

And to my fellow leftists: Focusing on rearranging the extrinsic rewards of work (something that is necessary, but is far from sufficient), we leftists fail to discuss how *dehumanizing is the extrinsic rewarding of work itself*, indeed how dehumanizing is any activity that is a means to a dreary monetary or other extrinsic end. I will have more to say about the odiousness of extrinsic means–end rewards in Chapter 6 but three central points must be made here. First, means–end activity denigrates the import-ance of the means. If work is only a means to something, then it has no inherent value—no inherent capacity for producing happiness and well-being apart from the end to which it is tied. Second, a system of extrinsic rewards is bound up with hier-archy since the externality of rewards means rewards can be controlled by others and differentially awarded to us by those others. Intrinsic rewards are not controlled by others, hence they cannot be the basis by which society creates status differences. Finally, and perhaps most importantly, if work is motivated by external rewards—the production of consumer goods, the attainment of material rewards given to us based on the work we do—then work and its creative pleasures are destroyed. The extrinsic goal crowds out intrinsic pleasure, just as the anxiety of pursuing hierarchy crowds out the joys of living.

Rather than rethink the workplace, leftists should rethink work itself, rethink how to make work intrinsically pleasurable. If pleasure is not central to the discussion about work (or about school too), then progressive discussions are not really progressive, because they covertly endorse puritanical views that denigrate pleasure and the happiness that work and study can and should bring. Making work non-obligatory is not sufficient to make it pleasurable, but it is a big start. And any proposal that does not start from this place will be ignoring the real welfare of workers.

The past and views of work

The declining number of jobs in the future is perhaps the strongest argument for my proposal that work in Utopia be made optional and hence pleasurable. But a detour into the history of work also helps denaturalize it, that is, shows that its present nature is not inevitable. For it turns out that even in the past, while there might have been more work to be done, the nature of how work was obligated varied, from being coerced of no one, to being overtly coerced through slavery, to being morally coerced through a new ideology that saw the lazy non-worker as evil and debased—the view most of us, especially in the Anglo-American world, hold today.

If we are to change work, we must change how it is viewed. To do that we must see why it came to be seen as a virtuous burden. Only then can we come to take away the moral valence attached to work and replace it with an association to pleasure and happiness.

A history of work

We can begin our history of work long before the advent of the Industrial Revolution. I will start instead with hunting and gathering peoples, foragers, since all humans lived this way for most of our existence on earth, from our first appearance 200,000 years ago until the invention of agriculture 12,000 years ago.

Foragers did not tolerate coercion of any kind. No leader could make anyone do anything. They could persuade, but not coerce (Lee 1993: 95). Needless to say, work was not coerced. Individual men decided when to work, whether or not to go hunting for example, and women also decided for themselves whether or not they would work. Even parents could not control the labor of their children (Barnard and Woodburn 1991: 18–19). Children did virtually no subsistence labor, or even care of younger children, among the well-studied Kung foragers; Kung parents simply did not require their children to work (Draper 1976: 210–216). Woodburn, based upon his research on the Hadza of Tanzania, likewise says that children did little work and when they worked, it was by their own choice, not commanded or coerced by their parents or anyone else. He, in fact, views the children's autonomy from coercion by elders as socialization into a culture in which no one could be made to work for anyone else for that most essential item: Food (Woodburn 1982: 439–440). In summary, then, the lack of coerced labor is the earliest work condition of humans, and the most fundamental, in many respects.

When did work become coerced? No one knows for sure when and why slavery, the first form of coerced work, emerged, although it most likely arose with the first states, about 6000 years ago. Carneiro (1970), in an intriguing and widely cited theory for the origins of the state and the very beginnings of hierarchy, says that in regions where the population was growing, and where mountains or other natural or social features circumscribed the growing population, war was the only option, since circumscription prevented migration to less densely settled areas. Communities thus began to fight each other over land. Given the circumscription of fighting populations, the vanquished could not flee. They were captured by the victors, becoming the first slaves or at the very least the first populations compelled to give routine tribute (taxes) to their new overlords.

Such compulsory labor arrangements have, of course, been the most common form of compelling people to work for others. In feudal Europe landowners controlled access to land, so that the landless were compelled to work for them. This was common practice in Asia as well, and in the Americas too.

But then a profound transformation happened between the 1600s and the 1800s, beginning first in England and then the United States. This transformation changed the nature of work by changing what compelled it: *Overt coercion by an overlord was replaced by covert coercion by new moral norms promoting work and stigmatizing idleness.* Some might date this transformation to the first Enclosure laws in England, beginning roughly in the 1500s. These laws forced many landless English peasants into towns in search of factory work by creating boundaries, and strict notions of ownership, which enclosed landholders' land. With the formalization of land boundaries, those without land no longer had a place to graze their animals, as they had prior to the Enclosure laws. This led to their destitution, and pushed them into towns in search of work in newly forming factories. This transformation to work as morally coerced, rather than physically coerced, did not reach its full form until the outlawing of slavery in putatively capitalistic America, which only occurred mid-19th century.

In any case the Anglo-American (I call it this because it was in England and the US that the new moral ideology, in conjunction with capitalism, has had its most clear manifestation) transformation brought into existence the urban wage laborer, who worked in factories. The wage laborer came to replace directly coerced forms of labor, such as slavery or serfdom. The most visible manifestation of this transformation was the outlawing of slavery. The notion that someone was required to work for another person was replaced by the notion that everyone is "free." Of course, freedom was actually more ideology than reality, because unless you owned your own house and farm, you still had to work for someone else. The difference was that before the origins of capitalism and industrialization you had to work because of direct coercion. In the 1700s and 1800s the new form coercion took was indirect, and moral. Rather than compel work from slaves, or those deemed to be inherently inferior, the new ideology compelled work by giving it new dignity, and by adding new stigma to idleness and pleasure. This ideology told us: We are all free and equal and we can all work or avoid work. Work is hard and unpleasant yet morally virtuous, while the pleasures of life tempt us to avoid work and engage in sin. So let us all work hard. Those who work the hardest will become wealthy. Those who are lazy will fall into poverty. Thus wealth will reward the morally superior and poverty will punish the morally inferior.

The origins of the view that work ennobles yet requires sacrifice, ascetic discipline, is described in one of the most influential works in all of the social science literature, Max Weber's *The Protestant Ethic and the Spirit of Capitalism* (Weber 1958 [1904–1905]: See especially the final chapter, Chapter 5, for a summary of his views). This is one of my favorite works, because it shows a profound change and how it implicated religion and economics, views of work and sex, pain and pleasure, poverty and wealth. Everything is there. Weber's point is as follows. New Protestant denominations espousing new views of work, such as the Calvinists, arose in Europe beginning in the 16th century. The most well-known group in the Calvinist tradition was the Puritans and they are the ones who are a main focus of Weber's study. Weber shows that the Puritans (he also includes the Quakers, and the views of Benjamin Franklin) adopted new anti-aristocratic views about pleasure and work. English monarchs and nobles, and the society they ruled, viewed aristocrats' recreational and artistic activities—sports, theater, for example—as a mark of their high status and the pleasure from these activities as a sign of their privilege. But the new Protestant sects overturned this view, seeing pleasure and idleness as sinful, and work as ennobling, a "calling" (Weber 1958 [1904–1905]: 166–169). This was the new middle-class creed: Work is virtuous, not stigmatizing. Pleasure is opposed to painful work; indulgent pleasures, especially sex, are sinful. *Work = pain = ennoblement. Art, theater, music, sex, and all pleasures of the flesh = pleasure = sin.* Work and sex were opposed through their connections to opposites, virtuous pain/asceticism versus sinful pleasure. In fact the Puritan cure for sexual temptation was a cold bath, vegetable diet, and hard *work* (Weber 1958 [1904–1905]: 158–159).

Of course, these new views of work led to new views about social class. The poor, who had been seen in Middle Ages Europe as unfortunate but not blameworthy for their poverty, became society's newly reviled class, especially for their alleged laziness (see Weber 1958 [1904–1905]: 163, 177–178). The new views of the English and Americans held that the poor were poor not because they were unlucky, but because they were lazy, and by implication sinful indulgers in the pleasures of the moment. The rich came to be lauded not for their aristocratic heritage but for the hard work, and resistance to momentary pleasures, that their riches were believed to signify. Thus was born that view of the poor which is so familiar to Anglo-American audiences: The poor are poor because it is their own fault. Don't give them charity because that only rewards their sinful idleness and self-indulgence. I might add that along with this view of the poor, and of work, were also born new attitudes toward art and music, as anyone who has gone into a Quaker meeting house, with its lack of music or artistic decoration (ostentation was a sensual pleasure), can attest.

The larger goal of Weber's book is to show how religious views, like those of the Puritans and Quakers, are connected to a new economic form, the rise of capitalism. While Weber acknowledges that the pursuit of wealth is age-old, he argues that Anglo-American capitalism brought about new motives for this pursuit. Wealth was no longer pursued in order for the wealthy to indulge in the pleasures wealth allows. Puritan asceticism precluded this, thus fostering the pursuit of wealth for its own sake, giving work a spiritual validation as a "calling." Wealth was to be saved, and reinvested, not spent. This is, of course, a central principle of capitalism, the notion that wealth should be reinvested to make even more wealth.

Thus, work went from being something that debased one because it was a mark of low status—the sign of the debased slave—to something that ennobled one through the painfulness and sacrifice it was thought to require. Work was no less obligatory than in the past but the nature of the obligations changed. Whereas prior to the Industrial Revolution, workers had been overtly constrained and coerced to work by their bosses, with the origins of capitalism they became nominally free. Many might see this to be an advance for the worker, but we should not overlook the advantages to the boss, who no longer needed to fear conflict with an enslaved worker. The worker was further disempowered from rebelling by the promulgation of the new views, which told the worker that s/he had to work in order to be a good person and that failure was his/her own fault. In reality deprivation continued, as did hierarchy, but it took on new moral justifications. Those who were rich were deservedly so, because they had worked hard to get there. If they hired others, this was also a situation ostensibly freely entered into for everyone, and one affirmed by the assumed moral superiority of the abstemious boss in contrast to the less meritorious and less abstemious worker. Education only further reinforced this view, by giving bosses the diplomas that allegedly showed how hard they had worked when young, as students.

This historical review shows that work need not be thought of as unpleasurable. It is only constructed that way for historical reasons. Its unpleasantness comes from its obligatory nature, and from a society that has, for the last several centuries, come to regard work as something painful but noble, or noble precisely because it is thought to be painful, requiring sacrifice. I like to think of work, following Weber, as having become the Protestant monastery: A site for personal asceticism that is believed to make one virtuous. And I want to undo these notions, by making work truly free, and truly pleasurable. To do this will transform work. And it will transform human activity more generally because, as David Frayne so nicely points out in his social critique of work, the valorization of work in modern society acts to demean human activities that are not work:

> We … may be losing our grip on the criteria that judge an activity to be worthwhile and meaningful, even if it does not contribute to employability or the needs of the economy. Those activities and relationships that cannot be defended in terms of an economic contribution are being devalued and neglected.
>
> *Frayne 2015: 6*

A personal justification for work as pleasure

Let me finish my justification of my proposal on a personal note. Like many other people, I have known far too many people, including myself, who have found it hard, often very hard, to find a job. To me this is such a waste. Consider the following:

- A friend from elementary school, who wanted to be a physicist all his life, went to a good grad school, got a PhD, and couldn't find a job. When he applied at his local store to bag groceries, he was turned down for a job there, since he was told he was too well-educated. I can only imagine how worthy this must have made him feel.
- A PhD anthropologist I know could not find a job, as happens so often in academia, and he ended up flat on his back for several weeks in a row, so depressed that he couldn't get out of bed. He finally found a position as a researcher in a lab, not what he had trained for, but something to help pay the bills. But after doing that for a few weeks, the lab budget was cut and he was let go.
- An artist I know, who has painted all her life because she has enjoyed it, plans to "paint until I croak" because she never earned enough to save up money for her old age. She could find another job, and has done so, as a painting teacher, but she is an adjunct professor and is paid so little that even full-time work brings in wages that put her below the poverty line.
- Not all of my examples are of underemployed academic and cultural elites. In 1983 I was a "job developer" at a social service agency on the West Side of Chicago. My job was to find basic jobs, at fast-food restaurants or supermarkets for example, for unemployed Chicago youth on the city's West Side. What so amazed me about working at this agency, however, was that the hundreds of youth I met were not angry but rather depressed, and in despair. They were bored at home and felt useless. They wanted to do anything in the world just so they could have a sense of personal worth, and a place to go during the day.

  I still remember how overjoyed one young late teens woman was when she found, by herself, a part-time bubble gum factory job out in the suburbs. Even though it would take her two hours of commuting each way on nearly non-existent buses to get to the factory, and she was going to be part-time at minimum wage, she was overjoyed to have a job. The same was true of a young man, for whom I found a job at a hotel, working as a janitor. He was overjoyed. These are, incidentally, the very same people whom President Ronald Reagan was belittling at the time as "welfare cheats." They were all on welfare, but they all wanted to work.

When I tell these stories to people, many are deeply moved, and feel the sense of sadness that I feel about lives wasted. But many people say, "Well, that's life. It is what it is." My response: It may be how things are, but there is no reason they need be this way. The reader will notice that the examples above do not include any from

China. In the 1980s, when I first went to China, every college graduate was guaranteed a job in their field upon graduation. I knew one student who majored in history and ended up working in his hometown's small historical department. His American counterpart at the time would have been unemployed. (Unfortunately, I *do know* his counterpart, someone who is incredibly gifted in the social sciences but who remains unemployed.) The Chinese view of keeping someone like that unemployed is, "What a waste of talent. A smart person like that is needed to build up our country." The Chinese have a different notion of labor than Americans. For capitalist Americans, labor is dispensable. If PhD's drive cabs, that is okay. To the Chinese, labor is a societal and national resource and talented people should be used. Granted, the Chinese in the 1980s assigned college graduates to jobs and then told them they were so valuable to society that they couldn't leave that job for life—nor ever be fired. I knew one teacher who wanted to quit her job to work as a translator in English. She tried being an irresponsible employee at the school where she taught so they would fire her! She kept telling me she hoped to be fired. Nonetheless, the school said it needed her too much, because she was a valuable "experienced teacher." They wouldn't let her quit, nor fire her. This is, of course, a pre-capitalist notion of labor, a feudal one in which the problem of the employer is not what to do with so many talented people but rather how to keep talented people willing to work for you (or, in feudal Europe and elsewhere, compelled to work for you).

I mention the Chinese example not to hold it up as the ideal; binding people to their jobs is sad too, just as sad as not giving them jobs that fit their abilities, the American model. I mention the Chinese example rather to show that there are alternate ways of thinking about people's talents. I do think that the Chinese are better than almost any nationality I know at thinking about how they can use someone's talents. Almost everyone I meet in China begins thinking the moment they realize I am a native English speaker who is fluent in Chinese. They want to "start a business in teaching English, with you as the teacher," or many, many other ventures I could never even dream of. Is this simply a strong entrepreneurial attitude, characteristic of the Chinese? Yes, but it is also an attitude encouraged by the fact that the Chinese, at least in the past, have not been treated as a dispensable commodity if they have something they can do for society. Even though China is several times larger than the US in population, in the very recent past (things are changing more recently) China has tried to use talented people and viewed their talents as a necessary contribution to society.

Eliminating hierarchy through the basic guarantee and freely chosen work

While I'm not proposing 1980s-style Chinese socialism, which has many drawbacks too numerous to describe here, I do think society should value the talents people have, and provide them with jobs in their chosen fields, not compelling them to stay at those jobs as the Chinese might do, but giving them the opportunity to have such jobs, unlike the Americans.

To me, these are basic and intuitive ideas. It's all the more surprising to me, then, how few policymakers, on the right *and* the left, have ever talked about the import-ance of the *enjoyment* of work, just as few policymakers, or any really, ask how school can be made more *enjoyable*. School, like work, is always a means to end—a more productive economy—and never a pleasurable end in itself. I suspect the Protestant work ethic, and its inherent asceticism, has affected most thinkers, both in America and abroad, for whom production of goods and services is the key, rather than worker happiness. The worker becomes a means, with the consumer and consump-tion as ends. It is true that consumerism is not really consistent with the Protestant work ethic, but enjoyment of work is even more antithetical to it, and hence work enjoyment has been overlooked even by many of the thinkers on the left with whom, in other respects, I am in agreement.

My proposal here is thus not only directed at moderates and conservatives. It is a call to leftists as well, whose inherent tendency toward material asceticism and more general ascetic movement discipline (anyone who has been involved in leftist politics will know what I mean—my reference here is to the self-sacrificing ten-dency of many leftists, admirable in some respects but detrimental in a larger sense) vitiates clear thinking about pleasure. It *is* necessary to advocate higher wages and better conditions for workers, but this is not sufficient. We must go much further, advocating that the very *purpose of work* be transformed, so that work becomes an end in itself—the fulfillment of our very human desire to create.

By providing every human with the basic necessities of life, and by making work something that is freely chosen rather than something we do to earn a living, the most fundamental hierarchies of modern society will be eliminated. The basic guarantee ends our obligation to work, and the means by which others can make us work, and make us work at a particular job (one we may not like) in a particular way. It gives us something like the proverbial freedom of the person winning the lottery, who now has the freedom to tell the boss "I don't have to listen to you any-more." But unlike the lottery winner, we do not just go off into consumer oblivion, but continue to work and create, but this time doing it for the pleasure that it brings us and others, our audiences.

The valorizing of work—seen as painful yet virtuous—brings about yet another subtle hierarchy. It is a hierarchy of work over play, and hence of adults over children. By erasing the distinction between work and play, we will also erase the hierarchy of "productive" unfun activity over "*un*productive" pleasur-able activity. This is a fortunate erasure of a very strange dichotomy. How can we pursue happiness when pleasure, that concomitant of happiness, is viewed with suspicion, a suspicion that is a legacy of the Protestant work ethic? How can we be happy if we feel guilt when we enjoy ourselves, guilt that we "ought to be" working? In the new society activities of all kinds that are pleasurable will be merged, so that "work" versus "play" will no longer be a meaningful distinc-tion. Work and study can, and should, become more like play itself. And with the work-versus-play distinction gone, the notion that there are productive and unproductive members of society, adults versus children, will diminish. Children can and should create, so that they will no longer be seen as of lesser importance to society than "productive" adults.

The abolition of meritocracy

Another hierarchy will end: Meritocracy. The question will no longer be raised: "How good is someone at doing something?" This will no longer be a basis, with its implicit connection to the morality of the Protestant work ethic, for judging people. Audiences will still respond to performers, giving positive feedback when they enjoy a good performance. But the emphasis will be on this positive feedback being the only "reward" for a good performance. No exogenous rewards for merit, like money or fame, will exist.

All well and good, I can hear many readers say, but how in the world can we end meritocracy? Will we allow simply anyone to commandeer a high-energy physics lab? What if an amateur wants to do surgery? Should s/he be allowed? Who could take the risk of being that surgeon's patient? And what if a doctor develops a new procedure? Isn't there someone who will use his/her connections to become the first patient? Isn't that a continuation of hierarchy?

These are thorny problems and ones that must be dealt with. Let me address each in turn.

As for thousands of wanna-be physicists or surgeons, I don't see a problem with this! Interest in one's work, rather than merit in doing it, is what will "qualify" one to do it. Meritocracy will be abolished and replaced by the opening up of all jobs and occupations to anyone and everyone—anyone with enough interest to give the occupation a try. This might seem shockingly risky to many readers, especially if we talk about a life-or-death matter like surgery. Can just anyone operate on anyone else? Isn't lengthy training required to do surgery, and shouldn't someone test surgeons—as state licensing boards now do—to make sure they are qualified to operate?

The answer is yes, but the real key is how merit is determined. Let me begin my critique of conventional merit and meritocracy by invoking a scenario I know will be familiar to many American readers. Many of us have gone to a doctor who seems rushed and hurried, more interested in churning us in and out the door than giving us adequate care. The pursuit of money—hierarchy—trumps the doctor's concern for our genuine medical welfare. We often feel that the quality of care we receive is diminished by the doctor's pursuit of high earnings. Sometimes even famous doctors, or famous artists, musicians, writers, etc., turn out to disappoint us too, seeming less competent than they should be, given their renown.

At the very least, these experiences should make us question just how good the current hierarchical system is at determining who should be a doctor or an artist, and who deserves fame for their work. The current system is, in fact, not all that genuinely meritocratic. To begin, we all know that we can sometimes get a good position in society through luck, connections, self-confidence, and other non-merit-related conditions. Even when it comes to merit, merit is really more appropriately characterized as the ability to conform to established colleagues' views and values—those who are the ones determining whether we have merit or not. Conformity to establishment values does not necessarily make one a good doctor or artist, and meritocracies, thus, are often more meritocratic in principle than in reality. In China, with its strong meritocratic tradition (dating back to Confucius, one might argue), I discovered that everyone gave the greatest esteem to older English-language teachers, who could barely speak English, rather than to younger teachers whom I could easily tell were clearly superior. They told me this was a judgment based upon merit, despite the very obvious inferiority of older teachers. When I confronted Chinese friends with my puzzles over their judgment, they told me that the old are better at anything by definition. They thus saw the older teachers as necessarily the best, even though, in reality, they were clearly deficient and less well-qualified than their younger counterparts. (In this specific case older teachers had studied Russian rather than English, so their English-language skills were *clearly* sub-par.) What this shows is the unmeritocratic nature of a famously meritocratic society. China is well-known among social scientists for its long tradition of, and articulation of, meritocratic ideals, and rejection of ascribed status. But what I found in this example, and many others, is that this famously meritocratically principled society is, nonetheless, unable to override the non-meritocratic means by which the putatively meritorious are accorded power.

In a fascinating column *New York Times* columnist Nicholas Kristof begins by asking a poignant question: Ever wonder how financial experts could lead the world over the economic cliff? He describes one tale after another of the lack of merit of those people otherwise deemed famous due to their merits:

> The expert on experts is Philip Tetlock, a professor at the University of California, Berkeley. His 2005 book, "Expert Political Judgment," is based on two decades of tracking some 82,000 predictions by 284 experts. The experts' forecasts were tracked both on the subjects of their specialties and on subjects that they knew little about. The result? The predictions of experts were, on average, only a tiny bit better than random guesses — the equivalent of a chimpanzee throwing darts at a board. "It made virtually no difference whether participants had doctorates, whether they were economists, political scientists, journalists or historians, whether they had policy experience or access to classified information, or whether they had logged many or few years of experience," Mr. Tetlock wrote. Indeed, the only consistent predictor was fame — and it was an inverse relationship. The more famous experts did worse than unknown ones. That had to do with a fault in the media. Talent bookers for television shows and reporters tended to call up experts who provided strong, coherent points of view, who saw things in blacks and whites.
>
> *Kristof 2009*

History is filled with examples of people whose work was not accorded the merit that it deserved. Only decades, or sometimes centuries later, were the merits of their work recognized. (The opposite is also true. There are many composers famous in their day whom most of us have never, and will never, hear of.) Nicolas Slonimsky (2000) has done a great service by collecting scathing reviews of compositions later considered to be wonderful works. I will cite a few examples from his book, in order to show that music critics, major deciders of merit, can be famously wrong about what is good and what is bad:

> We find Beethoven's Ninth Symphony to be precisely one hour and five minutes long; a fearful period indeed, which puts the muscles and lungs of the band, and the patience of the audience to a severe trial (The Harmonicon, London, April 1825).
>
> The merits of Beethoven's Seventh Symphony we have before discussed, and we repeat, that … it is a composition in which the author has indulged a great deal of disagreeable eccentricity ….Altogether, it seems to have been intended as a kind of enigma—we had almost said a hoax (The Harmonicon, London, July 1825).
>
> *Slonimsky 2000: 44*

Beethoven was popular in his day, and many listeners greatly admired his work, but his critics could be unrelenting. The following quote shows that "merit" is often really about conformity: "Beethoven's style … is nothing less than a violation of fundamental laws and of the most elementary rules of harmony … intolerable to anyone who is not completely deprived of the auditory sense" (A. Oulibicheff, *Beethoven, ses critiques et ses glossateurs*, Paris 1857 quoted in Slonimsky 2000: 51).

Beethoven was by no means the only one subject to severe criticism. Tchaikovsky's First Piano Concerto, "like the first pancake, is a flop," wrote one critic (Nicolai Soloviev, *Novoye Vremya*, St Petersburg, November 13, 1875 quoted in Slonimsky 2000: 205). A French critic wrote that Verdi "is a musician of decadence. He has all its defects, the violence of the style, the incoherence of ideas, the crudity of colors, the impropriety of language" (P. Scudo, *Revue des Deux Mondes*, Paris, December 15, 1856 quoted in Slonimsky 2000: 220).

There is no perfect solution to this phenomenon of good works of all kinds being deemed deficient by those granted the power to make this decision, but a good start is to widen access to creative facilities, create new audiences, and steer clear of an emphasis on merit and the inegalitarian conditions it seeks to justify. Let all people have access to the means necessary to create whatever it is that pleases them. Let all people as well have the means to judge each other's creations, or practices. In my medical example let patients and non-patients alike scrutinize (with proper protection of patient confidentiality, of course) diverse medical approaches. Let all of these criticisms, and praise as well, be made public. Subject the critiques themselves to praise and criticism—something that we are reluctant to do today because of the way hierarchy protects the judgements, even when erroneous, of elite critics.

The result will be far more robust genuine thoughtfulness about practitioners and practices than if a few chosen elite individuals, the top of the hierarchy, do the judging. No one will be believed in simply because the establishment says they should be believed in, nor will anyone be disbelieved due to establishment pressures. Instead, all people and all of their ideas will be open to thoughtful scrutiny and debate, and it is on this basis—the essence of genuine science, after all—upon which judgements about medical practices, or symphonic masterpieces, will be made. My proposal here is not only a scientific one but one which I find, surprisingly, echoes some of the conventional beliefs about how capitalism is supposed to work—letting all people produce and all have the right to judge each other's productions. (In capitalism the judgment is made with dollars; we purchase the goods and services of the supposedly meritorious.) The reason this process so often fails in current society is because the means to really evaluate others on our own—to know who is the good doctor, for example—are often kept hidden from us. And a huge industry of advertising interposes itself between us and our own common-sense evaluations, so that we don't trust our common sense, but listen to what the advertiser says or even simply deem a product good because we've heard of it through advertising.

The real key is to democratize and de-hierarchicize criticism of worker-creators and the determination of their works' merits. A further key is that evaluations will be made not in order to reward individual creators with money and status but to esteem and appreciate their individual *creations*, for the pleasure and well-being they bring us. This delegitimizes status-linked money and power and affirms the real reward that humans most genuinely feel: The ability to please and help others. And isn't that what we, as medical or artistic consumers, want most, after all: To be pleased and helped, not to be a spoke in the wheel of a producer's money-making gambit?

So, in a field like medicine, will there be no regulation? There will be, but not the kind of regulation we have today. I will have impartial medical judges—selected by all informed and interested lay persons—deliver verdicts upon various treatment options and their practitioners. These will not be verdicts, however, that have coercive effects. Some consumers, duly informed, can still try treatments or practitioners not sanctioned by the regulators. Further, my proposal, although not directly aimed at increasing transparency and patient education, has that effect, since we can all have access to medical labs, medical lectures, and the open-hypothesis testing that doctors will now conduct in public settings. With money gone as a corrupting motivator for selecting one treatment over another, I have much greater confidence that good medicine will result, and good practice of any and all kinds of work.

More evidence that hierarchy corrupts, rather than confirms, merit

The prime route through which people today are granted the right to practice medicine, and the status that comes with it, is through medical education. The same goes for many, many endeavors. As an educator myself, I am all in favor of more education, but as an educator, I also see how often hierarchy interferes with genuine training/education, hindering rather than promoting creativity, and more generally hindering real learning rather than facilitating it. Let me return to my medical example to explain what I mean, but with a detour about a relevant anthropological concept, rites of passage.

Rites of passage are rituals designed to take a group of individuals from one status, such as the status of "child," and elevate them to a higher status, such as that of "adulthood." Coming-of-age ceremonies are good examples of rites of passage. When looked at from the outside, the things people believe they must do to raise their status seem quite bizarre. In Chapter 2 I described how, in New Guinea, the Sambia believe that a boy cannot become a man unless at age 7–10 years of age he leaves his mother and all other women to live in the male clubhouse for the next 10 years, during which time he cannot have any contact with any woman (even looking at them is forbidden), even his own mother. During this time he undergoes a series of rituals to rid him of feminine contamination, contamination derived from contact with his mother in utero, and from proximity to menstrual blood acquired as boys touch their mothers and other women when young. (Adult men believe sex with their wives can also contaminate them.) Since contamination from the boy's mother and other women resides in his nose, boys are taken by older males into the ritual cult-house and then to the forest to be nosebled, the practice of men putting sharp cane grass up boys' noses to bleed out female contamination. This practice, plus ingestion of semen (through oral sex, a practice described in much greater depth in many of Herdt's other publications), turns boys into men (Herdt 1982).

Now, as an anthropologist, I believe in the integrity of these beliefs, and accord them due respect. But I offer them to the reader because, as a Westerner, it is hard to believe that 10 years of putting sharp cane grass up one's nose can be the essence of turning a boy into an adult male. My skepticism here is relativizing: Our strong belief that much of what we teach to a medical student makes him a better doctor is, likewise, strange, when looked at with the skepticism of the outsider. Take, for example, the common requirement that medical interns and residents work 24 or more hours at a stretch. No one has ever given me a good reason for doing this. In fact there are numerous scary cases of patients who have died at the hands of exhausted medical interns. Clearly, this is not good medicine, nor good medical training. Yet it continues. Why? The answer is simple. Rites of passage all require initiates to undergo some hardship, meted out to them by their superiors, in order to justify their elevation in status. And once they have undergone this hardship, the experience of the hardship itself is often used to justify the newly acquired high status. (As Turner says, "for an individual to go higher on the status ladder, he must go lower than the status ladder," Turner 1977: 170). Fraternity initiations are a prime example. All of the seemingly strange things fraternities make pledges do— the humiliations, and the hardships such as binge drinking or finding your way back to town blindfolded—serve little to no genuine educational or training purpose other than to justify the initiates' status elevation. "I've gone to class in my pyjamas for a week, and have refrained from talking to non-initiates for a week [seclusion and cutting ties with the outside is a common practice in rites of passage] so I'm now worthy of being a member of fraternity X." Or: "I've nose-bled for 10 years so you bet I'm now a real man." We see how funny it seems when we are not involved but consider this: "I've stayed awake for 35 hours, so now I'm worthy of high status and high pay as a doctor." Not too dissimilar. We grant status to doctors, and often believe them, based on training that often has no real relevance to their ability to care for the sick. In fact I would argue that the sadism inherent in any rite of passage teaches precisely the wrong kind of values for those engaged in a profession, such as medicine, that should emphasize care and concern for others. Rites of passage teach one that arbitrary self-sacrifice raises one's status. The emphasis on such arbitrary practices is not one I want any doctor of mine believing in.

And the larger point here relates merit and hierarchy: The rite of passage is really a vehicle to convince everyone, after someone's temporary debasement, that they are worthy of elevation in status and worthy enough to join an elite club. It is a means to build hierarchy, nothing more, nothing less. It is also a means to instill loyalty, as some of my students have often pointed out to me, and blind loyalty to an elite club hampers, rather than fosters, good medicine, or creativity of any type. Rites of passage are symbolic training at best, and they do not offer any real training for the position that is sought after. Hence, the following conclusion about hierarchy's consequences: Hierarchy interferes with real training for merit, by substituting symbolic status elevation in place of genuine education. Thus, the elimination of hierarchy and even meritocracy—which, after all is still a form of hierarchy—will free us to act genuinely meritoriously, rather than making us symbolize our merit through arbitrary pseudo-sadistic practices. The elimination of hierarchy, rather than being anti-meritocratic and leading to less well-trained doctors, fosters better medical education, and better creativity in any type of endeavor, at the same time that it leads to more pleasure in doing medicine. After all, as exogenous motives for creation, like the pursuit of money and fame, are replaced by the desire to help and please others, one's actions will become more sincere and more helpful almost by definition.

My plan: The details

Here are the details of my overall plan for the economy in Utopia. This is both a summary, and a further elaboration, of what is above:

1. *Basic guarantee*: Guarantee basic needs are given to all humans, whether or not they "work." Basic needs should include, but perhaps not be limited to, food, housing, clothing, and health care as well as facilities to create. The basic guarantee is a moral right, and is independent of how much food and housing exists in the world. Although I have argued that food is not in short supply, if it should turn out that I am wrong, then I would advocate population control to bring about the feasibility of the basic guarantee, since it is fundamental and primary. No one should starve, nor otherwise be deprived of the basic necessities to live, because there are too many people.

2. *Minimal work requirement*: In the US a very small percentage of people can produce enough food for the nation's needs, and then some. The same can be true

for the entire world. I have argued this for food but it is likely true for housing too. We can meet our basic needs with little labor.

Thus, either a small number of people working full-time, or most of us working a small number of hours each week, can provide all of our basic needs. The latter is the choice that I propose, for obvious egalitarian reasons. Thus, everyone who is capable should be required to work a small number of hours per week in labor connected to the world's provisioning of basic needs. Other than these hours of work, labor will never be coerced nor required, and work will therefore cease to be "work." Children will be given the option of contributing to the minimal labor requirement when they are old enough to make their desires known. Neither their parents nor anyone else will be allowed to compel or persuade them to work since this would send the wrong message to youth if their parents were allowed to force them to work.

I know there are readers who will be seriously concerned with the details of how we will all contribute to this labor effort. Will all of us go off to the farms for two or three hours each week? How will we get there? etc. These are valid questions, and sometimes thorny ones, but, in the spirit of cooperation I will intentionally leave these details for others to work on. One question I will address is the situation in which some people refuse to carry out their work assignment. See point 8.

3. *Emphasis on work enjoyment*: The central purpose of the economy will be to provide the conditions in which people can work on creative projects that they choose and that they enjoy. The economy will also link creative workers with potential "audiences." Thus, consumption will not end but it will simply no longer be given priority at the expense of worker happiness.

With work and consumption both freely engaged in—unlike today's situation of relatively freely chosen consumption but obligatory work—producers and consumers can come into a truer equilibrium than could ever be achieved with coerced labor. It will be an equilibrium that is social, not purely economic. That is, equilibrium will be based on the notion that the pleasures of the producer and the pleasures of the consumer are both important, and that both should be synergistically reinforcing. This, to me, is equilibrium.

Some readers might ask if allowing people to create at will is simply a magnifying of the current economy, where we can engage in hobbies at will in our spare time. Nothing can be further from the truth. I can't stress enough how damaging I believe it is to creative endeavors today that they are put into competition with paid work. With paid work and hobbies dichotomized, as today, the former becomes serious and necessary, albeit a burden, while the latter lacks affirmation. The individual is torn apart, wanting to engage in creative pleasures, but knowing that the serious business of life is work. This is both a psychological conflict and a very real-life one. We all know how work and other obligations take up more and more of our time, and our serious energy, at the expense of what we really love to do. And the consequences do not just affect producers. Consumers devalue the "amateur" production so that audiences for hobbyists are diminished, while audiences for professional creators are large and attentive. If joyful creativity is to exist, it must have a central role in society and such centrality can only come about by eliminating such creativity's deference to obligatory work. And if such work is to find meaningful audiences, the stamp of approval given to the professional—pay and status—must be eliminated, so that all humans can create and have their creative endeavors attended to.

Finally, I reiterate the above point: The purpose of the economy is not only to free up people to create, but to provide the conditions for creativity and most importantly to provide audiences for individuals' creations. Utopia does not simply throw us all into unemployment to live a life of decadence and inactivity. It maximizes genuine creation and the interaction between creators and their audiences.

4. *End of money and no pay for work; an end to wealth and wealth disparities of all kinds*: Money as we know it will cease to exist because there will be no reason for numerical value to be placed on goods and services. If I produce something, it will have value because I enjoy producing it.

Numerical equivalences through money will not only be unnecessary, but would be destructive to the fundamentals of the system. The idea that the more you enjoy something (a good performer, for example), the more you should *lose* (i.e., pay), will be a thing of the past. Thus, no one will be paid for their work, nor will anyone be paid more than anyone else for any reason whatsoever, because of the work they do, who they are, or whatever. Thus, money and the disparities it so often gives rise to, rich versus poor, will be eliminated.

To the extent that a market is required at all, it will be a market of time and attention, since these are the real limitations on all of us, not those artificial limitations of basic goods and services posited by many mainstream economists, with their ideologically derived belief in scarcity.

In Chapter 1 I discussed a number of ways that audiences can be provided equitably for all people. One of my ideas is that people can trade time spent as audiences: I will listen to your scientific theory if you listen to my composition. Such reciprocity of attention will never be compulsory, although education will help persuade us to engage in such reciprocity, if, in fact, it turns out that we don't establish reciprocal attention markets on our own.

I know the ending of money and traditional markets will be heresy to some economists and readers. But consider the following. The last quarter of 2008 saw the world economy devastated by forces even my economist friends don't fully understand. Any downturn in the business cycle raises the question of why such downturns happen, but the suddenness and magnitude of this downturn really brought into relief the arbitrariness—and needless destructiveness—of downturns. People in December 2008 had the same needs they had in July, before the meltdown, and workers and organizations had the same skills to meet these needs. And yet everything came to a standstill, with tragic, real consequences. *There is absolutely no reason for this.* What I mean is that while there is some cause for the standstill, it is not one having to do with *actual* demand or supply, nor one that can be justified in any other way. If the market can make such depressions happen, so quickly and for no justifiable reason, then isn't there something seriously wrong with the market? Markets are supposed to excel at matching supply and demand. If the very mechanism of the market causes demand and supply to decrease, then the market is no longer an efficient means for matching supply and demand but a factor that distorts both. Clearly, the lesson we should learn from this downturn is an end to fatalistic acceptance of anything that the market god gives, or takes, from us.

One other among many imperfections of the monetary market that needs to be discussed: Many commentators compare the market to a democracy when they claim that people "vote with their dollars." But in a democracy everyone gets one vote. The market at time $t = 0$ may work this way, thus somewhat fairly matching supply and demand, but over time some producers accumulate more money than others. These producers therefore get more than one "vote," and many more "votes" than those who are not wealthy. The market comes to respond to the "demands" of the rich far more than the demands/needs of the poor. This is why fancy jewelry can be sold side-by-side with neighborhoods and people who are literally starving. The market—and money—*distorts* supply and demand in a fundamentally undemocratic way. Utopia, by eliminating this distortion, will help return the economy to a more fair, and also more efficient, system of balancing supply and demand.

I know that some readers will object that with money gone, there will be no way to guarantee that the needs of people can be met. Health care is guaranteed in Utopia and individuals can meet their minimal work requirement by participating in health care. But what if not enough of these people study brain surgery, so there is a deficit of brain surgeons, for example? Or what if everybody wants to volunteer for brain surgery but no one wants to grow food?

The answer is that since a minimal work requirement exists, Utopia's administrators can also reassign people to work in certain areas. If not enough people choose to grow food, the administrators can use a random lottery to assign people to food production for a given period. When their turn is up, new people will be randomly chosen to work in the needed area. And if it is an area, like brain surgery, requiring training, then the administrators will first seek those trained in this area to volunteer their services. If there is still a shortage, administrators will seek volunteers interested in this area to seek training with senior practitioners. Those receiving training, and working in the given short-staffed specialty, will receive credit, against the minimum work requirement, for all hours spent both working and learning, since Utopia will not prioritize work over learning.

Wouldn't it be easier in the above example just to reintroduce money, so that Utopia can pay brain surgeons more than food growers, if there is a shortage of the former? Why can't money or some other extrinsic reward be used to reward good work?

The answer is that any extrinsic reward, just like hierarchy itself, crowds out pleasure. Therefore, it is a central feature of Utopia to eliminate all extrinsic rewards. The minute activity becomes means–end, a means to garner an extrinsic reward that others lack, the whole system is corrupted.

5. *Providing work facilities for everyone*: What if a billion people want to be particle physicists? Who will build all their facilities? What if a billion people all want to travel to distant places to do anthropology? Who will build the planes needed to transport them?

I admit to loving the idea: A billion people who want to be physicists or anthropologists. This is a professor's dream! But lest one accuse me of elitism, I also don't mind the idea of one billion people choosing to sit at home and watch television. And this leads to my first response to the billion physicists problem. My friends always critique my economic proposals by asserting that people are inherently lazy. But they also wonder if everyone can be accommodated as a physicist. Clearly, if both problems are true, they help cancel each other out. The two contentions taken together suggest that, probably, people will work at constructive endeavors despite the laziness fear, but the number of such physicists, and the time they will engage in such work, won't be so extreme as to overwhelm the ability of society to accommodate their work desires.

But even if a billion physicists emerge, it is their right to be physicists under my plan, and they must be accommodated. How can this be done? The solution begins by thinking about what makes anyone today able to be a physicist. Farming and the production of what we need to sustain ourselves does not require all of us to work all of the time. The billion physicists will work a few hours a week on food or housing production, and the rest of the time on physics. All of us will help build the facilities they need during our own compulsory labor time, and we will all labor at our chosen activities during the remainder of our time.

But wouldn't building all those facilities consume all the world's resources and swamp everyone's free time, because we'd all be compelled to be physics reactor-builders for most of our lives? The answer is no, for the following reasons:

a. *Technological efficiencies*: Just like the economy of today, the economy under my plan will use technological efficiencies to reduce the number of hours needing to be spent on non-desirable tasks. Just as robots today decrease the number of hours people must work on assembly lines, the robots of tomorrow will be programmed to build the facilities—be they physics labs or airplanes to carry us to anthropological field sites—to accommodate all of us in our chosen occupations.

b. *Sociological efficiencies*: Even more important, my plan significantly reduces the number of workers needed in today's market economy:

i. There will no longer be huge armies of salespeople and advertising people since selling to others will no longer be a goal of the economy. People will be consumers of whatever creative products make them happy, without the distortions of advertising and marketing. This will free up huge numbers of people, and hours upon hours of labor time.

ii. There will no longer be huge armies of supervisory personnel either, because there will be no need to have someone making sure that we work.

iii. Many of my friends and acquaintances spend enormous amounts of time looking for jobs. Sometimes looking for a satisfying job becomes a full-time job itself. In the new economy this will no longer be necessary. All of those starving writers, spending years trying to get their first novel published, will be able to feed themselves, and have their work attended to, resulting in much more writing and much less time spent trying to get recognized.

iv. Huge efficiencies will be gained by eliminating the conflict between public and private interests. There are so many examples of inefficiency due to this conflict today, it is hard to know which example to cite. One that stands out is General Motors buying up electric streetcar systems in cities throughout the US in the 1940s and 1950s in order to destroy them, so that people would have to buy cars, buses, and gasoline. This may have been good for General Motors but it certainly violated the public interest through its wastefulness. Such inefficiencies will end.

v. In Chapter 7 I will discuss plans to prevent war, and settle disputes without violence and destruction. This will bring about the end to the war economy, something not possible today because of the huge numbers of owners and workers who profit from it. Without a need for this profit, and with politics encouraging an end to war, all of the wastefulness and tragedy of war can be avoided, yielding a huge and very real peace dividend.

vi. At the college where I teach many people spend at least half their time protecting their job turf, and trying to politic their way into higher-paying jobs. Such enormous status-enhancement efforts are tremendously wasteful, as they contribute virtually nothing to the real goals of our college, teaching, and research. An end to hierarchy and the provision of the basic guarantee will end all of this enormous time spent by individuals, and bureaucracies, on preserving and promoting their own existence.

6. *Community of production and consumption*: I realize that not all creators can possibly know their audiences, nor all audiences know the creators of the music, art, sports, literature, or other creations. But to the extent possible, communities of producers and consumers, of performers and audiences, will be fostered.

The creation of communities of production and consumption—I'm using these conventional words interchangeably with "performer/creator" and "audience"—will take the following forms:

a. *Community of performance*: As creative production is magnified, our friends, neighbors, and family will all be creators. We may go to a concert hall as before to hear an anonymous performer, but we may also more frequently than today hear our own acquaintances perform, since so many more of them than at present will be creators, and their creative time will be increased from what it is today (usually nil).But who wants to hear all of our well-meaning but most likely incompetent acquaintances' performances? The answer here is that for music, art, and all other creative endeavors, new values will be promulgated in schools, emphasizing the importance of knowing and caring for the performer, and feeling his/her communication within the full context in which we know her/him. New performance values will also stress sincerity of creation over virtuosity, so that audiences will not feel disappointed and displeased when they hear less-than-virtuous performances by well-meaning performers we may personally know. I suspect many readers will already know how pleasing it can be to hear a performance by someone we know, even if they are not as "great" as a professional unknown performer.

b.   *Community of work*: Today we have a vision of the individual genius scientist, alone in her lab, or the individual artist, working alone on his creations. But in fact all work, especially all good creative work, draws from others' creations for its inspiration. There is nothing novel in this, but what my plan would add is a major magnification of communities of work. Just as new values will encourage new forms of performer/audience interaction, new values will encourage more collective work in general, and more testing of one's creations, be they artistic or scientific, against well-intentioned yet discerning audiences.

I imagine, for example, that those of us who are social science scholars, ironically among the most solitary of researchers in academia at present, will become genuinely social in how we do our research, not just in the nature of our research topics. I will take friends, colleagues, and students with me to the field, contrary to the common practice in anthropology today where we go to the field alone to do our research.

I also imagine that artists, writers, and composers will work on collective projects more than they do today. Physical and biological scientists, who already work together today, will nonetheless be encouraged to share their research with an appreciative audience of interested persons. This will happen much earlier than it does at present—not when one has definitive results for publication but when one has a hypothesis to share with interested lay people, who can help refine the hypothesis through questioning, debate, and constructive criticism.

With individual money and fame no longer a motive, or the motive, for work and creativity, individuals will be far more willing to collaborate.

c.   *Larger-scale connections*: While the small-scale, face-to-face nature of much creation is a virtue, there is a danger of parochialism from small-scale groups. If people do not circulate among different activities and performer groups themselves, then a voluntary process will subsidize individuals and groups to travel to each other's creative venues, so that creators in one area can learn from creators in another.

d.   *Larger-scale projects*: But what about projects that are large in terms of the number of creators needed? Could the pyramids have been built with voluntary labor, and without coercion or hierarchal leaders? This is, indeed, a nagging question and one that, I admit, has puzzled me.

We can begin to think about this issue by asking if there are large-scale creative endeavors that already exist, and that operate without coercion and coercive leaders.

The answer is that there are. One that is quite impressive is the online encyclopedia, Wikipedia. Wikipedia is an encyclopedia written in 287 languages, with over 30 million articles written entirely by volunteers across the globe. Not only is the encyclopedia itself a collaborative project, but each and every article is written by people who usually don't know each other. Someone may write a first draft of an article. Others add their own edits, and all changes, and disputes about changes, are openly tracked and available online. Anyone in the world has access to the system, so anyone can write an article, or edit an article previously written. Voluntary "administrators" oversee the larger process by, for example, blocking editors from outright vandalism of articles, or overseeing edits to particularly contentious articles (Wikipedia n.d.).

But such a messy process must lead to an inferior result, right? I was a major skeptic when I first learned of Wikipedia but I soon became a big supporter of it. The quality of articles, and the range of articles, is definitely more helpful to me than any other major resource I know of, including conventional paper encyclopedias as well as online ones written in the typical way, with paid persons who are supervised by paid professionals. I know many colleagues who feel the same way. And *Nature*, one of the very top science journals, compared 42 articles in Wikipedia to those in *Encyclopedia Britannica*, which is written in the traditional way, and found that the two were comparable in terms of accuracy (Wikipedia n.d.).

We have been led to believe that people will only work when coerced, either as slaves or in return for money. This is wrong. We have been led to believe that large projects, with many workers, cannot be self-organizing and need a system in which someone is the boss. This, too, is wrong, as Wikipedia illustrates. I'm sure that the reader can think of other examples as well.

Of course, it might be the case that some large projects require planning, even planning among volunteers. How will this happen in a democratic way, so that no large-scale planner uses de facto leadership status to accrue de jure hierarchy as a leader? The issue of leadership and planning will be one dealt with at greater length in Chapter 7.

7. *The organization of the "workplace"*: Much utopian writing about work and the workplace has focused on the nature of relations between workers and bosses. A common theme in much of this writing is the importance of worker democracy, where workers have a substantial say themselves in what they work on, and how they do it.

In Utopia, all work will be voluntary, so how will a workplace be organized? Will single individuals be allowed to start businesses? How will they get others to work for them? What if they can't find anyone to help them out?

These are good, and key, questions. First, it is important to say that not everyone with a good idea will necessarily be able to attract as many workers as they might like. Since the goal of all work is enjoyment, no one is compelled to work, nor is there any mechanism to compel people to work for a given person. If I decide I want to make a hand count of all the books in the Library of Congress, and I want ten people to help me do this, people will join me if they find the task rewarding. If not (as I suspect would be the case with counting of books), no one may join me in my task. Given that there *are* projects, such as Wikipedia, which have attracted huge numbers of volunteers, interesting and enjoyable collective projects will flourish; less interesting ones, like my counting example, will not. With the existence of the Internet it should be easy to connect individuals wanting to start a certain project with potential volunteers, who would be interested in working on the project.

Following are the details of how this will work:

a.   Anyone can start a collective project. The first and most important way someone starting a project, an "organizer," can recruit people to their cause is by describing online and in person what they are doing and how they will do it. This way, if the project interests a few people, those individuals may join the project and its organizer.

b.   Interest and the desire to cooperate with others on a mutually interesting project is a far more significant motivator of people than is money, so projects that are interesting should attract interested volunteers.

But will they be volunteers who know anything? What if complete amateurs want to help me with a book on Chinese history? Since the goal of work is interest and enjoyment, the ability of volunteers is far less important than their interest. Besides, humans learn best when they have an interest in something. There's no surprise here; the only thing that is surprising is that this seemingly self-evident truth is so blatantly ignored in workplaces and schools today. The corrosive nature of disinterest is front and center on my mind at the moment, since I am in the midst of correcting midterms for a class which students take as a requirement. The fact that the course is required, and the larger instrumentality of education today, works at cross-purposes to the interest the students might have in the subject. The result is dreadful. Their lack of interest results in inferior performance. Again, this is hardly a novel observation, but one that needs to be asserted and proclaimed nonetheless.

c.   Anyway, teaching and learning are such central pleasures that the workplace can and should make these central. It is only the creation of an artificial dichotomy between school and work, and childhood and adulthood, that sustains our contemporary notion that school is for learning, and the workplace is for displaying what you have learned.

If the workplace is for learning, then the organizer is like the teacher, a person who can train his/her volunteers to have the skills needed to carry out their work. (Of course, I am free to refuse someone whose skills might seem too low and I am definitely free to refuse someone who professes interest in my project, but actually evinces disinterest.) The workplace will thus come to resemble a hybrid between the school and the workplace we know today. The work organizer will recruit volunteers, and will train them. Then the entire group will work together to learn, and to create, with the organizer as a non-coercive facilitator, whose role is to guide others and enlighten them.

d. No doubt, there will still be problems that can occur. For example, what if someone becomes a famous artist, and thus easily attracts volunteers to join his/her project, to the detriment of those less-skilled artists who will be stuck working alone, because they can't attract volunteers to their cause. Doesn't this create a new hierarchy?

Yes, that is certainly possible, and it is a genuine concern. The problem should be alleviated, in part, by diminishing the cult of celebrity, which makes us believe that talent is in short supply, so that everyone flocks toward well-known people. But to further democratize the process, I would have an explicit rule whereby those who have organized projects but found fewer volunteers than others will have their projects placed at the front of the line in whatever media exist to advertise projects to potential volunteers. Displays of workplace results will also be democratized so that those whose work has been ignored will be given a chance to increase their audiences. This will give lesser-known individuals enhanced exposure, thus giving them the opportunity to attract more workers for future endeavors.

And just as there will be a reciprocity of audiences and performers, so will there be a reciprocity of volunteers. That is, a de facto, but not formalized, system of reciprocity will be encouraged, though not coerced, in which I can trade time working on your project for time you spend on mine. This system of reciprocity can also help alleviate work shortages. Someone with many volunteers will have no need to engage in worker reciprocity, but if I am starting a project and am having trouble attracting interested volunteers, then I might seek out others and volunteer on their projects, in return for their volunteering on mine. Of course, to keep work from becoming obligatory, this system of reciprocity will not be one in which I can compel others to work for me just because I worked for them, and any tendency in that regard will be strictly controlled.

Of course, if my work project is not an interesting one, one that does not lead to the enjoyment of my fellow workers, then I will ultimately fail to attract volunteers to my cause. And this is a good thing: In Utopia worker happiness is paramount, so if I can't attract workers, or can't keep them because I am not good to them, or because the work I have them do does not interest them, then I shouldn't attract cooperators, nor be successful in retaining them. In fact my desire to interest others in my project and to keep them on as volunteers will act as an informal check, albeit a potentially powerful one, to make sure that I keep my volunteers doing interesting work, and that I create a work environment that makes them happy.

e. Finally, some readers might say that I'm entrenching a certain neo-capitalist model above, in envisioning single individuals as the organizers of the workplace. What about cooperatively run endeavors?

Yes, such endeavors will definitely exist, and will be encouraged. In fact the reader should read the above sections, where I refer to an "organizer," as being in the plural. That is, an individual or a group of individuals may start a collective project, and recruit others to the project. If it is a group doing the recruiting, various mechanisms will be encouraged to keep the organizing group from becoming too authoritarian. First, the most important check on this process will be the voluntary nature of work. If I am a volunteer on a group project and am not treated well, I am always free to leave, just as I can leave an individual organizer. Second, groups might try rotating leaders, so that no one individual, or no one group, becomes the dominant one. Third, the new values placed on non-authoritarianism, and on non-coercion and compassion, will lead group members to care whether their new worker recruits are happy. That is key.

In fact since worker happiness is so key, Utopia might maintain a research database on different workplace models, and their relationship to worker happiness. Those organizing work projects could freely consult the database, so that they can modify their workplace arrangements, based upon the experience of other happy workplaces, in order to make their own cooperators happy.

8. *What to do if someone refuses to work*: If a specific person refuses to carry out his/her minimal work requirement, or claims to be incapable of working, I do not think there should be any punishment. I think it very unlikely that many people will refuse their work requirements, especially as compassionate and communitarian norms become widespread. As long as the number of work-refusers is small, nothing will be done to them.

I know that many readers may respond that my approach here will encourage laziness or selfishness. This may or may not be true, but even if true, it is a small price to pay in order to preserve the non-coercive nature of the system. Just as many religions believe one cannot be truly moral if one is coerced into moral action, I believe that people cannot be truly cooperative if the cooperative behavior is forced upon them by others. Coerced work, and coerced cooperation, are counterproductive.

But what if large numbers of people refuse their work assignments? In this case Utopia would create a special set-off place where those people could be sent. They would receive enough land so that they could raise their own food by farming but they would no longer receive the basic guarantee or other protections of Utopia (although their children would still receive their own allotment of food). This would not be jail or formal banishment. They could rejoin Utopia if they agreed to carry out their labor obligations, and they could do this rejoining at any time. They could also visit Utopia and Utopians could visit the set-off place. This way the non-coercive nature of Utopia is preserved. Anyone not enjoying it may leave at will.

9. *Progress?*: Will work of any kind accrue to any end benefit, besides pleasing performers and their audiences? Isn't a key human desire to see one's efforts produce a lasting legacy, one that might live beyond one's own lifetime?

This is an intriguing question. Buddhists of various stripes have, of course, criticized the human quest for immortality and fame and one response I might make would be to follow their lead. But if I were really of that frame of mind, I probably wouldn't be writing this book, which seeks to change and perfect society not just for my own benefit but for the benefit of generations to come!

My final answer on these questions is to remain agnostic. For some people, living in the moment of a performance, in Buddhist fashion, is a virtue. This view will certainly gain credence in a society in which work and creation are granted new statuses as ends themselves, rather than means to an end. But at the same time, humans love to learn, and so the culmination of creative activities, progress toward some creative goal, will not be discouraged. In fact I hope that a new synthesis of the Buddhist and Western views of activity will emerge, one that fully recognizes the vitality of the moment, and the value in spontaneous creation and pleasure, while at the same time acknowledging the pleasure felt by individuals and collect- ivities getting better over time, and learning greater skills and knowledge. Today the traditional view of work, as means to an end, prevents such a synthesis because we dichotomize work versus pleasure and play, dividing the pleasures of the moment from the pay-off that happens in the future. But as work and play, and work and pleasure, become one, this dichotomy should, happily, break down, allowing us to feel both the importance of pleasure in the moment as well as the desire to enjoy the longer-term effects of our creative efforts.

10. *Economic development*: There are ways to do things more efficiently and, as noted above, increased efficiency, especially in the provisioning of the basic guarantee, and the provisioning of work facilities, will be pursued.

But since the goal of work is the enjoyment of performers and their audiences, "development" will have a new goal: How can we make communication between scientists and their audiences, among scientists, between musicians and their audiences, etc. more robust, nuanced, meaningful, and honest (hence more enjoy- able)? This is an intriguing question, requiring a detailed response. It is, in fact, the subject of the next chapter.

Bibliography

Barnard, Alan and James Woodburn 1991. Property, power and ideology in hunter-gathering societies: An introduction. Pp. 4–31 in *Hunters and Gatherers, Volume 2: Property, Power and Ideology*. Paperback edition. Tim Ingold, David Riches, and James Woodburn, eds. Oxford: Berg.

Brown, Lester R. 2012. *Full Planet, Empty Plates: The New Geopolitics of Food Scarcity*. New York: Norton.

Carneiro, Robert L. 1970. A theory of the origin of the state. *Science*, 169: 733–738.

Clarke, Lawrence and Clare Bishop 2002. *Farm Power—Present and Future Availability in Developing Countries*. Paper presented at the annual meeting of the American Society of Agricultural Engineers/World Congress of International Commission of Agricultural and Biosystems Engineering (CIGR), Chicago, IL, July 30, 2002. Accessed March 18, 2018 at www.cigrjournal.org/index.php/Ejounral/article/viewFile/335/329.

DESA 2012. *World Urbanization Prospects: The 2011 Revision*. New York: United Nations Department of Economic and Social Affairs, Population Division. Accessed March 18, 2018 at www.un.org/en/development/desa/population/publications/pdf/urbanization/WUP2011_Report.pdf.

—— 2017. *World Population Prospects: The 2017 Revision, Key Findings and Advance Tables*. New York: United Nations Department of Economic and Social Affairs, Population Division. Working Paper No. ESA/P/WP/248. Accessed August 14, 2018 at https://esa.un.org/unpd/wpp/publications/files/wpp2017_keyfindings.pdf.

Dobbs, Taylor 2013. Farms of the future will run on robots and drones. *Nova Next*, July 9, 2013. Accessed March 4, 2014 at www.pbs.org/wgbh/nova/next/tech/farming-with-robotics-automation-and-sensors/.

Draper, Patricia 1976. Social and economic constraints on child life among the !Kung. Pp. 199–217 in *Kalahari Hunter-Gatherers: Studies of the !Kung San and Their Neighbors*. Richard B. Lee and Irven DeVore, eds. Cambridge, MA: Harvard University Press.

FAO 2000. *World-wide Estimates and Projections of the Agricultural Population and Labour Force, 1950–2010*. Rome: Statistical Analysis Service, Statistics Division, Economic and Social Department, FAO of the United Nations. Accessed March 14, 2018 at www.fao-ilo.org/fileadmin/user_upload/fao_ilo/pdf/World-Wide_Estimates__Projections_of_the_Agricultural_Population__Labour_Force_1950-2010__3_.pdf.

—— 2007. *Labour-saving Technologies and Practices: Draught Animal Power and Implements*. Rome: FAO of the United Nations.

—— 2009. *How to Feed the World in 2050*. Rome: FAO of the United Nations. Accessed March 14, 2018 at www.fao.org/fileadmin/templates/wsfs/docs/expert_paper/How_to_Feed_the_World_in_2050.pdf.

—— 2011. *Global Food Losses and Food Waste: Extent, Causes and Prevention*. Rome: FAO of the United Nations. Accessed March 14, 2018 at www.fao.org/docrep/014/mb060e/mb060e00.pdf.

—— 2012. *The State of Food and Agriculture 2012*. Rome: FAO of the United Nations. Accessed March 18, 2018 at www.fao.org/3/a-i3028e.pdf.

—— 2013. *Food Wastage Footprint: Impacts on Natural Resources*. Rome: FAO of the United Nations. Accessed March 14, 2018 at www.fao.org/docrep/018/i3347e/i3347e.pdf.

Foster, Andrew D. and Mark R. Rosenzweig 2010. *Is There Surplus Labor in Rural India?* Paper written for Yale University Economic Growth Center, October 2010. Accessed March 14, 2018 at https://economics.yale.edu/sites/default/files/files/Working-Papers/wp000/ddp0085.pdf.

Frayne, David 2015. *The Refusal of Work: The Theory and Practice of Resistance to Work*. London: Zed Books.

Ganzel, Bill 2006. *Bigger and Better Farm Machines in the 1950s*. Accessed August 14, 2018 at https://livinghistoryfarm.org/farminginthe50s/machines/.

Harvey, Fiona 2014. Robot farmers are the future of agriculture, says government. *Guardian*, January 9, 2014. Accessed March 4, 2014 at www.theguardian.com/environment/2014/jan/09/robots-farm-future.

Herdt, Gilbert H. 1982. Sambia nosebleeding rites and male proximity to women. *Ethos*, 10: 189–231.

IFAD and FAO 2003. *Labour Saving Technologies and Practices for Farming and Household Activities in Eastern and Southern Africa*. Rome: International Fund for Agricultural Development of the United Nations and FAO of the United Nations. Accessed March 14, 2018 at www.hiproweb.org/fileadmin/cdroms/biblio-reference-0912/documents/RRD-23-labour%20saving%20technologies.pdf.

Kristof, Nicholas D. 2009. Learning how to think. *New York Times*, March 26.

Lee, Richard B. 1968. What hunters do for a living, or, how to make out on scarce resources. Pp. 30–48 in *Man the Hunter*. Richard B. Lee and Irven Devore, eds. Chicago: Aldine Publishing.

—— 1993. *The Dobe Ju/'hoansi*, 2nd ed. Fort Worth, TX: Harcourt Brace College Publishers.

Mechanical weed control n.d. In *Wikipedia*. Accessed March 2, 2014 at http://en.wikipedia.org/wiki/Mechanical_weed_control.

Rifkin, Jeremy 1995. *The End of Work: The Decline of the Global Labor Force and the Dawn of the Post-market Era*. New York: G.P. Putnam's Sons.

Rosner, Hillary 2009. The future of farming: Eight solutions for a hungry world. *Popular Science*, 275: 38–44.

Slonimsky, Nicolas 2000. *Lexicon of Musical Invective: Critical Assaults on Composers Since Beethoven's Time*. New York: W.W. Norton.

Turner, Victor 1977. *The Ritual Process: Structure and Anti-structure*. Ithaca, NY: Cornell Paperbacks.

USDA 2005. *The 20th Century Transformation of U.S. Agriculture and Farm Policy*. Economic Information Bulletin No. (EIB-3). Washington, DC: United States Department of Agriculture, Economic Research Service. Accessed March 14, 2018 at www.ers.usda.gov/publications/pub-details/?pubid=44198.

——— 2007. 2007 census of agriculture. Demographics overview in *Fact Sheets: Demographics*. Washington, DC: United States Department of Agriculture. Accessed March 28, 2018 at www.agcensus.usda.gov/Publications/2007/Online_Highlights/Fact_Sheets/Demographics/demographics.pdf.

——— 2016. *Farm Labor*. Washington, DC: United States Department of Agriculture. Accessed March 18, 2018 at www.ers.usda.gov/topics/farm-economy/farm-labor/.

Weber, Max 1958 [1904–1905]. *The Protestant Ethic and the Spirit of Capitalism*. Talcott Parsons, trans. New York: Charles Scribner's Sons.

Wikipedia n.d. Wikipedia. Accessed May 30, 2014 at http://en.wikipedia.org/wiki/Wikipedia.

Woodburn, James 1982. Egalitarian societies. *Man*, 17: 431–451.

World Bank n.d. *Arable Land (% of Land Area)*. Accessed April 2, 2018 at https://data.worldbank.org/indicator/AG.LND.ARBL.ZS?end=2015&start=1998&view=c hart.

5

COMMUNICATING WITH SINCERITY AND COMPASSION

Language is central to life. It is through communication that we construct our relationships, and display love, anger, sadness, hate, and other emotions. It is through language that we express our perceptions about the world, and how we formulate theories that help us explain that world. It is through language that we learn and teach, relate and create.

Given the centrality of language to life and life's pleasures, it is surprising how hard it is to communicate well. Many of us may try our hand at literary, musical, or visual arts but few of us seem capable of making art that is truly pleasing, to others and even to ourselves. Sometimes we communicate in ways that ring hollow, ways that are not pleasing. Yet sometimes those very communications can attract the most attention. Why is this? What kind of communications attract our attention, and what kinds genuinely please us? And why are these not in sync?

Just as hierarchy provides compensatory feelings that are not really satisfying, so too with communication. We often attract attention with communications that are less than truly satisfying. In order to understand why some communications are so popular but not ultimately pleasing, let's look at videos that have garnered huge amounts of attention and analyze why they are so popular. To many readers familiar with popular YouTube videos, it will not be surprising what makes for a video with a huge following and many viewers. While there are many popular video subjects displaying a range of emotions, many of the most commonly forwarded videos, those going "viral," are often humorous videos. And they are often humorous because we witness someone's embarrassment—such as their failure to perform an athletic stunt they are attempting, or their intentionally embarrassing behavior.

Any list of viral videos can provide plenty of examples. One list of top ten viral YouTube videos (with the exception of music videos) (http://stylecaster.com/most-viewed-viral-videos-on-youtube/) includes "The Ultimate Fails Compilation." This popular video, the list's longest video, shows nearly 19 minutes of people in mildly unpleasant and/or embarrassing situations, such as a skateboard jumper whose stunt goes wrong, an officer who loses his hat during a ceremonial shooting by a row of officers, a basketball player whose attempt to make a basket causes the basketball net to come down, a seductive dancer who falls from stage, etc.

"The Evolution of Dance," the second most popular video in the list of ten viral videos, is one that shows a somewhat heavyset dancer, dressed in a T-shirt and blue jeans, smiling as he dances in different styles with a consistent lack of inhibition. He smiles (seeming to laugh as well) as the audience, who are not seen, show their pleasure by cheering. I admit that, to me, it is hard to see the video's appeal but the audience seems to like the quick transition between different styles of dance—all of which seem uninhibited, with none that are restrained. The dancer's willingness to dance without care is a major factor in this video's popularity. (Not all of the top ten videos fit the humorous video/embarrassing moment scenario. The top-ten list includes, for example, Susan Boyle's performance on *Britain's Got Talent*. It might be noted, however, that the most popular video on the list by far, "Charlie Bit Me," is of a toddler bitten by his infant brother. It much more closely resembles videos in which we laugh because of some unexpected yet innocuous hurtful mistake— in this case the child being bitten when he puts his finger in his infant brother's mouth—than to those videos popular due to their intended beauty.)

I want to turn now to a more extended analysis of one of the most popular videos ever on YouTube, to make the case that this video, like other mono-emotional communications, amplifies a singular emotion in a facile way. As such, it lacks nuance, understanding, true compassion, and true intimacy. It can please us only so far, as the many critical comments about it suggest. The reader will most likely know the video to which I refer since it is not only one of the all-time most viewed videos on YouTube, but is a video which has been seen over three *billion* times as of May 2018—not necessarily by three billion people because of repeat viewing, but certainly by a large segment of the world's population. The video is by a South Korean singer named Psy, and it is entitled "Gangnam Style" (www. youtube.com/watch?v=9bZkp7q19f0). It is the first YouTube video that reached one billion views (Gangnam Style n.d.).

I must say that I do not want to see videos such as this disappear; I readily admit seeing some of its charms. But what does disturb me is that this video consumes a great deal of attention at the expense of music and art that is more complex and compassionate and ultimately more robustly pleasing. I will argue below not for an elimination of videos such as this, but for a change in the underlying dynamics of hierarchy and shame that make this video so popular today. And I will argue, above all, that as those dynamics are transformed, this video will lose its immense popularity, even though it may still be well-liked by many for its good humor. It will not disappear, nor should it, but more meaningful communication will no longer be sidelined by it.

When I first looked up the video of "Gangnam Style," I was quite surprised to discover how negative the vast majority of viewers' comments were. If it is so popular and so effective, why are so few willing to proclaim its merits? Why, indeed, are so many viewers quite angry about the video's popularity? Here is a very small sampling of their comments on YouTube:

- "Wtf [what the fuck] almost 2 billion views. I don't get it." [Written when the video was at two billion views.]
- "This song is so fucking retarded no one should ever dance like that."
- "This vid is rubbish why does it get so many views."

I showed the video to one of my college classes. All but one student out of a dozen had seen the video and all said they hated it. (Ironically, I found myself defending the video.) I really do not know why there is so much reluctance to admit to liking it. Perhaps this is a rebellion against the winner-take-all celebrity on a medium, YouTube, that invites everyone to compete democratically for attention. Perhaps there is jealousy at how much money people assume Psy to have made with his video. These sentiments came up in my class discussion, especially anger at lots of money easily and "unfairly" made.

But I do think the negative comments show one thing. Their mono-emotional tone—anger—is unintentionally channeling, hence revealing, the basic mono-emotional nature of the video itself—its appeal to our desire to reduce shame. The video seems to me to succeed because, unlike so many music videos that portray sexy and rich stars, this one features a singer, in this case a Korean man, who is overweight and not particularly attractive but who is, nevertheless, unfazed by the glamourous people and images of wealth that surround him—the icons of Gangnam, a region of Seoul, South Korea known by Koreans for its wealth. In fact, not only is he unfazed, but he does a very silly dance, dancing as if he is riding a horse. And, even more importantly, the glamourous people around him, a young man and a young woman, join in his silly dance. The video is, in part, a critique of wealth and facile sexualized glamor. It is what I will call a "shame catharsis," because it works by making us feel less shame. We see a young man who is a seeming "loser" act in a truly embarrassing way and yet become a winner on his own terms—not by becoming glamorous but by recruiting glamourous wealthy youth to join him in his otherwise embarrassing dance and by poking fun at those with social class and gender pretensions: "[T]his song is actually poking fun at those kinds of people who are trying very hard to be something that they're not," Psy has explained (Gangnam Style n.d.). Thus, the shame we might feel at being unsuccessful in our own work or love lives is partially calmed by seeing someone even more shameful win in life precisely by acting shamefully, and by seeing the wealthy and proud brought low.

"Gangnam Style" also invokes a particular kind of shame-anxiety: The animal-like nature of humans, as evidenced most directly by Psy dancing like a horse. Many of the most popular viral videos follow a similar format. They portray humans acting shamefully, like animals (the very taunt of being like an animal is tantamount to saying one acts without human shame), or animals acting like humans. In the top-ten list referenced above, in fourth place, is a human off camera talking teasingly to a dog, who talks back. A list of the 40 most viral videos for

2013 (https://mashable.com/2013/12/27/viral-videos-2013/#f_e7ST2ffmqI) includes "What Does the Fox Say?" a musical video with a Norwegian band of pop singers singing in English about animal sounds, interspersed with the singers' own somewhat funny and raucous imitations of animal sounds. Toward the end, in what might seem to be the highlight, a standing computer-animated fox sings what seems to be human language nonsense syllables (ba dee bop, etc.). This video now stands at three-quarters of a billion (yes, billion) views on YouTube! "Grumpy Cat Does the Harlem Shake" shows a sleeping cat failing to respond while jazzy music plays. "How Animals Eat Their Food" has two young men sitting at a table eating with soothing music playing in the background. The serenity is disturbed when the one man asks the other: "Wanna see how animals eat their food?" His interpretations disturb the tranquil scene, as he makes raucous noises, movements that crash the table, and repeated plunging of his face into his food as part of his imitations of various animals. Another video is "Taylor Swift Goat Duet" which intersperses Swift's singing with goats screaming. It is interesting to look closely at the way the animal/human divide is portrayed by these popular videos. Unlike, say, Disney movies, which give human personas to animals but do so in a way that is usually endearing, these videos do not calm us by showing human-animals, but intentionally provoke shame, embarrassment, anxiety, and hence laughter and amusement with their portrayal of humans and animals acting like each other.

It is not surprising that shame and humor are connected. Shame is central to much comedy. Many comedians discuss their own embarrassments but in ways that transform the shame into laughter. This is a cross-cultural pattern as well. Shame is every bit as central to, for example, Chinese humor as it is to American humor. But shame also takes a central role in media that do not aim to be humorous. In the 1990s American talk shows followed a common format in which a lower-class person, like a freak at a circus, is put on stage to talk about how they have sex with their multiple wives, or their children, or something else scandalous, after which the audience is allowed to voice their moral outrage and anger. Here we feel a catharsis because the freaks are acting shamefully, and we can shame them and, by implication, say we are better than them because we do not act so shamefully. In the recent decade or more, reality television has also portrayed people's intimate lives in ways that often show them doing things that are shameful. A common dynamic on some of those shows is for the participants to act in shameful situations without showing any apparent shame, providing for us a way to rid ourselves of shame by indulging in it. They do this precisely in order to gain wealth—the low turned high. *Jackass*, a popular MTV show, follows this formula. Young men do embarrassing and even masochistic stunts, putting firecrackers in their anuses, for example, for the amusement of the audience.

Shame or shamelessness? Let me admit here that many of my students have contested my analysis of the shame evident in the above genres by noting that the participants in these shows seem to be shameless. In addition my students tell me the participants or contestants have a chance to become famous, so that riches and renown are their motive, trumping shame. True enough. The contestants may be shameless and that is partly what is therapeutic for the viewer. By watching others acting shamelessly, or being shamed, we feel a catharsis: "They have endured more shame than I ever will." Or: "They are a model for me: they have overcome shame and triumphed in the face of it." Or: "Shame is usually so painful but these people have turned it into a machine that mints money for the television networks and for themselves."

It is true that not all popular media are shame catharses. But like such catharses, many popular media attract our attention when the communications amplify our very easily amplifiable emotions—the negative emotions of fear and anxiety, anger, disgust, and, of course, shame. As I write this, the media have been consumed with telling Americans, literally, that "Western civilization" is being threatened by terrorists in Iraq, and that all of us are vulnerable to Ebola, a deadly virus. Of course, what stories about these issues do is replace the more complex emotions (and, above all, thought and understanding, the kind of thought and understanding that *can* give us pleasure) with easily amplifiable emotions. They also, of course, distract us from the many real threats to our well-being that exist, such as continuing joblessness or genuine health problems such as cancer. To the extent that these stories please us, they might make us respond: "Oh, well, we are all together in the same sinking boat"—a feeling of community that is quite clearly spurious. A spin on this dynamic is that many communications give positive feelings, such as they are, by making us glad that we are *not* sinking in the boat along with other people. My father calls this the "I'm glad it's not me" motivation of so much American local news broadcasts, with their repeated stories of awful local tragedies—people killed in auto accidents, people burned to death in fires. (As an aside I would note that the very ritualistic nature of such news, which runs in the same form night after night, is a strong hint that it is playing on our anxieties. Anxiety drives compulsion and compulsion looks for ritualistic sameness and, frankly, leads to monotony.) The "I'm glad it's not me" dynamic implicates hierarchy quite clearly because these stories appeal to *Schadenfreude*, the sentiment that we should feel better because other people are much less fortunate than we are.

One might argue that these stories do arouse our compassion (although the existence of *Schadenfreude* might suggest otherwise). After all, who can't feel sad hearing a child talk about losing his mother in a massive house fire? But this is compassion that lacks any cognitive understanding and that, in its mono-emotional nature, deprives us of the ability to relate to other humans in all of their complexity, rather than just in the monotonous way: "I'm sorry for your loss." And when we lack complexity of interaction, we become bored and lose interest in our communicants. Moreover, our mono-emotional understanding of them impedes intimacy and sincerity, since these are only possible when we know each other in all of our emotional complexity. True compassionate understanding is not possible with stereotyped singular emotional communication. We are, if I can be a bit colloquial, wired to enjoy communication, but communication that is complex and not mono-emotional.

The negative effects of shame

The divisive dynamics of shame

I now want to return to shame and focus on its dynamics. Shame in communication, and shame more generally, is particularly important to analyze, because it is so central in producing banality and precluding complexity. Other mono-emotional communication does this too, as discussed previously, but I see the challenge to shame as the most central way for communication to be transformed, hence my focus on it in this section. I will discuss how shame impedes communication, real robust communication, and I will discuss shame more generally, apart from communication, before returning to its effects on interaction.

Shame interferes with genuine intimacy and thereby prevents robust communication from taking place. An appeal to our intuition, to start: We all know how shame can affect communication since I think it is a nearly universal human experience to hold back on approaching a person to whom we are attracted, fearing that if they know of our interest in them, they will not requite our strong feelings, leading us to experience the despair and embarrassment of rejection. I know people who have endured painful months of unspoken love for someone else, just because the fear of shame and rejection (not exactly the same, I admit, but closely related) paralyzed them. These types of experiences are the most obvious ways in which shame can inhibit intimacy and quite literally our ability to talk to one another. But there are many other ways in which this happens. Let's consider what shame is and how it operates, so that we can understand its intimacy-inhibiting dynamics more fully.

Shame is thought to be a uniquely human emotion and it is one of the most toxic feelings humans can have. Shame and low self-esteem are directly connected, and thus shame is clearly bound to depression—and to anxiety too, since it is not just shame that affects us but the fear of shame as well. Shame is both *uniquely* human and *universally* human. It is present even among foragers and its role there is to prevent people from engaging openly in selfish acts, such as not sharing food. Humans also have profound shame around sex, and this sex shame is another unique human specialty, according to biologists (Douglas Futuyma, personal communication). Exactly how shame and sex became connected during the evolution of our ancestor hominins, why this connection arose, and when it happened, are all unknown and, ultimately, unknowable questions. Sex is critical to the reproduction of species so it would seem that anything interfering with it must confer a huge advantage to compensate for its potential anti-sex effects (if we are following conventional evolutionary theory). I would offer as a reasonable hypothesis that since shame is so often the enforcer of prosociality among humans, its role in sex must be similar. Shame must have evolved to allow communities of people to control their members. It is a weapon used by society to encourage its members to act prosocially, i.e., for the greater advantage of the group, even if individuals' desires for food and sex are compromised in the process.

My focus here is shame, but a fair question is: How does guilt figure in? Let me take a detour from my discussion of shame to answer this question, since it is hard to discuss the one emotion without a discussion of the other.

Shame and guilt are closely related in that both are unique to humans. Dogs may feel uncomfortable when we rebuke them, in a way that looks like shame to us, but truly ashamed reactions are limited to humans. Part of the evidence for saying this is that dogs, unlike humans, do not blush (Boehm 2012: 20–23). Shame and guilt are called the "social emotions," along with love and empathy, because they are emotions engendered by social interaction. Despite the similarities between shame and guilt, there are, of course, differences. Ruth Benedict, an anthropologist, famously distinguished between them and, more importantly, between societies that use shame for social control, "shame cultures," and those using guilt, "guilt cultures." Benedict's explanation of the distinction appears in her book about Japanese culture, and she describes East Asia as the predominant shame culture area, with the West being the predominant guilt culture area (Benedict 1974: 223). Other anthropologists, including me, have followed her lead (Schoenhals 1993).

But in this chapter I will focus on shame, and on the indictment of its effects. I will do this because, first, shame is strongly felt and strongly present even in cultures which tend, according to Benedict, to rely more on guilt for social control. This is the primary reason for my focus on shame—it is universally felt. In addition, second, shame and guilt are much closer in their dynamics than they often appear. Social analysts hold that the major difference between them is that shame, on the one hand, requires an audience, or at least the fear that there is an audience watching us, who will shame us if we act immorally or incompetently. Guilt, on the other hand, is said to be internal; we can feel it even if no one knows we have acted poorly. But the internal/external distinction is not hard and fast, since shame can be felt, and often is felt, even if no one knows anything about our shameful deeds. This is true, for example, in the realm of sex, where we can feel shame about our desires even if no one knows what it is that we feel. We might feel guilt about such desires too, or an emotion mixing the two, thus suggesting that our lexical distinction between them is imprecise. And if shame can be internal as well as external, the same is true for guilt. We might feel guilt if no one knows what we have done, but others can induce us to feel it by "laying a guilt trip on us," according to common parlance. That is, external knowers of our badness can refer with disdain to what we have done and to its consequences, thereby making us feel guilty. I know that there are lumpers and splitters in this world and the splitters will be unhappy at my conflating shame and guilt here, but I hope that the main point, that shame is ubiquitous even in guilt cultures, will be enough justification for my focus on shame, even if my argument about the similarity between them does not convince the splitters among us.

So, back to shame and my indictment of it: While we might accord shame respect for playing such an important role in promoting human prosociality and selflessness, empathy is an emotion related to shame, another social emotion, as noted above. Empathy can encourage prosociality too, and it does so without the toxic pain of shame. In fact my argument will be that the toxicity of shame, both to individuals and to their connections with each other, is so great that shame should be minimized in Utopia as much as possible, with empathy taking its place. Shame not only adversely affects intimacy but also foments hierarchy. Even though it may have evolved to enforce prosociality (or, at least, it is such a powerful weapon that prosocial-seeking hominins and humans used it, and continue to use it, for this purpose), its side-effects are precisely the opposite of what is intended for it. As I will describe here and again in Chapter 8, since shame does not directly encourage prosociality in the way empathy does, it often leads individuals to create counter-norms and counter-hierarchies in an attempt to dispel shame. The result is that shame can end up creating new hierarchies and new narcissisms, the very things that it was intended to counter.

Empathy, however, works directly on prosociality, free of such side-effects. It establishes real and direct connections between people, since the good we do for someone else redounds to us as well: If we give pleasure to another, that gives us pleasure. Empathy, on the one hand, when operating to its fullest extent, is tanta-mount to love, in that both establish the virtuous cycle of mutual pleasuring. Shame, on the other hand, allows us to feel anything we want toward another, as long as we do not publicly reveal self-interested and even hostile feelings. Thus shame is incap-able of fully establishing the non-zero-sum dynamics that are central in Utopia. It is true that shame encourages some humility in humans, and this humility can be important in encouraging prosociality. It is also true that the vulnerabilities that we feel because of shame can bind people together. But these feelings are always undercut by the possibility that our real feelings will be exposed. Empathy can replace the toxic humility of shame with a softer version, one that encourages us to not place ourselves above others, but to do so because of the feelings we have for them. And empathy, of course, can genuinely connect us to others, because of its centrality to love.

Let me expand on the above summary of shame's effects on intimacy and explore further how it cuts off genuine communication and connection between people. There is, first of all, the very way that shame operates. Shame compels conformity to social convention by inducing a toxic emotion if and when our non-conformity is made public. Thus, shame divides our personas in two. We have a public self, the one vulnerable to shame, and we have our private self, the one we hide from public view.

Which one is the real us? There are anthropologists who point out that many cultures don't care about the beliefs behind actions. If the action is done right, that is what really matters. If you show proper deference, for example, culture X might not care if it is real. The important point is that it be shown. Or in ritual: It is enough to please the gods by conducting the ritual. Your private feelings do not matter.

But the emphasis on sincerity, inner belief, and on the private self over the public self and ritualistic action is not merely a Western notion. China is one of the most shame-based cultures there is; Goffman, writing on face, took China as a major source for his discussion of face, what he called face-work (Goffman 1967). Yet I cannot think of a single one of my friends in China who is not bothered, sometimes traumatically, by the public/private divisiveness of shame. And this is true not only of urbanized Chinese. One of my Han Chinese friends grew up in a village on top of a mountain. He once said that shame paralyzed him, since he feared that people could look right through him, a clear articulation of a typical shame-based anxiety: We fear that the division of public versus private will not hold, and our private bad natures will become known to those around us.

Despite my own writings about the Chinese concept of face, I have had to admit to myself and others that I frequently heard the Chinese criticizing the quest for face. I thought this critique might be a product of contact with the West, and hence most prevalent among Westernized intellectuals, but it turned out that the anti-face values were fascinatingly emblematic of non-elites, a reaction against the elite quest for fame and face in China (Schoenhals 2005). It is true that face-conscious leaders often want ritualistic affirmations of support, ones that seem to ignore private belief. But even face-conscious elites are plagued by a desire to know what others *really* think about them. This is not just true of the high leaders, for whom such knowledge could be useful in squelching dissent. A very common way to know if someone really is loyal to you as a friend, a student, a classmate, or whatever, is if they are willing to tell you what other people around you really think about you, and say behind your back. I suspect that the power of gossip is universal precisely because it derives its power from its ability to undermine the public declarations of affirmation that any of us receives. Gossip is the backstage and often sincere feelings, knowledge of which all of us really crave.

My discussion here is a response to those who would say sincerity is a modern Western virtue only. It is a Chinese virtue too, one confirmed by my research. It is not just a value held by those with time on their hands, time to wonder what others are thinking, as some scholars have suggested. The Yi minority in China are subsistence agriculturists living in the high mountains of southwest China and during my year among them I heard over and over again from the Yi how much they hated the Chinese (the "Han"). When I asked why, the answer was universally the same: "The Chinese are fake and insincere. They will flatter you to your face and yet stab you in the back. We Yi let you know where you really stand."

I have given the Chinese and Yi examples not only to show how widespread is the value for sincerity, but also, more importantly, I have wanted to show the social conditions in which sincerity, versus ritualism and face, are implicated. Ritual is thought by many anthropologists to be opposed to sincerity, since ritual is action in which inner personal belief is unimportant. But rituals are most often employed in order to compel conformity, and they are often used to compel conformity by those in power. I suspect the same is true of most small-scale societies and their rituals. The rituals teach conformity and they often teach values of deference to those in power. One reason that anthropologists so often come away with the belief that other cultures do not care about sincerity is because we spend so much time among the powerful, people for whom ritualistic action supportive of conformity—versus sincerity—is often (but not always) esteemed.

So the divisive nature of shame is cross-culturally recognized as problematic by people in diverse cultures, with a yearning for sincerity also a widespread, and perhaps even universal, virtue. The reason that the dividing of the self by shame is detrimental to intimacy is that we come to feel, as the Yi attitude quoted above about face and shame shows, that our inner self is more real and honest than our outer one. I think we could justifiably argue with this contention, of course, and a good psychologist might tell my traumatized Chinese friend that his public persona is as real, if not more real, than the shameful hidden self that he fears will become exposed. But, nonetheless, when a fundamental category such as the self is divided in half, the way is paved for one half to be seen as more real than the other. And this is what often happens. People around the world come to feel as my Chinese friends do, that their most genuine selves are the hidden ones. And given this feeling, it is not hard to see how shame interferes with intimacy. If our real self is hidden, then who can really know us, and like us? We live in fear that if people knew our private self, or if that self were revealed, we would be unliked, unloved, and cast aside. Our divided self makes us feel as though others cannot really know us. And there is some truth here. What we keep hidden are the very things most troubling to us—our shameful secrets, and our vulnerabilities. If no one around us knows these, they don't really know us, nor can they really sympathize/empathize with us. We are left alone precisely at our most vulnerable points and aloneness exacerbates any negative emotion, especially one as potent as vulnerability. Ultimately, by hiding the things most troubling to us, we not only prevent others from knowing us, but prevent them, as well, from helping us. Ironically, shame has prosocial goals but, like any evolutionary adaptation, it has a strong side-effect: It prevents the mutual helpfulness that is central to prosociality itself.

And even more than this: Although happiness-displaying Americans may find it hard to believe, there are some cultures in which happiness is hidden, along with sadness, since too much public happiness is considered akin to bragging; it is a form of selfishness. By not displaying their greatest pleasures publicly, people in these cultures preclude the sharing of joys that is so important to bringing people together.

Given the trauma of the divided self, it is not surprising that we seek to reveal our inner selves at select times, and make the revelation or confession of shameful secrets a prime basis upon which to enhance the intimacy we feel with others. We only have to consider how central confession is in so many cultural domains—from religion to television—to understand its potency and the relief it can bring. As a gay man I know these feelings all too well. Like every LGBT person, I lived during my early youth with the knowledge that I was different from others because of who I loved. When I finally told someone that I was attracted to men, it was an amazing feeling. Finally, I could be who I am. I'd never have to live with a double self again. This was a huge catharsis.

Or so it seemed at the time. I later came to feel a sense of "now what?" I had told my secrets, but now I had to find the love I really wanted. Telling my secrets, and coming out, allowed me to search for this love, but it did not guarantee that it would be there. My point here is that the shame catharsis from confession is never permanent, and doesn't forge the real intimacy that we actually crave. Moreover, the intimate feelings confession brings between a confessor and confessee are skewed. The intimacy is based only on the revealing of one's vulnerabilities and selfishness. But we are more than just our most negative hidden selves. Thus, we establish bonds based upon, again, a falsehood, or a distortion. Our intimacy becomes one of shared suffering, at the expense of the sharing of the whole range of emotions that we feel.

People trading stories of suffering and vulnerability—sharing suffering—is a powerful theme throughout human history. Turner (1977) discusses the universal tendency for people to bond through shared suffering. A good example is religions, which call upon people to engage in the same sacrifices at the same times—fasting, self-flagellation, etc.—in order to achieve a sense of holiness and also what Turner calls *communitas*, a feeling of belongingness induced by common suffering. One can also see this dynamic at work in everything from natural disasters, which encourage a sense of togetherness lacking during normal times, to fraternity hazings, military boot camps, to the group asceticism of revolutions, and, most tellingly for those of us who teach, the bonding of students, whose favorite topic is to trade stories among a group of peers about how much they are suffering at the hands of their professors. (But what students don't know is that we professors bond by trading stories about how much we are suffering because of them!) There may be genuine unhappiness in schools—I'm sure there is—but there is also a ritualistic aspect to the complaining, parallel to a rite of passage. As with a rite of passage, everyone must not only suffer but also be seen to be suffering, so that no one can easily sit out the trading of stories of hardship. I've asked students to challenge the bonding-as-suffering dynamic by having them claim to be stress-free and happy about their classes. Students easily get the point: The non-sufferers are putting themselves above others, at the expense of group bonding, and my students engaging in the experiment return with tales about how hard it is to be happy in a group of complaining students. (And, yes, there is another motive to the assignment, but I'll keep that a secret!)

As Turner so astutely points out, the dynamics of rites of passage and their analogues implicate equality and hierarchy. In most rites of passage, and in religions too, you grind yourself down with a group of others, in order to gain equality and brotherhood or sisterhood with them, and a simultaneous show of self-debasement before your superiors: Military officers, full-fledged fraternity members, or a holy being. How unfortunate that humans need to suffer to bond; it almost seems masochistic. With diminished shame, and a society that encourages egalitarianism achieved without martyrdom, bonding and intimacy can occur through happiness, as well as through sadness. And happiness, as well as suffering, can be more robustly shared as a result.

And this leads back to my discussion above, in which I critique the media obsession with showing people in shameful situations. The problem with these portrayals is parallel to the problems with confession and shared suffering. A bond between the shamed person and others is forged based upon a limited set of emotions—all negative, shameful ones, and all vulnerabilities that are not actually overcome, even if they are made temporarily less intense by being shared with others. The media shame portrayals, like confession more generally, make a pretense of telling us some-thing intimate, and they make a pretense of forging a bond between us as audience and those doing the shameful telling, but ultimately the intimacy is as skewed as is the public face we put forth toward the world, the revelations being simply the inverse of that face.

Further, the dynamics between the teller and audience are distorted. In many of the media portrayals people intentionally engage in shameful acts for public con-sumption. I think one can easily intuit the motivation here: "If I shame myself and display it to the world, no one can harm me by shaming me, because I've already done it to myself." There is a parallel here to the logic of masochism, a taking con-trol of pain by inflicting it on oneself, and a celebrating of self-suffering (more reli-gious analogues here, of course). Thus, one is not really being humble or vulnerable. There is a conflicted dynamic, in which one goes higher by going lower, gaining attention by doing that for which people normally are ostracized. I don't want to minimize how therapeutic this might be for many people, but if genuine attention to others is a key to prosociality, then acting shamelessly can hardly be said to be such prosociality. In many ways it is just the opposite: More narcissism. And the reactions of the audience to shame are likewise antithetical to genuine intimacy. We may feel our own sense of relief but it is a relief that has at least the patina of *Schadenfreude* to it: "I'm so glad that my life and my actions are not as shameful, and not revealed as widely, as these shameless people." Both sides, teller and audi-ence, seek redemption through self-elevation, obviously not a basis for a genuine connection or empathy between people and, ironically, a hidden and insidious div-isiveness that replaces the divided self with a self still divided from others.

The insidious tragedy of "going through the motions"

Before giving a series of solutions to shame-based insincerity, I want to consider one related phenomenon. I confess that lately I've been nearly obsessed with the idea that I must write clearly about the dangers of insincerity, and more particu-larly my conviction that "going through the motions"—that is, acting superficially, without feeling and deep sincerity—is a central cause of human misery. It might seem harmless enough when store cashiers in America thank us for shopping at their businesses and wish us a nice day. We know it's insincere, a going through of a ritualistic politeness routine. But what about going through the motions in school? To me, it seems an unspeakable tragedy that the most central human pleasure—the desire to learn—is corrupted by "going through the motions." In the case of school most young people learn to bury their early childhood curiosity about the world lest their peers ostracize them for showing such curiosity (something especially true in America but also in many, many other cultures). Instead, youth learn that the only "valid" and socially acceptable response is to act and react to the extrinsic hierarchical motives of our hierarchical society—grades and the promise of a good job if you do well in school. I'm convinced that we all still *really* want to learn for pleasure. After all, the desire to know is the real pleasure versus the seductive yet false "pleasures" of hierarchy. Deep down our sincere motivation persists, but it is obscured by "going through the motions" of learning and teaching in schools where the passion to know the world has been pushed aside by money and status imperatives that make us act insincerely. Hence passionlessness and falsity pervade institutions ostensibly dedicated to the passionate search for truth, institutions that *could* make us happy if they really freed us to enjoy such truth-seeking, openly and with sincerity.

Equally tragic is going through the motions in love and sex. For those of us who are gay, this is a commonly experienced situation, as LGBT peoples prior to coming out often force themselves to perform love and sex acts based not on real desire but on a compulsion to follow society's sex and gender dictates (i.e., to feel and display heterosexual love and desire). To me, coerced sex of any kind is close to rape, even when the coercion is by societal dictates. I know many conservatives, and even moderates, will disagree with my claim that social conformity in love and sex is a lot like rape, but there is no denying the profound unhappiness caused when gay people form relationships based on falsity.

Less dramatic, perhaps, but no less tragic, is anyone who foregoes real, sincere romantic and sexual desire in order to fake it, so as to gain the acceptance of peers, or religious institutions, or their families, and/or the wider society. When a man goes through the motions to "score" with a woman, this is acting falsely, in denial of real emotion. The falsity is hence a source of ultimate, albeit insidious, unhappiness and depression. So too a woman who must manipulate her actions to appear a certain way (godlike in her purity), a way that is false to how she really feels (a human with desire).

I admit that there is a potent desire to belong, to belong to a clique, a group, or to the society of which you are part. And one of the prime ways in which we achieve such belonging is by "scoring" (I use the crude word intentionally), by making our outer persona one that will gain us acceptance due to the sexual and romantic prowess we display. We gain such acceptance by the group even if our inner persona is secretly bored, restless, and unfulfilled.

But just as the quest to be top in the hierarchy is motivated by potent but ultimately unfulfilling desires—the desire to achieve the illusory security that a top status promises us—so too with going through the motions. Ultimately, we must always fear that our inner self will be revealed, that deception once revealed will shame us, and that our fundamental real aloneness from the group will come crashing through. This description should sound familiar: It is the fear of shame.

The shame of not belonging, of being outcaste if one does not achieve what others achieve in the realm of sex and romance is a feeling I'm sure will be familiar to a majority of readers. But let me explain exactly how shame works its effects, and in so doing promotes falsity and insincerity—and new hierarchy too—at the expense of genuine intimacy. I said above that shame evolved to compel individuals to conform to group norms such as refraining from too much self-indulgence in food at the expense of others, or too open an indulgence in sex, also a fundamental group antagonist. But as I will explain momentarily, the divisiveness of shame creates conflicting feelings and these, in turn, give birth to conflicting groups. In the case of sex, the overt large group of society is opposed by smaller groups—think religion/parents versus adolescent peer groups here. And these opposing groups build their group solidarity precisely by opposing society as a whole, and its norms. Youth peer groups, for example, take the sex-refraining norms of society and turn them on their head. They define non-engagement in sex as a failure of youth norms, and indulgence in it to be the badge of status by which one affirms allegiance to the peer group and, most importantly, the means by which the group lets one in. Some readers might think that I would see as important youth rebellion, but the problem with the rebellion by youth against shame is that it is not a rebellion that challenges shame and intimacy directly. Rather, it simply negates everything that parents and society affirm, thereby ultimately working within the terms of the system itself, rather than genuinely changing those terms. And so just as the shame induced by the larger group and its anti-sex norms can prevent intimacy, so do the norms of the opposition peer group. The overt norms say "Don't have sex. Don't fall in love." The peer group norms say "Show us you belong by having sex, and displaying love." In both cases individuals must present a false public self in order to satisfy the group.

I hope I don't have too much explaining to do to convince any reader how odious this is. Love and sex are among the most fundamentally (potentially) intimate things we do, but by turning them into acts that are symbolic of allegiance to a group, and by having the group hold a gun to our head—the threat of ostracism—if we do not display our status symbols publicly, well, you get the picture: Groups compel love and sex, and compulsion is antithetical to real intimacy. Further both the larger and the smaller groups make an end run around pleasure itself, by putting the emphasis instead on what we publicly display as most important, rather than how we feel, or the pleasure we bring to others. And, of course, both groups introduce hierarchy into the equation, by making our overt actions a means by which we can climb high enough to be worthy of group membership. Thus public displays of status symbols, display of our love and sexuality, keep us from being pushed out by the group, thereby preventing us from falling down the hierarchical ladder into the position of loser and outcast. Shame, potentially a humility-inducing emotion and a prosocial one as well, foments hierarchy, a narcissistic competition for status through sex, and the exclusions and exclusiveness—ostracism, caste, and outcasting—that result from these dynamics. Once again we have hierarchy crowding out pleasure, and hierarchy and group symbolism overriding sincere pleasure-giving between individuals in the realm of love and sex, ironically the realm most potentially capable of leading to intimacy and pleasure. Truly tragic.

I've actually thought most about the emptiness of going through the motions while in musical rehearsals in the many choirs to which I've belonged. So many well-trained and well-intentioned musicians will sing or play precisely as the composer's score, or the conductor, tells them to perform, getting loud if they are told to be loud, and soft when they are told to be soft. These seemingly fine musicians do so, however, without any understanding of why they are being asked to get loud or soft. They only respond to the desire to please an authority figure, be it the composer or conductor, rather than to please themselves by conveying deeply felt emotions to an audience. I'm convinced that even untrained audiences know when a player is just going through the motions, just reading the music like a recipe followed blindly. We may marvel at the technique with which the player is loyal to the score or the conductor, and we marvel too when fingers fly fast over the keyboard. But ultimately we feel the lack of passion, the lack of emotions, and the lack of fundamental profundity. We are left cold and empty, even when we don't fully understand why we feel this way.

To summarize: The fear that we will not conform to an authority's wishes (the conductor) or that we will fail to do what is necessary to maintain our group membership (the peer group, or groups found at school) is the fear of shame. The group and authority figures both pressure us to conform by threatening shame if we fail. And as shame works on the public display and ignores the private self, we interact, and communicate, based not on what we feel internally, and sincerely, but what we think will most conspicuously symbolize our merits, and our allegiance to the authority of the superior or the group. We engage in potentially pleasure-inducing and intimacy-creating activities—learning, love, art—but we do so symbolically, publicly, and falsely, while pushing aside our very real desire to please others. Empathy and sincerity are sacrificed in order that we may gain acceptance. This is "going through the motions" and its fundamental dishonesty leads to cynicism and gaminess that destroys, albeit insidiously, any real chance of sympathetic communication with others and the joy that brings.

Shame and its dichotomies

I have already exposed much of shame's toxicities, but there are additional adverse consequences of shame that need explication. Shame not only divides us into a public and a private self, precluding honest communication, but also it tends to be divisive of all of our emotions.

Shame produces its effects upon love and sex, and other emotions in which selfishness and selflessness are implicated, in ways that are not always emotionally healthy. For starters, shame presumes a division between ourselves and others. Rather than promoting a generalized care for all conspecifics, ourselves included, shame makes us yield to others at the expense of ourselves. In the extreme this can lead to martyrdom or even its inverse, narcissism. Because shame does not challenge the self/other distinction, it actually ends up strengthening that distinction, because it adds its potency to it. Not only does shame reify self-versus-other, but us-versus-them as well. Among the Chinese, for example, you share pride and shame with your own group, your own family, your own region, and ultimately your own nation. And pride and shame are given to you by those *outside* your own group, those witnessing your goodness or badness. One could say there is a seed of something positive here, since shame connects the Chinese to the larger world outside their own groups. But as anyone who knows China well can attest, the shame and face dynamics may serve to incite attention to the outsider, and to the foreigner, but this happens in a way in which the Chinese/foreigner distinction is maintained. And it is maintained, just as it is partially created in the first place, by shame. Thus shame at once links the Chinese insiders to outsiders, and yet does so in a way in which the insider/outsider distinction persists. This results in conflictual feelings. In the case of China, the foreigner is both loved and hated, an object to become close to but one ultimately from whom one maintains distance. The conflictual feelings here are especially pronounced among the Chinese but they are no less common among the rest of humanity. The I/you and us/them conflicts engendered by shame keep humans in all contemporary societies from experiencing a strong sense of connection to others, and the joy that would go with it.

Shame creates other dichotomies that are sources of conflicts. It foments a good/bad distinction but one which, like the us/them distinction, is full of confusion. While shame is attached most paradigmatically to human sexuality, sex often becomes for many, ironically, a time to rid oneself of shame, to invert sexual shame into shamelessness, as when people deliberately degrade themselves in sex in order to overcome shame. The problem is that the overcoming of shame through shamelessness is superficial and compensatory and, like many human inversions, ends up ironically confirming the very thing that it challenges, all while eliding the compassion and humanity that would be the real challenge to shame. In Chapter 2 I have discussed the attraction in sex to the "bad" boy or girl. This attraction derives from the dichotomies and contradictions of shame. That which is publicly declared as good becomes considered "bad" and that which is publicly bad becomes good and attractive in the less public realm of peers and sexual desire. To handle the contradictions that result, some people engage in sex dissociatively, as an escape, a kind of escapism that becomes a pattern of living more generally. This is a major problem. And equally problematic from a psychological sense is that the good/bad duality forces us into polarized categories, ones that ultimately dehumanize us. One person is the super-sexed man or woman, or the unbelievably hot "sex god." The other is the whore or the loser—the anti-Christ. The polarity creates hierarchy. And partial reversal of the hierarchy by deeming the "bad" to be hot and good does nothing to challenge the fundamental inequalities produced by the good/bad division. It simply makes us embrace the other pole, in a way confusing and damaging to our psychic sense of integrity, all while reaffirming the very polarity and hierarchy that should be challenged.

While we all develop strategies for dealing with our dual selves, the ubiquity of religious conceptions of dueling forces of good and evil suggests that the conflict is never resolved. Far from it: The pervasiveness of the images of good and evil and light and dark, and their overwhelming potency, is testimony to the heavy angst that a divided self brings upon us. And those familiar with Levi-Strauss and structuralism will know that the power of myth, according to the structuralists, is that it tells a tale in which fundamental opposites are reconciled, thus providing further support for the contention that the dichotomies are fundamentally disturbing, and that there is a powerful yearning to overcome them.

A number of other dichotomies that I indict in this book have their roots in the dynamics of shame and guilt. Transforming shame and guilt may not be sufficient to end these conflicts but it is a beginning. One that is especially vexing is the division between pleasure and work. Work has not always been considered good but it came to be seen that way by Anglo-American Protestants such as the Puritans and Quakers, who were simultaneously rebuking the pleasure and work-free lives of the aristocrats as well as the presumed idleness of the poor. As work came to be seen as good and noble, it was opposed to anything sensual or sexual, now seen as bad. The reason that shame is implicated in the work/pleasure dichotomy is that the dichotomy is a moral one and, like the good/bad dichotomy more generally, it is founded on shame and guilt. Shame attaches to those whose pleasurable indulgences become known. Pride, the opposite of shame, attaches to those who are conspicuously hard-working. A series of allied dichotomies results: Future orientation versus present orientation (akin to work versus pleasure), school versus pleasure and *play*, selflessness versus selfishness, and many more.

The reasons for indicting these dichotomies—and for my ultimate goal of justifying the need to transform shame in Utopia—are as follows:

1.   The dichotomies create social constructions that deny pleasure in certain realms. As I will discuss further in Chapter 6, school and learning can and should be the ultimate pleasure. But the existence of the Puritanical ethic constrains students from feeling this way, and even involves them in policing the ethic themselves, by awarding the greatest stigma to the person who finds pleasure in school (the "nerd" stigma). The dichotomies thus serve to make us deny a fundamental pleasure to ourselves and others around us.

2.   The dichotomies give us inner conflict: Should we put off pleasure for future gain, or should we indulge in present pleasures? Whether we do one, or the other, or even both, we can never be truly fulfilled. If we seek pleasure, we feel guilt and shame. If we work, we feel pain, but also pride and an absence of guilt. We can't win nor can we be truly free, because these constructed dichotomies constrain all our actions.

Why can't we feel the pleasures of love and sex and the pleasures of creativity—work—simultaneously, rather than experiencing them as forces pulling us in opposite directions? If we could do so, we would not feel a conflict between life in the present and life in the future, and we could feel the pleasures of love and work simultaneously—restoring to our lives a holistic fullness that it lacks today.

3.   The dichotomies lead to social conflict as well: Individuals and groups rebel against public, overt cultural norms as described earlier. The conflicts this causes between the rebels and their parents, and the adult world, are all too well-known.

Some readers will rightly question whether the conflicts I am describing are only products of a certain place and time—industrialized, urbanized society. While it is true that society has a role in determining what causes shame and what leads to pride, it is also true that shame and pride are universals, and that shame, to one degree or another, is most implicated in sex while pride is most paradigmatically implicated in its opposites: Abstinence and self-sacrifice (sacrifice through work, sacrifice for family, sacrifice for the protection of one's community or nation, etc.). We see this in all the major religions, which oppose the carnal to the spiritual. We see it too in attitudes to work, even among non-Western non-industrialized peoples. On Goodenough Island, off the eastern coast of New Guinea, there is a society of people whose lives are non-urban and non-industrial, yet they also have strong concepts of shame connected to sex, which is opposed to work. Their views are amazingly similar to the Puritans. Goodenough Islanders see sexual indulgence as in conflict with the hard work of gardening and a speaker might address his rival with the following insult:

> You think we are birds or dogs and can't plant food? You think we remain idle all our lives? Well, we'll show you! You'll see who can plant better! We don't spend all our time copulating with our wives like you!
>
> *Quoted in Young 1971: 198–199*

What follows is a competitive exchange of food in which the one giving the most food shames his rival and opponent. My point, again, is to show that shame, especially sexual shame, is not only a product of "modern" societies, or of "modernity."

It is true that there may be some cultural and social concomitants to the production of these dichotomies. After all, that is the theme of this book: Society matters. I do admit that patriarchal societies are much more likely to have heavy-handed shame attached to sex for at least some members of the community—usually women. It is true, too, that earlier religions in many agricultural societies celebrated fertility as akin to holiness, thus connecting sex and goodness.

But even though the extent to which shame is attached to sex varies from society to society, shame is a universal human emotion, as is pride, and no people can be free of shame and pride. And since shame and pride force us to divide a public versus a private self, this distinction must be overcome. By overcoming shame and its dichotomies we can temper the angst that it creates, the separation from other humans that it causes, and most importantly the lack of true communication and understanding between us that is its most unfortunate consequence.

Solutions

How can we overcome the insincerity, falsity, and cynicism induced by shame? How can we promote interaction and communication that is genuinely intimate, that genuinely connects people in a way that establishes empathy between them? If we do this, if we can promote genuine communication, then we have a hope for such empathy, because with genuine communication we can have true mutual understanding of each other, in all of our variegated emotions and feelings. Such understanding itself, to me, is both a pleasure and an ultimate form of community and solidarity between people. With genuine empathy between people, there is a chance, a very strong chance, that the hurtful actions of groups can be overcome as individuals within them challenge those who seek to hurt others, with helpfulness between people maximized. And this is the *real* prosociality toward which all of us should aim.

1. Minimizing shame

A fundamental step in promoting deep sincerity and intimacy between people is to do as much as possible to minimize shame. How do we transform shame? Should it be ended? If so, what replaces it? These are such huge questions that I will not give a list of how change in this area can be made. Instead, I will narrate how the ending of hierarchy and all of the methods for encouraging non-zero-sum compassion will, in turn, transform the toxic dynamics of shame, while preserving the attention to others and the basic selflessness that is the good component of shame.

To begin: Shame rests upon a distinction between ourselves and everyone else in society. It undoubtedly evolved among humans, or our earlier hominin ancestors, to encourage cooperation by engendering feelings of embarrassment at any display of our selfishness. Good enough—this was a major evolutionary advance. But wouldn't it be better if, for the purposes of prosociality, society didn't counsel self-abnegation and the maintenance of a distinction between ourselves versus others but instead promoted a notion of equality: All people should be treated equally, and that includes ourselves. We should be good to all people, ourselves included, but no better to ourselves, or to any other group, than we are to all people. This is the morality of Utopia. It is not a morality based upon self-sacrifice for others but rather an exhortation to treat all people, self and others, the same, with goodness. This morality has transformative implications for shame and pride, since both emotions are founded on a self/other distinction, and both traffic in the language of hierarchy.

Furthermore, the dynamics of groups and our obligations to them are central to shame and guilt. In shame we are threatened, above all, with loss of esteem and, in the extreme, with ostracism from the group to which we belong. With guilt we imagine we might lose the love of others, because of what we have done. On the guilt front Utopia will work to preserve and strengthen the love between people, by encouraging understanding and empathy. Where love is imperiled, courts will step in, as I will describe in Chapter 7. This should help with guilt.

As for shame, in Chapter 3 I described a variety of mechanisms to challenge ostracism, and to change the nature of groups. If groups operate in a non-invidious manner, encouraging all to join them at will, then the threat of expelling one who doesn't belong, one who doesn't live up to cultural norms, is likewise challenged. This will also diminish the phenomenon of going through the motions. When groups are tightly bounded, and shame present (shame and bounded groups go together, since intense shame is engendered only when groups are bound tightly enough so that expulsion from a group is hurtful, and when other groups are so impenetrable that joining an alternate group is not an easy option), then there is a tendency for people to signal their affiliation to the group symbolically and ritualistically, as I've described. Status symbols work the same way. Status objects that can be possessed in an observable way mark one as a person worthy of group membership. Failing at an action or the pretense of an action (I include as an action the acquisition of status objects) that the group deems to mark your worthiness for membership in the group, leads the failing individual to feel shame and alienation from the group. This whole dynamic is particularly odious because real pleasure, which is not easily observable to the group *(or at least not observable in the absence of real sincerity and empathetic understanding)*, and which is not clearly status-marking, is downplayed, and its place is taken by symbolic action to demonstrate one's allegiance to an invidious and hierarchicizing group.

The transformation of groups will end shame. It will likewise inoculate us against the seductiveness of marking our membership in groups ritualistically, in a pleasure-denying manner that leads to the tragedy of living life robotically and without care for self and others.

A new sexuality, one that privileges goodness and compassion over badness or narrow conformity to compassionless virtues, will do perhaps the most to undercut shame. So too will the mechanisms described in Chapter 3 for moderating the conflict between love of natal family and romantic love, the natal/affinal conflicts that are such a human universal. With this primordial conflict blunted, we need no longer have the feeling that we must maintain a double self, a public self that shows duty to family versus a private self that indulges in sex and love at the expense of the group and the natal family. We can be both loving and compassionate to ourselves and others at the same time. In fact, doing so is humans' greatest strength. Our own happiness and others' happiness can and should interact synergistically, if empathy is truly functioning properly. It is only zero-sum thinking, the thinking of hierarchy, that prevents us from seeing this clearly.

2. Widen the meaning of intimacy

And as shame goes, sincerity can replace it. Without shame, intimacy and sincerity need not be defined as only confessional, as only the communication of negative or secretive emotions to others, or the revealing of mundane daily issues. Sincerity can widen to the whole panoply of complex emotions, thus combining the honesty that is sincerity with the wider nuance that makes our honest communications most interesting. I will call this deep sincerity, sincerity that is both true and also complex—not just focused on revelations of negative hidden emotions.

Deep sincerity is important because it allows for a deeper empathy. Shame makes us feel that we don't really know someone unless we know their inner secrets, and their shameful feelings. But in reality people are more than agglomerations of negative emotions. With deep sincerity people can communicate the wide range of their complex feelings, and this will allow us to know a person in all their genuine nuance—their sadnesses and weaknesses, but also their happiness, and their ambivalences. This is what good music and art does—communicates a wide range of complex emotions. Good interaction can and should do the same thing. When we know the full range of emotions of a person, we can really reduce that existential gap that exists between individuals, as deep sincerity leads us to deeper empathy and understanding between people.

In order to encourage people to connect intimacy to the whole range of emotions, Utopia should try to establish equivalence between happiness and sadness discourses. There might, for example, be set occasions, even set days, when people can tell intimate sadnesses to others, and other days for telling happiness, so that neither happiness nor sadness is masked and so there is an important cultural symmetry established between them (symmetry in the sense that neither sadness nor happiness is seen as making one a better person, or a less shameful person; note that I am not saying people need to feel equal measures of happiness and sadness but rather than there should be equal cultural encouragement for displaying, or talking about, both negative and positive emotions).

I also think that the zero-sum nature of happiness should be countered. I do think that the basic guarantee will be a big help in this direction. If money and other instrumentalities of well-being are not seen as limited in supply, in zero-sum fashion (so that my gain is someone else's loss), then emotions will consequently be freed up from a zero-sum dynamic.

But how else might individual X's happiness be genuinely shared with others, without causing those others to feel left out and less emotionally adequate? Perhaps X can invite randomly chosen others, strangers even, into the happy situation. At the same time person Y, experiencing sadness, can invite random others into the sad situation. A scientist excited by a new discovery should take the time to invite strangers to sit in her/his seat, to see what the pre-discovery situation was like, and then take the audience through the steps leading to the discovery. The emphasis should not be on recreating only the knowledge that the discovery created but the feelings that the scientist experienced in leading to the discovery.

Regarding sad occasions, the reader may shirk at the idea of being brought into someone else's sadness, but if this is not also done, along with happiness displays, then sadness and happiness discourses will become asymmetrical and that is fundamentally antithetical to an empathetic and sharing good society.

My students have convinced me of the toxic effects of shame and its dichotomizing of sad and happy communications and the importance of communication that transcends this dichotomy. For them, the dichotomy exists most explicitly on social media, especially in the way that individuals portray their dating lives. My students in New York and in North Carolina have talked passionately about the way people portray their dating and love lives as uniformly successful, showing off to friends and anyone else how successful and happy they are. Students know everyone is engaging in such false advertising. One student remarked humorously that a friend of his spends hours on weekends and vacations taking photos to post on Facebook, in order to show what spontaneous fun he has with his friends! Another student said her boyfriend has low self-esteem so she encourages widespread advertising of their relationship success on social media. This way, she says he will know their friends can see how happy and successful he has become in his dating life.

Despite their own engagement in the false advertising, students also talked passionately about how damaging this advertising can be to their psyches. Many said they feel truly bad, and even depressed, reading friends' happy dating posts, because they fear they have not achieved the same level of happiness and love success as their peers. This was a widespread sentiment—feeling that one-sided social media posts make everyone unhappy. In fact students told me that many of them have recently created alternate social media sites for their friends only, often using a fake name (they called these sites "Finsta" or fake Instagram sites, a rather ironic term), so that their close friends, but no one else, can know the *real* nature of their love lives and their life more generally, with all of its imperfections. Obviously, these hidden sites are understandable but less than ideal. Social media in Utopia needs to encourage more honest and sincere communication among all people and it can do this by merging the beautiful and ugly communications into one site, full of honesty and full of complexity. Doing so would allow my students, in fact all of us, to know about, *and more importantly learn from*, each other's relationships in all their complexity. It is rare that people talk about *both* the good and bad of their love lives, work lives, or social lives, but it is critical that they do so. Only by knowing the full story, can we really learn what works and what doesn't, and what works intermittently. This is a help to us as audience, as well as a pleasure too, since the nuance of non-dichotomizing communications is more pleasing to us. And by knowing our friends in their full complexity, not just the good or bad, we will be better positioned to help them, since we will know them in their full authenticity. This is knowledge all of my students crave, despite their reluctant interaction in the inauthentic dynamics of the social media present.

3. Sincerity of expression

The arts can, and must, play a key role in challenging cliché, and in fostering sincerity. My proposals here focus on reform of musical performance and pedagogy, since I am a musician; I invite others to offer suggestions for the reform of other arts education and art practice.

I have described above the emphasis of many good musicians on getting the notes "right" and playing the "right" dynamics (loudness or softness, which should be a key to expressiveness) and how this results in an emphasis on technique over expression, and a going through the motions musically that elides sincere emotionality. To challenge this, Utopia must alter musical pedagogy and performance. Musical students should be encouraged to play a piece first following the musical commands of the composer, and then play it again while violating those commands. They should be taught to play around with dynamics—loudness and softness—trying out not only those dynamics that are the opposite of what is on the page, but also their own dynamics. I would even ask performers to play as *un*musically as they can. If the piece is a lyrical one, for example, they should be asked to play it without lyricism, like a march.

The goal is to encourage playing with understanding and sincerity, rather than playing with a sense of obedience. Players and singers should only follow the composers' instructions if they think they are good. Nothing should be done without reason and understanding, and without the prior reflection that can lead to such musical understanding.

It might seem that the "only" result from the above process would be better musical playing, but I would point out that in at least one musical tradition, from India, there is a belief that genuinely feeling the emotions of the music is seen as a way to overcome one's own egotistical self-involvement by becoming spectators to others' emotions. Many of these emotions might be painful if we experience them ourselves, but they are joyful when experienced at the distance the theater provides, where we see others acting them out. This emotional experience takes us away from our own egotistical concerns (Paranjpe 2009: 4). This fascinating belief is consistent with my own views that sincere emotional expression is a key to compassion for others.

4. Meaningful intimacy and deeper empathy

To me, one of the most important ways to improve communication and sincerity, and thus the very possibility for empathy, is for Utopia to institutionalize a diversity of means by which we can understand each other, and even walk in each other's shoes. I would start with the telling of life stories as a way to reveal ourselves to others. I want to encourage a whole industry, if I can use that word, of life-story-telling. In order to make for the requisite audience for such telling, I would have the telling process be collective, and then disseminated widely. People should interview each other about their lives. Youth should interview the elderly, but so should the elderly interview the young. People from one culture should interview those from another culture. I have done this in my beginning anthropology classes and have found students quite excited at what they discover about fellow students from other cultures.

Stories could be supplemented with videos of the places the story-teller and his or her interviewer discuss. Creative people would then produce videos of others' lives, to be distributed widely through a worldwide channel devoted to life-story-telling and portrayals of the lives of average persons. As an anthropologist, I love the life-story medium, but I suspect that even non-anthropologists will be fascinated by hearing tales of other people's lives. I would also take the anthropological perspective about stories and not just tell those that are provocative or heroic, but those that might be boring, tedious, and mundane as well. For the anthropologist, nothing is truly mundane, and the life-story media should adopt this view. There is, admittedly, some resemblance here to Twitter and Facebook: The emphasis on the mundane. I have noted several times that Utopia should take popular or pervasive cultural forms from today's society, and change them so that they better serve the principles of Utopia. In this case the mundane would be portrayed, but only with the intent of providing a fuller and deeper understanding of those portrayed, not as a substitute for it. With shame minimized, the mundane could portray daily happinesses, as well as the details of our life that we usually hide from others. This is just one among many examples of how the portrayal of the mundane can grow in its significance, and its robustness.

I would also have people tell each other's stories in play form, and act them out in theatrical performance. This could have an empathetic and therapeutic effect, in that stories could be changed, so that problems confronted would be solved by an author writing a different ending to a problematic situation. Different emotional interpretations could also be given, so that the story-teller, and audience, could see a multiplicity of ways to respond to the same narrative situation. In addition story-tellers with similar stories could be linked electronically or in real life, to feel a sense of community with others. I would also make an art form out of how stories are categorized. Artists would be encouraged to find similarities between otherwise seemingly dissimilar stories, so that the linking of people with similar stories would not be facile or reductionist.

Telling of stories in this way would be prosocial, and pleasurable, because it would promote empathy and understanding between people. And rather than the listener/interviewer merely responding with some banal sympathetic comment, the process of re-telling others' stories, and doing so in a creative way, would promote much greater empathy of all involved. In fact I even like the idea of people trading places for a day or two, so that a professor would take on a truck driver's job for a day, to see what it is like to be in his/her shoes.

Needless to say, story-telling can also counter the cult of celebrity and the feeling that what one says doesn't matter, because there's no audience. If anyone and everyone, high and low, can tell about their life and see it acted out, retold, and portrayed on a worldwide channel (with the teller's permission, of course), then a real democratization of speech, and challenge to hierarchy and celebrity cults, would be achieved.

5. Deeper empathy leads to a proactive approach to others' pleasures and pains

If Utopia radically expands the means by which people can get to really know each other, including those remote from their daily interactions, then it promotes understanding. And understanding is the basis for deep empathy, which in turn leads to greater helpfulness among people, both those who are family and those who are more remote. Thus, better communication and wider communication leads to at least the possibility—I know the skeptics will be at work here—of true worldwide love.

Here's how I conceive of this happening. Utopia will institutionalize attention to all people, and a desire, a curiosity, to understand them in all their complexity. It will extend our current curiosity about our intimates, and/or our fascination with celebrities, to all humans. It will generalize as well our desire to seek to respond to what we come to understand about them. If someone is in the middle of a conflict with someone else, the amelioration of that conflict will not just be the privilege of those charged with this responsibility (although there will be formal conflict resolution, to be described in Chapter 7). Anyone watching the conflict will seek deep understanding of the conflict, and will work to redress it. Redress will not be punitive in nature but rather restorative, in the sense of seeking to restore equality between people and establish virtuous cycles. It may be the case that one person is acting unfairly, seeking hierarchical advantage at the expense of the other person, or attempting to acquire more from someone than they give back. In that case deep sincerity and empathy would operate not to condone this action, but to find a resolution that maximizes the happiness of both parties and restores equality.

I know many readers may be thinking that it is very hard to solve someone else's conflict, and that is precisely my point here. Knowing why a person acts one way requires formidable skills of understanding. We know how hard it is for therapists to understand why many of their patients do what they do, and how hard it can be for therapists to convince their patients to act in a more self-affirming way. The same is true in Utopia, where all people will be amateur therapists, albeit better-positioned in that we will have the access to observe people in their daily lives that therapists usually lack. In addition, amateurs will possess the social resources, in ourselves and through our wider networks of sympathetic friends on whom we draw, to make genuinely social interventions—that is, to change the unequal, or conflictual, or unloving, social conditions in which people find themselves, rather than leaving it up to clients to find their way in an unfair world.

I know that some readers might find the idea that everyone should act as an amateur psychologist to be perhaps too invasive of privacy. Who wants everyone around us prying into our affairs, some might ask. I would respond that the concern for privacy is a valid one, but when we have a physical accident, we expect bystanders to help us out, and all of us who see such aid are grateful. I'm asking that people adopt the same responsibility to help bystanders psychically and socially as we do when they are in physical danger.

6.   Empathy and non-human animals

I'm often pleasantly surprised at how much empathy humans can display toward their pets and even toward other people's dogs and cats. In New York City, otherwise aloof people out walking the streets—those who wouldn't give a second glance at another person—will talk lovingly to a stranger's dogs. There is, admittedly, something a bit sad about this situation. (A Puerto Rican friend of mine once commented how strange he finds the continental way of relating, where people don't have the politeness to say hello to others on the street, unless those others are with a dog. He noted how alien it seemed to him that people he encountered never remembered his name but did remember his dog's name.) But at the same time, it is a very hopeful sign that animals can turn the most hard-hearted of us into compassionate beings.

How can this be widened further? How can compassion for animals help with compassion for human animals, and for other living things? One possible solution responds to both questions simultaneously. What is needed is for people to widen their empathy from dogs and cats to all living things, something religions such as Buddhism often preach (compassion for all). Widening compassion to all living things might help make those who are otherwise alienated from humans feel greater empathy for each other.

How can this widening occur? There is, of course, far more to be said about respect for the environment generally, and adherence to sustainable living, than

I can possibly describe. All of these goals are important, as so many others have articulated so much more eloquently, and with far more detail, than I can do.

But a start could made by having education, especially in biology, include the close parallels between human emotions and those of animals. They are not the same of course (as mentioned in the discussion on shame), but we all know there are more homologues than many scientists might like to admit. Humanizing the non-human will, ironically, lead to more humane treatment by humans of humans.

I also think a non-hierarchical society might be better at teaching a non-hierarchical approach to all living things. Such an approach is taken today by biologists, but their teaching often has to work against the commonplace notion that human imperatives trump all others because humans are somehow more "evolved." With greater emphasis on non-invidious (human) community (as described in Chapter 3) can come more attention to the interconnections of all living things. The biological understanding of the interconnectedness of all species can penetrate more deeply into everyday thought and action, as we come to respond with compassion to all living things, both those that are large/complex and those that are small/"simple."

7. Replace hierarchical evaluation with pleasure

In this section I give a long and much-needed discussion on criticism and praise. Since good interaction between people is so crucial, it's important to discuss the domain of evaluative interaction. We all know how great it feels when someone tells us we are great, or demonstrates their appreciation of our performance non-verbally with loud applause or smiles. We also know how devastating criticism can be. Thus, if we are to reconstruct communication, we must address one of the most potent forms it takes: Evaluation. Doing so is key, too, to blunting shame, because shame comes from others evaluating us negatively, especially negative evaluations done without compassion.

It is especially critical to address evaluative communication because it is the base upon which meritocracy is built and meritocracy, in turn, is today's most common form of hierarchy. If the experts say an artist is outstanding, we all go see that artist, and the person becomes a celebrity, with all the trappings of fame and fortune that (usually) accompany it. Given the connection between critiques and hierarchy rationalized as legitimate due to its basis in merit, we are faced with a difficult choice: Should we abolish evaluative merit altogether? Or, perhaps, we should only encourage praise. The latter, of course, is one of the solutions put forth by progressive thinkers today, and an approach common in liberal American conceptions of teaching and parenting. While that approach is not without its own merits, if the pun can be pardoned, pure praise seems almost as problematic as the Old World pure criticism it seeks to counter. Both approaches tacitly acknowledge that the worth of an individual depends on whether others tell them they are good and bad. Pure criticism seeks to instill humility and obedience through incessant criticism; pure praise seeks to do the opposite. Both, ultimately, are ways to elevate the critic, often at the expense of the person being critiqued: I will freely admit as an adolescent discovering that I felt much more worldly myself when I could make a piercing critique of a musical performance I'd heard with my friends. We all bought into the notion that being able to tear someone down shows one's own intelligence and sophistication, an Old World attitude I again confronted in college, where I saw grad students and many of my own professors trying to outdo each other in how viciously they could critique a lecturer's talk.

As a teacher I tried hard to undo such viciousness, knowing how destructive it could be. My solution was neither pure criticism nor praise but instead a move to side-step the whole issue by writing lengthy comments and questions in response to my students' papers. I expended a great amount of time trying to write comments that neither directly praised nor criticized. When I first started teaching, I did the same in class, responding to a student comment with a comment back, rather than an exclamation of "good" or "not quite." I must say that I still like the intent of my idea, but I also must admit how confused it seemed to make students feel. I could see that my students were waiting for a final declaration on my part, following my evaluation-less response, that their comment, or paper, was good or not good. When I did *not* give the evaluation, all I saw was dejection and frustration, frustration that a hoped-for positive reward from the teacher never materialized.

So, what to do about evaluation? Sometimes I ask my students to let their inhibitions go, so that they can come up with a wacky idea. I will tell them not to think anything intelligent, that I will reject their answers if they are "too smart," and that I want them to put forth an idea that is as ridiculous as possible. (I must say that this approach has unfrozen more than one self-conscious class.) I am going to do the same here, with an idea I know some readers will think is ridiculous. It may indeed be ridiculous, but I beg your indulgence and the suspension of any critique!

Let's first discuss the evaluation of aesthetic productions, after which I'll discuss whether the ideas here are applicable to the evaluation of science, or whatever word we choose as the complement to "aesthetics." When we attend the theater, or a concert, we want to receive pleasure. However, our entire discourse about the performance justifies our pleasure based upon whether the performance was good or not. Yes, one could say that meritorious performances and pleasurable ones are the same. But the shift to merit is not innocuous. By shifting to the discourse of merit, we do two things. First, we seek to place the performer in a hierarchy. This is bad at face value. Also, we put the onus all on the performer for what happens in the performance. This is equally bad because it elides the very interactive nature of every human endeavor that I want to promote.

Thus, here is an alternative way of "critiquing." Suppose that all audience members at any aesthetic performance are given their own machines, with a dial that they can turn up when they like what they hear or see in the performance, and turn down if they don't like it. This is not as strange as it might seem since this method is used by political consultants to analyze, moment by moment, how an audience, and potential voters, react to political candidates. The dials have the advantage of revealing not just whether a candidate is liked as a whole, but what specific aspects of the speech—themes, tone, emotions—audiences most like.

Simultaneous audience response is also common among many African-American audiences, when audience members in churches, movies, and even in class will give immediate affirmative nods or utterances (and, interestingly, no negative reactions) in response to parts of the whole that they like: "That's right!" I must say that, as a professor, I truly appreciate the simultaneous response of many black students, in contrast to the deafening silence of many white students, whose lack of response leaves me without any means to gauge whether they agree, disagree, or are even awake! I know, too, that every colleague I talk to values student response—the more, the better.

With dials we have a moment-by-moment audience reaction. The total audience moment-by-moment dialings would be aggregated and projected where the performer could see them. I know that many readers, especially those of us who perform, might not like my suggestions here. Let me cite several potential objections, followed by my solutions to them:

- "Moment-by-moment reactions reduce a performance to its parts, ruining the effect of the overall performance." This is a valid objection but various strategies can address it. Some audience members might have dials that allow a response not at any second but, say, one response every one minute. Or the performer might activate a button calling for audience responses any time s/ he wants it—to find out whether the audience likes a certain segment of the performance.
- "This approach will make a performer too self-conscious and too servile to audience approval. You should just do what you believe is good, without regard to what people think. There's already too much pandering in society today, and this would only increase it." Much truth here too. But I would start by noting that great performers are already attuned to the micro reactions of audiences. They listen, not always happily either, to the rustling of programs and the coughs that reveal audience boredom, and even hostility. The dial approach gives more data, and positive data as well as negative data.
- "What about the fine arts?" I am not a visual artist, and my own predilections inevitably are manifest in that I think of art performatively. I would suggest that one approach might be to have an audience responding as a painter is painting. Another might be for viewers of an art work to scan the work carefully from top to bottom, dialing as they do so.

And here are other ideas to vary the dialing approach:

- The performer might dial his or her own minute-by-minute feelings of pleasure as s/he performs. The audience might see this projected before them, so that their own responses could take account of what the performer is feeling. (Re dialing logistics: I'm envisioning a pianist who, say, has a dial that can be activated by the left foot, or by some other appendage not involved in the performance.)

- One segment of the audience might be chosen by lottery and designated as the intentional contrarians. Any and every time they disagree with their audience-mates' reactions, they could dial a dissenting opinion which the performer would receive along with regular audience dial responses.
- Collaboration: This is, perhaps, the most important variant. Today there is an implicit antagonism between any performer—whether teacher, musician, or researcher—and the audience charged with evaluating her/his work. The antagonism derives from hierarchy and from the zero-sum nature of contemporary society: If we, the audience, laud someone, they gain, or maintain, the fame and fortune that accompany our praise. If not, they are consigned to oblivion. Thus, an audience has power over the performer that the performer cannot directly counter. And there are all kinds of motives—from jealousy, to personal animosity, to the sheer feeling of the power given—that might induce audiences and critics to exercise their power unjustly and unwisely, as so many good performers often complain.

But the idiom of *pleasure*, in contrast with merit, is not zero-sum. If two performers compete for a merit prize, only one can win, but if both please us, no problem—the more pleasure, the better. Further, a performer may win a prize and feel no pleasure but, ideally at least, the performer feels pleasure most when the audience feels pleasure as well—the virtuous cycle of pleasure I've referenced frequently. Thus the idiom of pleasure eradicates any antagonism between performer and audience and makes their goals inherently collaborative and synergistic.

To really capitalize on the mutuality of pleasure, I would give the performer an opportunity to perform, *for the same audience*, multiple times. The first performance the performer would learn what the audience likes and dislikes and they, too, would learn what s/he likes and dislikes. In fact to really equalize the communication here I would not only allow the performers to dial their own feelings about the performance but also allow them to dial their pleasure or displeasure with the audience's reactions. Unlike merit-based evaluation where the performer has a single goal, to be deemed "good", with pleasure the performer might be displeased if the audience likes something, a segment played insincerely, for example, or s/he might be displeased that the audience is displeased.

The goal of multiple performances would be to strive for mutual pleasure—not necessarily maximal pleasure, but enough to satisfy most people in the audience as well as the performer. Of course, dialing is an important contribution to this collaboration, but it is only the start. Dialing only communicates the fact that one is pleased but it doesn't make overt *why* one is pleased. After a first performance, I would have the performer and audience discuss why certain passages were pleasing and why some were less pleasurable. I realize this is no simple task. What pleases us, as important as that is, is notoriously difficult to put into words. Yet this is a task worth learning. The better we are at understanding, in *any* domain, what brings us pleasure and why, the more we can control our own pleasures and help others to please us. Therefore, the performer/audience collaboration in seeking greater pleasure for everyone is both a metaphor of, and model for, the learning of two sides to better love each other. Exactly how to create a discourse of pleasure could be the subject of an entire book, but let me give a simple example of what could be done. Audience and performer might create new words for different types of pleasure (words which languages other than English sometimes have in greater abundance). There might be pleasure from sorrow, pleasure from excitement, pleasure from sincerity, etc. In fact, given the importance of sincerity to pleasure and communication, one alternative to dialing based on pleasure, and talking about pleasure, might be to dial and dialogue about sincerity.

Could the dialing approach, and the emphasis on mutual pleasure, work for science too? One could argue that the arts aim to please, so that my proposal for foregrounding pleasure makes sense for them, but that science aims to know rather than to please, making an emphasis on pleasure less logical. But let me rebut this objection:

- First, I have made interactive joy central in the good society. This is true for *all* enterprises. Thus, if a scientist and her/his audience feel mutual pleasure from doing science, then the goals of Utopia are achieved, even if the science is not "good."
- I know the above point will arouse many readers to indignation: "If the goal of science is pleasure, science will not progress, and humanity will suffer." Thus, I would hasten to add the following: Pleasurable science and truthful science are not opposed; in fact they are mutually reinforcing. What makes more pleasing activity of any kind is interaction. But what makes for more thoughtful science, as well, is interaction. A good friend of mine and an eminent scientist said he feels the same way that I do. We both agreed that if we lack interaction, if there is no one with whom we can dialogue about our ideas, then our thinking becomes sterile. Our ideas suffer and our capacity to produce them suffers as well, since without interaction we feel the same as a performer playing without an audience—sterile and insignificant. It is only our cultural myth about the lone, brilliant scientist that keeps us from seeing the importance of community and interaction to good science. Our hierarchical and anti-communal values distort our own perception of how good science actually operates.
- For those readers who remain skeptical, and just as an interesting variation, I would propose in addition to pleasure dials, that there could be other types of dialing. In the case of any truth-oriented enterprise (I realize "truth" and science versus art and pleasure is not a perfectly clear distinction; many physicists talk of being led to their theories by attraction to what is "beautiful"), the audience members might dial up or down based on their moment-by-moment *understanding and conviction*. If the scientist makes claim X based on data Y, and the audience finds the evidence-based claim convincing, they dial

up. The same process could be used in a debate between two researchers with the audience responding moment-by-moment to indicate which side is more convincing at a given moment.

- Other variations are possible. Dialers might be asked to dial up if a given point seems especially significant, i.e., if it raises a whole range of new and interesting objections and/or has many implications. The reason I like this idea is because far, far too many academics today do research without thinking through its importance. In interviewing candidates for social science tenure-track positions, I always ask the significance of their research. Shockingly, few can answer! I don't know why this is. Perhaps many academics think, wrongly, that what makes research academic is that its importance is self-evident. Nothing could be further from the truth, of course, and this view fosters the insular elitism captured in the image of the ivory tower and, in fact, in the pejorative meaning of the word "academic."

- Collaboration, again: Just as collaboration in mutual pleasuring is the goal of aesthetic performances, so too with science: Mutual pleasuring, mutuality, and collaboration are the ultimate goals. In Chapter 6 I explain how lay publics can often be better interlocutors for scientists and researchers than their professional peers. But let me anticipate that argument in saying that just as audiences to aesthetic performers should become collaborators with the performer, so too in the case of science. Today if we hear a scientist speak and we are unconvinced or disinterested, we tend to chalk it up either to our own ignorance or to the lack of merit of the scientist. What I want to happen instead is for a scientist and audience to work together to create a convincing and interesting statement about the world. In order to do this the first step is, as described above, for the audience to dial their response to the scientist, indicating what they understand and find convincing and significant.

The next step is for both sides to work together to make the science more convincing and significant. The audience can first explain to the scientist what they don't understand and some audience members might propose a reframing of the scientist's point to make it clearer. This activity is not a trivial one. I am fully convinced that there is truth to the belief that you don't really know something unless you can teach it. In this case if you can't communicate something, then there might actually be a problem with your own logic, or a hole in the data. Audiences need not be experts to detect holes in data or logic. In fact I have often found that untutored audiences are actually far better at getting to the heart of the matter than educated audiences. The latter accept conclusions on face value because all of us in a given field "know" something to be true; lay audiences don't do this, and in rejecting conventional explanations, the lay audiences are actually more enlightened than those of us who are "experts." Nothing should ever be accepted based upon convention and we must go outside conventional groups in order for our conventions to be questioned.

The same is true of significance. Academics often give significance to certain approaches and insignificance to others, but our basis for doing this is convention. In anthropology it has become conventional not to compare cultures; we believe our research is meaningful if it is not comparative and we denigrate those who compare. No one bothers to question this view except for non-anthropologists. But in this case, the non-anthropologists are right in wondering of what use our research is if it has no comparative value. The anti-comparative stance of the field is a product of history that needs to be reinterrogated, and it is lay audiences who are best at getting those of us who are "expert" anthropologists to do it.

Thus, I imagine that the boundary between audience and performer, between scientist and lay public, will break down. We will all be scientists, and we will all take turns questioning each other, and helping each other formulate more meaningful, more significant, and therefore more pleasurable statements of findings about the world.

Equality, hierarchy, and good and bad communication

During the 2008 election season I visited a good friend at the University of Virginia. We walked along the main street of Charlottesville, where the University is located, and came upon a public blackboard. I immediately liked the idea. Here was a place for anyone to write anything that came to mind, on a public space provided by some innovative city planners. But when I looked at what people had written, things like "Obama's great" and "McCain sucks," my heart fell. Even worse, most of the blackboard had nothing written on it at all. "Such a nice space to say something truly thoughtful and meaningful, and yet only empty slogans," I thought to myself.

The sadness turned to irony when I recalled my time in China during the 1989 student democracy movement. During that movement, students all over China wrote "big character posters," their own political manifestos, and put them up in public settings for all to see. China, despite claims to the contrary, does not allow free speech, so the people writing and displaying these posters were taking big risks. A dissident posting a big character poster in the late 1970s was put in jail for 18 years for his manifesto advocating democracy, and most knowledgeable Chinese knew this at the time of the 1989 student democracy movement. Students' posters were not signed by their authors and were put up surreptitiously, often under cover of darkness. Nonetheless, their content was rich, full of thoughtful prose and sometimes poetry, and frequently accompanied by vivid cartoonish drawings. They criticized the Chinese leadership in no uncertain terms, calling for their overthrow, and mocking them with sarcasm and plays on words.

Plainclothes police were all around the poster display area on the campus where I lived, but nevertheless onlookers thronged the poster sites. I frequently saw students talking into tape-recorders to record the content of the posters, and many people took photos of the posters as well. My student friends were quite clear about the intentions behind their archival activities. They were doing this for purposes of historical documentation, for posterity.

This was a heady time, filled with excitement and hope at the possibility of great change happening. Friends would visit me and relay news of the content of the latest big character posters. They often quoted from posters displayed in Beijing, about 700 miles away, content they knew because students in Beijing transmitted the content of their posters via faxes and express-mail letters to their classmates in distant cities. (This was before Chinese had their own cell phones.) Many scholars of China transcribed the big character posters too, and the transcriptions have been published in numerous books.

The irony, of course, is that in the land of free speech—in the shadow of Thomas Jefferson's home and the university he founded—no one says anything when given the opportunity to do so. In the land where speech is heavily criminalized, where a very powerful big character poster by a famous dissident in 1978 landed him in jail for years, meaningful things get said in the taboo forum.

What made the Charlottesville speakers write with such banality while the Chinese democracy protesters wrote with such nuance and significance? One of the main explanations for the difference, I believe, is the presence or absence of an audience. The American public blackboard elicited only the most mindless slogans because the writers knew that, in reality, no one would really be paying attention to what they wrote. In China, in contrast, anti-government speech garners great attention. This is true to this day. Anyone speaking in opposition to the government, or in fact in opposition to any authority figure, attracts a great deal of attention, and empathy too. Therefore, dissident speech is complex and well-argued because the speakers know there is an important audience for what they say, and one listening closely and sympathetically.

This is a valuable lesson for speech, and for communication more generally, in Utopia. In the Chinese example it is people without power who really attract a listening audience. But in most cases, not just in China but anywhere, what really determines whether or not there will be an audience for someone is whether or not they are high-ranked. Attention goes to the powerful and they have far more outlets for attracting audiences than those without status.

Given the importance of audiences to good communication, let's consider some specific instances of hierarchy's effects on the presence of an audience and the resulting nature of the communication occurring. One example is the arts, both popular and high. In either case there are celebrities and there are those wanting to be celebrities. The former have the opportunity to perform and the latter do not, or their opportunities are far fewer in comparison to the stars. There's nothing at all surprising about any of this, of course, but it needs to be said in order to raise the next question: Why is it this way? Many readers will respond that it is this way because some people are better than others and we, as audience, want to see those who are best. This contention, of course, is less obvious. I'm sure all of us know someone who is a great actor, a great musician, a great artist who, for a variety of reasons—bad luck, lack of connections, etc.—fails to attract an audience. In fact one of the reasons for the phenomenal success of shows such as *America's Got Talent* and its analogues in other countries is that these shows bring to our attention precisely those often outstandingly talented individuals who had previously been neglected. I think there is both a huge vicarious joy that we feel in seeing the neglected gain the attention they deserve, as well as a feeling that the more democratic and popular methods of determining talent on these shows (albeit not entirely democratic nor entirely devoid of manipulation, I fully admit) will bring us into contact with better people than the normal top-down Hollywood and music-industry methods of finding talent.

Thus, these shows are important for what they reveal to us about talent. Although my contention here is not one that can be "proved," I would argue that these talent shows suggest that there are many more people who deserve to be attended to than our normal institutional methods select as worthy of attention. That is, merit is distributed much more widely than our star system, our celebrity cults, recognize. The celebrity cult system derives from, and reinforces, the myths of hierarchy and of capitalism: There are only a few truly outstanding people out there, capable of being experts, or capable of running a company. Thus, when we give all the money to these few people, it is because of their merits, and the scarceness of good talent itself. My counter to this is that I recognize that some people are better than others (although the issue of whether even this statement can be objectively demonstrated—ultimately it cannot—is worthy of a whole book), but there are far more talented people in existence than we will ever see making it to the top. *This is because our society limits the number of top positions.* This limitation of the number of positions is an artificial construct of society, not a reflection of the nature of human talent. It is a construct fomented by those at the top, who want to preserve their privileges by restricting audience access to a few top stars. And, admittedly, it is a construct further preserved by those at the middle and bottom, who have come to believe that talent is rare. In fact this is a very common sociological pattern. Those of lower status often help preserve the status system from which they seem to suffer, by receiving some compensation from their support of it. In this case, fans of celebrities can feel that they share in some of the star system's restricted status by being a celebrity's fan. Hence fans, too, are reluctant to deviate from a system that gives them vicarious attention, even if this attention is illusory and not ultimately fulfilling.

There is a huge literature on the sociology of the arts, and I could continue this discussion about the artificial construction of merit for several chapters, but I will refrain from doing so. But I do want to make one further contention, one that extends even beyond what I have said so far: Each one of us has something worthy of attention. We all know that sometimes we enjoy being an audience for someone we know, a friend or child, for example, more than for celebrity stars' performances. While we may argue that this is not due to the merits of the performance, but our relationship with the performer, this is precisely my point: Merit is not the only thing that can attract our attention. Listening and talking are the ultimate social activities, and so are the artistic versions of these activities. Therefore, we can find interest in them, great interest, if the social conditions in which they occur are good. Conversely, if we are alienated from those conditions—if we are an anonymous member of an audience for a great performance, for example—the performance might very well not please us, even if it is, by whatever measuring, outstanding.

My point here is to say that there are valid reasons for giving all of us an audience, and for dethroning the celebrity cult that makes society limit our attention to a few chosen stars. There is also an implied point, one that astute readers will have noticed. The artificiality of the system today not only hurts non-stars, by denying them an audience, but also it hurts stars too, because it gives them an audience often for reasons having little to do with what it is that they communicate, or how they do so. Both conditions, no audience or an arbitrary one, produce similar effects: If no one is listening or if people are listening out of hierarchical obligation—the obligation to attend to the star or the powerful authority figure—the result is the same: Communication that is ritualistic and banal. This is true for much of what is produced by Hollywood and it is equally true of Chinese authorities, whose mind-numbing political rhetoric is in sharp contrast to those dissidents who garner genuine, interested attention.

Solutions

Here are some ideas for challenging the cult of celebrity and for bringing attention to all of us, the attention that will please us, our listeners, and give us the reason to talk that makes us say something significant in the first place:

1. As described in Chapter 1, performance venues and audiences will be democratized, so that anyone wanting an audience of any kind can have it. Audience reactions will be encouraged and even maximized, but reactions will be shifted from a merit-based idiom to a pleasure-based one, as described earlier in this chapter.

2. Life stories of average people: I described this earlier as a way to encourage greater empathy between people, but it has the additional benefit of encouraging us to attend to all people's lives, not just celebrities' lives. Thus, it is an important strategy for breaking down the cult of celebrity.

I know that some readers might object that average people's lives are not as worthy of interest as lives of great people, and that it will be hard to encourage audiences to listen to lives of the average. I disagree. As an anthropologist I am a proud member of a discipline that has consciously sought to turn the discourse hierarchies upside down, and inside out. Those of us from powerful countries go to remote parts of the world to listen to the country "bumpkin," the person often deemed not worth listening to. The whole idea behind anthropology, of making a large-scale discourse across disparate and diverse cultures, and stimulating understanding between them, is, at least in its ideal form, one of encouraging the breakdown of barriers to good communication worldwide.

I start with this observation about anthropology not just out of disciplinary pride, but also to show that interest in those with the least power and least "merit" is something that *can* occur, however imperfectly many of us who are professional anthropologists might do it.

3. Musical composition changes: I would also change the way music, and other arts, are produced. Anyone who wants to compose can do so, and can have their compositions heard. This is key because an audience that reacts to someone's creation helps the creator make things that are pleasing to others—thus fostering compassion in the form of musical creativity. Music composed for oneself, or for status, cannot be compassionate and ends up being, as is often the case nowadays, academic.

I would also encourage more personal interaction between the composer and the audience. For starters, the composer should be on personal terms with the audience, much as happens in small-scale societies, where music is written by someone you know for you and your friends to play and hear, and for a specific social purpose. One reason that I think that someone like Bach was so musically creative is because he had a standing audience, his church, and his music was written for that audience, and not for anonymous persons in posterity.

Similar changes would hold for all arts. I use music as an example here because it is the art form with which I am most familiar.

4. Hierarchy and talk: Let's consider a few examples of hierarchy's pernicious influence on conversation in particular, and possible ways to ameliorate it:

- Academics, for example, frequently can't talk across disciplines to each other, or even within disciplines, because we believe only those from our own subspecialties can understand what we have to say, and can recognize its importance. We fear being shown as ignorant when discussing things that are not our own specialties and therefore many of us (well, not me), avoid any discussion that is not centered on our own specialty. Specialization allows for a kind of status détente: "I'll acknowledge that you are an expert in X, if you acknowledge I'm expert in Y, and let's not threaten this détente by you talking about Y, my specialty, or by me talking about X." I've often heard academics proudly say, "I know nothing about Y." Why the pride? The pride comes from the implication in saying "I know nothing about Y" that there *is*, indeed, topic X about which I am king—insidious hierarchy, that corrodes our propensity to meaningfully converse with each other and, indeed, the potential for learning from each other.
- The Yi people I studied, many of whom have not had formal schooling, often felt reluctant to talk with me. They said only the schooled know valuable information, so I should seek them out, rather than interviewing the unschooled. This is, of course, part of a very widespread social class and educational divide, in which class and schooling erect barriers to dialogue and it is a divide that those without formal schooling help to maintain by claiming ignorance when an educated person wants to talk with them.

Needless to say, Utopia's ending of hierarchy has much to contribute toward better talk among academics, and between people of different social classes and educational backgrounds. If showing off is no longer a motive for talk, our talk can become more fluent, and more sincere—both key goals in the joy of communication. I can tell you about topic X because I'm interested in telling about it, and you are curious to hear about it.

But ending hierarchy in general is not enough. We need to end conversational inequality, through education. Specifically, I propose a proactive approach to eliminating hierarchy's effects by having young people, in school, conduct ethnographies of conversations they hear around them, to evaluate the inequality and banality they find, or the meaningfulness they find. I would also have students study, through ethnographic observation or by watching recorded videos of discourse, already existing discourse traditions seen as exemplary—those that privilege discourse equality. In Utopia, students will study these kinds of discourse traditions. This way they will learn how to discuss things in meaningful and hierarchy-free ways. The study of discourse itself, and the ways in which it can perpetuate inequality, will raise awareness of this inequality and lead, hopefully, to new discourse styles that challenge it.

5. Facilitating talk: Talking can be hard to do. For many readers a good example of talk's difficulty is the awkwardness of conversation during a first date, wanting to say something that will make a positive impression, but not knowing what to say.

Sometimes we know people well, but don't know what to say that we haven't said before. Our familiarity leads to a lack of conversational novelty. Sometimes we may be friends with someone, but different interests prevent meaningful talk. One person may like rock music, another baseball, a third person might like old movies. How can we communicate with each other when our interests differ? The seeming abundance of activities in modern life, and the plethora of celebrities and their diverse audiences, makes it hard for one person to share a fund of knowledge with others, thus precluding meaningful communication, or simply anything shared that can be talked about.

I know many people will find any "solution" to all of the above scenarios to be an artificial imposition on the natural awkwardness of interaction. If there is awkwardness, better to leave it alone, than to force an inauthentic solution upon people. I don't accept this belief. Therefore, I want to propose a means to institutionalize talk between people whose interests are different. Such talk will help us break out of the conventionality of our daily discourse routines, and it will help break the conversational barriers that both reflect and reinforce social divisions.

A personal example: As a classical music lover, I feel left out of many discussions among friends, whose musical passions center on popular music, or genres other than the classical. This phenomenon is widespread—different hobbies, different interests, etc. multiply the barriers to good conversation, often leaving us with little, if anything, to say to each other.

Since talk topics so often correlate with status and education, or at least pretensions to such, they become symbolic of these divisions in society, as well as divisions of gender and gender presentation, among other invidious distinctions.

Ending class and gender distinctions will depoliticize talk, so that talk topics no longer transmit messages about who stands where in the status hierarchy. This will go a long way toward helping communication, so that we can listen to someone who has knowledge of a topic we lack, without feeling that our own ignorance of the topic will show us up as too educated, too uneducated, too macho, too feminine, and so on.

But I think change is also necessary on the discourse end of divisiveness, as well as on the macro structures causing such divisions. There must be a way for people to be brought together to talk and listen to those who have different knowledge and interests. One way would be to create venues in which people could talk about things they're interested in, and take turns doing so. A group of people interested in classical music might go on stage (I'm speaking semi-metaphorically here, although an actual small stage might help by encouraging an audience that would feel bound to listen) to discuss their interests, and to explain them to those in the audience not knowledgeable about the subject. Even within the group of classical music talkers there will be diverse knowledges—about opera, about instrumental music, etc.—and so telling each other, and *teaching* each other, can also be a means to teach those in the audience. I can imagine, for example, that a group of opera lovers could play arias from their favorite operas for each other and for the audience. They would be sharing their passions with all involved. Then a group of rock aficionados would come onto stage to play recordings of their favorite pieces, and talk about them, again to each other, and to the audience of opera lovers. American children do something vaguely similar in school—show and tell—of course, and there's no reason why the turn-taking in talking about one's passions should not, and cannot, continue into adulthood. (In fact I think the fact that we share as children but not as adults is indicative. Our adulthood reluctance to do such turn-taking in sharing our interests derives from, and reinforces, the growing invidious social distinctions that dominate us as we "mature.")

In summary, if we can talk across different interest groups, and between the divisions that so often separate us today, we can start to develop bridges of understanding, and interest, between different groups of people. And how much more interesting will be our lives if we communicate more robustly and sincerely, with more frequent audiences for all of us, not just those who are stars. Communication will be democratized. So too will learning, a topic considered further in the next chapter.

Bibliography

Benedict, Ruth 1974. *The Chrysanthemum and the Sword: Patterns of Japanese Culture*. New York: New American Library.

Boehm, Christopher 2012. *Moral Origins: The Evolution of Virtue, Altruism, and Shame*. New York: Basic Books.

Gangnam Style n.d. In *Wikipedia*. Accessed May 29, 2018 at https://en.wikipedia.org/wiki/Gangnam_Style.

Goffman, Erving 1967. *Interaction Ritual: Essays on Face-to-face Behavior*. New York: Pantheon.

Paranjpe, Anand C. 2009. In defence of an Indian approach to the psychology of emotion. *Psychological Studies*, 54: 3–22.

Schoenhals, Martin 1993. *The Paradox of Power in a People's Republic of China Middle School*. Armonk, NY: M.E. Sharpe.

—— 2005. The opening and closing of China: The conflict of values in traditional and contemporary China and its significance for understanding the Cultural Revolution and China's subsequent opening up (*kaifang*). Paper presented at Harvard University's New England China Seminar, Cambridge, MA, November 28, 2005.

Turner, Victor 1977. *The Ritual Process: Structure and Anti-Structure*. Ithaca, NY: Cornell Paperbacks.

Young, Michael W. 1971. *Fighting with Food: Leadership, Values and Social Control in a Massim Society*. Cambridge: Cambridge University Press.

6

THE INTRINSIC PLEASURES AND PURPOSES OF LEARNING

One of the things that school teaches us, wrongly, is to place little value on personal experience, and much value on the testimony of experts. Many cultures that lack widespread schooling make a strong distinction between what you know based on personal observation and what you know based upon second-hand knowledge, and the former is valued over the latter. To me, this makes eminent sense. Why believe someone else's reported experience more than what you have seen with your own eyes?

There are pockets of our own society that are sensible enough to support the privileging of personal over second-hand testimony. Our legal system does this by making hearsay inadmissible. But in our schools most teaching is based, precisely, on hearsay. When I teach about China to students, they must accept what I say based upon my own testimony unless they have personally been to China and know the issues I'm discussing. Obviously, they *can* learn about China this way; if I didn't think so, I would feel little purpose in being a professor. And students can even bring in some of their own contributions to the discussion, by asking questions, by finding contradictions in my analysis of China, and so on. But I know all too well how remote China seems to most of them, and how colorless it feels to them to hear my descriptions of a place that they may never see and experience first-hand.

I say all of this to advocate more experiential teaching, not a novel idea of course, but also to validate what I am about to do, which is to follow my own advice, and use my own disappointments with schooling as a basis for advocating changes in education in Utopia.

As a young child, I had a passionate curiosity about the world. My mother reports that I often asked questions about whoever was driving down the street: "Where is she going? What is she doing?"—a young social scientist at work! My constant questioning was a real test of my mother's ability to create new and inventive stories that would satiate my curiosity.

I also loved technological things, as does my father, and he drew me pictures of how things worked. Often these pleased me, but sometimes I ended up asking questions that neither of us could answer. This pushed me on to further thinking about inventions and mechanics.

Being the passionate learner that I was, and with parents who encouraged my passion and helped feed it, I was shocked to find out that other kids my age did not even like school. Not only did they dislike it, but they believed that any cool kid was not *supposed* to like it. When I was in kindergarten I told my neighbor, who was in first grade, that I liked school. "You like school?" she asked with incredulity and derision. This was my first education in something seemingly more important than school itself: How to be a social success in American society. I learned that if you are to be a social success you must not admit to liking school. Well, I didn't really learn this, or accept it, since I've rebelled against the view that learning is uncool for my whole life. This chapter just continues the rebellion.

During my elementary school years, a move to an elite Detroit suburb, home to the leaders of what was, at that time, the lead weapon in America's arsenal of industry—the auto industry—brought me face-to-face with sustained anti-intellectualism. I'll spare the reader the specific details of years of feeling alienated and ostracized at school for being one of the school "brains." I know that such experiences will be familiar to many readers, even those in many countries outside America. After all, the Chinese put their intellectuals on stages during the 1966–1976 Cultural Revolution in order to torture them physically and emotionally, often for little cause other than the crime of being intellectual. I guess we American intellectuals should be grateful we weren't Chinese during those terrible years.

What really puzzled me the most at school, and continues to puzzle me to this day, was the dichotomy between the social and the academic. If you wanted to be liked, you couldn't be interested in school. And if you *were* interested in school, this led to varying degrees of ostracism from the world of friends and romance.

Since at home and among family I was quite social and loved to play outside with cousins and neighbors, I saw no conflict between being social and being smart, despite the dichotomy between these characteristics that existed at my suburban school. And because my parents had interacted so joyously with me during my early curious questionings, I saw thinking, questioning, and learning as the ultimate social and interactional act. Let me repeat this: *Thinking, questioning, and learning are the most social and interactive activities there are.* If there is interactive joy, learning is a prime source of it.

I knew that the joys of learning were most pronounced when shared in a meaningful way with others. I also knew, and continue to know, that my own ideas and research are vastly improved when I discuss and debate my ideas with others, something I had great and wonderful practice doing throughout my youth, with a mother who loved to play devil's advocate with me. In fact one of the outstanding experiences I did have in school was being on the debate team. Debate appealed to my penchant for intellectual interaction and play, in the sense of the play that characterizes any team competition. The legacy of my experiences with debate will be quite evident to the reader of this book.

So too with my musical life, which is the other sparkling exception to my youthful disappointment with school. I attended the summer music camp at Interlochen, Michigan, a music center attracting young music students from around the world, and it was there that I experienced an intense feeling of joy in combining music, which for me is a very thoughtful enterprise, with sociality. I realized then, as I realize now, that this sociality was especially reinforced by living with my fellow students and by the experience of performing for each other. While academia encourages us to create for status, with much of our work going unnoticed, *performance and audience recognition* are built into the very notion of music, which is why it has become such a great metaphor for me in this book: It has at its core interaction and the giving and receiving of pleasure, including the giving and receiving of a wide range of emotions. Music, at least when it is at its best (I know there is a whole critique one can make of the contemporary "serious" musical world today), does not dichotomize social interaction from achievement—as is the case with schools—nor does it neglect the importance of emotions and pleasure to our cognitive experiences, as so often happens in schools and even more so in academia. Good music pedagogy is inherently interactional, dialogic. You play for a teacher, who responds to each musical utterance, telling you if it is good or bad, pleasing or not. Second-language teaching, again at its best, is similar, and so it is a model, too, for good education. You talk, the teacher talks with you, understanding you, or corrects the grammar and pronunciation of what you have said. And if you are learning a second language to use it, by going to a land where the language is spoken for example, then such learning has purpose to it. Unlike so much of learning—which is merely done to get a degree, or a good job, or a promotion, and where the connection between what is learned and what you "use" it for is tenuous at best (more on this later)—second-language learning has an inherent and genuine purpose and the learning process is authentically social.

Despite these exceptions, inauthenticity continued in high school. In my public high school, being a good student was no longer completely reviled, as was the case in earlier school years. As my upper-middle-class classmates were getting closer to college, they knew they had to study hard to get into Harvard, and Harvard was, of course, the ticket to remain wealthy, and being wealthy was … well, it was just important for its own sake. Thus, studious students were no longer always reviled. *But* there was an important distinction made. If you studied for pleasure, you were still reviled, in the strongest terms possible: You were a "nerd." However, if you studied as a means to get into Harvard, you were tolerated, even respected. As long as you were just accidentally and mindlessly a good student, you were in good stead with the social powers that be. But if you were affirmatively and unashamedly smart, you were, like the openly gay person, "flaunting" your shameful desire—in this case a desire to study—in a way that made you seem to be selfish and conceited.

Note the bitter irony here: Studying for pleasure is, in actuality, highly liberating, because of the *internal* nature of the pleasure motive. If we study and work for pleasure, on the one hand, then the teacher or boss cannot compel us to act as they want, because grades and money have no meaning to us. On the other hand, studying to get ahead is the exact opposite. It lays the foundation for constraint and oppression because it gives significance and affirmation to the very external motives that others use over us: Money and status.

So when students tease and bully the classmate who studies for pleasure, while quietly approving of the ones who study to get ahead, they are according value to the very means used to control and coerce people. Students think they are being cool and anti-establishment in trying hard not to show pleasure in learning, but they are in fact actually being as pro-establishment as they can be. It is not only corporations and political elites that oppress us. We do it to ourselves, in schools, every time we revile the child who finds pleasure in learning. We create the means to oppress us. And we fail to affirm, and thus often fail to feel, the genuine pleasure of learning. We both imprison ourselves and suffer the denial of one of life's greatest joys.

Along with the denial of the pleasure of school, one of the other causes of my frustration and disappointment with school has been its disconnect from the rest of society and its usually very unsocial nature. School is for children and the imma-ture, but is not seen as having a real purpose of its own. To the extent that it has "purpose," its purpose is to validate who deserves a high place in society's hier-archy. I will have more to say about this, but for the moment some more personal reflections.

I always felt that there was something unreal and alienating about school and any time I step back into a primary or secondary school, these feelings come flooding back. It is hard to describe the nature of the alienation though I know many, many readers will have experienced something similar. For me, I always felt that much of the academic side of school, as opposed to the very consequential social side (the sports activities, school "spirit," etc.), was a kind of game, devoid of connection to real-life purpose. We might learn something fascinating in school but my classmates never reacted positively to this learning itself. They would never talk about the subject matter itself—the themes of Shakespeare, the origins of the universe, the causes of racism. Instead, they talked about whether these issues would appear on the test or not, whether a certain answer would get them an A or not, etc. Students talked, and teachers joined in this talk, about what we were learning in terms of the processes of school as a hierarchy-sorting grades-giving institution, and not about the content of what was learned. The paraphernalia of learning mattered, but not its essence.

School came to be about the smell of Dittos, the fear of tests, mindless conver-sation about how many points were needed for an A, and the sinking feeling that nothing really mattered because, after all, once we played the game and got into a good college, we would start over with a new game. To this day I am ashamed to admit a lingering disinterest in Native American issues because all I can think of when reading about such issues is the quizzes about Native American esoterica after a visit to a local museum (quizzes whose triviality made me hate the subject) and, even more strongly, the smell of old bologna sandwiches eaten by unruly kids at the museum. These are the images remaining in my memory because the true fascination that is another culture was killed by the gaminess of school. All that was left were the strange and disquieting sensory memories.

I will end here by citing one of my own student's insights about the gaminess of school. In a graduate education class I was teaching I had just asked the students why we do experiments in chemistry class whose answers we already know. We don't do this anywhere else, I said. "Why do we do such unnatural and abnormal things in school?" To this, my student replied quite aptly: "That's because school is a simulation." He was right. School simulates life, at best, but remains divorced from it, without genuine purpose. If school becomes a burden, it is partly because it has been created to be a burden, a burden we must endure while young in order to gain entrée into the seemingly meaningful adult activity of the working world.

The problem with education

To summarize: Learning is one of the most enjoyable and human activities there is, yet we have made it into a burden. We have deprived it of joy by making it a realm of hierarchy, a realm that builds and justifies the hierarchies that exist in life outside of school. We have deprived it of pleasure by making it anxiety-inducing and by making it a means to an end but not an end itself. We have structured schools so that individuals work alone, thus isolating people from each other and from the possibilities of co-learning and co-creation.

What we learn at school is sometimes pleasurable, but the pleasure motive is invalidated by society. It is invalidated by elites, who never ask how to make schools more fun, but only more efficient. Why shouldn't the former question be asked? The pleasure motive of school is invalidated as well by students themselves who, unknowingly, cooperate in their own scholastic imprisonment by stigmatizing those among them who dare feel pleasure at school. Feeling pleasure, openly and honestly, comes to be seen as disgraceful. Those who feel pleasure, and admit it, risk ostracism by many, or most, of their peers.

The dynamic of stigmatizing school's pleasures is not limited only to American schools. While American anti-intellectualism is far more potent than any such anti-intellectualism I know of in Europe, China has a bipolar nature. During China's Cultural Revolution of 1966–1976, it far outdid American anti-intellectualism. All schools and universities nationwide were closed and youth in groups tortured their teachers and professors in public criticism sessions.

I must also say that intellectuals have endured persecution in many nations and cultures around the world, not least because of our tendency to criticize political and economic elites and because we are in competition with those elites, since our own hierarchies are purchased with a much different currency than theirs (well, usually). I have had hundreds of students interview informants from different cultures about schools and the role of intellectuals in those cultures, and a wide variety of these reports have included accounts of anti-intellectualism, especially a tendency (e.g., in the Caribbean) to disparage males who are too studious. In many cultures educational achievement is gendered female, and homophobic and gendered taunts are used to keep both males and females from excelling. Girls who do too well in science and math are teased for being unfeminine and males who study with too much vigor and pleasure are teased for being unmasculine.

In many cases the pleasure stigma is played out by what is unsaid, not just by what is said. In my own research, and in my students' research, I've always asked if the genuine pleasure of school is ever acknowledged by policy planners as a goal in its own right, as *the* goal of education. Do policymakers ever say that we should make schools more enjoyable, so that people can have a happier life? The answer is no. Although American progressives acknowledge the fulfillment that learning can bring, even they seem to always go on to make this fulfillment a means, not an end. They will often say that if kids like school more, they will study harder. *Why doesn't anyone say if school is more pleasurable, this in itself makes for a much better and joyful society?*

This is an extremely serious question, and one that speaks to the whole issue of the debasement of learning, by tying it to an end, while devaluing its intrinsic pleasures. And it is a very specific means–end relationship. Even though any means–end relationship is problematic, and tends to devalue the means, the school means–end relationship is tied to the very building blocks of hierarchy: Money and power. We are told that if we do well in school, we will get a high-paying job, with high status. We are told that if our nation collectively does well in school, then our industries will flourish, and we will all be better off as a result. The idea of devaluing pleasure by making school, like work itself, a means to an end, rather than a pleasurable end itself, seems to me so odious that I considered making a critique of means–end relations the centerpiece of this book's critique. But hierarchy is equally odious, and directly tied to means–end relations, so it became the focus of my critique. In truth the means–end relations, and the debasement of pleasure, are intimately connected to hierarchy.

Students rebel against school, but they do so in a way that preserves, rather than challenges, school's hierarchy and its denial of pleasure. Just as work came to be seen by employers and employees alike as a noble burden with the development of the Protestant work ethic, so too with school, where sacrifice is lauded by teachers and students. Like workers, students internalize values that cast school as an ascetic burden, so that like workers they comply with what is required of them in order to prove their virtues through sacrifice.

The school as noble sacrifice dynamic also works against genuine, joyful communities of learning. Instead, to the extent that there is any bonding at school, it is bonding done by virtue of shared sacrifice and shared anxiety over school, rather than shared pleasure. Turner (1977) describes this process for rituals and religion, where hardship is used to bond initiates, or fellow congregants. In the case of religion we can think of all of the intentional hardships of the major religions, and the way these create community bonds. There is fasting, self-flagellation, celibacy, and other ordeals endured by monks and nuns, and so on. I like to tell my students that the Puritans made work and school their monastery.

School and work become seen as difficult, even ascetic, and society promulgates the illusion that these difficulties and unpleasantnesses create communal bonds just as do religious hardships. Just as the fraternity initiates who say they bond through hazing, so workers and students bond through their dislike of work and school. Just listen to how almost obligatory it is to talk about work, and school, as a burden. The talk is almost ritualistic and gives us that sense that we are all enduring this together.

Yes, work and school can be a burden, but I would ask the reader to try the following experiment: When you hear co-workers or classmates complaining of how much work they have to do, say to them: "I don't know what you're talking about. I love what we're doing here."

When I've had my students try out this mini-experiment, they can always predict the result. Others will respond to them: "You're crazy." Beneath this response is the anger that someone has placed themselves outside the mutual masochism circle. Pleasure comes to be seen as an anti-social act.

The communalism of suffering that has become school (and the workplace too) is a false sense of community, just as false as invidious community. It is false above all because it is suffering meant to validate hierarchy—the high-status jobs we get if we study hard. This brings hierarchy and suffering into a dangerous alliance with each other in learning environments.

In reality learning is the most communal of actions and one of the most pleasurable: Mammals learn from and with other mammals. Humans learn from each other, and build on what others have learned. Thus, learning is not selfish, or at least it need not be, nor does it need to be a hardship. It only seems this way because it has been so constructed by the Puritan ethic, and by the dynamics of community produced through suffering.

Hierarchy and education

The connection of schooling to hierarchy is implicit, and partly explicit, in my discussion above. Here in list form is how that connection is manifest in education:

1. Schools are hierarchical in that their role is to sort people into a hierarchy of achievement, a sorting epitomized by the grading of students and the focus of teaching and learning on grades.
2. Schools are hierarchical moreover in that the hierarchies created in school are used by society to create a hierarchy among adult workers. Only if you do well in school can you become a doctor or lawyer or other high-paying, high-status job. If you do poorly at school, you may face the punishment of a life of destitution (not always true in reality but true enough to shape the way we think of school).
3. And something obvious to me but needing to be said: The hierarchies of points 1 and 2 exist in schools worldwide. In fact the global spread of schooling is connected to the globalization of certain kinds of hierarchy, specifically meritocracies (or societies that make at least the pretense of meritocracy).

4. Since hierarchy crowds out joy, school hierarchy keeps school learning from being the joy that it should be. Like work, which is also unfun because of its hierarchical nature and because it is something we must do, so too does school become unfun because of hierarchy and compulsion. In fact school is directly conceived of as work. Americans talk of doing their "homework" or their "schoolwork."

5. Being work, school takes on all of the other cultural baggage of work. With the origins of the Protestant work ethic, work came to be seen as noble and virtuous precisely because it was painful, and was opposed to sinful pleasure (see Chapter 4). School is conceived in the same manner. Students feel that doing schoolwork is good, even if they don't always do it, and they know they should feel guilty if they have fun doing something that is not schoolwork.

6. In the next section I will show the history of the origins of these views, to denaturalize them, to show that they need not be this way, but at this point it is necessary to remind the reader of a point made in Chapter 4: There is nothing inherent in work that makes it odious. It becomes odious because of its connections to hierarchy and compulsion. So too with school. As one student told me, she loves reading history books, but if one she is reading is suddenly assigned, the pleasure fades and turns to a burden.

    I confess that I must fight this feeling myself. I have always felt the joy of learning and thinking, and yet the pressure of trying to earn money and fame through thought turns this lifelong joy for me into a chore. Even as I write this book, I am wondering if it will be well-received, and my anxiety about external motives for my work makes writing this book occasionally burdensome.

7. School's construction by our cultures as analogous to work sets up the same hierarchical dynamics that exist in the workplace. As in the workplace, where we work not because we want to but because we have to, so too with school. As with the workplace, the external rewarding by grades makes us controllable by others—by the teacher at school, by the boss at work. As at work, the rewards usually go to individuals, so that work and school are both similarly individualizing and anti-communitarian.

The consequences of how schooling arose

As with my discussion of work in Chapter 4, I want to turn to history. I will discuss the history of schooling here to denaturalize the ideas about education that we take for granted, just as I did for the ideas about work that we, wrongly, take for granted. By showing how the origin of institutionalized education is a product of history, I want to demonstrate that the nature of schooling and the way we view it is not timeless and inevitable, but rather is a product of recent history and, being a historical construction, is therefore changeable.

The first step in this denaturalizing of schools is to realize that while the education of some children—principally elite offspring, and usually male elite offspring—is age-old, the idea that *all* children, rich and poor alike, should be taught in institutions specifically constructed for them *by the state* is *not* age-old. It dates only to the 19th century, with the US and Prussia being the early leaders in widespread primary-school education (Go and Lindert 2010: 3). Thus, the view that learning is for children and work is for adults is not inevitable. More importantly, the means–end nature of learning—seeing it as giving us the credentials to assume our adult work roles—can likewise be challenged as a product of history, and a fairly recent one at that. Learning need not be seen as only a means. It can be, and should be, seen as an end in itself, and history demonstrates the possibility of re-conceiving of learning in this way. That re-conception is my goal for this somewhat lengthy interlude about the history of schooling.

My discussion here is informed by my own original research (Schoenhals 1986) on how universal schooling was first established in the US, with a focus on 19th-century Pennsylvania. Schools in the US were forged in the context of new views about the poor, the rich, children, and adults. School, seen as a form of charity, was originally provided for all poor, young and old, children and adults. But as charity for the poor came under attack in the 19th century, the notion arose that school is a form of benevolence that should be provided for all children, rich and poor alike, and not for undeserving adult poor people. The charity that was schooling was shifted from the poor to children in the 1830s in places such as Pennsylvania. This is how universal schooling as an institution was first created.

Since views of the poor were implicated in the establishment of universal schooling, let's begin with a recap of these views. I turn first to Europe, since European attitudes toward the poor affected American attitudes. Pre-capitalist and preindustrial notions in the early Middle Ages in Europe held that the poor were unfortunate and hence should be pitied, not despised. Poverty entered into voluntarily, through renunciation of wealth, even came to be considered holy, an attitude that Geremek (1997) connects in part to rebellion against growing Middle Ages wealth earned in towns and cities (32, 35). Above all, the dominant attitude toward all poor was one of charity. Charity to the poor was the means by which the wealthy believed they could redeem their sins (23, 36–52); in exchange for receiving alms, the poor prayed for their benefactors (47–48). Geremek cites many examples of the rich giving alms to the poor, such as the 1355 will of a wealthy man from Lubeck, Germany that instructed his estate be given as alms to the 19,000 poor out of a total town population of 22,000–24,000 people (37). He describes the "enormous quantity of alms which continued to be distributed [during the Middle Ages] and the ease with which the poor could obtain aid" (40). Individual alms-giving with time became not only a responsibility of kings and aristocrats, but of the bourgeoisie as well (42).

Charity was a prime mission of the Church too. In the early Middle Ages

> people intent on living off charity caused the agrarian civilization of Western Christendom no serious discomfort. It was the Church's mission to help the poor, and a *third or a fourth part of Church income* was to be allocated to them on a regular basis.
>
> *Geremek 1997: 17; emphasis added*

The distinction between the able-bodied poor, who were seen as less deserving of aid because they could work, and the infirm poor, was one made many times throughout European history according to Geremek. But the number of poor grew greatly in the later Middle Ages, a result of various factors such as the English Enclosure movement (which I described in Chapter 4) beginning in the 16th century. Poor English peasants, no longer allowed to graze their animals on wealthy landholders' land, flooded into towns and cities. In England, and across Europe, the result of huge increases in beggars in cities led town and city governments to create new forms of municipal poor aid, to supplement, or supplant, religious aid. Central to much municipal aid was an assertion of the dichotomy between the idle able-bodied poor, who were seen as wicked, and those who were poor because of infirmity or other reasons beyond their own control. In England Henry VIII in 1531 ordered a census of the poor. Those unable to work because of age, sickness, or infirmity were given certificates allowing them to beg in certain areas. Those able-bodied poor, however, were to be flogged if caught begging, and those giving them alms were to be fined (Geremek 1997: 164). Throughout Europe, governments in towns and cities established workhouses, places where the poor were forced to go to work. In the early 1700s England had nearly 200 workhouses and a 1723 law allowed parishes to refuse aid to any poor person who refused to work in the workhouse (218). Calvinists and Puritans saw poverty as punishment for idleness (246) and in its "war against 'idleness'" the Amsterdam workhouse locked up in a cellar filled with water those who refused work:

> In the cellar there was a pump, and the prisoner, in order to keep from drowning, had to work constantly at pumping out the water. This was considered an effective way of countering idleness and inculcating the habit of work.
>
> *Geremek 1997: 219*

The European situation prefigures the American one, with the notable difference that the transformation in attitudes and institutions for charity occurred, in the Pennsylvania example I will describe, during the first half of the 19th century. Prior to the mid-19th century, Pennsylvania hewed to a traditional notion of charity for the poor, which did not distinguish between types of poor. Pennsylvania colonial legislation made no explicit distinction between charity for the helpless versus the "able-bodied" poor in its 1771 poor law (Laws of the Commonwealth of Pennsylvania, 1810, I: 332–350). As an 1824 report presented to the Pennsylvania House of Representatives stated:

> [I]t must be admitted that the uniform practical construction of the [poor] law, both in England and in this state, has been, to place the relief granted to the able-bodied poor, on the same permanent footing with that which is extended to the old, the sick, the infirm, and disabled.
>
> *House Journal, 1824–1825, II: 173*

In the legislative session of 1833–1834 an act was proposed and passed that distinctly specified, as the 1771 law had not, that the overseers of the poor should provide work, rather than money, for the able-bodied poor (House Journal, 1833–1834, II: 324–325). As in Europe, poorhouses, which at the beginning of the century had been only found in a few places, came to be the dominant method of care for the "able-bodied" poor. Klebaner has called the rapid spread of the poorhouse "the most striking development in the field of public poor relief in the Atlantic States" (Klebaner 1952: 691).

Education was considered a form of charity (Schoenhals 1986) and so schools were provided free for all poor people in Pennsylvania prior to the changes in charity occurring in the 1830s. The 1790 Constitution of Pennsylvania, in Article VII, Section I called on the state legislature to "provide, by law, for the establishment of schools throughout the state in such manner that the poor may be taught *gratis*" (Minutes of the Pennsylvania Constitution Convention 1789: 218), and in 1809 a state law was passed acting on the constitutional mandate. The law required schools to accept poor children as students and instructed schools to obtain funds to cover this education from the counties in which the students resided (Statutes at Large of Pennsylvania, 1915, XVIII: 1171–1172).

But the provision of schools as charity for the poor came under attack. The rhetoric of the debates during the challenge to schools for the poor illustrates the dramatic transformation in attitudes toward the poor and children. Children replaced the poor as the targets of societal benevolence and provision of free state schools for all children, rich and poor, became the institutional manifestation of this dramatic transformation. Schools exist worldwide today and most of us have spent our childhoods at schools, ostensibly preparing for our adult lives. The widespread existence of schools today, however, should not blind us to how new and unusual a notion it was to create a state institution for all children in the 19th century. Not only was the creation of universal schooling a manifestation of a transformation in charity away from the poor and toward children, but also it grouped children together for the first time, across class lines, in institutions, schools, newly created for them.

This creation of a new category of children as the rightful recipients of societal adult-provided benevolence occurred at the same time that new views—reminiscent of the later Middle Ages and the modern period in Europe—sought to distinguish between the deserving and the undeserving poor. And the key trope in dividing the category of poor and unifying that of children was helplessness and innocence. In older times children had not been seen as innocent. Prior to the 19th century Protestant theology characterized children as evil beings, tainted with original sin. Puritan minister Benjamin Wadsworth wrote in 1721 that children's hearts "naturally, are a meer nest, root fountain of Sin, and wickedness … Indeed, as sharers in the guilt of Adam's first Sin, they're *Children of Wrath by Nature*" (Benjamin Wadsworth quoted in Heininger 1984: 2; original emphasis). But in the 19th century childhood came to be viewed as a time of universal innocence

(Heininger 1984: 2–3), a contrast to the able-bodied poor, whose presumed laziness and lack of a work ethic was assumed to derive from too much indulgence in the now-condemned pleasures of the body. Children were innocent because they were presexual. Adults could be held accountable for their own fates, and hence no longer deserved help unless they were, like helpless children, infirm and unable to provide for themselves. Children's innocence, too, was connected to their helplessness, in contrast to the ability of adults to work and therefore help—i.e., take care of—themselves. A newfound subject in the 19th century was the necessity of care for children, and the connection of this care to their helplessness. John Knox in 1834 delivered a discourse in the Dutch Church in New York, in which the helplessness of children was seen to necessitate parental care for them:

> In the whole range of human feelings ... where shall we find an affection so strong, so tender, so enduring, so invincible, so efficient as that of parents towards their offspring? ... The reason of this ... is to be sought for in the utter and long protracted helplessness of infancy.
>
> *Knox 1834: 24–25*

Let's look at the rhetoric from Pennsylvania legislators to see the new views of children and the poor, the way that the trope of helplessness and innocence unified all children and split the poor into categories, and the connection of all of this to the establishment of universal schooling for all children as a replacement for charity schooling for the poor, young and old. From its inception the 1809 law providing charity schools for all Pennsylvania poor people, children and adults, came under attack. The chairman of the Committee on Education in the Pennsylvania House of Representatives during the 1830–1831 session read a report criticizing the 1809 Act as follows: "This Act [the 1809 Act] in some measure militates with the spirit of our free institutions. They have an equalizing tendency; it, the contrary. They would confound all ranks, classes and distinctions; it marks, delineates and approves of them" (Fetterman 1831: 641)

In 1827 a number of prominent Pennsylvanians established the Pennsylvania Society for the Promotion of Public Schools. Although the Society functioned for only four years, its propaganda efforts were very important in paving the way for universal education. An 1830 memorial from the Society to the Pennsylvania Legislature urged that

> every child should have the opportunity of receiving an education which will fit him to fulfil all his duties. Happily ignorant of distinctive grades in society; aware that no one is debarred by our political constitution, from any station his talents and virtues may fit him to assume, they consider it a duty to establish a system of education, liberal and extensive as circumstance can possibly authorize.
>
> *Memorial to the Legislature 1830*

As a result of the pressure against the 1809 law, a Joint Committee of the Legislature was established to investigate the possibility of a system of universal education. Its report, issued during the 1833–1834 session, articulates the new ideology: Charity should go to all children, rather than to all of the poor:

> A radical defect in our laws upon the subject of education, is that the public aid now given, and imperfectly given, is confined to the poor. Aware of this, your Committee have taken care to exclude the word, poor, from the bill which will accompany this report, meaning to make the system general, that is to say, to form an educational association between the rich, the comparatively rich, and the destitute. Let them all fare alike in the primary schools, receive the same elementary instruction, imbibe the republican spirit, and be animated by a feeling of perfect equality. In after life, he who is diligent at school will take his station accordingly, whether born to wealth or not. Common schools universally established will multiply the chances of success, perhaps of brilliant success, among those who may otherwise forever continue ignorant. It is the duty of the State to promote and foster such establishments. That done, the career of each youth will depend upon himself.
>
> *Report of the Joint Committee 1834: 3–4*

The Joint Committee sent a bill to the floor for universal schooling, where it passed almost unanimously. The result was passage of a new law, in 1834, that replaced charity schools for the poor with schools provided statewide—funded in part through state funds and supplemented with a county school tax—for free to all children, poor and rich alike (Laws of Pennsylvania, 1833–1834: 171–179). (School attendance, however, was not yet made compulsory.) The Act of 1834 encountered opposition in 1835 but was saved from repeal. Thaddeus Stevens, a member of the Pennsylvania House, gave a speech that many testified had a great impact on them in encouraging them to vote against repeal (Wickersham 1969 [1886]: 333). Stevens' speech demonstrates the new view of children as innocent and hence, regardless of their parents' wealth or poverty, worthy of benevolence in the form of schooling:

> This law is often objected to because its benefits are shared by children of the profligate spendthrift equally with those of the most industrious and economical habits. It ought to be remembered, that the benefit is bestowed, not upon the erring parents, but the innocent children. Carry out this objection and you punish children for the crimes or misfortunes of their parents. You virtually establish castes and grades founded on no merit of the particular generation, but on the demerits of their ancestors; an aristocracy of the most odious and insolent kind—the aristocracy of wealth and pride.
>
> *Stevens 1904 (1835): 6–7*

During the 1837–1838 Pennsylvania Constitution Convention delegates sought, unsuccessfully as it turned out (since no consensus on a new clause could be reached), to modify Article VII of the 1790 Constitution, which had urged the state legislature to provide for the education of the poor. There was almost unanimous opposition to Article VII on the grounds that it singled out the poor as a separate class to receive educational charity. Delegates consistently referred to the "odious clause" that distinguished between the poor and non-poor, again reflecting the new consensus that children constituted a unified category, and one deserving of benevolence, while the poor no longer constituted such a unified category. The following quote by a delegate to the constitutional convention summarizes how the trope of helplessness was central to these new views urging benevolence to children, rather than to the poor. It nicely ties together, as well, all of the themes discussed in this section:

> Now he [the speaker refers to himself in the third person] apprehended that there was a substantial reason for confining this system of education to children. Upon what principle is it that the public at large is called upon to contribute funds for the support of these schools. It is because it is necessary for the welfare of the children of the commonwealth; and because they are altogether *incapable* of providing education for themselves. Then because they are *incapable* of making this provision themselves, it becomes the duty of parents to make it, and if the parents do not attend to it, it becomes the *duty of the government, as far as is in its power, to provide for the wants of that class of the community who are incapable of providing for their own wants. But, sir, this principle does not apply to adults.* Suppose a man of twenty-one years of age is uneducated, is he to be educated at public expense on this principle? Not at all. *He is able to provide for himself. The same reason does not exist, that the public should provide for his education as for the children.*
>
> *Proceedings and Debates of the Convention, 1838, V: 249–250; emphasis added*

The fundamental transformation I'm describing here was finalized later in the 19th century and during the 20th century Great Depression, when schooling was not only provided to all children, but was made compulsory for all of them, while work for children was newly outlawed. *Thus society was divided into two spheres, school for children and work for adults. And learning, concomitantly, was transformed into a means to an end—the preparation of children for adulthood and for adult employment,* at least for most males and many females. I should add that the fact that the means–end nature of schooling was/is fuzzier for women is consistent with the overall debasement of learning. Anything unpaid—whether going to school or doing the unpaid work in the home that is often consigned to women—is devalued by the very fact of its being unpaid.

Despite my obvious criticism of these transformations, I don't want to neglect the positive social consequences of schooling. The idea that even poor children will be educated for free, and in theory alongside the children of the rich, is a reasonably progressive notion, since it challenges rich/poor divisions (though not divisions of race) and reconstructs the most prominent societal division as one of child versus adult in place of rich versus poor. This is a potentially democratic notion. Theoretically, schools establish a meritocracy, in which anyone who is smart and who studies hard in school can achieve a good position in society. But, of course, that is theory and often not reality. I must also tell the reader that the elites who established Pennsylvania schools made it clear in their writings that their motives were *not* in sync with the democratic and social-leveling motives of the associations of working men in the state, groups that were also advocating universal schooling. It is interesting to note too that an informed reader might have guessed universal schooling would have been first proposed by industrialists, as a way to socialize lower-status children for the work discipline necessary for factory work. While there is a strong connection between schools and the Industrial Revolution evident later in the 19th century, the very earliest transformation was the shift in charity from the poor to children. Further, the leaders of that shift in Pennsylvania were not industrialists but legislators, especially lawyers (Schoenhals 1986), who were urged to establish schools so as to "mark your official career with an act which will indicate you as the chief benefactors of the commonwealth" (Memorial to the Legislature 1830).

The negative consequence of the social transformation wrought by universal schools for all children is that school came to be seen as more of a means than ever before. Learning became, as it is today, a childish activity, now that the schools walled off learning from most adults. (I know there are exceptions, but their exceptional status proves the rule.) *School was robbed of any genuine societal validation, because it is was and is now seen, along with work, as a means to pleasure but not a source of pleasure itself.* Contrast this with the role of learning among, say, European aristocrats (admittedly not an ideal example, but the point is still relevant). They pursued intellectual activities throughout life, and they engaged in them not only to symbolize their life of leisure but also one of the luxuries of that life: They had the time to enjoy learning and learning was one of their central pleasures. But not so in this new world of work and business, this new middle-class world. In this world, school and work are a burden to be endured on the road to vacations, the purchasing of consumer goods, and retirement—the ends that are supposed to give us happiness.

Moreover, the establishment of schools for children created a *greater* separation of means and ends than ever before. Apprentices had to "study" seven years before becoming a full artisan, but their learning and their future occupations were not segregated, since they learned at the workplace, from the master, a senior worker in their chosen field. But since schools are a general preparation for a general occupation that is years and years off, the conditions are established for the means to be more tenuously connected than ever before to the ends.

It is important to note that the basic transformations I have described here hold for schools around the world. All societies worldwide have created schools as institutions that are separate from the world and tied to it only by making school a means to an occupational end. One of the most noteworthy exceptions to this pattern occurred in China during the 1966–1976 Cultural Revolution, but even this is not as much of an exception as it seems at first glance. During that time

Mao declared that students, and their teachers and professors too, needed to be sent to the countryside to "learn from the peasants." I remember reading about this movement and the somewhat favorable reports from some American progressives at the time it occurred, who supported the seemingly populist notions of the Cultural Revolution, including the Maoist view that growing rice was more important to know about than "useless" book knowledge. I didn't exactly agree with what I knew about the Cultural Revolution as a young man, but I was intrigued, and this is partly what stimulated my desire to go to China in the first place, to study its education and culture in the 1980s. But I quickly learned that the Cultural Revolution had been neither pro-peasant nor a real critique of education. Instead, it was a way for China to punish the large masses of urban intellectuals, a term that includes students in China. As these groups threatened the stability of Mao's regime, he once again targeted intellectuals, as he'd done in the late 1950s, and he sent them to the countryside less as education and instead as punishment. I give the details of the Chinese movement partly to illustrate an exception to the usual pattern of education, since schools were closed and the often uneducated and sometimes barely literate peasants became the nominal teachers of the educated—youth and their teachers and professors. But more than this, China has returned to an educational system that has all of the characteristics I've described for school, hence showing that even in the most outlying of nations, the basic educational patterns—a division of adults versus children and work versus school—are in effect.

To summarize, this worldwide 19th- and 20th-century creation of universal schooling (or at least the ideal of such, since poor rural areas in much of the developing world still lack fully functioning schools) created the conditions for one of the most odious features of contemporary schooling to my mind—its lack of *intrinsic* pleasurable purpose and its tenuous connection even to any real extrinsic social purpose. Not only are its intrinsic pleasurable rewards devalued, but also the rewards recognized by society, entry into adulthood and a job, further serve to debase it, by making it childish—a preparation for adult life but not life itself.

School today, debased as a means to an end, but not a pleasurable end in itself

So, my critique of schooling as it exists today worldwide is not just that it is a means to an end. Even more so, my critique is of the nature of this means–end relationship:

1. The ends, a job and adulthood, are remote in time—years after the learning events.
2. The ends are ones not shared with one's teacher, or one's fellow classmates. That is, while you study side-by-side with your classmates, you don't share a communal job with them upon graduation. The rewards are individual and they separate those studying together from each other. Further, most of us secure a job that also fails to maintain our connection with our teachers; often they don't even know what becomes of us as adults. This divorce of teachers

from sharing in the achievements of their adult students is nicely illustrated in the Chinese belief that what is so frustrating about teaching is that you may never get to see what happens to your own students, thus never experiencing the fruits of your own labor.

3. Further, the ends—the rewards—are zero-sum. If I win at school, someone else usually must lose i.e., must be ranked below me. My win is someone else's loss. While we could imagine that society would create jobs for everyone qualified, the restriction of the number of jobs—a situation used to discipline workers and control them—means that school likewise must have winners and losers, and winners who win at the expense of others.

4. All of this serves to make school isolating, competitive, and anti-communal—the exact opposite of how learning should be.

5. Finally, the remoteness in time of school's goal, a job, and the radical separation between those who are your employers from those who are your teachers (we usually never see each other: I even don't know what jobs most of my college students finally obtain) means that there is space opened up for the means–end nature of schooling to become symbolic rather than real. While teachers like to say we are preparing students for their careers, much of what happens in school is more like a rite of passage, a hazing. It is an arbitrary erection of barriers, rather than any kind of real education with real purpose.

In Chapter 4 I discussed rites of passage and the way that, for example, medical education is a rite of passage. Interns and residents go for long stretches with no sleep. That this is not good medical practice should need no evidence but if evidence is needed it comes in the form of many young doctors making mistakes on patients because of sleep deprivation. Older doctors do not work these long, long hours so it would be hard to say that the long hours are anything but a kind of a hazing: "I did this so you must do this." Such hazings are typical barriers erected to screen entry into elite groups, and the hazing itself becomes a means for the group to claim eliteness. Doctors will justify their high salaries because of all the burdensome hazing/education they've had to endure. I've asked my doctor friends if the long hours of work have anything to do with preparing them to be good doctors, and no one has ever found a way to answer in the affirmative. How could they? Sleepless doctoring is bad medicine, and bad medical education, on the face of it.

What I am aiming to show here (and it is not an original point: I owe the observation of school being a rite of passage to Greg Urban, one of my favorite professors and the one who first taught me anthropology) is that school professes to be preparing us for something real. Sometimes this is the case but more often than not the things that happen in school have little real preparatory value. The more elite a school is, the more likely it is to put its students through hazings. When I started teaching at an elite liberal arts college in my first year of full-time teaching, I was told to increase the amount of reading the students were required to do compared to what I had previously required when teaching elsewhere. Why? No educational rationale was given. It was simply to conform to the "standards" of the elite place.

Students at that school cooperated, as usual, in their own debasement by reveling in their victimhood, using it as a badge of honor (and a means, upon graduation, to lay claim to a higher-status job, since they had endured a more "unique" experience than those at "easier" schools). They told me they played a game they called "misery poker." In misery poker person A says how miserable he is—how many papers he must write and books he must read all during the current sleepless night. Person B responds: "That's nothing. I have even more papers and even more books to read" and B specifies the exact amounts. Whoever is the most miserable is the winner—the one who is most virtuous because of enduring the greatest suffering.

Is this really education? What are these students really being taught? High anxiety typically interferes with cognition, so I highly doubt the winner of misery poker will remember anything s/he has learned during that sleepless night, or nights, other than being miserable and sleepless. It only provides these students with the war stories that students like to tell after graduation, recalling with bittersweet nostalgia the "hell" they have been through.

When one looks at other rites of passage, the real essence of what is being learned becomes clear. Ask any fraternity member what he had to do to join his fraternity. Often the initiation involves physical and emotional hardship. A common tactic is the use of shame—making students wear pajamas to class, or making them endure being urinated on by their "teachers." I've had a few students who have gone through military boot camp and they describe similar adventures—being publicly humiliated, being subjected to extreme heat and made to do extreme exercises in that heat. One student said that a number of her fellow boot campers became suicidal due to the physical and mental torment they endured, made all the more severe by a common rite of passage tactic: The isolation of the initiate from his/her friends and family. (Boot campers cannot call anyone outside the camp for weeks during their training).

To me, it is hard to imagine how any of this can be real, genuine training. In fact when I ask students what is being taught, they are quite clear: "We are being taught to be obedient. We are being taught by being abused to respect our abusers." They are, thus, being socialized for hierarchy.

Much of school is this way, and the more elite a school is, the more likely it is to create itself as a rite of passage. While schools, like any initiators, always make a pretense of the necessity of their rituals to making you into a good member of the club, the process is, in fact, arbitrary and ritualistic. It does little else than make you endure arbitrary hardship to teach obedience to the group, and to justify the group's claims to high status, due to how hard it is to enter.

I do not want to say that no useful learning takes place in school or that none of those of us who are teachers ever teach anything with social purpose. I wouldn't be a teacher if I thought that were true. But, at the same time, what I do want to assert is that we are salmon swimming against the stream. The nature of schools, and the value they are accorded as preparation for entry to a high-status job, if one can make it—this all works against those of us wanting to do something worthwhile in our teaching. I know, for example, that there are virtually no jobs in anthropology, so I am aware that while my field teaches fascinating and socially useful information, society does not use it. Thus, I feel a definite lack of purpose in my teaching, which I try hard to hide from my students! They know that the jobs that do exist are in more "practical" fields, and hence they too feel the socially constructed pointlessness of learning what I teach. I also have stumbled upon an unfortunate realization. If I make my teaching hard and stress the difficult nature of it, I can distract the students from feeling that what they are doing is pointless. In being subjected to hardship of any kind, they come to feel that what they are doing is meaningful, even if it has no meaning at all. I believe schools use this strategy to disguise the real arbitrariness of what we learn, and how we learn it. (The reader should note that I do not mean that what we learn is truly arbitrary, but rather that the way society treats learning and its end result makes much learning arbitrary.) By making students endure hardship, school becomes a rite of passage, and thus replaces real purpose with a ritualistic one.

School as simulation

No wonder school becomes a simulation. No wonder school pedagogy is unnatural in so many ways. School is about giving us status, and giving that status to us as individuals. It is not a collective enterprise in which we collectively learn how to make society better.

When I say these things to students, especially those wanting to become teachers, they not surprisingly debate me (which I encourage!). So here I offer only a few anecdotes to show the simulated nature of schooling:

- In classes the "why" question is all too seldom asked. We learn the history of the world, but we don't learn to question why certain things happened. I can remember catching my 10th-grade teacher off-guard by asking why there seemed to be no unified European empire after the fall of Rome. My chemistry teacher, considered one of the best teachers in our school, asked me to stop asking why and just memorize the equations.

  "Why" is a natural question that we ask of the world. So: Why is there such a disjuncture between the very natural asking of why in our daily lives and our tendency to not ask that question in school? I suggest that the disjuncture reflects the artificial nature of schooling. I also suspect that "why" is the most dangerous question and schools, geared toward teaching conformity and obedience, are especially sensitive to that question being asked.

- The nature of questioning: When we talk to friends and family, and ask them questions, they would think we had gone crazy if we asked them a series of questions whose answers we already know. "John, what is my name?" "John, what is the town where I grew up?" In conversation we ask questions to find out something.

But in schools we ask questions to test the knowledge of our students. This is perhaps okay up to a point. It is useful to ask questions to check student understanding. But the paucity of "real" and natural question-asking in the classroom makes inquiry there fake, a simulation.

Below I will suggest an alternative, but just a hint of that alternative now: Teachers should ask questions the answers to which we ourselves don't know. These might be questions such as "Student X, how many siblings do you have?" But they should also be questions which scholars have not yet answered: "Why do you think civilizations first arose 6000 years ago?" (Recall that Carneiro's answer to this question is accepted by many anthropologists, but not by all of them.)

- It never fails to amaze me that in science (e.g., in chemistry) class experiments are done by students who already know what outcome they will derive. What scientist would spend a good chunk of valuable research time doing experiments that have already been done, and whose results are already known? In real life we experiment to find out something. The fact that we don't do this often enough in school once again shows the simulated nature of schooling.

- In China: The Chinese know that their oral English skills are not that good and they also know that oral skills are often the most important ones for their interaction with foreigners. But the college entrance exam did not test oral English when I was an English teacher (doing my dissertation fieldwork) at a Chinese school in the late 1980s. As a result, students were as openly disinterested in my class as they could be. They would do other homework, play cards, not listen, talk to their friends. And this was one of the best schools in central China. Perhaps that was part of the problem. Being a good school, students had learned not to study that which is actually useful, but to study that which is useful in passing the college entrance exam. Of course, I can't entirely blame them. They must pass that test to go to college, to get the lifelong good job that college attendance guaranteed in late 20th-century China (no longer). But this is precisely the point. As long as school is tied toward an end that is remote, and individual, and hierarchical, it cannot genuinely serve the collective and contemporary needs of the society, nor will learning have the organic response to purpose that it should have.

I know that every American professor knows the American counterpart to the Chinese reaction. No matter how interesting something seems to us, students reduce us to size with that question we all detest: "Will this be on the test?"

I know some readers will be quick to cite teachers and teaching styles that are clear exceptions to what I have described above. In fact I would count myself as one of those exceptions. But as I've noted, I clearly realize that I can never really do anything close to what I want to do as a teacher, because of the structural patterns I've described. If education is to really be made enjoyable, major transformations must occur in both society and schools, and it is to this topic that I turn now.

Education in Utopia

Here I will discuss schooling in Utopia, but first I need to discuss some guiding principles. These eight basic principles are the foundation of my proposals for changes to education:

1. The hierarchy of schools, and the way schools support the hierarchy of society, must end. Schools today have as a central function the sorting of students into those who are good and those who are not so good. This sorting function will be eliminated in schools: No grades will be given in learning environments. Those who are "better" at learning—a dubious and problematic concept anyway, as any thoughtful teacher knows—will get no greater rewards than anyone else. In particular schooling will not be the entrée to occupations and work, and therefore being a better learner will not be rewarded by a "better" and higher-status job.

2. Learning will not be geared mainly toward children and the young. It will be lifelong and will be a central activity of all peoples in Utopia.

3. Since learning will be for young and old, and for pleasure rather than pain, it will not be considered work. In fact the dichotomy between work and play will no longer exist and the new nature of learning will have a central role in erasing this unfortunate division. I know that many of us will still want variety in our lives, and so certain natural dichotomies, such as activity versus quiescence, can still exist. This dichotomy is natural and reasonable since all animals alternate activity and rest, and it does not carry the cultural judgment of the sort made of "work" versus "play."

4. The ultimate purpose of learning will be pleasure. Any reform of learning institutions will be focused on making learning more enjoyable for all. The notion that school is only good as a means to an end—a good job for the individual, the production of ever more inventive consumer goods by the educated society—will end.

5. Learning will be collective to as great an extent as possible. The purpose of learning will be, above all, to please learners and teachers (who will also not be clearly dichotomized) *through interaction*. In fact learning might be best defined, then, as collective and interactional activity focused on participants jointly encountering novelty, and striving collectively to understand it. By seeking out novelty, by doing so collectively, and by combining the emotional experience of it with the quest to better understand it, novelty and the excitement it can so naturally bring to humans (and other animals too) will reach its full potential in Utopia. The excitement of the new will be a variation to, or an important addition to, joy in the lives of Utopians.

6. The gaminess of learning—learning as an inauthentic experience separate from other true learning—will end, as schools and learning are integrated with society. School will have genuine purpose, not fake purpose.
   Is there a contradiction here? After all, I have condemned the way that the means–end nature of schools is inextricably linked to hierarchy and makes learning into a simulation. If learning is to have a purpose, isn't this perpetuating a means–end

rationale for it? I have thought long and hard about this important issue. It is necessary to discuss with nuance what kinds of means and ends we are talking about.

In my analysis of school as a rite of passage, I wanted to demonstrate that the perceived means–end relationship of school as the means of preparation for obtaining an elite job was fake, fake in the sense that much of what we do in school often has little genuine function as preparation for elite jobs and is more a symbolic process to allow us to claim the status of those jobs by the usual rite of passage logic: "I've suffered hard in this rite of passage, so I deserve elevation into the elite community that has brought suffering upon me. Through having suffered, I am now worthy of that eliteness."

I also analyzed other factors of the school–work means–end relationship—such as the fact that the means and the end are so remotely connected in time and space, and the way in which this separates teaching and working, rather than integrating them. As a teacher, I discussed too the effects on teachers. Our teaching activity and the results of that activity, when our students purportedly use what they've learned from us in their work (to the extent that they do so), are not accessible to us because of the huge gaps in space and time between schools and the workplace. Teachers rarely, if ever, see the results of our teaching in action. At best we may hear our previous students discuss their work lives, but we seldom get to experience along with them the learning and working connection. This makes our teaching seem purposeless and simulated, since the purported end is remote and, so often, symbolic rather than truly related to our teaching activity.

So my critique is not just of means and ends but of the fake means–end relationship between school and later activity, activity remote in space and time and, in fact, in genuine purpose. The notion, however, that learning about X should have some purpose is to say that X and the world around us should be in interaction. Ironically, today's segregation of schools as means-making institutions separated from the "real world" is what makes so much of academia "academic"—in the pejorative sense of that word. Those of us in the upper echelons of teaching sense the gaminess of teaching, a good move on our part, but we make an unfortunate protest against it by saying that learning should be pure and devoid of any purpose. We revel in the notion that our research is pure and need not have any purpose. I have seen this quite clearly with so many job candidates who, when I ask them the significance of their dissertation research, cannot answer! Clearly, they and their professors have encouraged them to study things without thinking through why they are doing so. They cannot even answer the most obvious question, "What does your research contribute to the field of anthropology" (these are anthropology job candidates), so their research not only lacks "practical" and "real-world" purpose but also purpose and relationship to the activities of other academics in their same field, within the rarified world of academic anthropology.

While the professorial reaction to means–end teaching is understandable, it unfortunately does not solve the problem we intend to address. In fact, by being academics who research for no obvious purpose, our research becomes something like the activities of the aristocrat learner: "I am studying this not because it has merit in being studied. I am studying this because I am so elite that I don't have to care about whether it has merit or use. I am so elite that these issues need not concern me. I can live apart from the world." The result is, ironically, to connect our putatively pure academic activity to the world of hierarchy and status, and to the world of the aristocrat. Like the aristocrat, we set ourselves off from the common folk not only by refusing to address their "needs," but also by talking to each other in specialized language inaccessible to common people, and even inaccessible to other academics who do not belong to our increasingly narrow specialties. Our well-intentioned reaction against means and ends has made us indulge in narrow and elite language, without much of an audience for our work. The effects of the lack of an audience for our work is especially evident in academic music I think, as anyone who has listened to much (though not all) of this music can attest. The general recognition of over-specialization throughout the academia hints strongly, as well, at the harm done by having no audiences, or only limited ones.

So rather than eschew all ends, we need to think clearly about what kind of ends to learning are acceptable and what kinds are fake and corrupting. I want to assert that, above all, we introduce the concept of learning that is "relational," as opposed to learning that is a means to an end. Relational learning is desirable. It does not avoid ends and means but does not make learning the means and everything else the ends. First of all, learning about A will be deemed better if it can relate to learning about B. In this formulation, A is not subservient to B, nor B to A. Rather, connections between them make them more interesting (and pleasurable too). An example: Say I find (this is a real example from my current research) that Chinese elderly peasants say their 1949 revolution was not a peasant revolution. Say, too, I find that they do not talk of revolution in the nationalistic terms so common among Mao and his followers. This finding is not an isolated one, but it relates to larger discussions about nationalism as motive (or not) of the Chinese revolution and relates as well to the longstanding view of that revolution as unique because of its nature as peasant-led. The finding, too, has additional relations, with comparative social movement research, which uses the Chinese revolution to theorize about revolutions generally. Citing the significance of my research and seeking to connect it as broadly as possible to research outside China, and to fields other than anthropology, makes the research both more related to what others are studying, more significant because of this relationship, and, frankly, more interesting. (Ironically and sadly, I've often found that journal critics dislike research that seeks broad connections, because they believe that disinterested and disconnected research, and esoteric discussions, are often the most "academic." How wrong this view is.)

Relational learning also means learning that relates to the world around us, and to our own lives. With the deinstitutionalization of schooling, that which happens in our world and that which we understand about our world can become two sides of the same coin. Neither activity, living in the world nor our quest to better understand it, is given the priority as an "end." This will sound cliché but the cliché has merit: We will learn by living and live by learning. There will be no separation between these activities and, in the best-case scenario, we will be like babies who live and learn simultaneously. The speed with which infants learn, and the joy with which they do so, shows the wisdom of erasing, as much as possible, distinctions between inquiry and life. If I can display some disciplinary chauvinism, I think that the anthropological idea of learning about the life of a given people by entering their society and living along with them demonstrates what I am discussing here. Daily activities of the anthropologist become the method to garner an understanding of the culture in which one is living. We do not learn something separate from life but we learn by living.

So relational learning is learning that has a purpose, but a purpose not of greater value than the learning process itself. Relational learning also does not overspecialize. It always seeks significance in its findings, striving to relate finding A in field A to finding B in fields A and B. This significance, again, does not make A or B means or ends. It just means that A and B are related, a far different statement from the hierarchy of a means–end relationship. One should note here that, when comparing, say, cancer research with philosophy, neither will be deemed more worthy, more purposeful, than the other (consistent with the general dehierarchicizing of everything). Philosophy that relates A to B, or philosophy that engages a large audience, might be more relational, hence more significant and purposeful, than cancer research that is esoteric, or cancer research conducted in a remote laboratory. And the fact that the metrics for measuring purpose in Utopia are no longer monetary, or otherwise reductionist (e.g., physical health as opposed to happiness and mental health), a new technological finding, or even a new finding on cancer, will not automatically be more useful to society than a philosopher saying something that is truly significant due to its relation to our lives and the joy of greater understanding it gives us.

Above all, relational learning is relational in the sense of being communal. Learners will come together, but so too will an active audience to the research in which the learners are engaged. Just as music or acting without an interested audience becomes sterile, so too with any other activities in school or in the academy. Thus even the most seemingly esoteric research will be open to an interested audience. After all, as so many authors and academics can attest, it is in seeking to communicate our findings and ideas to others, such as students or a book audience, that we come to best understand our own material. Only with an audience can we truly learn and create and do so with the interactional joy that is so central to human life including, *and especially*, that most potentially interactive of all activities: Learning. Thus relational learning, purposive learning, is not inconsistent with pleasure, the pleasure that I have said is the ultimate purpose of learning. It is, in fact, the best way to find pleasure in learning.

7. Learning and research will be open to all interested people, not just those who specialize in the field. This openness is of course a key requirement, since it gives researchers and learners the audiences so critical to enjoyable learning. But for those skeptics among the readership, I want to argue here that interactive learning, and the opening of elite research to an interested lay audience, will also lead to much better research.

I have often found that my own students, uninhibited by the kinds of questions that academics know we should not ask, end up asking some of the most penetrating questions. One reason this is so is because academic research, like anything else, is subject to pressures for conformity. Among academics those who say what everyone already knows (or believes) get acclaimed, especially if they can say it in a fancy way. In anthropology Clifford Geertz is a person who took the basic assumptions of anthropology and rendered them in an elegant fashion. Little of what he said was new, but by invoking philosophy, literary criticism, and other fields, academics were easily seduced into thinking that what he was saying was somehow special. I can remember knowing that I was supposed to think his work was profound. I kept wondering, as a "naive" second-year undergraduate, why I was failing to understand the profundity of Geertz. It is interesting that while Geertz's works were the bibles of the 1970s and 1980s, it has been over a decade since I have even heard his name mentioned at anthropology conference sessions I've attended. Clearly, my young and naive self was onto something.

So too was my friend, Douglas Futuyma, the eminent biologist, when I told him that anthropologists believe that there should be no comparison of different cultures. I also told him that I do not believe this myself but that it is standard orthodoxy. My last book elicited from an anonymous reviewer the comment: "Doesn't Schoenhals know that comparison in anthropology went out of date long, long ago?" Doug, not knowing this, was aghast: "How can you be scientific and learn anything meaningful without comparison? An enormous amount of what we know about biology comes directly from comparisons among species." He's quite right. There are reasons that anthropologists don't compare, and having studied our field's history (anti-comparison was advocated by the Boasians to challenge 19th-century ethnocentric methods and beliefs), I know what these are. But Doug's question was exactly the kind anthropologists don't ask each other—the question of the intelligent lay person. These are the kinds of questions needing to be asked. Perhaps comparison has its faults, but the anti-comparative stance should not be accepted by our field as unquestioned orthodoxy.

The naivety of the young and those without training is often precisely what is needed to make for the best research and creative activity. The "naive" person asks questions based upon interest and pleasure, rather than based upon a dichotomy of good/bad, a dichotomy largely fashioned around disciplinary platitudes. Thus, just as an audience reacting based upon pleasure is a better audience for a musician, and a more natural one, so too with any creative endeavor.

One of the best examples of this comes from medicine, from AIDS research. People with AIDS have taken a huge interest in the research of AIDS scientists and have challenged their methods and the focus on limited treatments. The result of the attention by lay people is that AIDS researchers were forced to rethink their approaches, a rethinking that significantly improved AIDS research and the resulting treatments (see Epstein 1996: 337–341).

8. Will there still be schools? Where will learning actually occur? Since institutionalizing learning in schools built by the state for children makes education

means–end and divorces it from a genuine purpose, much of education must be deinstitutionalized. The research and learning groups referenced previously, and discussed in more detail below, will be a primary place where learning will occur and these groups will be neither age-limited nor age-segregated.

Also in the section below on group learning I address the issue of "teacher" and "learner." I do not think that these roles should be totally eliminated but they must be increasingly democratized. In research groups there may be leaders of the research who will play the role of teachers. In other contexts some people may act as teachers, but this will not preclude students from also assuming a teaching role, nor will it preclude the teacher from being in a learning role.

Here are a few specifics on how the above can happen. In this discussion I am using "teachers" and "students" loosely of course, and these words should not be seen as analogous to the words, and the roles, they designate today:

- Teachers will be encouraged to ask questions to which they don't know the answer. For example, anthropologists don't know, for sure, why hierarchy arose 6000 years ago. I have cited Carneiro (1970) in this book, but his hypothesis is untested. One of my own favorite classes in teaching undergraduates is to assign them Carneiro to review his theory and then ask for pros and cons. I also ask students to come up with their own theories of the evolution of hierarchy and the state, something they are far more willing to do once I tell them that the question, "How and why did hierarchy originate among humans?" is not solved. The fact that I am asking them to speculate on a genuine question, rather than one whose answer is already known, makes the discussion seem real, not a simulation.
- Teachers will not have authoritarian and punitive power.
- Discourse will be democratized. The teacher will not necessarily control the topics to be discussed, nor the questions which everyone should answer. Anyone can pose a question to be discussed. I realize many readers may foresee chaos in this process, but such chaos really only occurs in classrooms today, where the hierarchical nature of the teacher–student relationship invites discourse chaos—students talking out of turn—as a challenge to the teacher's status and to the overall hierarchy.

  If there are discourse problems, groups can experiment with different methods of discourse moderation. For example, there might be a discourse moderator who is entirely separate from the research leader/teacher. This would help ensure that the teacher does not gain undue power.

But isn't there a need to have separate schools for the very young, to teach them things like reading and basic arithmetic, for example? Yes, there are things that young people need to learn. I will concede this point. Thus there will still be schools, established by volunteers and voluntarily attended by youth (yes, this can work: In places like rural mountainous China where schooling is a luxury, I've known many kids begging their parents for the privilege to attend school). These schools will be for children during the first few years that it takes them to learn basic skills. There will be no grading in these schools. The curriculum will be as integrated as is possible with the activities and interests of children occurring outside of school. There is, of course, much to be said about how to do this—how, for example, to make reading a naturally occurring activity, similar to the learning of the ability to speak. I won't give more specifics here, however, only because so many others before me have done that part so well.

So there will be teachers too, but these individuals may or may not spend their whole time as teachers. That will be their choice. I think that the healthiest approach would be for these teachers to not be full-time unless that is their true passion, so that teaching, like schooling, does not become any more segregated an activity than it has to be.

The specifics of learning in Utopia

1. *The nature of the groups in which learning occurs*: What will the research groups be like? How will they function in a manner that is most natural and sincere? How will they be organized to generate the most enjoyable learning?

To a certain extent, once humans are given the ability to learn free of coercion and free of judgments that affect their future and free too of the anxiety and often depression this induces, they should do so readily, and with pleasure. In some ways I hesitate to say anything more—one of the reasons writing recommendations for this chapter has been difficult for me: I almost don't see the need to do so.

But a few issues need to be addressed. If hierarchy crowds out joy, then we must make sure that there are no new hierarchies in these research groups. So let me describe more about how the research groups, the inquiry groups, will operate.

As noted in this chapter and Chapter 3, groups with similar creative interests and learning interests will form together. Consistent with the eradication of the division between work and learning, they will both create and learn together; in addition they might also live together. For example, those interested in experimental physics, will form a study/research group. Unlike physics or any field today, "experts" and lay people will be grouped together. In some cases the lay people will be the audience for the work and findings of the experts, but I would alter that often as well.

Who will lead these inquiry groups? I propose two alternatives:

> *Alternative one*: Experts will continue to lead the research endeavors but lay people will join in the research as full co-researchers and co-questioners. The search for answers will be the responsibility of all group members, whether expert or amateur. So, too, with the formulation of questions. Today questions that are deemed relevant to research are defined by those with power and authority. It should not be this way. Anyone, not just the leaders, will be given the right to ask a question interesting to them and relevant to the group, and have it considered by the group. The equality of this process—the full

involvement of the lay amateurs and in particular their ability to contribute questions that interest them and have them considered seriously as possible research agendas for the group—is a way of honoring them as full members of the group. I know that many readers will object that this will destroy research. But I remind these readers of my discussion earlier, in which I point out that even today many of the most astute thinkers are amateurs, untainted by "knowledge" of what we professionals have defined as good questions to ask, and ones that shouldn't be asked. And that is today, with a system that makes questioning and learning into a simulation. When this is no longer the case, there may still be people who are more knowledgeable than others, but they do not deserve a monopoly on the right to research and question. By democratizing these rights, the full talents, and the full curiosities, of the widest possible spectrum of humans will be put into play.

Alternative two: No one will lead the group, or experts and amateurs alike can take turns leading it. This might not work out—I truly don't know for sure— but it might also work well. Utopia should be empirical and scientific in all respects, including experiments upon itself. I encourage trial of this alternative; if it is too democratic and too anarchic, it can be dropped. Or those who want a different approach, can simply form expert-led groups. Then there will be the widest possible array of groups, and individuals will be free to join whichever group they find most meaningful and enjoyable.

2. *Pleasure and the "use" of learning*: A major theme of this chapter has been that education today has a use that is not real—sorting youth into adult positions. What we learn in school and the end for which we learn it have little relationship to each other. This leads school to be a simulation, an insincere exercise that has little to do with real learning or curiosity.

Utopia must be different. It should be relational, as described above, and one important way for it to be relational is to connect learning to a real use. Thus, for the sake of good learning and for the sake of a better society, I want to propose that there be continual experimentation and learning directed toward improving Utopia itself.

Let me give some specifics for how Utopia-oriented learning could occur. In the last chapter I suggested that there be life-history media, devoted to portrayals of average people. In the course of assembling life histories, ethnographers will collect information on what makes people happy about Utopia and what makes them unhappy. Based on this information, reformers—individuals or groups of reform-interested individuals—will propose changes in Utopia (within the bounds of the basic principles, which will be summarized in the next chapter). Reformers will then debate each other's proposals. They will be required to give evidence from life-history research to support their proposals. Reformers might also do research on change-making, a sorely under-researched issue today, in order to craft implementation strategies. They could collect information on past changes in Utopia, how these were implemented, how people reacted, and so on, so as to arrive at a plan for how to make changes in the most efficient *and* happy way. Reformers would thus debate proposals and implementation strategies, arguing for both the change and the method of bringing it about. Based on these public debates, individuals who are convinced of the merits of a particular reform proposal will volunteer to be the test case for it. They will form a small test community, and the proposing individual or group will implement their changes in this test community, broadening it to wider communities as the desire arises.

The idea of doing all of the above is not only to make learning useful in Utopia, but also to encourage learning about society by acting upon it. I often feel that much social science research and teaching today is voyeuristic. We learn about problems, almost with the glee of the nosy bystander, but we rarely use our learning to do something about the problems we observe. I want learners to be proactively involved in creating the kinds of worlds that they want (again, as long as those worlds are consistent with Utopia's basic principles). Since the world we live in is something that profoundly interests all of us, it should fascinate us to debate what this world should be like, how it might be improved, and what means might be used to implement improvements. And it will be more fascinating still to be real empirical scientists, who experiment with new ideas, to see how they function, rather than merely discussing them in a classroom, with no attempt to implement them. Formulating new ideas and implementing them makes learning truly engaging, and it will also make Utopia a truly living and breathing society, in which its residents can feel that they have contributed to its continued refinement.

My advocacy of learning geared toward improving one's society responds to what I see as a major defect in education and politics today. I often feel that my students are disenfranchised from both school and the world around them, since they feel they have so little ability to positively affect that world. This disenfranchisement leads to an understandable depression and apathy. By giving people the power to make changes and by also institutionalizing change-making that is driven by knowledge and experimentation, both learning and politics can be mutually invigorated. Learning will have useful effects and individuals can play a role in using their learning to put those effects into place to improve their own, and others', lives. Thus empowered, learners will debate the world around them not as voyeurs, but as real participants.

Although most of the concrete proposals in this book can only really succeed if the full changes of Utopia are instituted, I do think that learning and research aimed at making positive change is a pedagogy teachers can, and should, implement today. Let me formulate a specific example, to further illustrate how this proposal could work, whether today or in Utopia.

Let's take the aging of the population as an example. Students–researchers could interview the elderly about their desires and needs. They could conduct cross-cultural research on the meaning of aging in other societies and the cultural values underpinning pro-elderly values. They could also go to other cultures to observe the treatment of the elderly in pro-elderly cultures. Thus enlightened through direct research, they might formulate proposals for ameliorating the problems of aging in a society such as the US. They would then form groups, each of which would advocate a specific proposal to an audience of elderly Americans. Those eld-erly who like group A's proposal would then volunteer to form a small community for testing out A's ideas and group A would then implement their proposal and carry out assessments of it, to be compared to other groups, and their proposals and implementation. After implementation, student leaders (or teachers) could then reconvene groups for more debate and discussion of the merits of the various proposals, and they would also lead analysis of the larger social principles under-lying the success of some proposals. To me, this kind of learning is real and useful and hence pleasurable. It helps others, helps ourselves too (since, in this case, we will all be old one day), and it does so not by distant learning—voyeuristic learning of society—nor by simple involvement in society's already-existing remedies, such as volunteering at nursing homes, as important as that is. Instead, learning's aim becomes the creation of new and better social practices, something we usually only allow adult workers to do today, and, I might add, something we do poorly because of the division of learning for youth, and work for adults. This division frequently makes those of us involved in change-making undervalue the necessary research that must go into change processes. I have seen this undervaluing at work even among my graduate students in international development, a field devoted to change. My students think that learning occurs in the classroom. When I have pushed them to do ethnography before implementing their projects in countries abroad, they frequently rebel, believing, wrongly, that real knowledge is found in books, rather than learned through their own engagement with the world. And who can entirely blame them? Learning about South Asian women's needs by living with them costs little. Learning about their needs while an Ivy League stu-dent is extremely expensive. Thus my students have come to believe that the latter learning is the most valuable because it is the most costly, when in fact it is the former learning that is truly invaluable.

One type of ethnographic learning that I think would be especially useful, and which should be institutionalized as a regular feature of research in Utopia, is the ethnography of hierarchy. While Utopia will aim to eliminate hierarchy and will hopefully succeed in doing so, hierarchy might still exist in subtle ways. I have had my own students conduct ethnographies of life around them to discover the subtleties of existing racism, sexism, and class hierarchy; Utopia researchers could do likewise. For example, one of my most clever student papers examined where the server in a restaurant placed the bill when there was a male–female couple being served. This student observed this issue in both family restaurants and fancy ones, thus examining the conflation of class and gender. Interestingly, though perhaps not surprisingly, the bill was most often given to the man in the fancy restaurant, while in the family (non-elite) restaurant the bill was most often placed in the middle of the table, between the man and woman (suggesting, perhaps, that class eliteness reinforces traditional gender roles). I have had other students look at the holding open of doors as it relates to gender, age, and race; seating on public transport and race; and many other interesting issues. With similar research regularly conducted in Utopia, all Utopians will become attuned to noticing hierarchy whenever and wherever it exists. And, of course, when they discover it existing, they can propose changes to ameliorate the problem.

3. *Experiential learning*: Researchers/learners will not only study society but also will participate as much as possible in that which they are studying. In anthropology we do not denigrate knowledge gained through direct and personal experience. Indeed, we realize that if you want to know how a Chinese peasant lives, for example, the best way to find out is to live with Chinese peasants, and do whatever they do. Today schooling tends to prevent such experiential learning, since the school, like the museum, encloses its activities from the rest of society. And if we actually do carry out experiential learning in today's schools, the fact that grades and a future job are the "real" motive undercuts the meaningfulness of the immediate experiences.

I want to change this as much as possible and democratize the learning curriculum to its fullest extent. This is why I like the idea I presented in Chapter 5 that we take a simple person, and study them by living life in their shoes. This kind of learning gives value to ordinary people, by making them objects of study. And the experiential teaching process by which we find out about another person is simply a formalization of what we do when we are creating a relationship, and learning to feel compassion and love for someone. This teaching method thus combines the best of learning with the best of compassion—we learn about another ordinary individual, and we come to really understand them by being them, or by writing and acting out dramas about their lives. Such democratization of the learning curriculum and of pedagogy is what is needed to make school genuinely purposeful, purposeful in an egalitarian way, and in a way that makes learning naturalistic, by breaking down the false division between what we do while learning and what we do while living. Best of all, there are enough people in the world, in enough variations, that we can never run out of people, or situations, to experience. Boredom is the enemy of happiness, and a broader view of learning, one that makes everyone a worthy topic of "study," will guarantee that there is always something interesting to learn.

A historical dimension could also be added to experiential learning. Individuals or groups can reenact the lives and actions of past historical periods, something already done by many historical groups. But, in addition, groups should reenact the lives and actions of everyday peoples, the people not usually found in history textbooks. This would include reenacting the lives of one's own forebears, as a way to understand them better, and bring the concern with ancestry into the present.

4. *Science learning*: I am a social scientist, so my ideas about teaching that field, such as the proposal above, are the most well-worked out. But I have always had a strong capacity for math and physical sciences too, and so I am going to draw on this capacity and interest to describe science teaching in Utopia.

First an observation, and an ironic one: While social scientists recognize the importance of social interaction to humans, we devalue it in the way that we do our research. The scientists and mathematicians I know are much more collabora-tive than social scientists, with the exception of psychologists who, for some reason (maybe greater funding opportunities), research and write collectively. So science learning has partially overcome one obstacle that social science learning must sur-mount: The need for interaction and collaboration.

But where I think science and math teaching fails is in emphasizing equations and processes for problem-solving, at the expense of greater understanding. Like so much else (here I think of musical pedagogy), we learn to comply with what some authority figure has already worked out for us. This, to me, is dreadful learning—boring at best, disengaging to many (the cause of so many students saying "Why is it important to learn this equation?" "Why should I learn math?"), and defective above all in being a simulation of inquiry rather than the real thing.

But how can students learn basic math and science without the teaching being, at some level, inauthentic? After all, Newtonian mechanics is already known, but it needs to be learned by youth before they can learn anything else. How can it be learned in a meaningful way?

I am all too aware that these questions, perhaps most especially for math teaching, have already been tackled in great depth and I am familiar with some of the solutions, since I grew up learning the new math in the 1970s. Its emphasis on process over solutions is good, but the spirit of making math learning organic and less rote needs to be carried much further.

Let's say, for the sake of argument, we are studying geometry. I think I would have students arrive at as many geometric principles as they can without studying anything that has come before, thus almost reliving the process of past geometers. This is not reinventing the wheel, because in the process of reliving this process, students might come to think of things differently than did ancient students of geometry or they would raise questions that the ancients never answered. In fact that would be a goal: To realize the things that are *not* known, as well as what is known. True understanding of anything, and true description of anything know-able, requires us to specify both what is known and what is not known, so the pro-cess I'm proposing here is useful and pleasurable too because students can relive the experiences of ancient mathematicians.

Once having tried their hand, perhaps not very successfully, at querying the geometrical world themselves, then students can learn what is already known, by studying conventional geometry as it has always been taught. But even here I would want them to recreate as much as possible of, say, Euclid's study conditions. What did he know first? What questions did he ask next? What did this lead to? This is the real process-over-product learning because students will be learning not just what others have come to know, but *how* they came to their conclusions.

I have several purposes here. First, consistent with a general Utopian principle of having people live in the shoes of others, I want the same to happen for intel-lectual understanding: Live in the shoes of those who have made important dis-coveries before. Experience their discovery process in as close a fashion as possible to how they discovered it. I might even add that students could study the lives of the discoverers and try to live out some of these conditions, in the interest both of good science and good history of science. Second, I want to teach a critical skill: Epistemological rigor. I want them to think about how things are known, and have come to be known, by enacting that process for themselves. Third, I want to give students as much of a chance to feel the pleasure of discovery as past mathematicians and scientists did. And why not? They no doubt experienced pleasure in making their discoveries. Why should the fact that they have done it before preclude us from having that same pleasure, that same sense of discovery that they had?

But this is only the beginning. The next step would be for students to compare their own geometries with conventional geometry. What differences exist? What questions, especially, does conventional geometry overlook? What questions does it fail to answer? How can we answer these questions? This last question becomes the ultimate aim of continuing scientific study. And the unanswered questions that anyone formulates could then be entered into a world database, so that anyone can address questions of interest to others.

5. *Humanities*: Just as much social science learning and research is voyeuristic and inorganic, so too with much learning in the humanities. Much of this field is devoted to activities secondary to the creation of the arts themselves. So many humanities teachers take as their goal guiding students to learn how to talk about art already created.

A quick fix to this problem would be to say that all learning about art and music should be done by creating it oneself, individually and in groups. But I do recognize the value of audience reaction to art and music, of course. After all, this is an integral part of the interactive joy that I want to be maximized in Utopia. But I think that the nature of audience reactions has to be rethought.

I have done much already to problematize this issue in my discussions in Chapter 5. I have suggested new ways to have audiences react, ways that elide meritocracy and the building of hierarchy, but which, nonetheless, give meaningful feedback to performers. Even in the absence of a performer, the same process can be used. If we are reading a classical literary work, the emphasis will be on enjoying it and/or making it more enjoyable by discussing how it might be altered. Yes, I am advocating that Utopians take Shakespeare and rewrite him to suit their own desires. I know this will offend literary purists, but that reaction is indicative. It is a reaction that builds up individual human creators and their creations as godlike, above change. I want to involve people in a process of creation even as they read Shakespeare, reliving the way he wrote it, and perhaps altering some of the ways that he wrote. This process will be more enjoyable because artistic works will be interacted with and a discourse and discussion of pleasure will be stimulated. Nothing, even the greats, will be taken for granted as good and pleasing. This is one way to further diminish the cult of celebrities, in this case literary and artistic ones. And it is a means to make enjoyment of great works, rather than recognition of their merits, the centerpiece of our engagement with them, thus furthering the goal of affirming pleasure over means–end merit.

One caveat: I am acutely aware how difficult it really is to describe what pleases us about a work of art, just as it is difficult to really specify what makes it good. This is one puzzle, among many, whose answer is very important, but whose answer continues to elude me.

6. *Recreating older schooling traditions*: The reader might be surprised by this suggestion. One of the activities of inquiry groups will be to study different pedagogical traditions through time. They will then appoint someone as teacher, and the remaining group members as "students" and they will recreate those different teaching traditions, by teaching following the exact pedagogies, and content, as existed in those traditions. I am thinking that students could study the way Confucius taught his students and also the way Confucian schools through the centuries taught students—the memorizing of Confucian truths. The same with Socrates and the Socratic method. Different pedagogies existing through time would be studied by recreating them, and learning according to their methods.

My reason for advocating such an approach is that I want everyone to become aware of the way that pedagogy and content reflect the sociology of the historical context in which the education took place. This is important to know not only for historical reasons, but also to denaturalize any way of teaching—that is, to see that what we do as teachers and learners is always contrived in response to historical and social demands.

Once all of this is done, the inquiry group then will play with the idea of pedagogy and will advocate as many creative new traditions as they can think of.

7. *School and the making of community*: Education appeals to two of the most profound human desires, the desire for learning and the desire for community. Or, at least, it has the potential to appeal to both. Schooling today combines the worst of individualism and community. Students are judged as individuals, usually learn individually, and yet do everything else in school as a community (sports, social clubs, the ordinary life of the school). Thus, they come to see learning and community, and learning and their social lives, as opposed. This is especially true of those cultures where parental authority over marital choices has weakened. Where there is arranged marriage, or strong parental authority over marital choices, parents and adults set the tone by making sure that well-educated youth (with the significant exception in some countries of females, for whom education is not always a plus) are most desirable in the marriage market. But in much of the world, doing well in school is seen as an impediment to finding friends and lovers, since those who do well in school are seen as validating through their scholastic achievement values often seen as antithetical to the peer culture of friends and lovers. Achievers are— or are socially constructed to be—individualistic, to value study above sociality, and to affirm their loyalty to parents and adult culture, in opposition to the peer culture.

If learning is to be made communal, it must, for starters, challenge these dynamics. In Chapter 3 I describe new arrangements to break the natal/affinal conflict, which also plays out among youth as a conflict between parents and youths' search for love. This will go a long way toward blunting anti-learning and anti-intellectual orientations toward youth. So too will the Chapter 5 challenge to shame since, as described there, shame plays a major role in creating opposition peer groups, with opposition values, in the schools. And, of course, the dismantling of the hierarchy and competition, which pit students against each other, will be a major help.

But learning must be made intrinsically compatible with community and sociality. To me, the lack of community and meaningful interaction in learning communities today is one of its most tragic failings. There are so many ways that learning and community could be merged and I would hope that this topic can be one for ongoing discussion and experimentation in Utopia. But let me offer just a glimpse of what is possible on this front. One important process would be for inquiry groups to exchange findings, *and exchange members*. This way learning new things and having new social experiences can be even more tightly connected, further reducing the learning versus sociality opposition that holds today. And this also establishes the kind of social dynamics that can make for the most robust, non-invidious group feelings.

Also, if a major part of contemporary schooling's inauthenticity is in artificially segregating learning and production, and institutions for children from institutions for adults, then Utopia must experiment with ways to break these inauthentic dichotomies. Learning groups should be intergenerational; if they are not, non-coercive measures could be used to mix them. People might live, too, with their inquiry groups, with care for younger members of the group the responsibility of older members of the inquiry group. Groups should mix family and non-family, too, so that people work and study with those they most deeply love as kin.

And the work versus play dichotomy must be broken. This should happen automatically as the hierarchical sorting functions of learning are eliminated; school can be fun in the same way as play. In both play and non-hierarchical schooling, fun is the goal and anxiety over the consequences of what you are doing is at a minimum.

8. *Debate as a central feature of centers of research and learning*: This one should be obvious: If we are to really collectively pursue novelty, then heterodox ideas must be brought forth constantly to challenge orthodoxy; otherwise, we will come to believe things just because they've always been believed. Debate is a prime way to institutionalize such challenges, because the idea behind debate is that any idea can be, indeed should be, open to challenge; subscribers to orthodox views must respond to challenges through debate, defending their views with logic and data rather than merely relying on invocations of conventional belief as the defense of their positions.

Debate is also key because it encourages the formation of antitheses and any knowledge only has real meaning if it is controvertible, i.e., essentially debatable.

To me, debate is one of the most enjoyable learning activities that exists, because it is interactional, meaningful, and meaning-making (rather than sloganeering), and because it introduces the novel ideas that are at the heart of learning. But it is important to specify some stipulations for what makes for genuine debate, since as can be seen by the "debates" so often held on American television between political candidates, it is easy to call something a "debate" even when it is really two people with opposing views, merely stating those views while standing next to each other.

Thus, debate must be genuinely interactional. If X puts forth proposition x, then debater Y must respond to x, either conceding the point or debating it. If Y debates the point, Y's argument can rely on facts and subjectivities *but* Y must clearly distinguish—must clearly say—what parts of the argument are pure fact (something that can conceivably be verified against the nature of the world that exists) and what parts are subjective assumptions (something that relies, ultimately, on humans to define what is good and bad).

9. *Unsolved puzzles*: In the spirit of following my own advice on the importance of stating what you know and also what you *don't* know, and also raising questions to which you don't know the answer, I will describe here major pedagogical questions whose solutions continue to elude me:

a. Is teaching the giving of knowledge or the cultivation of a skill? American professors are fond of saying that we seek, above all, to teach students to think; we are coaching them in a skill rather than merely giving them knowledge. I am definitely sympathetic to this approach. After all, no one needs a teacher to learn the facts about a field; we can get those from books or, now, from the Internet. Those of us who believe we have honed our research and analytical skills over the years believe teaching these abilities as skills is what we can best pass on to students.

But not all people agree. I was so baffled the first time Chinese teachers and students asked me, in all seriousness, "How did you learn Chinese so well? Can you tell us how to learn English?" When I told them the skill-oriented answer, that language is simply something that they must practice with someone like me, a native speaker, over months and months, they looked frustrated. They felt that would take too long and that my answer was not explicit enough. Couldn't I simply "give" them the "knowledge" I possessed, in order to make them into knowledgeable native English speakers?

This idea of teaching as the giving of knowledge cropped up repeatedly during my years in China. A math teacher told me that all students can learn math, since doing math is not a skill open only to a few but knowledge that can be acquired by anyone diligent enough to put in the effort. I liked this democratic approach to math teaching and the rejection of the American notion that only a few geniuses can understand higher math. In fact I believe the Chinese do better in math because of this democratic and demystifying approach to the subject. There's something appealing about the idea of learning as the acquisition of knowledge. You don't engage in some implicitly defined skills-based process to learn a difficult field. Your teacher gives you the knowledge and you take it in. Once you've done that, you're on the same playing field as anyone else, in terms of your competencies.

But if we *really* could reduce complex skills, such as the playing of the piano or the composing of good music, or the speaking of a foreign language, to a set of knowable principles, then we should be able to capture Beethoven's essence in some basic principles that anyone could replicate. This is not, however, the case. Even the most sophisticated of music critics end up either describing what Beethoven is doing in a given symphony ("it is written in A-B-A form; it has x number of themes in y key signatures, etc. etc.) or they resort to seemingly metaphysical and abstract description of his work—calling it "universal," "triumphant," covering the full range of "human emotions"—that could never suffice as knowledge that we could follow to compose like Beethoven.

Is it then impossible for certain "skills" to be taught as knowledge, as principles to be communicated overtly to students? If this is so, is this impossibility due to problems with verbal language? (Think of trying to describe a great painting using words. It's hard to do. Describing a great-tasting meal is equally difficult. Why is this so?) I have yet to fully come up with an answer to these questions but I do know one of the problems with teaching as the giving of knowledge is that when we state basic limited principles, they are so abstract and vague as to be almost meaningless. (What 10 principles, for example, might you come up with to describe how to teach students to think?) We need to concretize the process by giving examples, by modeling thought processes, etc.—all non-knowledge-giving teaching—the kind of teaching that my American self still esteems the most highly, despite the intriguing Chinese challenge to my beliefs. I often think of learning something like the piano. You can talk about principles, but it is only by playing specific pieces, and having a teacher or knowledgeable person react to them, that we learn the skills of being a good musician.

So I am left with the puzzle of why we cannot specify the principles of good musicianship in a way that those principles could simply be applied overtly and openly by any student who learned them. In fact, good teaching is the same way. Much of it is a skill and, as a skill, cannot be easily written about in language. This is why this chapter has often frustrated me. I know that describing a skill like good teaching is somehow, and for some reason, ineffable. I don't know why this is so, nor am I fully convinced that it need always be so, and that is the puzzle here, one of major consequence I believe: Can anything truly nuanced, like good scientific thinking, good musical playing or good acting, be truly and fully taught—rather than somehow cultivated, rather mystically and ineffably, as a skill, immune to linguistic representation. I'd like to think the answer is yes—that the process can be overt and "scientific," but I am still at a loss about how to describe how this can happen—a huge pedagogical and philosophical puzzle that Utopian pedagogues can hopefully confront.

b. Evaluative versus non-evaluative teaching: This conundrum follows from the skills/knowledge puzzle. When we teach, teachers want to evaluate their students, to tell them what they have done right and "wrong." But there are several problems with how we actually do this. First, American and other Western teachers (not the Chinese) may say there are no wrong answers, especially to essay questions, yet we grade as if "wrong" is a clearly delineated concept. We try to tell students what is wrong. This is the first problem—contradiction between our professed neo-relativism and our absolutism of judgement.

And the evaluations we give are, as discussed in the last section, in language that is ineffable. That is, we can't "tell" students in 10 principles how to write a good paper and have them do it. Once they do it, we can point out problems, but this doesn't fully suffice to get them to, at one huge transformation, become great writers. Again, there is something, at the very least, insufficient in our dialogue about what students have done "wrong."

Further problematic, to me, is the fact that our reactions are evaluative. I opened this book with a story of the musician playing for competition versus the musician playing for an audience. The audience reacts with pleasure, while the judges react with judgment. The musician playing for an audience often leads to the most genuinely musical playing, while the one playing in a competition plays mechanistically, seeking to avoid making obvious "mistakes." This approach reduces music-making to a mechanical and largely unemotional process. When I first began teaching anthropology, I decided to try a more naturalistic discourse approach in the classroom—more like an appreciative and responding audience than an authoritative and evaluative judge. Thus, I wanted classroom discourse to be less evaluative and more reactive. When a student made a comment, I wanted to respond not with "good" or "not quite" but with a comment further extending the student's point—hoping to teach them, through modeling, how to extend on the thoughts they were having. For example, if a student suggested something interesting—one student asked, for example, if the American emphasis on looks is related to our racist heritage (an amazing insight and one that I think is correct!)—I would say, in this example, "That's really interesting. How might we test this hypothesis? What kinds of data would we need to collect to see if it is true?" I think what I was doing was clever but it didn't sit well with the students, who wanted me to give them that nice compliment they craved, rather than my longer, seemingly ambiguous reactions.

I also tried a different way of grading their papers. Typically, my own professors would either tell me all the bad things I did in my paper or simply say "great work." This obvious asymmetry implies a refusal, or inability, to talk about what's good with as much nuance as how we discuss that which is bad. Therefore, I decided to write more comments on better papers than on problematic or uninteresting ones and to, as before, be less evaluative than naturalistically dialogic, telling my interest in certain parts of the good paper and how those parts relate to larger questions. This practice worked better than my classroom non-evaluation, but only when I told those with good grades that my page or two of typed comments meant I liked their paper. They had been so accustomed to only receiving comments if their paper was "bad" that they assumed my many comments were a sign of my disappointment, despite their high grades.

But the conundrum that remains for me is whether naturalistic and relatively non-evaluative reactions on my part are capable of teaching students. Well, I know it does teach them certain skills, but as with the skills issue above, how much is this approach actually teaching students, and what are the inherent limitations to my ability to teach something that, again, is not fully reducible to a number of simple maxims? And can we really teach without being evaluative? I think we can do so, but I can't fully describe how and why this is the case!

c.   Unanswered questions and the lack of resolution: I have described how I will ask questions, such as students' own theories about how hierarchy might have evolved, following on their reading of Carneiro's (1970) theories. I love doing this—asking a question that I, too, don't know the answer to, and guiding students in articulating their own hypotheses, as they think through what data supports and refutes their own hypotheses. This feels so much more interesting to me as a teacher, and I think to them as students, than simply telling them what someone else has proved about the origins of hierarchy.

When I explained that I didn't know the answer, nor could give them the answer to the fascinating question of the origins of "civilization" and hierarchy, one student in my class expressed dismay. "I hate unanswered questions," she exclaimed. I understand her feelings. Ultimately, uncertainty is intriguing since it invites our thoughtfulness but certainty gives us a sense of resolution. And many of us might feel best if a great uncertain question can be answered through our discoveries, so that the tension and excitement of the unknown are released by the pleasures and joy of knowing.

My own as yet unanswered question, here, is how to answer the students' discomfort—how to encourage students to experience thought about the unknown without the frustration that often comes with that process. Perhaps the answer, here, is not that profound. I often suspect if students were taught to ask more questions to which no one knows the answers for certain, they might become more accustomed to the pleasures of the process of thinking through difficult problems, rather than feeling facile satisfaction at being given the answer by the all-knowing teacher. But is this sufficient to overcome the desire for certainty? This is another question to which I do not know the answer.

Bibliography

Carneiro, Robert L. 1970. A theory of the origin of the state. *Science*, 169: 733–738.

Epstein, Steven 1996. *Impure Science: AIDS, Activism, and the Politics of Knowledge*. Berkeley: University of California Press.

Fetterman, N.P. 1831. Report relative to a general system of education. *House Journal of Pennsylvania, 1830–31, II*. Harrisburg, PA: Henry Welsh.

Geremek, Bronislaw 1997. *Poverty: A History*. Paperback edition. Agnieszka Kolakowska, trans. Oxford: Blackwell.

Go, Sun and Peter Lindert 2010. The uneven rise of American public schools to 1850. *The Journal of Economic History*, 70: 1–26.

Heininger, Mary Lynn Stevens 1984. Children, childhood and change in America, 1820–1920. Pp. 1–33 in *A Century of Childhood, 1820–1920*. Mary Lynn Stevens Heininger, ed. Rochester, NY: The Margaret Woodbury Strong Museum.

House Journal, II 1824–1825. Report of the Committee appointed to Enquire into the Operation of the Poor Laws. Harrisburg, PA: J.S. Wiestling.

House Journal, II 1833–1834. Harrisburg, PA: Henry Welsh.

Klebaner, B. 1952. *Public Poor Relief in America, 1790–1860.* Ann Arbor: University Microfilms.

Knox, John 1834. *Parental Responsibility and Parental Solicitude.* New York: H.R. Piercy.

Laws of Pennsylvania 1833–1834. Harrisburg, PA: Henry Welsh.

Laws of the Commonwealth of Pennsylvania, I 1810. Philadelphia: John Bioren.

Memorial to the Legislature from the Pennsylvania Society for the Promotion of Public Schools 1830. Philadelphia: Penna. Society for the Promotion of Public Schools.

Minutes of the Pennsylvania Constitution Convention 1789. Philadelphia: Zachariah Pouson.

Proceedings and Debates of the Convention of the Commonwealth of Pennsylvania, to Propose Amendments to the Constitution, V 1838. Harrisburg, PA: Packer, Barrett, and Parke.

Report of the Joint Committee of the Two Houses of the Pennsylvania Legislature, on the subject of a system of general education 1834. Harrisburg, PA: Henry Welsh.

Schoenhals, Martin 1986. Educational benevolence: The origins of public schools in nineteenth century Pennsylvania. Unpublished paper.

Statutes at Large of Pennsylvania, XVIII 1915. Harrisburg, PA: William Stanley Ray.

Stevens, Thaddeus 1904 [1835]. *The Famous Speech of Hon. Thaddeus Stevens of Pennsylvania in Opposition to the Repeal of the Common School Law of 1834.* Philadelphia: Thaddeus Stevens Memorial Association of Philadelphia.

Turner, Victor 1977. *The Ritual Process: Structure and Anti-structure.* Ithaca, NY: Cornell Paperbacks.

Wickersham, J.P. 1969 [1886]. *A History of Education in Pennsylvania.* New York: Arno Press and The New York Times.

7

POLITICS IN EGALITARIAN SOCIETY

Utopian writers are often criticized for being authoritarian. We want our Utopias to function as we prescribe, with no changes allowed—or so it is often said of us. I admit that my first impulse is to believe that my Utopia is a good idea, a great idea, that it is good for everyone, and that it should simply be put into place, functioning on auto-pilot. But my impulse is not very consistent with my democratic and non-coercive values, so in this chapter I will address the politics of Utopia, politics consistent with the equality that is an essential feature of Utopia. This chapter answers the following questions:

1. How will Utopia be instituted? Who will establish it, and following what kind of process?
2. How will Utopia be administered? How will conflicts between individuals or groups be handled?

Instituting Utopia: Who belongs?

No one will be forced to join Utopia. This is a good principle in the abstract, but harder when we confront the details of how this voluntarism will be enacted. Where do non-Utopians go? Do we send them to Siberia? What if the non-Utopians are imperialists, who try to conquer Utopia and take our land? Or what if they violate fundamental human rights? Should we ignore this, or should we intervene?

For starters, if Utopia is to be egalitarian, it must provide equal land per capita to non-Utopians to found their own societies as alternatives to Utopia. Further, Utopians can leave Utopia at will and non-Utopians can always join it. However, both Utopians and others will subscribe to a charter of basic human rights, building upon the Universal Declaration of Human Rights. The charter will include an agreement by all societies not to intervene in each other's affairs unless one of them violates the charter. The charter will also include a right of anyone to leave or to join any society freely and at will. In the event of charter violations, all non-violating societies will join together to stop the violation, in a manner agreed upon by all at the time of the writing of the charter.

What about small-scale rural societies—what will happen to them in Utopia? The general principle articulated above, that any human should have the freedom to join Utopia or to stay away holds equally for rural and indigenous peoples. If a large group of these people want to maintain their own culture, they should have a right to do so, and they should be provided land and resources on which their current culture can thrive. But if any of their members want to join Utopia, they should be free to do so.

And I cannot justify giving these societies a blanket right to exclude others, so if there are those from Utopia or elsewhere who want to join an indigenous society, they too should be free to do so. The latter movement might threaten indigenous society, or introduce changes into its traditional culture and I know some readers would argue against allowing freedom of movement into small-scale cultures. Others might allow such movement but ask that Utopia help protect these cultures from the change that outsiders might bring. However, just as the basic guarantee is something that should be central to all cultures, so should freedom of individuals to join or leave any and all societies be a central value. Exclusion of others is such a perniciously dangerous dynamic that if one society were allowed to exclude others, the principle of exclusion might spread to other societies, and we would end up with a kind of new nation-state system, with societies guarding their borders. This is not tolerable. Therefore, even though allowing outsiders to join small-scale cultures might threaten to change their natures, I do not believe these cultures should be granted any exemption from the basic right of any individual to join or leave any society, Utopian or not.

Basic egalitarian principles

What will Utopia's government be like? My aim is greater genuine engagement by all Utopians in implementing and administering Utopia. To me, this is necessary for genuine democracy. Voting for leaders is not sufficient. All Utopians must have the opportunity to participate in their government actively by making policy choices and by serving to adjudicate cases of conflict.

Here are five foundational practices that will promote greater citizen engagement and prevent the development of political hierarchy:

1. *Selection and rotation of personnel*: When thinking of contemporary practices in which power does not become entrenched, I've often returned to the model of American juries. I can think of many cases in America's clearly flawed democracy in which democratically elected politicians' power becomes entrenched—but not juries. The fact that the jury pool (though not jurors themselves) is chosen at random works to prevent entrenchment. So too does the fact that jury service ends when the case is over.

Thus personnel for administration and courts in Utopia will be like juries, chosen at random (e.g., by lottery from among a pool of individuals volunteering to work in the administration and courts), with strict rotation off service when a case, or administrative project, is finished. Unlike juries, however, no one will be compelled to serve; judges and administrators will do so voluntarily. Also, unlike juries there will not be lawyers who can disqualify anyone willing to serve. And Utopia's government personnel will not be compensated for their service other than, perhaps, to have such service count toward the minimal work requirement.

With voluntary and term-limited political service, and a random element introduced for choosing government personnel, Utopia's government can be like juries, with their lack of entrenched power.

2. *Choice*: The ability to leave Utopia at any time is another safety valve preventing hierarchy. If Utopia were to become ruled by a tyrant, the ability to move to another society, a right that will be enforced by all societies, would allow Utopians an escape. In contrast to today's world, where accidents of birth confine us to live in particular societies (that is, within particular nation-states), Utopia and all other societies will have open borders.

Of course, there is no perfect guarantee against a hypothetical tyrant closing the borders, but just as we accept borders today as legitimate due to their existence, the pervasiveness of choice in Utopia will legitimize openness, making borders very difficult to legitimately establish. Besides, tyrants in the past have needed monopoly over land and wealth for a critical purpose in the closing of borders: Compelling individuals to become the enforcers, police or military, of borders. But no Utopian will have this land and wealth monopoly, nor will they have any means to compel work from others—a reason why the basic guarantee and *voluntarism* of work are so important. This will make it very difficult for anyone to become a border-closing tyrant in the first place.

3. *Engagement in Utopia's ongoing improvement*: In the previous chapter I discussed how reform of Utopia will be allowed and encouraged, as long as the basics of the Utopian constitution are followed. The reason for discussing this practice in the chapter on education is that I want to encourage learning that is connected to real uses, in this case the improvement of one's own society. Such practices will promote genuine engaged learning.

I wish to promote engaged politics too. By asking all Utopians to be involved in a constant process of improving Utopia, society will not be passively received by individuals but will be actively constructed by them in an ongoing process. Engagement in Utopia's ongoing improvement creates robust democracy, in contrast to the passivity of today's system, where we delegate the care of our own society to politicians. The passivity of today's process promotes apathy, apathy that allows our "democratically elected leaders" to take control of the political process for their own benefit. Engagement of all citizens in the governance of Utopia, however, will challenge this self-serving hierarchical dynamic by promoting the egalitarian notion that every individual can and should participate equally in the maintenance and improvement of their society.

4. *Constitution and laws on hierarchy*: Utopia's constitution and its laws will protect its fundamental egalitarian principles, and these will be enforced by the courts. These issues are discussed in more detail in the following section.

5. *Scale*: Throughout this book I have cited foragers as evidence that humans have the capacity to live egalitarian lives. Foragers are known not only for their economic equality but also for their political equality; so too is the case with small-scale agricultural (nonforager) societies, such as the Yi whom I studied.

But an important question arises: Can humans live in *larger-scale* communities and still maintain sharing and equality? What is the impact of the size of a society, "scale," on human egalitarian capacities?

At the most basic level, I cannot answer this question. I am not advocating that Utopians live in the small camps of only a few dozen people characteristic of foragers, or in the villages of small-scale farmers that have one thousand or fewer inhabitants. Utopia has never existed. If I am to be an honest empiricist, as indeed I believe is the right approach, I must admit that neither I nor anyone else can know, at least with certainty, what will happen in Utopia until it is up and running.

There are reasons for skepticism, as well as reasons to be hopeful. Regarding skepticism: I often teach about scale to students by appealing to their intuitive sense that it is much harder to refuse to share when you are confronted face-to-face in a small village on a daily basis with needy people whom you know than when confronting a needy person in a large anonymous urban context. When we pass a homeless person in New York, on the one hand, we can walk by without giving a penny, secure in the knowledge that no one will gossip about our stinginess. Everyone in such encounters is usually anonymous so the giver, receiver, or non-giver can all act as they wish, without considering the social repercussions of being observed. In many small-scale societies, on the other hand, all of our actions are seen by people among whom we may live for life. We need their esteem for so many reasons, not only psychological ones, so if we are stingy—often one of the most reviled of traits in small-scale societies—we will be gossiped about mercilessly, gossip aimed at goading us to be less stingy. If we still persist in our stinginess, we may face extreme social ostracism as the ultimate response to our anti-social behavior. Thus, the dynamics of the small scale are a powerful force to ensure that people share, and these dynamics are essentially absent in large-scale contexts.

Yet people in our large-scale contemporary world *do* give money to strangers, and charity is a central provision of the world's major religions. This should remind us that while scale may matter for purposes of sharing and egalitarianism, scale is not everything. Humans do share with other humans they may see only once, or may not even know, and they do so not only in small village society.

Further, as biologists know well, different environments bring out different animal behaviors. The chimps foraging in the wild studied by Jane Goodall and others were surprisingly egalitarian (Chapter 1). But when the chimps were fed by Goodall in concentrated areas, conflict over food ensued, and these same chimps became war-like and hierarchical. It would be simplistic to say that human hierarchy can be fully solved by ending conflict over food, but doing so can certainly be a stimulus, akin to a changed environment, toward egalitarianism. And when we add to egalitarian food provision interventions to counter gender, ethnic, and other forms of hierarchy, sharing and generalized egalitarianism are the likely consequence. Ending the concatenation of hierarchies—such as the gender and class hierarchies that so often reinforce each other, for example—creates an egalitarian synergy, a culture of equality.

But here I will add more nuance to the issue of scale, so that some *small* scale within Utopia's larger-scale society can help engender the prosociality and egalitarianism reminiscent of small-scale societies. To begin: While we will not live in isolated small villages, the reader will note that much of Utopia will take place in small groups. There will be creative groups and learning groups, for example, that will have limited numbers of people (at least in most cases, though not always, see Chapter 4)—I'm imagining only one or two dozen for many such groups. These small groups will exist within a larger-scale society and small and large scale will be intermingled. Here are a few ways this will happen:

a.   *Circulation between groups*: Utopia will combine small groups with large-scale circulation freely allowed, and encouraged, between any and all groups (work groups, learning groups, and any groups formed that have political functions). Small groups will promote solidarity and egalitarianism while freedom of movement will prevent the stultifying feeling sometimes characteristic of small-group life.

Further, group circulation will prevent the in-group/out-group dynamics that can often be the foundations of hierarchy in contemporary society. It will serve to bind groups into larger entities, but will do so through *face-to-face contact*. While today a large-scale polity such as a nation is formed from often invented senses of connection between individuals who do not know each other, in Utopia there will be no coerced and enforced connection between people operating at a large-scale. The connections made by individuals will be their own, and they will be face-to-face ones.

b.   *Judges and groups*: All who serve as judges could be required to live temporarily in the small groups that are home to judicial complainants whose cases they hear, so that judicial intervention does not come from on high. This living requirement could be in effect for, say, several months after their judicial term of service has ended. Since most judicial resolutions will not be punitive, but will aim to restore community harmony, living among someone against whom you have ruled will not create the same possible dangers as it might today, were judges to live among those they convict.

In fact judges could also be required to live among complainants *during* a case over which they preside. This would give them a better chance to understand, ethnographically, the roots of any conflict and it would ensure that they would act with greater face-to-face knowledge of, and compassion for, any and all complainants.

c.   *Scale of administration*: Utopia will need to plan for the production of food and its distribution. This might be fairly straightforward, but plans for allocating minimal required service to other domains besides food will be more difficult: Will labor service go for improved medical care, new transportation technologies, or something else? These issues will need to be decided and planned.

Will these decisions and their implementation occur at a world level, or will it be done locally? There are pros and cons to both approaches, of course. World planning could be more efficient than planning done in small localities. In addition localism, often celebrated by the left, is not always so progressive. In today's society, devolution to the local level can lead to control by local elites, an undesirable situation. But world planning is of such large scale that it might not be responsive to individual community needs.

Therefore, Utopia might take a mixed approach. Large-scale planning could be carried out, but planners would be required to live among many different communities in many different places, both during and after the planning process, so that they can interact face-to-face with those for whom they are planning. Also, with the easy transportation and communication possible today, something non-existent in forager societies, people with ideas that differ from those of the planners will be encouraged to present their alternative ideas during planning sessions. These ideas will be presented personally when possible, and through the Internet if personal travel to present the ideas is not possible. Finally, individuals from one region, or from multiple regions, who are still dissatisfied with the plans made for them might form their own region, and plan according to their own desires, as long as the basic constitution is followed.

This way no planners will have jurisdiction over all localities. Localities and individuals can argue for plans that better meet their own needs, and planners might accept their wishes, after robust discussion and debate. And if this doesn't happen, any Utopians are free to go off on their own, to experiment according to their own ideas, needs and desires, whether in a sub-region of Utopia itself or in a non-Utopian society.

Now that I have discussed ideas to promote engaged politics and ways to prevent the formation of political inequality, I will describe in more detail the political system of Utopia: Its constitution, courts, and administration.

The Utopian constitution

All societies in the world, Utopia and non-utopian, will be required to subscribe to a basic charter of rights. The basic charter will be based on the Universal Declaration of Human Rights. All societies will also agree to allow any individual to join or leave their society at will and will pledge not to interfere in each other's affairs, unless a society is in violation of the basic charter.

Utopia will also have its own constitution with rights as outlined in the next section. The working draft of the constitution will be based on this set of rights. However, in order that Utopians proactively accept the constitution, and fully understand its rationale, I suggest that each right in the constitution be debated, with an affirmative and negative debate team, and with a team of judges deciding based upon reason and evidence which side has won. If the negative side wins, they can present an alternative constitutional plank, or a modified one. If accepted by the judges, their plank will become part of the constitution.

All debaters and judges will be volunteers and non-experts, chosen by lottery from among a pool of all Utopians. Debates will be open to all who wish to attend and will be widely available on the Internet, as will commentary on the constitutional proceedings. In order to encourage greater debate on the merits of provisions, any provision accepted by judges will continue to be "tested" by being debated in further rounds, rounds in which supporters will become opponents of the provision and opponents will become supporters. The entire constitutional process will be repeated at least once each generation so that Utopia's basic provisions are always open to change and never passively accepted nor accepted without full understanding.

Basic constitutional rights

An end to hierarchy is central to individual happiness, to collective happiness, and to establishing a virtuous cycle of compassion so that individuals' happinesses are mutually reinforcing rather than in conflict. Therefore, equality in all dimensions will be the primary right in Utopia, and in its constitution.

Since humans' food needs are essential, and since denial of access to food has been a central means throughout history to establish hierarchy over others, the right of all humans to food is a central egalitarian right—the most central egalitarian right. So too is the right of all to other subsistence needs—housing, medical care, basic clothing, and anything else that might be determined as necessary at the time of the adoption of the constitution.

All humans need to give and get attention, which is tantamount to love. We all need love from family and friends, from the groups to which we belong, and love for our creativity—our "work." To the greatest extent possible, Utopia will guarantee, as a right as basic as the right of subsistence, affirmative attention to everyone. Consistent with equality, Utopia will seek to end inequalities of attention—more love to the "beautiful," more attention to the "meritorious," the winner-take-all system of celebrity. Romantic love, love from the groups to which we belong, and love for what we create, will be redistributed in Utopia, as described in previous chapters, so that love can be generally equalized. The basic right to be loved will also be enforced by Utopia's judicial system, as described in the following section. The right to be cared for if one is ill or incapacitated, and the right of all people—including (especially) the elderly—to enjoy friendship and companionship will also be an important right guaranteed in Utopia and one institutionalized through care mechanisms described in Chapter 3.

Utopia will be fashioned so as to challenge the segregations and ostracisms that give rise to hierarchy—the segregations of gender, sexuality, race, ableism, ethnicity, and any other invidious and exclusionary categorizations of humans. Ending war and the nation-state, progenitors of some of the most odious hierarchies, will be a central goal of Utopia. Utopia's judicial system will monitor all domains to ensure equality.

Hierarchy and means–end activity are closely related. One might even argue that they are the same. When we must work for someone else for our subsistence, we are unequal to them due to their coercive power over us. If we feel we will starve if we do not work, our work becomes obligatory and motivated by anxiety, hence crowding out the pleasure of creation. The right not to be compelled to work, beyond the minimal work requirement, will be guaranteed by Utopia. No individual can make us work, nor can the threat of starvation make us work, nor can we be encouraged to work by the awarding of an external reward. All such work situations are to be eliminated, since they are the concomitants of hierarchy. Instead, work will be voluntary, so that it can be intrinsically pleasurable, and a significant contributor to our general happiness. Further, Utopia will facilitate our desired creative endeavors and will provide audiences for what we create, so that interactive joy can be maximized. Provision of the facilities for creation, for "work," will be part of the basic guarantee.

As is the case with work, learning must not be coerced, nor can it be rewarded by extrinsic rewards such as a job or increased status. Extrinsic rewards for learning, as for work, create hierarchy by giving others the power to obligate us to study and to differentially reward us for our learning. The obligation and the means–end motivation of learning, motivation by means of external rewards, crowds out pleasure just as hierarchy crowds it out: In both cases existential anxiety—fear of failure, ostracism, and shame—overrides joy.

Utopia will, of course, also guarantee freedom against harm to persons. This will include Utopia itself: Utopia will not have the right to kill anyone, and punishments for crimes will be limited, as described in the next section.

Exceptions to basic rights: One might reasonably ask, as many of my friends have, how Utopia will produce food or health technologies without coerced labor? If we all create according to our desires, what if no one does work to make medical advances, for example? Does Utopia forego such advances?

This is, indeed, a difficult question since it pits basic needs, in this example the right to health care, against the voluntary nature of work. Let me begin by noting that while there is a limit on how much food we can consume, there is no limit on how much we might improve health care. Thus critics of Utopia could always say it does not do enough to improve health care. The reader should note, however, that the same could be said of today's economy. While no system can provide a perfect solution to satisfy all critics, I hope the following seems reasonable enough:

1. The minimal work requirement in Utopia can be satisfied by working on health care research, including new cures, or on any research related to processes to better satisfy basic subsistence.
2. The hours required to be worked each week will be the same for all people but they can be increased from five to, say, ten (a top limit will be

constitutionally specified) upon a majority vote of Utopians. Utopia's lottery-chosen administrators may also propose such a change and, upon debate, this can be implemented.

3. Utopia's administrators may decide to shift person-hours from one subsistence need to another, as long as basic needs are still met. For example, they might shift a small percentage of person-hours from the construction of housing to health care. Those with an interest in health care, in that case, would be asked to shift voluntarily. If not enough individuals volunteer, then a lottery could be used as a last resort to shift people from housing into medical care.

4. Utopia's administrators may make other administrative laws as necessary, as long as these do not conflict with the constitution.

Finally, there are a number of issues that might not be direct and basic rights but that have an impact upon those rights. These will thus be secondary rights and they will be given any and all primacy as long as they promote, rather than negatively affect, basic rights. Among these secondary rights are the right to transportation, to energy, and a focus on efficiency. Since freedom of movement is important to Utopia—to challenge invidious groupings, to facilitate learning between groups, and to allow people to come and go from Utopia at will—transportation is necessarily important, as is the energy needed for transportation and for the production of basic subsistence needs. Energy and transportation thus will be secondary rights, and priorities, of Utopia. The same will be true of efficiency since increasing the efficiency of production can reduce the number of hours Utopians must work. Since a limited work obligation is a basic right, efficiency will be a right and priority too, as a means to achieve that basic right and to improve upon it by reducing the number of hours Utopians must work.

And what about environmental rights and priorities? I know there are those who strongly feel that the rights of animals are as important as the rights of humans. I know some readers will reasonably argue that compassion toward humans entails compassion for animals and, indeed, for all living things. Therefore, Utopians, when writing the constitution, might wish to add, as a *basic right*, protection of the environment and the rights of all living things, not just humans. Or they might wish to make this a secondary right, akin to the right to transportation, energy, and efficiency. At the very least, however, reasonable protection of the world's environment, including its climate, has a bearing on such key aspects of human lives as food production. Therefore, Utopia's constitution must protect the environment so that the natural resources necessary for human life are preserved.

So many others have written well about the details of how to preserve the environment and how to promote sustainability that I will not give further details here. But the lack of such details should not overshadow the issues of sustainability implied in the earlier sections on social scale, and the requirement that the protection of the environment will be given a central place in Utopia. The monopoly of nature by the powerful is clearly fundamentally inegalitarian and it has been a key source throughout history to further foment inequality—I'm thinking of inequality in landownership, a cornerstone of much traditional disenfranchisement over the centuries. Natural resources must be preserved and conserved and this must be done with total equality.

Utopia's judiciary

How will the constitution be enforced? How will conflicts within society be addressed? What kinds of punishments will there be? Utopia will differ fundamentally in its judicial system from judicial systems of today. I don't think I will have to argue too hard to make the case, well-known among many social scientists, that property, hierarchy, and the formal prosecution of crime are inextricably linked. If the reader just thinks casually about criminal law, and civil law too, a central focus is the protection of the rights of property and wealth. And the disposition for violations of property rights is either punishment of the perpetrator and/or compensation of the victim.

Utopia's absence of personal wealth renders unnecessary a judicial focus on wealth and property protection. Punishment of violators is also not a necessary focus. The central purpose of Utopia's judiciary, instead, will be to preserve equality in all forms, prevent violation of any other rights, and, of course, protect individuals against bodily harm.

How will the judiciary do this? Will it have coercive power? How will violators be handled? The answers are complicated—complicated in an interesting way. Let's begin by thinking about how equality might be violated. Just as I have raised the hypothetical, though unlikely, scenario of a tyrant closing Utopia's borders, we might imagine someone refusing to step down from his/her administrative position, or someone trying to commandeer more than his/her fair share of Utopia's food or other goods produced. We could also imagine a group of people forming an exclusive club, perhaps based on ethnicity, and restricting membership of outsiders. Or perhaps a group of men might form such a group and restrict women.

A first impulse for dealing with such violations would be to have an armed police force arrest perpetrators and punish them with confinement, on the model of contemporary judicial systems. But once a group of people is armed, they could, themselves, become an anti-egalitarian force, so this process is problematic. Instead, Utopia will have protectors, chosen for limited terms of service by lottery from a pool of volunteers, who will be "armed" only with tranquilizer weapons that can sedate another person. In addition, these arms will be programmed by Utopian technologists to have a time-limited efficacy, so that they cannot be used at all after, say, one or two months. Other safeguards will be taken as needed to prevent any individual from having any means of force that is permanent (and, yes, Utopia will not allow individuals to possess real firearms or other deadly weapons). Perhaps, too, the tranquilizers can be programmed to only fire at people who have been convicted of "crimes." All of these safeguards will prevent tranquilizers from being used for any other purpose than subduing violators of Utopia's constitution in order to bring them to court or to deal with them after a judgment is rendered.

And what guiding principles will there be for courts to follow? There is a longstanding debate about "crime" and individual responsibility. Conservatives want to punish wrongdoers, while liberals often want to reform society, while lessening the punishments meted out. To me, in a society that seeks to be as non-coercive as possible, and one that seeks to continually improve itself, the liberal approach makes much more sense. Therefore, one set of judges will exist, again a temporary set chosen by lottery, to continually monitor any violations of equality. They will be proactive by living among other Utopians to monitor any potential violations of equality. Their main goal will not be to punish any individual but to try to prevent inequalities from occurring. Let's say, following one of the cases above, that a group of men forms a clubhouse that restricts women—fomenting gender exclusion and hierarchy. The first approach of judges will be to ask the men to voluntarily stop their behavior. Judges will informally talk with the men and try to persuade them.

If they refuse to cease their violations, they will have a chance to present their arguments to judges, and those disagreeing with the men will present their case. The men might argue, perhaps, that they are not in fundamental violation of gender equality. The judges will weigh the arguments based upon the constitution. There will, however, be a heavy burden of argument placed upon any potential violators of equality so that, in this example, the men would most likely not win their argument before the court and the court would rule against them. In this case, they will be required to cease their hierarchical behavior. If they do not, they will be required to leave Utopia for another society willing to take them or to establish their own society. (This is where protectors with tranquilizers might need to be used.) If they leave Utopia, they will not be in jail, since they will be able to come back to Utopia periodically to visit friends and family for short periods of time. If they choose to found their own society, they will be given their own land on which to live. And friends and family members from Utopia can visit them in their new society. The idea will be to remove the threat, rather than to punish the wrongdoers. Maintaining equality will take precedence over "punishment."

One of the characteristics distinguishing Utopia from contemporary society, as well as from many previous leftist proposals for socialist and progressive societies, is that equality of love will be regarded as seriously as equality of wealth and power. Courts will play an important role in enforcing this equality. Despite mechanisms to help us all find romantic love, some individuals might attract greater attention from a greater number of potential romantic partners than others. One response to such a situation, probably a common one of many readers, would be to say, "You can't legislate love. How can you make someone love someone else?" Fair enough. No one should be compelled to feel something they don't feel, or to act sexually or romantically in a way inauthentic to their desires. That would violate the extremely important value for sincerity that I've described in Chapter 5, and would also be an extreme case of coercion. But courts worldwide do intervene *today* in child custody, marriage, divorce, and so on, so it is not unreasonable to suggest that intervention in relationships should be a domain of court action.

The reason this is especially important in Utopia is because of the close connection between inequality of attention and other inequalities. When someone accrues years of feeling disrespected or unloved, this often sets the stage for anti-social behavior, including the anti-social behavior that is a refusal to share and show compassion. The pursuit of wealth and power is often a psychological compensation for the anxiety and pain produced through accumulated feelings of disrespect and love-hurt. I am not, of course, making an excuse for individuals' responses in this case, however. Hierarchy is clearly odious. I simply want to analyze its causes and eradicate them as much as possible, and one main cause is inequality of attention. Taking this inequality seriously is important in its own terms and it is important for challenging other forms of hierarchy connected to it.

Furthermore, I think it is essential that inequality at the micro level be taken just as seriously as inequality at the macro level. I'm sure anyone who has worked among leftist activists can attest to the hypocrisy so common among them: Those espousing equality in society often reproduce the most unequal social conditions within the very groups working for macro equality. Such hypocrisy is insidiously toxic, making a mockery of the principles of equality. Therefore, what might seem to some readers as "small" inequities, ones that are personal and private, need to be taken just as seriously as those that seem to be "larger." Courts, therefore, will be open to the adjudication of any conflict arising from inequality, no matter how large or small, no matter whether its provenance is the "public" domain or the "private" realm.

So how could courts enforce equality of attention and love? An outline of how this will happen follows. While these principles and practices apply specifically to cases of inequality of love, they might also be an important model for Utopia's judiciary in general:

1. Who can bring cases? It is essential that the courts be open to all people, so any group, *or any individual*, who feels himself/herself to be a victim of inequality, can petition the court. Also, individuals who are not themselves victims can bring cases on behalf of anyone else, based on compassion for that person or persons. Let's say that I encounter someone who seems socially neglected. With that person's consent, I can bring a case to court seeking redress of the neglect faced by that individual.

2. What actions can the court take? The whole panoply of remedies described in previous chapters for equalizing attention, such as using media to bring attention to neglected persons (see Chapter 2), will be available to judges. A judge may issue a voluntary proclamation calling on media outlets to, say, increase their coverage of elderly persons. The judge may also call upon all people to increase their attention to the elderly.

If a person feels slighted not by society as a whole, but by friends or family members, or coworkers, then the court can, again non-coercively, rule in favor of the neglected party. In order to avoid coercion, the court would then call upon the parties to the situation to devise their own mutually agreeable solution, and the court would monitor the progress of the solution. If this process fails, the court may devise its own solution. The court, of course, may be free to say that two parties may continue their relationship, and in a way rectifying its inequality, but the court may also prescribe a breaking and ending of the relationship.

Key to rectifying any inequality is strengthening the virtuous cycles of compassion, so that there is mutual understanding and mutual care between individuals. I don't know whether I would claim equality to be foundational to compassion or vice versa, but it is clear they are as inextricably related as are their opposites— hierarchy and a zero-sum approach. Therefore, another central component of a judicial decision will be to challenge any causes, large or small, disturbing the basic empathy existing in Utopia. The idea of walking in another's shoes is a truly old idea precisely because it is so powerful. Judges, thus, would ask petitioners to take on each other's roles, and learn about each other, following the strategies described in Chapter 5. I know this is a technique already used in therapy and informal conflict resolution, but its formalization in the judicial system will help ensure that empathy is maintained at the forefront, along with equality, as a key virtue to be rectified in case of conflict.

In fact, empathy and understanding can be seen as helping to prevent conflict. Therefore, courts will seek to prevent conflict by promoting greater empathy. In particular, judges will monitor societal conflict, and any time there is a pattern detected indicating inequality and lack of empathy in a particular place, or societal domain, judges will be able to issue noncompulsory edicts to address this pattern— by, for example, prescribing greater involvement in walking-in-others'-shoes types of activities.

I cannot stress with enough enthusiasm how important it is for the courts to prevent erosion of empathy and virtuous cycles. Humans, like our primate relatives, have a supreme ability to pay back both the good and the bad. If there is a pattern of inequality and hurtfulness occurring, the victims and even bystanders will tend to propagate the hurt more widely. Just as states and courts in the past often arose to intervene in cases of feuding, there is an analogous, yet ultimately more transformational power, which they will have in Utopia. They will keep cycles of revenge or zero-sum hurtfulness from occurring, and they will preserve the virtuous cycles based on empathy and mutual understanding that are so centrally human, and so foundational to societal peace and love.

3. No zero-sum decisions: Where money and power exist, then conflicts often take the form of a zero-sum contest between two parties to a conflict. One will win at the others' expense.

But in the absence of zero-sum possibilities, court decisions about attention will not produce the kinds of winners and losers so common in today's court proceedings. Where a group of people, or an individual, feels a lack of sufficient attention, there is little, if any, zero-sum dynamic possible. Attention is not an inherently limited commodity. I can sit in someone's presence and ignore them or attend to them. To do the latter only takes focus on my part, and it takes away nothing from me or from anyone else to do so, except maybe depriving my wandering mind, temporarily, of its wanderings! In fact, how many times do so many of us "give time" but not genuine attention to those we love—a major cause of complaint and conflict between long-term partners, family, and friends. We all know that we can increase our focus and attention, without losing anything but a wandering mind.

The lack of a zero-sum dynamic in Utopian justice is important to stress. In today's judicial system, even a fair decision still contains the seeds of the vicious cycle of zero-sum dynamics, since someone is a winner at someone else's expense.

But Utopia's courts, by meting out justice that is not zero-sum but rather restorative of virtuous cycles, can be seen, *in their very functioning*, as embodying the principles of empathy and non-zero-sum logics that they seek to promote among the courts' petitioners.

4. Negative rulings: Sometimes we feel we are not receiving sufficient attention when, in fact, we really aren't being ignored. These feelings can be especially strong in depressed persons. If a judge feels that a complainant's case has no basis, no one will be punished, and the judge may rule against the complainant. What such a ruling means is that the judge will kindly explain, with the help of court assistants, all of the attention a person is really garnering, and will seek to show, indeed to prove, that the complainant is not deficient in attention received. *Such a ruling, in fact, should not really be deemed "negative" since it is instead a way to reassure a person of that most fundamental human desire: Yes, despite our fears, we are, indeed, loved, and loved as much as others.*

5. The judges: Who will they be and how will they be chosen? One way would be that already described: A lottery to pick term-limited individuals to be judges, with judges receiving no compensation or privileges.

But let me also propose a variation on this method. The judges might be chosen by lottery from among each of the following pools of candidates:

a. Earlier I described how people may bring to the court cases of inequality affecting those other than themselves. Anyone who successfully brings such cases ("success" means the judge affirms the alleged inequality) will be in the first pool of judicial candidates. The rationale here is that those who are most sensitive to the equality needs of others deserve to serve as judges.

b. Successful past complainants in equality cases will comprise the second pool.

c. Random individuals will comprise the third pool.

d. Actors or artists who portray the resolution of hierarchical conflicts will be the fourth pool.

6. Will the judges of cases of inequality of attention be able to coerce others, based upon their rulings? This is, indeed, a tricky question. However, the reader might guess my answer: No. No coercion, simply persuasion. This is, in fact, the way chiefs in small-scale societies operate. If their views are persuasive and correct, then the chief keeps power. The same with informal judges such as the *ssa hxuo* among the Yi, who have no coercive power.

The absence of coercion will work to ensure that no judge gets too much power. But, in addition, the emphasis on persuasion over coercion is consistent with the freedoms that Utopia must value. If I take a friend to court claiming he is demeaning me, or neglecting me, a ruling against him would not seem viable were he to be coerced, in some way, to attend to me. But a well-respected outside observer issuing a non-binding ruling in my favor is a different matter.

I know some readers may see even persuasion as a form of coercion, but I disagree. Non-coercive determinations are more like a form of teaching. My friend is free to ignore the thoughts of the judge, but it is the fairness and compassion of the judge which may make those thoughts, and the judge's ruling, difficult to ignore. In fact, undesirable to ignore as well: Since Utopia and its judges' rulings are non-zero-sum, the ruling is one that seeks advantage not for me at my friend's expense, but to improve the equity and balance of our relationship as a whole, which is to the benefit of both of us. If my friend ignores the ruling, then I can at least feel a sense of third-party vindication of my feelings, which in itself is a way to rectify the hurts of an inequitable relationship. But in most cases a ruling that seeks benefit for both parties, and is convincing, would persuade my friend to change his behavior through his own volition. This preserves both freedom and equality simultaneously.

7. Lawyers: Will they exist? It is important to make court action transparent, and lawyers and legal jargon might interfere with this goal. Further, no one would be paid for providing legal services. Therefore, I'm inclined to say that the complainants should give their cases in their own voices, supported only if desired by a friend or family member who may help them present their case.

Administration in Utopia

Utopia will not only need conflict resolution, but also administration. What happens if everyone wants to study particle physics, and there aren't enough particle-physics reactors? Who will build them and who will plan and supervise their building?

As a utopian, I want to assume Utopia will run on its own. My friends like to burst this bubble of mine, by asking me questions such as those above. Those are fair questions, since societies can't run on auto-pilot, of course. So how will the administration of Utopia take place, and who will be its administrators?

Is it possible to have administration that is non-formal and voluntary, as proposed? Can such an administration accomplish anything? This might seem difficult to do but, as I argued in Chapter 4, the Internet provides nice counterexamples. Wikipedia is a huge and growing academically oriented encyclopedia written, organized, and administered almost entirely by volunteers. I'm sure the key to Wikipedia's success, and the key to the successful administration of Utopia, is that administrative positions, like anything else, will not be zero-sum. So, to start off, I'd allow anyone who wants to be involved in the planning of Utopia to have a role in doing so. Where power and money are involved, then positions of influence become limited by the limiting nature of the rewards, but there is no reason to limit the planning functions to a small number of individuals. The only reason for limitation will be logistical reasons (you can't have a meeting with three million people), so, when necessary, a lottery will choose administrators from among a pool of volunteers. And as described previously, administration will be like a jury, in the sense that service will be term-limited, so as to prevent the entrenchment of any administrative elites.

An important corrective to the political dysfunction of today will be to encourage decision-making based on clear thinking and analysis. To do this I would encourage very carefully structured political debates:

1. Anyone will be allowed to come to any Utopia policy debate, to participate, judge, or just listen. By policy debate I mean a debate over what administrative decisions will be taken in Utopia to satisfy the basic guarantees (e.g., whether to build more physics facilities for the huge number of people wanting to study physics).

2. In these debates, people will argue for different positions, but the debate rules, worked out in advance and in more detail than I will give here (I welcome here the assistance of readers to supply further details about the debate structure), will specify that debaters must not only advance their own positions, but also must address and confront the positions of others—both those with whom they have agreements and those with whom they have disagreements. By confront I mean that a debater A who disagrees with a debater advocating position B, must argue clearly against B. The argument can be based on controversy over facts, or it can revolve around principles. However, in the latter case, no principle can trump the basic holistic egalitarian principles of Utopia, of course.

To me this is a key point because the sense we often have of people talking past each other in disagreements is quite literally true. People today often do not listen to each other carefully and do not address each other's points. In Utopia listening is a critical component of compassion for others, so Utopians must always listen carefully. They do *not* need to agree, but they must hear what others are saying, even if they disagree, and even if they believe their opponent's views are totally wrong or completely immoral. After all, understanding someone's point of view is in no way equivalent to condoning it: Police trying to find a mass murderer are aided by understanding his or her thinking. Knowing how the perpetrator thinks clearly does not mean they approve of those thoughts and actions.

3. There will be an audience of debate adjudicators. They will not just decide who "wins," but also will attempt to clarify the nature of the agreements and disagreements. In particular, it is extremely important that these debate analysts separate objective elements of the debate from subjective elements and clarify the axiomatic assumptions beneath people's arguments.

4. The debate can be resolved in one of the following ways:

a. Everyone comes to an agreement, as unknown facts clarify the issue and as opinions and subjectivities are unmasked.

b. Disagreement remains, but the sources of that disagreement will be made clear to all:

i. Is it that one speaker doubts another speaker's facts? In this case debate adjudicators might prescribe more fact-finding.

ii. Is it that one speaker holds to an axiomatic value that is antithetical to the basic values of Utopia? If so, that person should be overruled, unless and until s/he counters the basic egalitarian values of Utopia with evidence and argument of his/her own.

c. Disagreement exists, but both sides modify their axioms in various ways, or acknowledge the reasonableness of certain elements of each other's axioms, to reach some albeit not full agreement on axioms—what we might call "soft" agreement, as opposed to total agreement.

I may be an idealist, but I strongly believe that clearly reasoned debate can lead to better administration of Utopia—indeed better administration of any society.

Utopian universalism: No more nation-states and no more war

End war. End the nation-state: Two of the biggest causes of hierarchy in history are war and the nation-state. War is a great cause of human misery and so is the nation-state—which so often foments war, at least in the absence of a world government and world judiciary to settle conflicts. Thus, Utopia will strive to end war, nationalism, and the nation-state, in favor of peaceful settlement of conflicts by a body beholden to no nation or sub-group. Individuals' welfare will no longer be tied to the sub-group or nation into which they are born and to which they are bound. Utopia will make freedom of movement a common practice, eliminate borders, and establish universalism within the entire Utopian community.

Let me give the reasons why it must do this, starting with the connection of war to hierarchy, followed by the nation-state's connection to hierarchy. In Chapter 1 I discussed Carneiro's (1970) classic theory about the origins of the state (*not* the nation-state, which is different from the state) and the first hierarchy among humans, about 6000 years ago. War was central to his theory. He argues, in brief, that war in certain conditions led to the taking of captives by the winners in warfare, captives who became slaves. The resulting division of society into slaves and their masters marks the first formal hierarchy ever in human history, a history that had been virtually egalitarian since the first appearance of humans on earth nearly 200,000 years ago.

Fast forward thousands of years after the first hierarchy and state of 6000 years ago and we find the nation-state being established for the first time. The exact time of its origin and place of origin are in some dispute but there is basic agreement that the first nation-states arose in the West, either in Europe or the Americas, beginning perhaps in the late 18th century (with the American and French Revolutions) and reaching a climax beginning in the late 19th century and throughout the 20th century.

The nation-state, unlike most empires (or what others call "states") that preceded it, urged a congruence between the ethnic background of the rulers and the ethnicity of the people they ruled. Another way to say it is that a territory should be inhabited and ruled by those whose ancestors, and culture, belonged to that territory (with some immigration allowed, often with great opposition, however).

There is a seeming reasonableness to this idea, of course. "People should rule their own land"—democracy—rather than being ruled by outside invaders. But as the history of the United States illustrates, democracies are often in reality quite undemocratic. With the American denial of rights to indigenous peoples and to Africans brought to the nation as slaves, as well as the denial of rights to women, it is clear that the seemingly democratic and simple notion of "the people" is ideologically constructed to give the right of belongingness to certain classes of people at the great expense of the rights of others also inhabiting the national territory. Indigenous peoples, women, and ethnic and religious minorities all lost out and they are the worldwide losers of so many nation-states.

There were many groups who lost out in empires too, but in the empire brute force, in the form of huge armies, was the means of winning or losing. In the nation-state brute force continues to exist, but to this overt power is wedded a seductive covert power—the emotions attached to the idea that "this is our *home*," "our national family" (note the national terminologies of "homeland," "motherland," "fatherland,"). As I have argued elsewhere (Schoenhals 2003), the nation-state is the exclusionary caste and its segregating and hierarchicizing sentiments wedded onto land. The desire of imperial rulers to extract wealth from subjects who were often multi-ethnic (and why not? The more subjects giving taxes, the better for the ruler) was replaced by the desire to decide who belongs and who doesn't belong *in your home, with the nation as home*. And when these domestic and familial emotions, the most potent of emotions, are wedded to the political and economic spoils of belongingness—jobs and the opportunity to be a ruler in that home—the combination of emotions and incentives becomes toxic. Elite political motives are aligned to both mass economic motives (rights to a job based on one's nationality) and to mass socio-psychological feelings—the idea of belonging to a large community of those defined as being the same (ancestry, culture) as you, in opposition to a world outside your borders filled with strangers. Nationalist elites in the modern era have used popular sentiment to bolster their own power and to recruit soldiers motivated to serve by new feelings that their polity is their own home.

No wonder that, in the extreme, the nation-state uses its military and police powers to purify the "homeland" of "outsiders" just as is done on a more micro level, and without the full apparatus of violence at its disposal, in caste societies. And national leaders are supported in this purifying process by the nation's "democratic" masses, both those serving in the police and military, and those who participate in extra-legal and often very violent movements against minorities. This dynamic leads to the genocides that became such a common feature of the 20th century.

The realization that the world would be better off without war is probably as old as war itself, and the same with nation-states, whose intrinsic divisions of humanity into exclusionary territories, and the resulting nationalistic warfare and genocides that sometimes ensue, are clearly visible to any casual student of 20th-century history. These are all very good reasons for ending war and nation-states, but I am adding here the relationship between hierarchy and war, and hierarchy and the nation-state.

I could write a whole chapter elaborating on these relationships. After all, war not only produces slave–master hierarchies but it also produces patriarchal societies that come to demean women. This is a complex story but one I can only allude to here. And to the divisiveness, often extreme, of nationalism I have added its caste-like, exclusionary nature. Since caste and its segregations (see Chapter 2) are central to the hierarchies it produces, I am arguing that the nation-state with its caste-like nature cannot coexist with genuine equality. Again, I could write a whole chapter relating the nation-state to hierarchies: It is centrally related to racial oppression, to ethnic-minority group oppression, and to the oppression of women (by denying women the right to vote, the right that is central to power and belongingness in the nation-state). And I can only allude to the potent and toxic relationship between nationalism and war itself.

But rather than further detail contemporary ills, which are all too familiar to many readers, I want to sketch how Utopia will end war and the nation-state. Let me begin by arguing why an end to war is not as unrealistic as many might think.

I begin with an observation made by another scholar and friend. Slavery in the 19th century might have seemed to have been an inevitable part of humanity, but in the 20th and early 21st centuries there is a universal consensus that it should no longer exist. Likewise, war, which seems so intrinsic to the human condition, need not be. Like slavery, it too can be ended. In fact, the silver lining in the dark cloud of 20th-century warfare was the establishment of international organizations, such as the United Nations and the International Criminal Court, devoted to preventing war and to handling inter- and intra-state conflict judicially rather than militarily. With our 21st-century myopia we often forget that the other contribution of "civilization" is not just warfare but judicial systems for resolving conflict within societies. As Frank Fukuyama points out, the advent of a disinterested third party to resolve disputes between two parties to a conflict is a significant human development. Fukuyama includes independent judiciaries as a key component of his discussion of the "evolution" of political order, leading up to the rule of law, accountability, and so on. All of these resolve conflict, and they even do so between a ruler and his followers, by institutionalizing the means for controlling the naked abuse of power by the ruler himself (Fukuyama 2011: See especially 254–261).

Thus, genuine third-party resolution of all conflicts is a genuine accomplishment of humanity, and one that arose with "civilization." It is a significant accomplishment because it establishes a peaceful means to resolve conflicts, and one in which conflicts can be resolved based upon justice, rather than based on the strange notion that the stronger person should win. In fact, the reason civilized societies are deemed civilized in the first place is because of the pacification that holds within their domain, a pacification made possible by judicial settling of conflict.

Where I am going with all of this is simple: If "civilization" is in large part synonymous with the notion that conflicts should be solved peacefully and judicially between two parties, and if these principles can exist within societies, then *why not between societies as well?* Why couldn't nations resolve their differences through judiciaries, rather than through warfare?

Only our own myopia prevents us from seeing that a long-term trend in human history is moving us in the direction of a worldwide judiciary. That trend is the gradual enlargement of the domains over which judicial, rather than military, conflict resolution takes place. While early 20th-century Europe saw brutal wars between nations, later 20th-century Europe created the European Union and its administrative, judicial, and legislative bodies in large measure in order to prevent war through the settlement of conflicts by peaceful means. Why can't the next step be world justice? Why shouldn't it be so? Isn't it inevitable that we have been heading in that direction for hundreds of years anyway? I think so.

One way war will be ended is implicit throughout this book. By ending property, wealth, and status—the spoils of war—there will be no reason to go to war. Conflicts will still occur, and they may make individuals or groups quite angry, perhaps even prone to violence. But if any individual or group is truly unhappy, they can leave Utopia and found their own society. And if they use violence when in Utopia, this will be a clear violation of the constitution, to be dealt with by the judiciary. One of the reasons war exists today is that the injunction against killing other humans is not universalized, an amazing inconsistency to me considering how central universalism is to the world's major religions. In Utopia, all killing will be wrong and therefore any conflict will be dealt with through peaceful means.

Key also to ending war is to abolish the nation-state. This will be done by eliminating all borders and allowing anyone to travel, temporarily or permanently, anywhere within Utopia. This might seem to be a radical suggestion, but the really radical idea is that we would *not* be able to travel freely or live where we want. After all, if freedom is a virtue, then freedom of movement is essential, not only the freedom to move within one's own land, but also between all lands. It is a bitter hypocrisy that right-wing authors trumpet freedom's virtues, but they are the pillars of resistance to free international movement (except for the free movement of capital, which they love, since this is a freedom allowing them to move factories to wherever labor is cheapest).

If borders were opened up today, it is true that a flood of people might pour into the US, Canada, parts of Europe, and the few other "wealthy" countries around the world. But that is because those countries have more than their fair share of wealth to begin with. If every single human was guaranteed basic subsistence, and jobs no longer were required, then the attraction for going to one place over another diminishes. It is true that natural beauty might make more people flock to, say, the

Swiss Alps than those mountains could accommodate. In that case a purely egalitarian mechanism, such as a lottery, could be used to determine who could live there. I would still allow all people to visit anywhere, however, and I think it entirely possible that no restrictions on residence would be necessary. Recall that notions of what is attractive about people will be democratized. The same dynamic might operate to make people think differently about what counts as natural beauty too, so that some people will see beauty in, say, a stark desert scene, rather than in snow-capped mountains.

Bibliography

Carneiro, Robert L. 1970. A theory of the origin of the state. *Science*, 169: 733–738.

Fukuyama, Francis 2011. *The Origins of Political Order: From Prehuman Times to the French Revolution*. New York: Farrar, Straus and Giroux.

Schoenhals, Martin 2003. *Intimate Exclusion: Race and Caste Turned Inside Out*. Lanham, MD: University Press of America.

8

UTOPIA'S SOLUTIONS TO UNIVERSAL PSYCHOLOGICAL DILEMMAS

The proposals in this book cannot end all unhappiness, nor make everyone happy. But because we are social beings, the societies in which we live profoundly affect the way we feel. This truth is perhaps most obvious about unhappiness. Hierarchy produces so many social conditions directly implicated in human misery—war, genocide, poverty, slavery, the oppression of women, the persecution of ethnic minorities and sexual minorities—that it does not seem terribly controversial to say that ending these will greatly elevate our opportunity to achieve happiness.

But I want to conclude this book by considering ways in which Utopia addresses widespread human dilemmas, ones that we usually characterize as psychological and therefore immune to being affected by social change. My goal here is twofold. I want to remind readers once again of the powerful effect on our psychologies that can result from social transformation. And in doing so I will show the interconnections between the many changes prescribed in the book's previous chapters, an especially important task given the wide range of issues the book covers.

The real versus the ideal

Because humans have the capacity to think about things not in our immediate environment, we are able to imagine conditions different from our present existence. We conjure up dreams of a happier world, of friendlier friends, more loving lovers, and of ourselves as more perfect, more loveable and admirable than we really are. This capacity is quintessentially human and is thus universal. Popular opinion, and some popular scholarship, sometimes asserts that reflection and dreaming is a condition that only arose in the West with the Industrial Revolution, once we had the time and luxury to worry about something other than "our next meal." But aside from the incorrect view that the Industrial Revolution ended subsistence worries, rather than exacerbating them, it is also incorrect that people who are poor and/or parochial have no dreams. Dreaming, hoping, longing—these are central activities of all of us.

As any reader knows, the gap between our reality and our dreams can often be a source of great pain. Buddhism, in fact, makes yearnings for money, sex, and love a central cause of human unhappiness. And a major tenet of a multitude of religions and philosophies is that one should be grateful for what one has. In the secular realm, American cognitive psychology counsels us to reframe our reality in a more positive light; in feeling less of a gap between dreams and reality, it is believed we will become happy.

Leftists, Marxists in particular, have been deeply critical of counseling people to accept their fate, especially when the person giving such counsel represents the elite and when the counselee belongs to an exploited class. Leftists *are* correct that those living in poverty can be made happier by improvements to their external conditions. But we all know too many people who remain unfulfilled despite seeming to have acquired so much of what others lack. Why is this? Why is there a gap between our lives as they are, and our dreams?

One major force driving our anxious dreaming and longing is our fear that others might be better than us. We know there are others richer than us. But we also imagine that others might be feeling more love, having better sex, and being pleased in ways that elude us. The fear that we are missing something that others have makes us worry that we are being left behind—isolated, ostracized, abandoned—lacking something that many other humans have. One measure of the potency of this fear is the craving to know that we are "normal" in what we feel and do. If we believe we are "normal," this reassures us: We are part of a majority; we belong.

If a major cause of the real/ideal gap is our fears, real or imagined, of being deficient compared to others, then the egalitarianism of this book offers a powerful antidote. Living in a society that tries to guarantee equality can reassure us that we will not be left behind. In particular:

1. Equality in all domains: In this book I have differed from much conventional left thinking by advocating equality not just of money and power, but equality too of love, of gender, and of any other form of human interaction. This broad-based egalitarianism is key to ending anxious longing. Since the longings all humans have, and the gaps we imagine might exist between us and others, are not just monetary, but focused on inequality in the spheres of intimacy as well, equality in all spheres of society is the only real way to end the gnawing feeling that reality doesn't measure up to what we imagine it might be, or what we imagine others might have.

2. Dealing better with difference: Yes, many readers will quickly object that no two people can ever be truly equal in the pleasure, love, and respect that they feel. True. But there is a huge difference between a society in which people only feel good if they outpace others, versus the society I imagine, where others help us acquire what we lack.

Further, today so much of our anxious longing is intensified by never really knowing where we stand relative to others. This is especially true of inequality of love and sex, since what people do and feel in this realm is so much less visible than in the realm of money, where status goods are often clearly on display.

Compare these two scenarios:

Scenario A: X knows he has less pleasure in sex, and/or has sex less often than Y. In fact, he knows exactly how much he differs from Y. Y knows this difference too, but takes no pleasure in the inequality itself (i.e., feels no *Schadenfreude*), and maybe even wants to feel a bit less pleasure so that he will be more equal to X. (Wouldn't that be amazing?!)

Scenario B: X suspects Y feels more pleasure in sex, or has more pleasure, but doesn't know for sure if this is true, nor does he know by what magnitude he differs from Y. Y, for his part, suspects his own superiority although he's not absolutely sure of it. As a result, he manifests an outer air of exaggerated self-confidence, and a disdain for X, in order to try to achieve a feeling of superiority over X.

As I have argued above, in scenario B, today's situation, X can be driven to longing precisely because he doesn't know by how much he is behind Y. In addition X's sensing Y's happiness at his expense further injures X's self-esteem. If other people become complicit in the inequality—granting esteem to Y for his apparent superiority and self-confidence—then X's insecurity becomes even more intense, and justifiably so.

And Y, never knowing if he really is ahead, must keep striving himself. His actual pleasure is never stable, because he knows X, and others, are doing what he himself does—trying hard to put on an act of self-confidence which, if successful, can embolden himself and hurt others' esteem. Y's insecurity, indeed everyone's insecurity, becomes the cause of obsessive thinking and actions. And Y's outer self-confidence and inner fears might conflict enough so as to cause angst and shame—the shame that the real insecurity will show through.

These dynamics are nearly eliminated in scenario A. Not only is love equalized, as described in Chapter 2, but the various mechanisms to encourage honest communication, sincerity, and integrity of inner and outer selves, as described in Chapter 5, defuse the mystification of inequality of scenario B. Knowing what others actually feel—and studying their lives and acting out others' lives (see Chapter 5)—reduces the existential fear that we are alone—alone in what we feel, and vulnerable to being left behind because of it.

3. Means–end: A means–end orientation is the foundation upon which the mystification of point 2 is built. If we seek pleasure in love and work for its own sake, then our love and work cannot become a means for our self-aggrandizement, and the debasement of others. The connection of means–end behavior to hierarchy is a key reason for eliminating it.

4. Real community: The prescription for real community (Chapter 3) further challenges the existential fear. Even if we feel less pleasure than others, the fear of

isolation this might cause is mitigated by a greater sense of belonging. And we can take pleasure in others' pleasure, even if we have less. Moreover, greater community can lead to greater shared pleasures, further diminishing the inequality that leads us to feel a reality/fantasy gap.

My point here is simple: The painful gap we all feel between what we have and what we imagine we might have derives from inequality itself, because it is seeing others whom we imagine are happier or better off that provokes us to believe we lack something. Ending hierarchy and instituting genuine communication between people will go a long way toward ending anxious longing, that source of so much pain and angst through the centuries.

Free will and happiness

For Americans, the idea of being in control of our own lives is a powerful one. I know some readers, especially Americans, will dislike the idea that we should depend on others, and on society and its transformation, to make us happy. They will say such dependence absolves us of the responsibility to care for ourselves. We should create the conditions for our own well-being, they will add. Conservatives, in particular, may express disdain for yet another leftist analysis that places blame for our suffering on social conditions, rather than on ourselves, and our own errant thoughts and actions.

While I do not share the self-reliance critique, it *is* appealing to imagine how we might acquire the power to please ourselves. If we could do this, if we could make ourselves happy at will, wouldn't this be ideal? Indeed it would. The question is: *Why can't we please ourselves at will?*

The aim of this book has been to emphasize our social nature. We need to interact affirmatively with others in order to feel happy. Thus, we cannot make ourselves happy if social conditions interfere with the quality of our relationships with other humans. While the belief in our own independence is seductive, it is factually inaccurate to say that we can make ourselves fully happy independent of the nature of the society in which we live. Moreover, the belief that we can be robustly happy by ourselves, devoid of connections to others and obligations to them, is a conservative fantasy that not only seems impossible, but is also heedless of moral responsibility, an irony since we leftists are often the ones accused, at least by those on the right, of neglecting morality.

My proposal in this book is a moral one. Its emphasis on pleasure is not on self-indulgent pleasure but on pleasure deriving from mutual obligations to care for others and to be cared for by them. This mutual care and concern is, to me, the real essence of morality.

My proposal also does not run counter to self-reliance but embraces it. It does so by advocating the creation of the social conditions allowing people to feel pleasure and happiness much more easily, at will, independent of means–end externalities. The very reason that so many people cannot bring themselves pleasure at will in contemporary society is because they either lack the basics of pleasure—access to work or love—and/or their position in multiple hierarchies produces the depression that saps the ability to feel basic pleasures from everyday life. It is well-known that depression has this role, but the pathologizing of mental health precludes our realization that *all of us in hierarchical society* suffer the disempowerment induced by a kind of collective depression. I have tended to emphasize the anxieties produced by hierarchy (and these too sap pleasure), but hierarchy also produces psychological hurts to our fundamental sense of self-esteem, be it the hurt of feeling we are not sufficiently recognized for our work, or the feeling of shame that we are insufficiently feminine or masculine.

If these hurts existed in only one domain, such as on the job, we could seek refuge from the pain away from our workplace, but the multiplicity of hierarchies ensures that they are omnipresent. And, as I have argued, even if we seem to be high up in the hierarchy, we are not relieved of these hurts. In fact, those who climb up the ladder of hierarchy not only continue to fear they will fall back down, but they also come to believe their ladder perch is never high enough. Lack of self-esteem thus haunts even those at the top, sometimes even more than those at the bottom, a dynamic we can easily see by watching the tragically self-destructive lives of so many celebrities.

By ending all hierarchy, we can end the hurts to self-esteem that are caused by it. By ending these hurts, we eliminate the soft but insidious experience of depression ever-present in contemporary life. And by ending this pervasive depression, we allow humans to be the social and compassionate animals that we can be, those who easily derive pleasure from even the most mundane and trivial instances of such sociality.

And in addition to ending depression-inducing hierarchy, Utopia makes it easy for people to work, and to work creatively at endeavors that stir their passions. Think how empowering that would be. I know so many amazingly creative people, who either must forego their passions to make a living at a boring job, and/or who spend years and years writing books, singing songs, and thinking great thoughts that go unnoticed. They spend countless years trying to obtain that most basic human need—attention. The experience of repeated failure in obtaining notice for their passionate creations lowers their sense of self-efficacy and leads to depression. They develop a sense of the lack of their own power to bring to themselves what they need and want.

Utopia aids self-esteem and self-efficacy not just by changing how we think about the world—a goal of much therapy—but also by actually changing that world, so that the multitude of forces denying us access to love and work are reduced. The end to today's artificial restrictions on access to attention, work, and love will in turn diminish learned helplessness and restore to us a feeling of self-efficacy, powerfulness, and, above all, self-esteem and happiness.

Means and ends

A central theme of my book has been that humans should act for pleasure, so that their actions are not means to an end, but an end in itself. I argue this based partly on the seemingly obvious notion that if pleasure is a key component of human happiness, then present pleasure, rather than future rewards, should be the only aim of our actions (and given that pleasure is experienced during action itself, "aim" might be an inappropriate term; it is revealing that our language makes it difficult to talk with sophistication about means and ends). I argue it, too, because hierarchy is always a means to some other end, by its very nature, so that challenging means–end action, in schools and work, for example, leads us to challenge the pursuit of hierarchy itself.

But I need to admit that some psychological thinkers do not see present pleasure as always being the force for the greatest happiness. Csikszentmihalyi suggests, in a remarkable work (1990), that we feel greatest pleasure in pursuing a challenging goal. Who is right—those advocating means–end action or those, like me, disparaging it? I will take a compromise position, conceding reasons goals might be attractive but reformulating the kinds of goals that could be tolerated in Utopia.

First, goal-driven achievements satisfy us in our present system because we have been socialized to seek extrinsic rewards for our actions, rather than to feel pleasure in the actions themselves. This could, and should change, as the social conditions underpinning the desire for extrinsic reward change, thereby reducing the pleasure gained in achieving extrinsic rewards. Second, there may be a tendency for us to construe our activity as goal-directed in order to satisfy our desire for immortality, or at least our desire for something beyond our own lives. We might feel that if we accomplish something, that our activity will have meaning for posterity. This desire might or might not change with Utopia. (It could change if, for example, the maximization of attention by Utopia is satisfying enough that we no longer have the urge to become known, or remain known, after we are gone.) If the desire lingers in Utopia, there might be legitimacy to conserving some goal-directed behavior. Finally, I think it is possible that the distinction between goals, on the one hand, and actions that lead to goals, on the other hand, might be attractive to us because they give a rhythm to life, one in which there is action, satisfaction, and then rest. This same rhythm might also add variety—actions and their consequences.

But even if I were to concede that humans can achieve legitimate satisfaction from goal-driven behavior, there is nonetheless a significant difference between a goal pursued in pain and distress versus one pursued with perhaps some pain, but with a sense of desire for, and excitement about, the ultimate goal. That is, the climax itself depends on the nature of the lead-up to the climax. If the lead-up to the climax does not produce a feeling of *pleasurable* tension, then the climax cannot satisfy, and the result will be the obsessive repetition of the goal-driven behavior, driven by the desire to attain the elusive satisfaction. But if the means, that is, the behavior leading up to the goal, is one of excitement and even pleasurable tension, then the attainment of the goal is satisfying. It is these waves of pleasurable tension and the attainment of pleasurable release from that tension that help humans feel happy. Conversely, it is inattention to the means, and a failure to see the means as necessarily pleasuring, that leads to a lack of satisfaction even when a goal is reached. Thus, even if we strive for some delayed or distant goal, in which we seek a sense of pride and larger pleasure, we must still feel pleasure during our actions in pursuit of the goal. Only this way can the goal fully satisfy us when it is achieved. And, if the goal is not attained, we will not feel cheated out of a pleasure we had convinced ourselves was forthcoming, a pleasure we wrongly believed would compensate us for the pain involved in pursuing delayed pleasure.

I sincerely believe that the main reason humans so often emphasize the need to delay pleasure in order to pursue distant goals (thus overlooking the possibility that both the goal *and* its pursuit can and should be pleasurable) is because we live in hierarchies. Those on top rationalize their status based upon having gone through the appropriate painful rites of passage—the long hours put in to become a doctor, for example. And the teachers, parents, and friends of those on the top use the ostensible pain-for-gain rhetoric to control the pleasures, especially the sexual pleasures, of the strivers. (This is very clearly in evidence in China, where studying and dating are culturally constructed as virtually inherent opposites. Yes, I admit that romantic and sexual attractions can, in fact, be true distractions from study but the desire that others not feel more pleasure than oneself is a powerful motive for the polemic that study and work require pain and sacrifice.)

Were we to openly admit that the rite of passage was a pleasurable one, or were we to make it so, then the whole moral superiority of the pleasure-denying upper class, and its attendant superabundant wealth and power, would be undercut. (And, conversely, the consolations felt by the lower status—that at least "we had more fun than the wealthy did"—would likewise be challenged.) The familiar refrain, "no pain, no gain" also implies "if you've gained, you must have pained." In reality, there is no reason that it must be this way, or even that it is socially and psychologically desirable to live this way.

Hierarchy and invidiousness versus belonging and empathy

The more I have worked on this book, the more I have come to realize how connected are the different phenomena I've been indicting. In Chapter 5 I described the connections between shame and hierarchy. But let me reprise and expand that argument, since it helps unify key themes found throughout the book.

Shame is a uniquely human emotion that animals do not feel and it is a universal emotion too. No individual or culture fully escapes it. Shame is related to the other social emotions of love, compassion, and guilt. It likely evolved to encourage prosociality, the goal of Utopia, but it does so in an imperfect way. It works by inducing extremely toxic pain if our private selfishness or other anti-social impulses are revealed. This is an indirect mechanism of social action. Rather than getting us to act prosocially because it will please ourselves and others, shame incites us to make a *pretense* of acting prosocially so that we can avoid the intense punishment of feeling shame. Clearly, this is not the best route to genuine prosociality.

Because shame is so toxic, we seek ways to challenge it. A real challenge would be for humans to work collectively to eliminate it, using other strategies instead to encourage prosociality. But we don't take that route. Instead, we either adopt public actions to hide our true negative inclinations or we do the opposite, indulging in shameful actions as an attempted rebellion against shame. In sex we may act shame-lessly in order to counter sexual embarrassment. We may use sex as an arena for showing off, indulging in the narcissism and obsessive self-interest that make us feel less shame-based humility. We may attempt to expel the vulnerability we feel from shame and replace it with an invulnerable sexuality, lacking tenderness and compas-sion. These moves may give us temporary relief from shame, but they preclude the compassion and attention to others that is the basis for real human interactive joy.

We counter the effects of shame, too, by creating new groups with values exactly the opposite of those of the larger society, so that what is shameful in the larger society becomes honorable in our smaller sphere. But these groups, such as ado-lescent peer groups, do not implement a direct challenge to shame and hierarchy, but recreate new shame, new hierarchies, and, above all, new ostracisms if we fail to conform, such as outcasting us if we fail to perform to the group's sexual standards. The result is hierarchy, dehumanization, bounded status groups maintained through outcasting and shame, and the unfreedom and coarseness that destroys joy, sincerity, and real empathic connection to other humans.

And a vicious cycle is established. The shame of these new would-be rebel groups makes some individuals flee back to the larger society, often as new advocates for that society's norms. Those individuals seeking to escape shame through shameless sex, for example, sometimes feel the emptiness of their escape, and they often form the very constituency that promotes fundamentalist religious ideologies as a back-lash against their own previous would-be rebellion. Both the "rebel" groups and the fundamentalist backlash groups establish rigid hierarchies, with firm criteria for deciding who gets welcomed into the group and who, failing to measure up to the group's norms, must be turned away.

In narrating this process as a reaction of peers to shame, and then a counterreaction against peer-based shame, I do not intend to suggest this is the necessary order for the process. Written description is necessarily linear but the process I'm describing here is one in which shame and hierarchy in one domain produces new shames, hierarchies, and exclusions in another domain, with the opposing domains intensi-fying the toxicity of each other's anti-social dynamics. I also do not mean to imply, in using sex as an example, that shame's dynamics operate only there. Shame's div-isive dynamics operate in all human spheres, from love to work to learning.

And finally I want to acknowledge that the operation of shame takes place in a historical and cultural context to which I can only briefly allude in this book. For example, hard work has not always been a source of pride and dignity. In the West, the pride of work and the shame of idleness were values first popularized in Puritan/Protestant Britain and America. Prior to the Puritan ascendance, indulging in idleness and pleasure was a badge of pride, because it meant you had enough status and money to amuse yourself. Pleasure and an idle, non-working life were the privilege enjoyed by aristocrats, privileges denied to those with less societal honor.

But despite the historical contingencies, I know from my own research in China, and from life in America, that puritanical and anti-puritanical values coexist, with the former culturally dominant and the latter culturally dissident (yes, I know even this can be debated!)—not surprisingly, because the ubiquitousness of shame creates dominant and dissident groups with opposing values. Thus while values for hard work may have changed over time, and among different social classes, there is no doubt in my mind that honor and shame have always been salient with regard to work, just as is the case with love and sex. It is shame's universal salience in the key elements of human life that makes it possible to discuss its pernicious effects generally and to summarize how these can be overcome cross-culturally, as I will now do.

Shame engenders (albeit unwittingly) the following pleasure-denying and intimacy-denying hierarchical dynamics:

- self-love at the expense of love encompassing self and others;
- the elevation of the self and one's own groupmates through the exclusion of others, others defined as not measuring up;
- the resulting creation of exclusionary and exclusive groups;
- the creation of the hierarchy that is a concomitant of exclusion;
- public displays of group allegiance and of one's merits, in place of embrace of inner pleasure and sincerity; and
- the resulting insincerity of going through the motions.

The only way out of the vicious cycle of shame is not to create new escapes from shame that then recreate new shames, but to embrace new social dynamics that genuinely replace shame with prosociality:

- the creation of open and welcoming groups, which do not seek to exclude others;
- the elimination of hierarchy;
- the elimination of public/private dichotomies through an affirmation of sincerity and inner feelings, such as pleasure; and
- the mutual pleasuring and empathy as a direct replacement for shame.

Only with the above new social practices can the contradictions that shame produces, oppositions between sex and spirituality, between work and play, between learning and sociality, be eradicated.

The importance of eliminating these contradictions cannot be overstated. They are a source of a divided self, a self at war with itself. Today the anxiety, hierarchy, and obligation characterizing work makes us distinguish it from play. When we work, we do not feel a sense of playfulness; we only feel that sense when escaping from work. That escape offers us temporary relief from the pressures of work, but we feel guilty or ashamed while at play since play is defined as selfish/nonproductive indulgence. We are trapped, caught in the division of work from play.

But Utopia breaks down the work/play distinction. It does so by eliminating hierarchy, so that our creative lives will no longer be riddled with the pleasure-denying anxiety linked to hierarchical striving. It does so too by making work optional, just as play is optional—something we want to do rather than something we are made to do. With work no longer an obligation, and hierarchy gone, the difference between work and play ends, as both are now optional and equally pleasurable. Eliminating the artificial work/play dichotomy will infuse work with playfulness and play with a sense of the creative seriousness that is work. This allows for a reintegrated self and more meaningful work/play. And it will deepen our most meaningful relationships since we will no longer dichotomize those with whom we work and those whom we love. We will play and work with family and friends, deepening the love of these relationships with the new opportunity to co-create with them.

Utopia also eliminates another fundamental artificial distinction: The opposition between learning and sociality. Learning and socializing are opposed today as a result of the same dynamic that separates play from work. Learning, like work, is obligatory, anxiety-producing, and often unpleasurable as a result. And learning is construed as an individual act, in contrast to the sociable play that is our escape from school. School pits us against others in an individualistic struggle to gain a merit-based perch in the hierarchy of achievement.

And as underachievement at work leads to shame, so too in school. Many failed learners challenge this shame (though in vain) by creating peer groups that shame those who *do well at school!* Anyone who finds pleasure in studying is outcaste as an asocial and, by implication, a selfish, self-interested "nerd" (and this outcasting occurs in many more cultures than just the US, as studious friends from different parts of Asia have often reported to me). The studious individuals, *especially* those studying because they seek pleasure in learning, are too often denied friendship and love precisely because of their desires and abilities. Ironically, would-be rebel peer cultures, seeking to challenge adult values, actually end up reinforcing the ascetic/pleasure-denying alienation of the adult world: Learning, that most sociable and pleasurable of human activities, is construed by youth culture, as it is by the wider adult culture, as unpleasurable and anti-social, an activity that too often comes at the cost of love and friendship. Thus the young get caught in a false dichotomy of their own partial creation, one that pulls them in opposing directions and precludes the sense of belongingness and sociality that learning should actually engender.

Utopia must reject all false dichotomies created in the crucible of shame and hierarchy. For learning this means challenging the notion that it is not a social process. It means creating learning environments that are supremely communal. We need feel neither shame nor selfishness in pursuing joy from learning because such joy, in Utopia, no longer comes at the expense of others, or our communion with the crowd. With shame and hierarchy minimized, we can gain pleasure, and give pleasure, as we love, play, create, and learn. Uniting these dichotomies so that we can live our lives with a sense of fullness and integrity is one of the key transformations of Utopia.

New and old

One of the most profound capabilities of humans is our ability to embrace that which is new. We can see this in our mammalian heritage, a heritage that transformed the reptilian fear of strangers into a desire to approach novel conspecifics, starting with the mammalian practice of nurturing our own offspring, rather than doing what our direct reptilian ancestors did: Abandoning, or even killing, their very own offspring due to fear of the novel stranger.

We can see the human capacity for engaging novelty too in our passion for learning, since learning is a yearning for cognitive and experiential novelty. While humans have taken learning capacities to their apex, the response to new stimuli in our environment has ancient origins. The most elementary forms of life needed to recognize new stimuli in their environment in order to protect themselves from predators that might eat them. Thus they developed an aversive reaction to anything new in the environment, an aversion leading to withdrawal (fear) or aggression and a fighting stance toward anything novel. But ancient and elementary life forms also needed to respond affirmatively to new stimuli, since such stimuli might be a source of food that could be eaten. This led to an approach response, the source of animal interest and curiosity.

Psychologists and biologists have written voluminously about the human and animal interest in novel stimuli. They have also written about habituation to new stimuli, the feeling that the new no longer seems new, and begins to lose interest for us. Some have argued that this habituation process keeps us from exhausting ourselves. Were we never to lose our fascination with a singular new object, we would focus all of our intense perceptual energy on this object, an attentional obsessiveness that is, quite likely, the source of human obsession. By encouraging us to tire of the new, our perceptions keep attuned to that which is even newer, when it enters our field of perception.

But there is a downside to this habituation process: Boredom. What is familiar can fail to energize us. And even novelty can seem less novel, and learning a chore. The flagging of interest in the new is a major source of human unhappiness. The excitement of a new lover turns to the contempt we often feel as they become too familiar to us. The childhood excitement from engagement with the world turns into the cynical adolescent's boredom and disdain for everything. Religion and love, often its secular counterpart, may seem to revivify us as we enter adulthood, but the resuscitation easily flags.

How does Utopia address this universal human problem—the contempt for the familiar and reduced desire to encounter the new? This is a question begging for an answer, because joy is a fine emotion, but even it can turn sour if it lacks the excitement that is its counterpart, positive emotion. An often-heard critique of utopian experiments is that if they bring us all happiness, we will all end up dying of boredom, since unchanging happiness seems, for many, devoid of the necessary drama of life and living.

Here is my response:

1. *Tipping toward the positive:* While joy has a completely separate evolutionary history from the negative emotions, making them function quite differently from joy, the same cannot be said of excitement and interest. As just noted, these are among

the more ancient of organic responses, and they are paired with fear as well. Love and the other social emotions—shame, for example—are among the newest of evolved emotions, often thought to be unique to humans. But the attention and excitement, and the desire for the novel, that are such an important part of romantic love, have their origins in the ancient response of interest. Thus, while eliminating the causes of anti-joy can allow joy to flourish, the process of producing excitement and love is more complicated. Because these emotions are paired with negative counterparts, the approach that Utopia must take is to tip the scales, somehow, toward the positive part of each pair—excitement versus fear; love versus hate. How does society do this?

The answer is that Utopia neutralizes the potency of the negatively valenced side of fear/excitement, and hate/love. It does this using multiple tactics. First, if we encounter novelty collectively, it is less likely to induce fear, and more likely to induce excitement. This is why it is so important that learning be carried out collectively. This is also why it is so important that learning be construed as pleasurable. Utopia must do everything possible to make the engagement with novelty so characteristic of the learning process into a positive experience. Today, even good students come to feel that learning something they don't know is an admission of failure, rather than an opportunity to expand oneself into newly interesting terrain.

By reformatting school and what I call "research" (adult learning) as pleasurable and exciting activities, Utopia toggles the novelty response back toward the positive, thus satisfying that most basic hunger (an intended pun!) of all animals. And by reconceiving of learning not as a childish activity whose goal is achievement of adult capacities but as a lifelong central human process, Utopia returns to adults, as well as to children, the joy and excitement that learning can bring.

2. *Love and hate*: Psychologists recognize that frustrated love, and sexual frustration, can turn love into hate. Readers will easily recognize that dynamic, and the tendency of the excitement of love to turn into the contempt for the familiar. So too a lover's betrayal, which turns former love to hate.

There is a huge literature on how to keep love alive, how to rekindle the flames of passion and romance, and how to overcome jealousy. But that literature makes the task of keeping love alive into a responsibility of the individual, with no contribution from society. In so doing it neglects the larger social and biological dynamics at work in our response to the new versus the familiar.

One critically important dynamic, and it is a dynamic that is either uniquely human or at least one that reaches its apex in humans, is the capacity to integrate the novel and the familiar, and to do so in creative and new ways, so that novelty and excitement are no longer dichotomously opposed to familiarity and boredom. Perhaps the paradigmatic case of our capacity to do this is seen in how we learn: When we are at our best in learning, we relate new facts and findings to what we already know, combining our experience of the present with our memories of experiences from the past. We do this too in artistic creation, seeing familiar things in new ways. We combine the old and new through marriage as well, taking a new person into our familiar, family realm. And, unlike so many of our primate relatives, we strive to sustain lifelong and emotionally meaningful relationships with our own offspring and often, too, with those who are our romantic and sexual partners. In fact we find warmth and interest in the familiar, not only in the unfamiliar. And as someone becomes more familiar to us, they can become more interesting, rather than less so.

But in order for all of this to happen, some quintessential conflicts need to be overcome. Chief among them is the natal family/affinal family conflict—that is, in-law problems—as described in Chapter 3. This conflict is founded on social conflicts between a person's loyalties to older family (the family of birth) versus loyalty to new family (affines), and it is a conflict enhanced by feelings of jealousy and fears of abandonment. By overcoming it or at least making an attempt in that direction as suggested in Chapter 3, the socially new need no longer be opposed to, and in conflict with, the socially old.

In fact, throughout my proposals in this book I strive to reduce stranger/family conflicts. Chapter 3 prescribes many means for attenuating invidious groupism and its most pernicious manifestation, the nation-state; the ending of nationalism and its replacement with universal principles is, indeed, a key theme of Chapter 7.

Throughout the book, too, I emphasize the importance not just of learning, or learning with others, but of learning *about* new others, and carrying out this learning with a community of familiar co-learners. My intent is to make any stranger into an object of curiosity, interest, and excitement—a potential love object, a dynamic furthered by ending gender dichotomies, since these create a division between those others who can interest us, and those others about whom we should have a restrained interest, an interest bounded by disgust should the interest ever veer toward the sexual.

In Chapter 5 I describe how a key process in Utopia will be to produce media about all individuals (not just celebrities), enact stories about them, and seek to understand them at both the cognitive and experiential level. Utopia will encourage such experiential learning about both others who are new to us, as well as those whom we already know. After all, how much do any of us really know about those familiar to us? Not fully knowing what even our most intimate friends and family think of us underlies quintessential human existential angst. This angst is potentially devastating to all of us, and induces dread, and great anxiety, but it is a lack of knowledge that can be made to reanimate our interest in those whom we otherwise think we already know well, turning the anxiety of not knowing something about our intimates into the excitement that sustains our interest in them. There is always, after all, much more to learn about even our closest family and friends: Who were their friends? What games did they play? What were their favorite activities? How did these change over time? Can any of us clearly answer all these questions about the person we know best? I doubt it.

Thus, Utopia will make the familiar seem newly strange, and thus exciting, and it will make the strange seem less threatening, more familiar and hence more loveable. Challenging the stranger/familiar dichotomy may not completely end our boredom with the familiar, but by encouraging us to seek new perspectives about anything that seems familiar, or anyone familiar to us, we can keep alive the excitement that more primitive organisms lose when the novel becomes the known. For humans, unlike other animals, there is always more to learn about those we already know.

Final thoughts

This book has described my own visions for a better world. It is, indeed, a new world, one very different from the one we know. I hope that its newness can be a cause for excitement rather than fear. I hope, too, that others can experience the same pleasure thinking about it that I have experienced in writing about it. And I wish, above all, that you will add your own voice to mine. The epitome of community is to think and talk collectively about our desires and dreams. Please join me in describing your own response to that profoundly intriguing question: What, for you, would an ideal life be like?

Bibliography

Csikszentmihalyi, Mihaly. 1990. *Flow: The Psychology of Optimal Experience.* New York: Harper and Row.

INDEX